Propositional and Doxas

This volume features original essays that advance debates on propositional and doxastic justification and explore how these debates shape and are shaped by a range of established and emerging topics in contemporary epistemology.

This is the first book-length project devoted to the distinction between propositional and doxastic justification. Notably, the contributors cover the relationship between propositional and doxastic justification and group belief, credence, commitment, suspension, faith, and hope. They also consider state-of-the-art work on knowledge-first approaches to justification, hinge-epistemology, moral and practical reasons for belief, epistemic normativity, and applications of formal epistemology to traditional epistemological disputes. Finally, the contributors promise to reinvigorate old epistemological debates on coherentism, externalism, internalism, and phenomenal conservatism.

Propositional and Doxastic Justification will be of interest to researchers and advanced students working in epistemology, metaethics, and normativity.

Paul Silva Jr. is Junior Professor at the University of Cologne. He received his Ph.D. from the University of Connecticut and has publications in *Philosophy and Phenomenological Research*, *Australasian Journal of Philosophy*, *Philosophical Studies*, and other journals.

Luis R.G. Oliveira is Assistant Professor of Philosophy at the University of Houston. He has published numerous articles in refereed journals, on topics in epistemology, ethics, and religion. He is also the director of the *LATAM Bridges in the Epistemology of Religion*, an international project focused on connecting Latin American philosophers to the Anglophone philosophical world.

Routledge Studies in Epistemology

Edited by Kevin McCain
University of Alabama at Birmingham, USA

And Scott Stapleford
St. Thomas University, Canada

Ethno-Epistemology
New Directions for Global Epistemology
Edited by Masaharu Mizumoto, Jonardon Ganeri and Cliff Goddard

The Dispositional Architecture of Epistemic Reasons
Hamid Vahid

The Epistemology of Group Disagreement
Edited by Fernando Broncano-Berrocal and J. Adam Carter

The Philosophy of Group Polarization
Epistemology, Metaphysics, Psychology
Fernando Broncano-Berrocal and J. Adam Carter

The Social Epistemology of Legal Trials
Edited by Zachary Hoskins and Jon Robson

Intellectual Dependability
A Virtue Theory of the Epistemic and Educational Ideal
T. Ryan Byerly

Skeptical Invariantism Reconsidered
Edited by Christos Kyriacou and Kevin Wallbridge

Epistemic Autonomy
Edited by Jonathan Matheson and Kirk Lougheed

Epistemic Dilemmas
New Arguments, New Angles
Edited by Kevin McCain, Scott Stapleford and Matthias Steup

Propositional and Doxastic Justification
New Essays on Their Nature and Significance
Edited by Paul Silva Jr. and Luis R.G. Oliveira

For more information about this series, please visit: https://www.routledge.com/Routledge-Studies-in-Epistemology/book-series/RSIE

Propositional and Doxastic Justification

New Essays on Their Nature and Significance

Edited by Paul Silva Jr. and
Luis R.G. Oliveira

NEW YORK AND LONDON

First published 2022
by Routledge
605 Third Avenue, New York, NY 10158

and by Routledge
4 Park Square, Milton Park, Abingdon, Oxon, OX14 4RN

Routledge is an imprint of the Taylor & Francis Group, an informa business

© 2022 Taylor & Francis

The right of Paul Silva Jr. and Luis R.G. Oliveira to be identified as the authors of the editorial material, and of the authors for their individual chapters, has been asserted in accordance with sections 77 and 78 of the Copyright, Designs and Patents Act 1988.

All rights reserved. No part of this book may be reprinted or reproduced or utilised in any form or by any electronic, mechanical, or other means, now known or hereafter invented, including photocopying and recording, or in any information storage or retrieval system, without permission in writing from the publishers.

Trademark notice: Product or corporate names may be trademarks or registered trademarks, and are used only for identification and explanation without intent to infringe.

Library of Congress Cataloging-in-Publication Data
Names: Silva, Paul, Jr., editor. | Oliveira, Luis R. G., editor.
Title: Propositional and doxastic justification : new essays on their nature and significance / edited by Paul Silva, Jr and Luis R.G. Oliveira.
Description: New York, NY : Routledge, 2022. | Series: Routledge studies in epistemology | Includes bibliographical references and index.
Identifiers: LCCN 2021052398 (print) | LCCN 2021052399 (ebook) | ISBN 9780367431686 (hbk) | ISBN 9781032246871 (pbk) | ISBN 9781003008101 (ebk)
Subjects: LCSH: Justification (Theory of knowledge)
Classification: LCC BD212 .P76 2022 (print) | LCC BD212 (ebook) | DDC 121--dc23/eng/20211202
LC record available at https://lccn.loc.gov/2021052398
LC ebook record available at https://lccn.loc.gov/2021052399

ISBN: 978-0-367-43168-6 (hbk)
ISBN: 978-1-032-24687-1 (pbk)
ISBN: 978-1-003-00810-1 (ebk)

DOI: 10.4324/9781003008101

Typeset in Sabon
by SPi Technologies India Pvt Ltd (Straive)

This book is dedicated to our epistemological predecessors, who first noticed the surprisingly important difference between justifiedly believing and merely having justification to believe.

Contents

Contributors ix

Introduction 1
PAUL SILVA JR. AND LUIS R.G. OLIVEIRA

PART I
Foundational Questions 5

1   The Plenitude of Justification and the Paucity of Knowledge 7
    ROBERT AUDI

2   Theoretical Unity and the Priority of Propositional Justification 27
    JONATHAN L. KVANVIG

3   What Does Logic Have to do With Justified Belief? Why
    Doxastic Justification is Fundamental 40
    HILARY KORNBLITH

4   Justification *Ex Ante* and *Ex Post*: Why We Need Both
    Notions, and Why Neither is Reducible to the Other 59
    RAM NETA

PART II
Reasons, Basing, and Justification 77

5   Factive Reasons and Propositional Justification 79
    DUNCAN PRITCHARD

6   The Epistemic Function of Higher-Order Evidence 97
    DECLAN SMITHIES

7 Doxastic Justification and Creditworthiness 121
ANNE MEYLAN

8 Does the Basing Demand on Doxastic Justification Have Any Dialectical Force? A Response to Oliveira 131
PAUL SILVA JR.

PART III
Other Attitudes and Justification 139

9 On Suspending Properly 141
ERROL LORD AND KURT SYLVAN

10 Propositional and Doxastic Hinge Assumptions 162
ANNALISA COLIVA

11 On Behalf of Knowledge-First Collective Epistemology 181
MONA SIMION, J. ADAM CARTER AND CHRISTOPH KELP

12 Faith, Hope, and Justification 201
ELIZABETH JACKSON

PART IV
New Horizons for Justification 217

13 Doxastic Rationality 219
RALPH WEDGWOOD

14 Intersubjective Propositional Justification 241
SILVIA DE TOFFOLI

15 Knowledge-First Theories of Justification 263
CLAYTON LITTLEJOHN

16 Epistemic Consent and Doxastic Justification 286
LUIS R.G. OLIVEIRA

Index 313

Contributors

Robert Audi is John A. O'Brien Professor of Philosophy at the University of Notre Dame.

J. Adam Carter is Reader in Epistemology at the University of Glasgow.

Annalisa Coliva is Professor of Philosophy at the University of California, Irvine.

Silvia De Toffoli is Postdoctoral Research Associate in the Philosophy Department at Princeton University.

Elizabeth Jackson is Assistant Professor of Philosophy Ryerson University.

Christoph Kelp is Senior Lecturer in Philosophy at the University of Glasgow.

Hilary Kornblith is Distinguished Professor of Philosophy at the University of Massachusetts Amherst.

Jonathan L. Kvanvig is Professor of Philosophy at Washington University in St. Louis.

Clayton Littlejohn is Professor of Philosophy at Kings College London and a Professor of Philosophy at the Australian Catholic University.

Errol Lord is Associate Professor of Philosophy at the University of Pennsylvania.

Anne Meylan is Assistant Professor of Philosophy at the University of Zurich.

Ram Neta is Professor of Philosophy at the University of North Carolina at Chapel Hill.

Luis R.G. Oliveira is Assistant Professor of Philosophy at the University of Houston.

Duncan Pritchard is Distinguished Professor of Philosophy at the University of California, Irvine.

Paul Silva Jr. is Junior Professor of Philosophy at the University of Cologne.

Mona Simion is Professor of Philosophy at the University of Glasgow.

Declan Smithies is Professor of Philosophy at the Ohio State University.

Kurt Sylvan is Associate Professor of Philosophy at the University of Southampton.

Ralph Wedgwood is Professor of Philosophy at the University of Southern California.

Introduction

Paul Silva Jr. and Luis R.G. Oliveira

Epistemologists distinguish between two notions of epistemic justification: *having justification to believe that p* and *justifiedly believing that p*. To keep track of these notions, epistemologists typically refer to the former as *propositional justification* and to the latter as *doxastic justification*. The most obvious difference between these notions is that propositional justification does not require belief: one can have justification to believe that p without actually believing it. Consider, for example, someone who knows that Tom said he would be home and knows that Tom is reliable. Other things being equal, this person could go on to justifiedly believe (that is, to have a doxastically justified belief) that Tom is probably home. But this person might simply not have this belief at all. In such a case, one would still have propositional justification to believe that Tom is probably home.

Most epistemologists, however, tend to think that there is more to doxastic justification than believing that p when one has propositional justification to believe that p. Most agree that having a justified belief depends on there being an "appropriate connection" between one's source of justification to believe that p and one's actual state of believing that p. Someone who believes that p on a whim, for example, lacks a justified belief that p even if she has fantastic reasons for believing that p that were left unengaged. Typically, this "appropriate connection" has been identified as *the basing relation*, although the nature of this relation, of course, is a matter of debate.

The distinction between propositional and doxastic justification, and the related idea of a basing relation, have been of undisputed theoretical importance in a wide range of contemporary epistemological debates. For example: it has been used to undermine coherentism, and if it does then it casts a shadow over subjective Bayesian epistemology as well; it has been used in defense of liberalism about perceptual justification; it has been used to justify phenomenal conservatism; and it has also been used to justify non-factualist views about reasons. Yet despite this central importance, there are a host of surrounding issues that have rarely been discussed in connection with these notions. With this lacuna in mind, this collection brings together chapters that advance the state-of-the-art on propositional and doxastic justification, and on the basing relation. These chapters explore how this distinction and this idea both shape and are shaped by a range of contemporary topics in epistemology.

Part I focuses on foundational questions about propositional and doxastic justification, and Robert Audi's "The Plenitude of Justification and the Paucity of Knowledge" provides a penetrating overview of the collective wisdom regarding almost every aspect of the notions of propositional and doxastic justification. Focusing on the special case of memorial justification, Audi discusses issues about the varieties, sources, and relations between these two central notions. One part of this collective wisdom, in fact, is the idea that propositional justification is more basic than doxastic justification, and thus that doxastic justification is to be understood in terms of propositional justification. Jonathan Kvanvig brings into focus and defends this position in his essay "Theoretical Unity and the Priority of Propositional Justification." But this traditional idea can be also reversed, where doxastic justification is taken as more basic than propositional justification, and where propositional justification is then understood in terms of doxastic justification instead. Hilary Kornblith defends precisely this reversal in his essay "What does Logic Have to do With Justified Belief? Why Doxastic Justification is Fundamental." A further alternative to orthodoxy here is to deny that either one can be reduced to the other. In his essay "Justification *Ex Ante* and *Ex Post*: Why We Need Both Notions, and Why Neither is Reducible to the Other," Ram Neta argues that the function of our concept of propositional justification (i.e., *ex ante* justification) is to identify prospective attitudes that conform to regulative epistemic norms, while the function of our concept of doxastic justification (i.e., *ex post* justification) is to explain the epistemic behavior of agents. Thus understood, Neta argues, we should not reduce one normative status to the other.

Part II explores substantive constraints on propositional and doxastic justification. In his chapter "Factive Reasons and Propositional Justification," Duncan Pritchard argues that the core motivations driving internalism about propositional justification are better served on a *disjunctivist* view that allows there to be a difference between one's factive and non-factive mental states as sources of propositional justification – something that classical internalism denies. Declan Smithies' "The Epistemic Function of Higher-Order Evidence" focuses on *higher-order evidence*—evidence that bears on whether one has justification to believe p without bearing directly on whether p—offering a novel account of how and why higher-order evidence defeats knowledge, doxastic justification, and propositional justification. Next, in her chapter "Doxastic Justification and Creditworthiness," Anne Meylan argues for a virtue-theoretic account of *proper basing*: the widely recognized, but hard to pin down, requirement that doxastically justified beliefs be based on sources of propositional justification "in the right way." And, finally, Paul Silva closes Part II with his chapter, "Does the Basing Demand on Doxastic Justification Have Any Dialectical Force? A Response to Oliveira," by continuing and reinforcing his previous argument that the notion of doxastic justification cannot play the extensive dialectical role that it has played in epistemology.

Part III explores novel extensions of the propositional/doxastic distinction. In their chapter "On Suspending Properly," Errol Lord and Kurt Sylvan argue that a *Kantian reasons-based* approach to justification provides a unified account of justified (dis)belief and suspension. In her chapter "Propositional and Doxastic Hinge Assumptions," Annalisa Coliva further defends her overall *hinge epistemology*—one where perceptual justification depends on general propositions that are just assumed without reasons—by bringing the resources of the propositional/doxastic distinction to bear on the nature of hinge assumptions. In their contribution "On Behalf of Knowledge-First Collective Epistemology," Mona Simion, J. Adam Carter, and Christoph Kelp explain how a knowledge-first approach to *collective epistemology* allows us to remain neutral on the nature of collective attitudes while allowing for substantive non-reductive theories of group knowledge and justified group belief. Finally, in her chapter "Faith, Hope, and Justification," Elizabeth Jackson spends some time discussing the nature of the attitudes of faith and hope—especially their contrasts with belief—and proceeds to explore how the distinction between propositional and doxastic justification can be applied to them as well.

Part IV brings chapters offering novel accounts of epistemic justification. In his chapter "Doxastic Rationality," Ralph Wedgwood starts from the observation that justification and rationality are closely related and proceeds to develop a new virtue-theoretic account of what it is for any attitude whatsoever to be *rationally held*. In her chapter "Intersubjective Propositional Justification," Silvia De Toffoli draws on mathematical propositional justification and argues that whether an agent has propositional justification to believe p modally depends on the possibility of having doxastic justification (given some limited idealizations of the agent). In his chapter "Knowledge-First Theories of Justification," Clayton Littlejohn begins by highlighting the way in which knowledge-first accounts of the possession of evidence and propositional justification are inconsistent with the view that the possession of evidence and (mere) propositional justification are prior to both doxastic justification and knowledge. Taking his cue from an earlier exchange between Timothy Williamson and Anthony Brueckner, Littlejohn then defends the knowledge-first approach. Finally, in his chapter "Epistemic Consent and Doxastic Justification," Luis Oliveira defends an account of doxastic justification where it is by virtue of doing well or poorly with respect to our own epistemic commitments, collectively and interpersonally understood, that we are properly said to be justified or unjustified in our beliefs.

Together, the contributions in this volume constitute detailed and exciting cutting-edge work on a topic of central importance to epistemology. We are extremely proud of the opportunity to bring them together in this way and we look forward to seeing their inevitable impact.

Part I
Foundational Questions

1 The Plenitude of Justification and the Paucity of Knowledge[1]

Robert Audi

Justification for believing—*propositional justification*—is wide in its scope and uncountable in its instances. I have justification for a multitude of propositions obvious in my environment: that the ceiling is not 102 feet high, that my chair is not teetering from an earthquake, that the piano is closer to me than the sofa, and many other propositions. I also have justification for believing indefinitely many propositions in the series, 1.1 is larger than 1, 2.11 is larger than 2, 3.111 is larger than 3, and so on. The number of propositions in this series that are *justified for me*—an alternative phrase for ascribing propositional justification— seems uncountable. I doubt that I believed any of these propositions until I (comprehendingly) considered them in framing these examples. When I did believe them, it was *justifiedly*—that is, I had *doxastic justification* for each proposition. It is widely held that what we justifiedly believe is *based on* something constituting a justifier for it—hence, that doxastic justification for a proposition requires propositional justification for it.

Many difficulties beset attempts to analyze any of these notions, but it is widely assumed that whatever knowledge is, it requires doxastic justification. This chapter will concentrate mainly on the relation between the two kinds of justification, particularly in one major case that helps to clarify both notions: memory. Among the difficult questions to be addressed are these. How does memory yield propositional justification? What is the scope, extent, and magnitude of the propositional justification it yields? What kinds of factors explain how memorial justification that is propositional can yield, for the propositions in question, doxastic justification or knowledge? And how is *remembering*—conceived as entailing memory knowledge—related to propositional memorial justification?

---

[1] An earlier version of this chapter was presented (online) at the Australian Catholic University's Dianoia Institute of Philosophy and I benefited from that discussion. For specific comments on earlier versions, I am grateful to Annalisa Coliva, Garrett Cullity, Rachel Dichter, Richard Feldman, Anna-Sara Malmgren, and Luis Oliveira.

Varieties of Justification

Doxastic justification, as the term "doxastic" should indicate, is a property of actual beliefs; having it is equivalent to justifiedly believing something. Propositional justification, by contrast, is, in the standard usage of the term, a property of persons (or anyway beings with minds) in relation to propositions. The former is important because beliefs that entirely lack it are defective in a certain way. Moreover, by and large—and, on some views, necessarily—they do not constitute knowledge. Both kinds of justification may be viewed synchronically or, since their status can change over time, diachronically. (Here I'll assume reference to a single time unless otherwise indicated.) Doxastic justification may be conceived roughly as justification that a belief has in virtue of being based on at least one set of elements that constitutes adequately strong propositional justification for S at the time.[2] Let us consider the main locutions important for understanding propositional justification.

The locution "p is justified for S" is a philosopher's phrase, usually explained in terms of the broad notion of having justification for a proposition, p, in a sense that does not entail believing p.[3] The locution can mislead by giving the impression that a proposition can be justified simpliciter. But there may be no single notion of a proposition's being justified simpliciter. Granted, one can ask whether there is any justification for believing something, say that New York City will someday be submerged. But this is a request for some set of true propositions—*evidence*, in one sense of the term—that objectively supports p and would constitute some degree of propositional justification for anyone who believed the proposition and had a certain kind of capacity to see how they support p.

Would it be better, then, to focus analytical attention on "S is justified in believing p," which does not entail actual belief but does ascribe to S the right normative status? There are a few cases in which believing is not entailed by a proper use of this attribution, but they are a small proportion. To see that there is no entailment, imagine someone's saying to a friend, "I'm surprised you don't believe your student will pass—you're certainly justified in believing that given the record." It may be that the locution captures the notion of propositional justification where actual belief is ruled out, as in the case just given, but not invariably otherwise. "They're justified in believing that" normally presupposes actual belief.

---

2 I have explicated the basis relation crucial for understanding doxastic justification in Audi (1986), and though the main focus there is inferential justification, much of the account of inferential justification holds also for non-inferential justification, e.g. for which many (though not all) of the same conditions hold.

3 Though the notions of propositional justification and doxastic justification apply to *de re* and other non-propositional beliefs, such as believing a plane *to be* landing, they will not be explicitly considered here. What emerges concerning propositional beliefs, however, can be readily applied to those cases.

Saying they *would* be justified does not presuppose it, but this terminology would not serve us well because of difficulties in specifying the relevant hypothetical conditions.

It may be that the best way to capture propositional justification is to begin with locutions of the form of "S has justification for (believing) p." This is of course both indefinite as to *possession conditions*—those that indicate what is covered by "having"—and also as to how much justification is in question. We cannot eliminate either case of indefiniteness by shifting to "S has *a* justification for p," though this may seem to imply (but need not imply) *sufficient justification*, a degree implying *overall* (thus undefeated) justification for believing p. It does appear, however, that if S is justified *in believing* p—in the sense in which that does not imply actual belief—this does entail that (other things remaining equal) S would not merit criticism for believing p on account of lacking sufficient justification. In any case, possession conditions are still left indefinite. They will be the main concern of Section 3.

At least one other way of conceiving propositional justification should be considered before we proceed. Is having propositional justification for p simply having evidence for it? If I have propositional justification and have a normal grasp of what justification and evidence are, then it may be natural for me to say, in reference to my justification, that I have evidence. But suppose I have just a memory impression that I told someone about a deadline. If you doubt that I did and ask if I have evidence for this, I would hesitate to claim this impression as evidence, even if I think it justifies my claim. If, by contrast, I had a recent diary notation indicating the intention to tell the person about the deadline, I would regard that as some evidence that I did so. Perhaps this difference is pragmatic: I simply do not want to call such weak, impressionistic justification, especially given its privacy, *evidence*. Another question is whether only propositions are, strictly speaking, evidence. I doubt that and, if so, then even the diary entry is not evidence, though the proposition that I have it would be. Perhaps we can say this: first, that if p is genuine evidence for q, it follows that p is true, and, second, that the proposition that there *is* evidence for p entails (even if no one has the evidence) that there is at least one true evidential proposition that supports p.[4]

Does the counterpart point hold in the same way for saying there is justification (even if no one has it) for p? That there is evidence that a tumor is cancerous entails that there is some true supporting proposition, such as that an X-ray indicates cancer. This evidence constitutes some justification for p. No one need have it but possibly someone could, so it

---

4 The term "evidence" is used variously but if we allow for the crucial "evidence of the senses," phenomenal states will count, and they are surely among the basic grounds of propositional justification. For extensive discussions of evidence see Conee and Feldman (2004).

could propositionally justify p (to some degree) for someone. But recall the memory impression that I told someone about the deadline: this can provide propositional justification for me even if its content is false and so does not constitute evidence. In virtue of a memory impression that I told someone about a deadline, *I* may have justification for believing that I did, but this impression may be false and its propositional content may fail to be genuine evidence. There is, however, corresponding, if very weak, evidence: the true proposition that I *have* the impression.

A useful comparison here is the notion of a reason. I can *have* a reason for believing p, in the form of q, which I believe on highly credible expert testimony, though q is false. Then q is not evidence for p (though some would call it misleading evidence). It would also be a mistake, however, to say here, "There *is* a reason for p, namely q." This locution is used factively: we may properly withdraw it if we find that q is false. One may now ask whether we do not also withdraw the claim that there is justification for p when we find that q is false. We likely would if we find there is no objective support for q. But suppose q is well evidenced, as where several experts testify that an X-ray indicates cancer. Here q, though false, has external objective justification. The difference is apparently that the proposition constituting the justification, q, can be false, whereas only true propositions constitute genuine evidence. Such *free-floating justification* will not be my concern. If S has it, S also has propositional justification of the person-relative kind I am exploring, but propositional justification for S (for p) is perspectival. Such justification may or may not be externally and objectively adequate—justification there *is*, for anyone—and so not person-relative. Propositional justification for S may entail S's having *presumptive* evidence, but it does not entail having the genuine article.

There are philosophers who take justification to be equivalent to rationality. I have argued that these are different and that, where both terms apply, the notion of rationality is more permissive.[5] This issue may be set aside here given the plausible assumption that whether or not rationality and justification are equivalent, we should understand a proposition's being rational for S and S's rationally believing it quite analogously to the way we should understand p's being justified for S and S's justifiedly believing p.

Justification and Knowledge

One reason for the importance of propositional justification is that there has long been a case, likely still accepted by many philosophers, that knowledge is built from, or anyway rests on, justified true belief. This (doxastic) justification must be sufficient and the belief constituting

---

5 I have argued for this in (among other works) Audi (2011, 2015). See also Siscoe (2021).

knowledge must be based on the justifier(s), but these conditions are often met. Suppose, however, that (as I have argued elsewhere[6]) knowledge is possible without the knower's having justification. Then propositional justification will not be necessary, at least on the highly plausible assumption that it is entailed by doxastic justification.

If justification should be necessary for knowledge, however, might we then say that given enough propositional justification for a true belief, one *can* know that p—at least as far as meeting the propositional justification requirement goes? One obstacle to a positive answer is the lottery problem. For any number of tickets in a fair lottery, a loser is in the same epistemic position as the winner, who clearly cannot know that the ticket the winner holds will lose.

A related question is this: Can't we have propositional justification for p but be unable to see how the justifying element(s) support(s) p? If so, then although we would justifiedly believe p *if* we believed it on that basis, we are not in a position to have propositional justification in the usual sense in which we are when we have justification for p (or, especially, are justified *in* believing it).

Such cases also show that, even where p is true, having justification need not put one in a position to know. Imagine someone who knows enough logic to understand a proof of p from q, r, s, and t, which the person justifiedly believes and which provide premises for a clear and cogent proof of p. Does this "possessed" justification for p guarantee being in a position to know that p—if that implies being able to come to know now without outside help? This is doubtful. The person might need Socratic leading questions to find the proof. Compare saying someone is in a position to stitch up a wound—having all the tools, good light, medicines, and so on—but lacks the ability to stitch it up. Perhaps the distinction we need—though it is not sharp—is between being in a position to know that p and being able (perhaps even ready) to learn that p. In any case, few philosophers would doubt that justification is important even apart from its importance for understanding or achieving knowledge.

Having Justification

However we explicate propositional justification, we need an understanding of what it is to have it—of its possession conditions. There is quite a variety of such conditions.

We have already seen the possibility of having propositional justification by virtue of meeting doxastic conditions: by having justified beliefs whose contents adequately support p, say as evidential premises. Adequate support may be entailment or strong probabilification. My space does not permit an account of these types of support, but examples

---

[6] Most recently in Audi (2020, ch. 6).

will indicate that the justified supporting beliefs in question may or may not constitute knowledge. Some of the examples will also suggest some roles knowledge may play in producing doxastic justification. We must, however, explore whether propositional justification for p may derive, not from having doxastic justification for propositions that support p—a kind of *premise-based justification*—but from having only propositional justification for such supporting propositions.

Consider the proposition that an applicant will be admitted to a PhD program. If I have read through the file, I may have propositional justification for several propositions citing strong merits of the applicant. This might imply my possessing justification for believing that the applicant will be admitted. Imagine, however, that I do not have premise-beliefs that support projecting admission, but simply form clear impressions of the writing sample and the supporting letters, yet am cautious about concluding anything and would have to reflect on these to achieve justification for the admission-implying propositions. I *have* the impressions; I know *how* to reflect on them and can conclude, with justification, that, for example, the applicant is talented, committed, superior to most in the comparison class, and so on. I could then have justification for propositions that would be premises and are such that my propositional justification for them suffices to give me such justification for p—in this case, that the applicant will be admitted. This seems a case in which having propositional justification for p does not require that it reside in justificatory *premise-beliefs* that support p. Propositional justification requires normative grounds, but these grounds need not be constituted by current beliefs that provide, nor need the grounds ever produce beliefs whose *contents* provide, adequate support for p. The grounds may, for instance, be information that is caused by non-propositional impressions that, when their possessor reflects on or otherwise gets them appropriately in mind, yield justification for believing certain propositions.

Call cases in which S has propositional justification for p *first level* when the justification resides in elements, such as an overall impression of a pattern, that do not themselves stand in need of justification. This is one case of a non-propositional ground of justification. In this sense, such justification is one level below p. This level of justification may be perceptual, memorial, or of other kinds besides the impressionistic, broadly intuitive kind just illustrated. Where propositional justification for p resides in justification for premises for p, as in the second variant of the admissions case, we might speak of *second-level* propositional justification: propositional justification for p based on the propositional justification for other propositions that, at the first level below p, adequately support p.

Could there be *third-level* propositional justification? This would be justification for which S's basis is having information that, on appropriate reflection, would lead to S's having propositional justification for propositions at two levels below p, that themselves constitute, for

S, propositional justification for propositions at one level below p, that directly support p. This seems possible. Might there be *forth-level* propositional justification and perhaps still deeper levels? I presuppose no answer in this plainly contingent matter. The answer depends on the complexity of S's mind and how readily S's seeking a justification for p would reveal to S the two layers of justificatory propositions to which S has an appropriate a kind of access. What is apparently not contingent—at least on the assumption that the minds in question are finite—is that the number of levels cannot be infinite.[7]

It may help here to make a comparison to knowledge. There is some analogy between being propositionally justified and (where p is true) being in a position to know. The latter, at least, rules out beliefs' constituting knowledge if they are, in a certain way, accidentally true or based on pure luck. Suppose S has what would otherwise be third-level propositional justification but can come to believe and know that p only if a nearby brain-manipulating machine is accidentally made to configure S's brain so that S can see how the relevant justificatory items combine so as to justify believing p. Second, suppose that, with extraordinary luck, S could hit upon a proof, proceeding from the third-level propositions as premises, to the second-level ones and from those, as premises, to the first level ones, and thence to p. This does not suffice for propositional justification for p. In neither case, moreover, that of accidental assistance or lucky discovery should we say that S is in a position to have knowledge that p, or propositional justification for p, though S may be in a position to be *taught* that p.

Whatever it is to have propositional justification, it is surely grounded in something to which S has an appropriate kind of access, and the number of levels in question is variable depending on the subject's mental capacities. Minimally, such access requires an ability to get the justifiers, whether propositional or, for example, experiential, appropriately in mind. Consider a financial analogy. One can in a sense "have" money in a foreign account to which one has no direct access, but one must have some kind of access that permits contact with it. This case is not like having a disease; that does not imply access at all. It is simply an affliction. Justification plays roles in our thought and action, and it is intrinsically relational, being *for* a determinate kind of thing. No account of it that fails to do justice to its function in the relevant roles is adequate, and

---

7 At some point, depending on the individual, at which S lacks propositional justification, there may be what I have called *structural justification* for believing p: roughly, accessible justificatory elements in S's overall cognitive structure that can, given appropriate efforts by S, lead to S's having propositional justification for p. The difference—which does not permit a sharp distinction—is explored in Audi (1991). Clearly propositional justification is a kind of structural property; but some structural justification would not meet the possession conditions for propositional justification—particularly if having it entails being justified *in believing p*, as that is normally understood.

the most plausible accounts require a kind of access that entails knowability—at least in the acquaintance sense—of the justificatory elements.

So far, nothing has been said about the relation between either propositional justification or doxastic justification and the process of *justifying*. This relation is important, in ways too rarely noted, for understanding justification. Clearly, having propositional justification for p normally puts one in a position to justify p—at least assuming conceptual capacity to understand what it is for considerations to bear on supporting p and also some ability to appeal to them in at least mentally justifying p. This capacity qualification is intended to allow for the—to be sure debatable—case of someone's having, say, perceptual justification for p but no capacity to do the kinds of things that constitute giving a justification. In any case, if what constitutes a basis of propositional justification is inaccessible to S, by reflection or introspection in the light of comprehendingly considering the question whether p, S cannot be expected to be able to justify p. This is not to deny that on being asked why p is the case, S might, by luck, think of some propositions, q and r, that objectively show that p. But adducing these will not count as S's justifying p in the sense that goes with the normal conception of expressing (a kind of realizing) a possessed justification for it. It is in a sense *invented*, and, if retained after the invention, will yield fortuitous propositional justification.

Accessibility also has a connection with doxastic justification. If S justifiedly believes p, this is not a matter of having a brute normative property. S will be justified on an appropriate basis, and we normally expect that, at least with some effort and perhaps skillful prompting, S can adduce, under some description, at least certain elements in that basis in a process of justification. The elements may be impressions or experiences as well as propositions. This normal expectation is not well explainable, if explainable at all, apart from an accessibility condition. For similar reasons, it is not clear that S (a normal adult with a mastery of a natural language) can count as justifiedly believing p if, asked why p is the case, S cannot—given guided reflection or relevant introspection, but without outside help—indicate some suitable set of elements that carry some justificatory weight.

Memory as a Source of Justification

The account of propositional justification so far sketched leaves open how "implicit" propositional justification can be. It might be considered implicit when it is, as it were, achievable only by the mediation of reflection or some other potentially connecting process that, for S, brings the justificatory elements in sufficiently close contact to p. Suppose one has justification, from a clear memory of a conversation, for believing that the other party (as often happens) mixed English with German but, being used to this mixing, took no notice of it and formed no belief to the effect that the person did this. This might be a case of second-level propositional justification. Here we have a propositional impression that the speaker mixed the languages. A related and arguably more basic case would be one in which S has a memory of a snippet of a linguistically mixed conversation. With that in mind, S could readily form the propositional impression. How much propositional justification is "implicit" in either of these ways is a contingent matter; but the limit seems to be that of the kind of accessibility noted here.[8]

The notion of what is "implicit" is vague, and I prefer to use the notion of an information base, allowing, to be sure, for false information, as with hallucinational sense impressions. Our information base includes what is stored in images as well as propositionally. Often, we are disposed to form beliefs when circumstances in some way call for it, say when asked the color of a car that went by at a time one was uninterested in it and merely formed an image rather than, say, a belief that it was a striking red. But a mere disposition to form beliefs, even if they would be true, does not imply propositional justification; it could be based on brain abnormalities that can trigger forming beliefs for which there is no justification. A brain defect could cause someone to believe, on seeing a cat and hearing its plaintive meow, that it portends a lightning storm. If propositional justification of many kinds implies a disposition to form the belief(s) it supports when they are not already possessed, dispositions to believe do not imply propositional justification.

Memory is an epistemologically crucial dimension of our normal information base, and there is much to be learned from considering memorial propositional justification as a special and instructive case.

Memory is a capacity manifested in part by our remembering propositions, but not all our memories are propositional. We also retain images, as where we have seen a lovely view. We may or may not have formed beliefs about what we saw or later imaged, but certainly will not form all the beliefs that our visual information would justify. But memory, like our senses, can be operative in the formation of misleading impressions or false beliefs, somewhat as our visual system can harbor illusions and hallucinations. This is important for understanding propositional justification because there is more than one kind of such justification that is broadly memorial.

---

8 This conclusion favors an internalist view of justification over a reliabilist view. Cf. Alvin Goldman's (1988) distinction between strong and weak justification and Conee and Feldman's (2004) "mentalist" view of the basis of justification. The mentalist view would normally entail accessibility. Both their view and Goldman's can make use of the account of propositional justification provided. Each will replace the accessibility requirement with its own candidate and can adopt the resulting versions of the substantive points.

Suppose one does not have a memory belief that p, where p is about the past, but would, immediately on considering the proposition, be justified in believing it and perhaps also justifiedly believe it. Asked if I had two eggs at breakfast, I may immediately believe I did not. This might be because I had none and rarely have any at all; but it is possible that I had one and needed to think about whether I had a second. My recall of the breakfast may or may not involve images. But quite apart from images, it might suffice to give me propositional justification for believing I had just one even if, being cautious, I withhold believing that.

Memory can also justify believing false propositions. Consider memorial images. We can recall a maroon car as black when, although much of our image is faithful to the car's actual properties, our recollection of color is illusory. If, however, there actually was a certain shadow on the car, we might have strong propositional justification for believing it was black. But propositional justification could also come from a vivid image of it as black, even apart from false lighting. Suppose, however, that, without supporting images, I simply have the memorial sense of the car's passing at high speed. Can't this sense yield propositional justification even if it is not supported by an image? It would seem so. Certainly the sense of remembering, say, that Malta is an island in the Mediterranean, can yield some degree of propositional justification even if not supported by either images or a sense of remembering either an assertion of it or some confirming proposition. The proposition in question here, however, is not perceptual, and I leave open the apparently empirical question whether the role of images in memorial propositional justification differs depending on the kind of proposition in question.

None of these points implies that remembering something or some proposition at a time when the memory is occurrent entails having a sense of remembering at that time. I think I can describe some routes to my home from memory both without imagining anything and so automatically that I need have no sense of remembering it. Indeed, this applies to much that we have memorized. If remembering that p entails knowing that p, and if justification in this case, in which I have p explicitly in mind, must be occurrent as I speak, then since that justification is not occurrent, the case provides some reason to think that occurrently knowing does not entail being occurrently justified. In affirming simple sums while teaching a child arithmetic, one exhibits occurrent knowledge, but one's justification need not be occurrent. Perhaps, however, propositional justification for p—which need not be occurrent, since S need not have the justificatory elements in mind—is all that is required by taking memorial knowledge, even when expressed in statements, to entail propositional justification for p at the time in question. That this justification would be present is supported by the point that if I should consider my description carefully, I almost certainly would have the (occurrent) sense of remembering the propositions in question. It is a very difficult question, however, what constitutes that special sense of familiarity that is naturally called a sense of remembering.

Memory has a further and quite subtle connection with both propositional and doxastic justification in relation to self-knowledge and self-ascriptions. Consider memories of some of one's dispositional psychological properties, such as beliefs and intentions regarding the next day. I may look ahead to a day I thought would be busy and wonder, what was I going to (intending to) do in the afternoon? Suppose it comes to me that I intended to talk with Ginger, a colleague. My memorial impression could give me propositional justification for believing that I intended to do so. But here is another possibility. A present desire to talk with her could be what *produces* the intention to do so. Suppose it does and that I never previously intended this. I might nevertheless have propositional justification, based on the newly formed intention, for believing I will meet with her. I could even have doxastic justification for believing this, since intending to do something is often an adequate ground for believing one will, and I could believe I will meet her on the basis of intending to.

I could, however, also retain propositional justification for believing both that I *originally* intended to meet her and that I have retained that intention; and from that justification (say, where I seem to remember promising to meet her), I might have propositional justification for believing I will meet her. But suppose I have entirely forgotten the original conversation. My propositional justification for believing I will meet her could lack even a supporting memory impression of the conversation and still be based on the newly formed intention. Whether I misremember or have entirely forgotten the original conversation with Ginger, this new intention could give me doxastic (as well as propositional) justification for the belief that I will meet her. Suppose I have not forgotten the original conversation. The newly formed intention might still provide no *causal* basis of my forming that (long-standing) belief, since, despite my memory impression of forming, at the time of the conversation, an intention to talk with her in the future, we merely discussed meeting, and there *was* no earlier-formed intention to serve as what yields doxastic justification of my present belief that I will meet with her. This and other cases show that one can have propositional justification for believing p over a period of time, yet come to believe p on a new basis—such as a newly formed intention—that was not the basis of the original propositional justification, but now is either the basis of an instance of doxastic justification (as the newly formed intention might be) or part of that basis. Here my propositional justification for p is overdetermined, resting on both a memory basis and a present intention. But my doxastic justification, since it is *based on* only one of the justificatory grounds I have for p, is not overdetermined.

Conceptual Conditions for Propositional Justification

In the cases of memory we have considered, there is no question that S has the conceptual capacity to believe p. We cannot have the sense of remembering that p if we do not have a minimal understanding of the proposition. The possibility of this sense seems necessary for propositional justification. But perhaps we should countenance a sense of "having a justification for p" not subject to this requirement. Consider having in mind a number of propositions that are good evidence for p, which is a technical philosophical proposition one cannot understand. They constitute a justification for p; one has them; and, we may assume, understands them. Still, if one cannot understand p, does one have propositional justification for it?[9]

We are pulled in two directions: negatively by the thought that, since S cannot believe a proposition without understanding it, S cannot have doxastic justification for p on the basis of S's "possessed" justification, and thus cannot even be justified *in* believing p; positively by the thought that S clearly has what constitutes *a* justification for p. I propose to call this a case of having *a merely evidential justification* for p. We can fruitfully compare it to something we must in any case account for: cases in which scientists have all the evidence—justificatory considerations—that they need for a theory, but, where the amount and complexity of the evidence is vast and they have not even approached formulating the theory, which they do not understand prior to some explanation. Here they cannot now be said to be justified *in* believing the theory, and indeed would not say they understand the theory.

In the case of inability to understand p just described, I have assumed a lack of basic semantic comprehension—p is technical, and S cannot make out what p says. We can imagine a similar case in which p is understood by S semantically but seems crazy or in some way absurd. "I just don't understand that at all!," S might say, as someone responds on being told that a man may be both father and grandfather of the same person.[10] Such cases illustrate *unintegrated evidence*: S may understand p in a minimal way yet be conceptually ill-equipped to bring together the propositions that jointly justify p. Note that in both cases, those of merely evidential justification for p and of unintegrated evidence for it, S cannot use the justificatory materials in a normal process of justifying p. The impossibility is, to be sure, contingent in the integration case, but in both cases S in some sense possesses a perfectly understandable justification for p but cannot justifiedly believe p or even, in the usual sense, be justified in believing p.

---

9 Compare having justification, simpliciter, as opposed to having *a* justification. The former is less specific and arguably is a better indication of what constitutes propositional justification.

10 This is a case (modeled on Sophocles' *Oedipus Cycle*) described in detail in Audi (2020).

There are, then, some conceptual conditions for having justification. It is not merely a kind of possession of evidence or, more broadly, merely having informational materials that constitute a justification for p in the abstract. Propositional justification is, as it were, designed to play a role in the normative status of a person's outlook and, in the social sphere, in explaining and justifying one's views. Once again, it is significant for understanding propositional justification that it is by its nature constituted by elements that are *fit for* citation in a process of justifying p. This is not to conflate conceptual with pragmatic questions. Rather, it reflects the fact that justification is in an important sense a *dialectical* concept and cannot be adequately understood apart from its essential role in intellectual practices.

Sources of Propositional Justification

It will now be evident how memory is a source of propositional justification. It is not, however, the only source, not even the only *basic* source—a kind that, without (evidentially) depending on another source of justification, provides grounds of non-inferential justification. Clearly perception, introspection (as an internal source of experience analogous to perception), and reason—intuition, in one sense—are also sources. If I see snow falling, I acquire justification for believing that the temperature will not rise to summer levels, but I do not normally form any such belief. Enthusiastic participants in a lavish dinner may feel sated without believing they are, but the feeling gives them justification for believing this.[11] And surely my information base gives me justification for believing that if 1/26th is smaller than 1/16th then the latter is larger than the former.

An interesting point of difference here is that the first two cases would normally issue in *non-inferential* belief that p if (as where one is asked whether p, say that snow is falling or that one feels sated) one formed the belief that p directly, whereas in the third case, the arithmetic belief would presumably be inferential. I *could* believe the arithmetic proposition non-inferentially—and do now since I now simply remember that it is true. But initially, I believed the proposition at least in part on the basis of recognizing (hence believing) that 1 divided by a given integer is larger than 1 divided by a larger integer. The three cases, perceptual, introspective, and intuitive, can occur in other forms. But they suffice to show both how perception, outer and inner, can yield propositional justification and that intuition, at least, can in quite ordinary cases yield either inferential or non-inferential belief when S's propositional justification

---

11 The view proposed here can be adjusted to take account of credences, at least understood as degrees of belief (a notion I grant may also need more explication than it is usually given).

for p produces doxastic justification when something engenders the belief that p on the basis of it.

All the sources of propositional justification we have considered—and these are the standard *basic* sources of it—have a kind of *seeming*, roughly a phenomenal sense of truth, as a normal element in considering p at certain times when S has such justification. Might we conclude, then, that the seemings are the basis of occurrent propositional justification—roughly, the kind one has in entertaining p in the light of justification one has for it—and that dispositional propositional justification is simply a tendency to have occurrent propositional justification? I believe not. There are at least two reasons to doubt this.

First, in virtue of what we justifiedly believe, we can have propositional justification for p even if, as with many arithmetic propositions that never come before our minds, we never tend to have the thought. I have never had a tendency for the proposition that 4,572.3 is larger than 4,572 to come to mind, but I have long had propositional justification for it.[12]

Second, one can tend to have it seem to one that p only because one's brain is manipulated in such a way as to make it likely that one will entertain p and have it seem true. This need not yield propositional justification in a dispositional form, since the seeming might have no accessible basis, such as a visual impression. It does not follow that no artificially produced seemings can yield occurrent propositional justification. Some can, and that shows that occurrent justification need not be a realization of existent propositional justification. One may have occurrent justification—both doxastic and propositional—if, for instance, one suddenly has a hallucination of a black cat and on that visual basis believes there is one ahead. The seen elements that underlie seeing that p may simultaneously be the basis of doxastic justification for p. Here both the propositional and the doxastic justification arise from the same basis; the latter is not a realization of antecedently existing propositional justification. This phenomenon is common with observing such significant events as people's waving at us, dogs barking, and cars crashing. This point is the kind that defenders of "phenomenal conservatism" have noted in the context of

---

12 I would have a conditional tendency: to believe this *if* asked whether it is true. The distinction here is not sharp; tendencies are, after all, manifested *given* eliciting conditions, and there is much variability concerning the difference between these conditions and factors that make the tendency conditional. In the cases in question here, a significant difference is that conditional tendencies to form beliefs are often to form them inferentially, whereas many propositions for which we have propositional justification we tend to believe non-inferentially, as with perceptual, intuitive, and many memorial justifiers. Where we see a green maple tree, for example, but are occupied with other things, there is likely no eliciting condition. But if we were choosing shrubs to blend with the green, we would form a non-inferential belief to the effect that the tree is a certain green.

arguing that the genesis, as opposed to the character, of a justificatory seeming is not strictly relevant to its normative power.[13]

Might we say, then, that propositional justification is (in part) a disposition—or anyway readiness—to have occurrent justification that *realizes* it? The underlying idea here is that propositional justification is *grounded* in elements that are appropriate support for believing p and, properly cited in an attempt to justify p, would succeed in justifying p. This is surely plausible, and it allows for a kind of priority of occurrent justifiers as central for the concept of justification. That concept must be understood partly in terms of justification one has at a time when what justifies p is in the mind of the person at the time. This is in part because dependence on memory would otherwise be a necessary element in having justification at all.[14]

The point that occurrent justifiers have a kind of priority also accommodates the role of justificatory elements in the process of justifying as central for understanding their normative power. They most clearly play this role when present in the consciousness of the person giving a justification. In normal human life, moreover, justification for p cannot normally be acquired without some kind of occurrent justification, though this need not be for p as opposed to some proposition(s) that support p. (An exception would be perfect duplication of a person: my perfect duplicate would presumably have all the propositional and even doxastic justification I have—but, significantly, not all the knowledge: even if, on being "born," he justifiedly and truly believes it snowed the day before, he would not know this, whereas I would.) Even misleading justificatory elements, such as hallucinational sense impressions, mistaken intuitions of the truth of a proposition one considers, and false memory impressions, are occurrent elements in consciousness. Beyond this, propositional justification is apparently in fact realized only in ways that embody phenomenal seemings, such as its now visually seeming to me that there is black print here.

It may appear that the realizationist conception of occurrent propositional justification just sketched supports the liberal view that just *any* phenomenal seeming that p provides some degree of justification for it. It does not. Granted, seemings that p normally provide some justification for p, but normal seemings represent the common basic sources of propositional justification, such as memory and perception. Suppose S believes p owing to mere brain manipulation and then entertains p. Imagine that it now seems true, but *not* memorially, perceptually, introspectively,

---

13 For papers clarifying and critically appraising phenomenal conservatism, including one of mine, see Tucker (2013).
14 Granted, propositional justification need not be realized, but even its becoming a basis of belief requires a passage of time, which would entail *retention* of the justifying element(s) whether or not we call it memory.

intuitively or in any way closely akin to these. This might be called a *merely representational seeming*: S cognitively leans toward believing p but not on any ground of the kinds that seem constitutive of justification. This may be a case where a belief that p which is not a realization of any basic kind of propositional justification can yield a kind of seeming, such as a felt attraction to believing p, that can in turn produce belief or at least an inclination to believe, but connects with no kind of evidence and fails to yield justification.

Compare "I don't know why I'm attracted to believing p" with "I can't give you any argument for p, but I seem to remember it" or "I can't show that p, but it's plausible." These and other cases of occurrent justification—the kind in question—might be considered *presentational* seemings. These are not easily characterized, though some connection with perception and the kinds of representational states it yields may be an element in the justificatory power of at least perceptual and memorial impressions. This is not the place for an account.[15] Memorial and intellectual seemings may be the most difficult to characterize, perceptual ones the least difficult.

In any case, there are apparently some ways p can seem true to S that do not entail S's having propositional justification for p. If we grant that p can seem true *in the light of* propositions that one believes, though they are not premises *on which* one believes p, then although one here believes or tends to believe p non-inferentially, one perhaps *would* answer "Why do you believe p?" by citing some potential premise for it, if only by way of rationalization or explanation. The belief might arise by a kind of *innocence by association*; p might be about a previously unknown person one learns is a member of a family one knows well. One might believe some positive things about the person even without *inferring* them through some argument from analogy to other family members, though one might also be disposed to *defend* them by such arguments if necessary. Here the influencing beliefs might not provide any justification for p but simply cause a felt attraction to believing it of a kind that qualifies as a seeming. This would be a *cognitively influenced* seeming, though not necessarily one that realizes a justificatory element—the influencing beliefs do not justify the belief, nor is p intuitive or even plausible. Other sorts of phenomenal seemings might also be the wrong kind to ground occurrent justification, but here I simply want to point out that there can be seemings that do not necessarily yield propositional justification.

The distinction between believing in the light of elements that are at least potentially justificatory and believing on the basis of actually justificatory elements is among the considerations that show why we should not conceive propositional justification as simply an informational condition

---

15 For detailed discussions of how phenomenal elements figure in justification see Tucker (2013) and Smithies (2019).

such that, if S believes that p in the light of its (accessible) elements, S justifiedly believes p. Such elements can pave the way for believing p on an inadequate basis. Imagine that I learn some merits of a literary work. They may move me toward a positive attitude toward it and, given that attitude, as lowering the threshold for positive appraisal, I believe it is excellent on the basis of *other* elements that I simply like in it. This does not entail that I justifiedly believe it is excellent. Granted, if challenged, I might adduce the enlightening elements; but this does not show that, *prior* to the challenge, I believed the proposition on an adequate basis. Once again, we can see both that propositional justification requires *having* normatively adequate grounds for believing p and that doxastic justification requires believing *on* such grounds. Considerations that cast light on p may or may not be such grounds, and they can lead to belief that is based neither on them nor on any justificatory basis. Such cases are among those showing that the *justifiability* of p for S at a given time does not entail S's already having propositional justification for it. What we can justify depends on our resources; our propositional justification depends on our grounds. It is an epistemic good that we can have such extensive resources. But to assimilate propositional justification to propositional justifiability is like treating the ability to raise money as already having it.

The Indefinite Expandability of Justification and Knowledge

If any proposition trivially entails its disjunction with any other proposition, then propositional justification for any proposition entails propositional justification for disjunctions that one can readily see follow from it. This is a huge number. If, moreover, we know elementary arithmetic, we have justification for a vast range of propositions, for example uncountably many in such series as $2 > 1$, $3 > 2$, and so on. Here and in many other trivial cases, propositional justification is indefinitely extensive. Moreover, retaining it requires memorial retention of only a small number of justificatory materials (such as formuli), whereas even where each propositionally justified proposition can be known, retaining that knowledge requires retaining the myriad beliefs constituting the knowledge.

Fortunately, there are many substantive cases. Just thinking about a philosophical problem—or indeed any intellectual problem one understands well enough for reflection on it—confronts one with many possible inferences—valid or at least highly probable. If we are justified in a simple view, for example that knowing entails believing or that believing is not a process, we have propositional justification for believing such apparently entailed consequences as that it should not be possible for a person to know arithmetic truths the person does not believe and it should be deviant to ask, for example, "what were the stages of the process of your believing that you missed the deadline?"

Examples like these make it easy to overlook the importance of defeasibility. Suppose it is true that propositional justification is to be understood largely in terms of a relation between a justifier, say a proposition one can understand, and accessible supporting grounds one has for that proposition, and that at least much doxastic justification can be understood as roughly a realization of propositional justification. Still, the realization of propositional justification may yield only justification that is immediately defeated. If S is appropriately aware of defeat, that may prevent belief formation; if not, and S forms the belief in question, doxastic justification may not occur. Suppose I want to give my friend Mark a razor-sharp carving knife as a house-warming present. Believing he loves carving, I may have propositional justification for believing he will be pleased to receive it. But, just as I form the belief that he will be pleased and reach for the knife, I recall something I had temporarily forgotten at the time I saw the elegant knife: that he once expressed the superstitious belief that weapons like knives should only be bought. I may now lose overall justification for believing he will be pleased and may withhold the belief and find a different gift.

There is a major issue here. If justification is *entailed* by a ground for it, then, given retention of the ground, its defeat will not eliminate it. If not, then a belief whose formation is a realization of propositional justification does not, by defeat, lose justification altogether. Here a certain kind of epistemological rationalism, favors a holistic *retentional* account.[16] I would retain prima facie justification but fail to be justified *overall* in believing my friend will be pleased; on the *eliminationist* view, open to epistemological empiricists and possibly some rationalists, I would retain none.

This issue is connected with the matter of why we have so much more justification than knowledge. As many of our examples indicate, we have justification for a vast number of propositions we do not believe and hence do not know. Moreover, beliefs constituting knowledge are invariably true; truth is not required for doxastically or even propositionally justified beliefs. The additional point shown by some of our examples is that the kind of justification required for knowledge is not just any kind or degree. There are many truths we believe with enough justification to avoid the charge of intellectual laxity, but do not know. Granted, if knowledge does not entail justification, this opens up the possibility of more of it than is usually countenanced even by non-skeptics, but instances of knowledge without justification seem quite limited in both variety and number.

Nothing said here undermines the point that our knowledge is indefinitely expandable. If I come to know that p, then I can come to know p or

---

16 An example of how defeasible but justification might persist even when defeated see Ross (1930), and for recent explication of Ross see Phillips (2019).

q, for any q that does not take me beyond my comprehension (or is such that for some reason I cannot *believe* its disjunction with p, as where, if I am about to form the relevant belief, a brain-manipulating machine prevents this). Happily, there are many kinds of non-trivial extensions of knowledge. It remains true, however, that extensions of knowledge require gaining beliefs, whereas propositional justification may increase with no such burden on the mind and comes, even in great variety, with ordinary thinking and everyday perceptions of the world.

Propositional justification resides in our grounds for believing—in such elements in our lives as perceptions, memory impressions, bodily sensations, and, regarding the abstract as well as the concrete, intuitions. Given even a single sighting of a passing car, we may have such justification for many propositions whether or not we entertain them or ever come to believe them. These include propositions that attribute to what we see certain of the properties by which we see it—properties represented in our visual field. But given normal intuitional and inferential powers, having propositional justification for any proposition can give us propositional justification for others that we can easily see to be entailed by it. In any normal person, this allows for a vast number of propositionally justified propositions. Many of these are trivial, many never actually believed. But given the power of imagination and the blessings of insight, there is a vast number of significant propositions we can have justification to believe. Propositional justification, then, is not itself a trivial status. In addition to giving us a multitude of normative rights, it is commonly realized in its doxastic counterpart: justified belief. Here beliefs whose doxastic justification is based on what also grounds the corresponding propositional justification can guide our actions and, if true, often lead us to goals worth achieving. Many of our doxastically justified beliefs are true, and many of those constitute knowledge. But knowledge requires truth, and we cannot be expected to know, or even be able to know, everything we justifiedly believe. For all that, the grounds that yield propositional justification are not only of the kind that yield its doxastic counterpart, but also of a kind that commonly yields knowledge. Propositional justification, then, when sufficiently strong, is a kind of right to believe; it is often realized in beliefs rightfully held; and those may reflect truth and constitute valuable knowledge.

References

Audi, Robert. (1986). "Belief, Reason, and Inference," *Philosophical Topics*, XIV (1): 27–65.
Audi, Robert. (1991). "Structural Justification," *Journal of Philosophical Research*, XVI, 473–492.
Audi, Robert. (2011). *Rationality and Religious Commitment*. Oxford University Press.

Audi, Robert. (2015). "Intuition and Its Place in Ethics," *Journal of the American Philosophical Association*, 1 (1): 57–77.
Audi, Robert. (2020). *Seeing, Knowing, and Doing: A Perceptualist Account*. Oxford University Press.
Conee, Earl, and Richard Feldman. (2004). *Evidentialism*. Oxford University Press.
Feldman, Richard, and Earl Conee. (2019). "Between Belief and Disbelief," in *Believing in Accordance with the Evidence*, edited by Kevin McCain. Springer Nature.
Goldman, Alvin. (1988) "Strong and Weak Justification," *Philosophical Perspectives*, 2: 51–69.
Phillips, David. (2019). *Rossian Ethics: W. D. Ross and Contemporary Moral Theory*. Oxford University Press.
Ross, W. D. (1930). *The Right and the Good*. Oxford University Press.
Siscoe, Robert Weston. (2021). "Belief, Rational and Justified," *Mind*, 130 (517): 59–83.
Smithies, Declan. (2019). *The Epistemic Role of Consciousness*. Oxford University Press.
Tucker, Christopher. (2013). *Seemings and Justification*. Oxford University Press.

2 Theoretical Unity and the Priority of Propositional Justification

Jonathan L. Kvanvig

Propositionalists hold that the basic kind of epistemic support involves a relation between semantic contents, and thus oppose doxasticism which maintains that the basic kind of epistemic support targets beliefs themselves as opposed to their contents. Other options might also be present, perhaps, as when we describe a person as being justified in believing something, but here the focus will be on the disagreement between propositionalists and doxasticists.

The fundamental argument for propositionalism is two-fold. First, there are the problems facing doxasticism. Second, there is the role that propositional justification plays in the wide territory of epistemology for which we seek adequate theories. Since I have been arguing the former case for nearly three decades, beginning with Kvanvig and Menzel (1990), and extending through Kvanvig (1992, 1996, 2000, 2003a, 2003b, 2003c, 2005, 2007a, 2007b) and most recently in Kvanvig (2014), I will here focus on the positive case for propositionalism in terms of its theoretical and explanatory virtues.

Before proceeding, however, it may be useful to rehearse what I take to be the fundamental problems facing doxasticism. As I see it, there are two main problems. The first is the problem of essential cognitive admirability, of the sort some classical Foundationalists think we have about basic beliefs. For such beliefs (typically reporting the contents of immediate experience or our awareness of our own mental states), such Foundationalists take us to be incapable of error. The class of such claims is not important and may vary across the range of possible individuals. So, for simplicity, let's identify the class of such claims for a given person S as Γ_s. The difficulty such possibilities create for doxasticism is that there is a need to explain how there can be justification for a claim one doesn't believe, and to give an explanation of such a case, doxasticists must turn to counterfactual situations where the belief is present in spite of being actually absent. But when the claim is a member of Γ_s, every possible situation in which S believes the claim in question will be a case in which S infallibly and justifiably believes that claim. Hence, every member of Γ_s

will get counted as a claim for which S has justification, even those that S actually knows to be false.

The second problem concerns claims that involve a kind of epistemic blindspot, as discussed in Sorensen (1988), claims that can be true and for which one can have justification, but which cannot be believed without destroying the justificational basis for that claim. Such claims are the most extreme examples of cases in which belief itself can both enhance and diminish the degree of justification one has for a claim. For example, upon first learning about the squaring function, one can acquire justification for the claim that one has never considered that $11^2 = 121$, perhaps on the basis of knowing that one has only been considering examples of squaring single digit numbers. The problem such cases present for doxasticists is that every counterfactual situation in which one believes the claim in question will be a situation in which the belief itself has undermined the justification for the claim in question. As a result, the propositional justification that can actually be present for such epistemic blindspots can't be accounted for by considering counterfactual situations in which the belief is present.

These issues put negative pressure on doxasticists, but a strong case for propositionalism requires something beyond pointing out difficulties for contrary positions. Here my goal is to lay out the positive case for propositionalism, to which I now turn.

Mapping the Epistemological Landscape

The positive case begins with a proper characterization of the landscape of epistemology. It is often claimed that epistemology is simply the theory of knowledge, but that characterization is mistaken. Epistemology is concerned with successful cognition from a purely intellectual or theoretical point of view, one that abstracts from other dimensions of cognitive success such as its practical, moral, or aesthetic value.

Once we focus on this particular kind of successful cognition, the landscape falls into two distinct regions, the evaluative and the normative, mirroring the divisions in ethics between the theory of value and the theory of obligation. We can thus ask about which cognitive accomplishments are good, better, or best from a purely intellectual point of view, and we can ask questions about which cognitive states are to be counted as permissible, forbidden, or obligatory from a purely theoretical standpoint.

Dividing the landscape in this way leads to a focus on the great intellectual goods of (factive) knowledge, understanding, and theoretical wisdom as well as to a focus on the normative dimensions characterizable in terms of justification, warrant, rationality, and reasonability, among other normative notions.

We might also wish to add a third region to this landscape, one concerning character traits related to the other two regions. Doing so brings with it the possibility of a virtue epistemology, though every epistemology will show some interest in what kinds of habits, dispositions, and excellences make successful cognition from a purely intellectual point of view more probable than it would have been otherwise.

There is also a cautionary note to include here about this characterization of the subject matter of epistemology. Some will note my reference to purely intellectual points of view and theoretical concerns and will resist such language because of an attraction for a pragmatic theory of truth or on an account of knowledge subject to pragmatic encroachment. Any such intrusion by practical considerations into key elements of a complete epistemology raises a concern about whether and how to characterize the kind of successful cognition that delineates the epistemic realm from other normative realms. This point is worth noting and acknowledging, but here I want to table this issue in order to pursue our main task, which is the issue of what kind of normativity is fundamental to epistemology. In brief, however, the options for response include (i) resisting such pragmatisms, thereby allowing the characterization to remain as is, a strategy I pursue in Kvanvig (2011), (ii) refining the account so as to allow some intrusion of practical considerations in a way that allows reference to intellectual concerns to be sufficient for delineating epistemic normativity from mere practical rationality, or (iii) giving up on the idea that there is any such thing as a distinctively epistemic kind of normativity. In my view, this sequence goes from better to worse options, but in any case, I raise this concern to table it for another time.

Returning to our tripartite map of the landscape, I will here focus primarily on the first two parts, since it is in these areas that the case for propositionalism arises. The third area concerns dispositions, skills, habits, or excellences that may need to be defined in terms of the conceptual machinery found in the first two areas, but even if the definitional direction is reversed so that we define the good and the right in terms of them, the case for propositionalism remains independent of that issue. So here I will focus on the tasks for the first two areas and the issue of how to organize these tasks to generate an approach to epistemology that identifies some notion or notions as fundamental.

In the evaluative domain, there is a tradition that can be traced to medieval times at least on which knowledge is fundamental in virtue of the possibility of defining understanding as knowledge of causes and theoretical wisdom in terms of knowing what matters, knowing what is important. If we embrace this tradition, then we are on our way to determining what is fundamental to epistemology more broadly, needing only to inquire about the tasks of normative epistemology and the relationship between it and knowledge.

I doubt that things are quite this simple in the evaluative domain, for I doubt that understanding is properly characterized as a species of knowledge, as I argue in Kvanvig (2003c) and is also argued for in Pritchard (2007, 2009) and Pritchard (2010). This is another issue that we don't need to pursue here, however, for even if understanding is not a species of knowledge, the search for what is fundamental in epistemology will look pretty much the same, requiring an account of the tasks within the terrain of normativity and an account of the relationship between whatever is normatively fundamental and the great intellectual goods of knowledge, understanding, and wisdom. The approach I have developed opposes the medieval tradition above, characterizing understanding primarily in terms of justification rather than knowledge, while at the same time holding that knowledge is also to be characterized partially in terms of justification. Given this combination of views, it doesn't much matter whether we adopt the medieval view or resist it—the case for propositionalism will remain unaffected by that dispute. Since the medieval view has a kind of simplicity and elegance to it, I propose to simply assume it for present purposes, treating it as the evaluative backdrop for the central focus here, which is on the domain of epistemic normativity itself.

The Search for Fundamentality

A standard practice in epistemology is to notice the multiplicity of epistemically normative terms (warrant, rationality, justification, etc.) and try to figure out the relationships between them. Our issue, however, requires abstracting from the specific properties involved to the structural level where we attempt to delineate the tasks we face, regardless of which property we focus on or what the connections are between them. At the structural level, the first thing to notice is that our tasks are at least two-fold, one of which is holistic in character and the other atomistic. The holistic task is that of characterizing an all-things-considered assessment of when normative adequacy (of a purely intellectual sort) has been achieved. The atomistic task is that of characterizing a relationship between individual items of information or belief and other specific claims or beliefs. On occasion, I'll refer to the holistic project as that of providing a theory of justification, and to the atomistic pursuit as that of providing a theory of confirmation; equally instructive, though, would be to refer to the former in terms of the theory of rationality and the latter in terms of the theory of reasons. Nothing turns on the terminology used, however, for as most recognize, the epistemological use of such language is best thought of as an engagement in the use of terms of art, so the key here is to get a grip on the structural distinction rather than trying to determine which particular term of art has some advantage over others.

I should note in passing that the focus should be on the holism/atomism point here, rather than on the rationality/reasons contrast or the contrast between justification and confirmation. The reason is that neither of the latter contrasts shows much promise of being exhaustive, since the notions of reasons and confirmation, though atomistic, aren't likely to be capable of giving a full explanation of reasoning itself. The theory of reasons and the theory of reasoning, though related, are distinct, for reasons underlying Harman's mantra that implication is not inference, a point he makes in several locations, but a really clear and straightforward account of the distinction is in Harman and Kulkarni (2006). Presumably there is some way of linking reasons and reasoning, evidence and logic, confirmation and change in view, but no simple identification is promising. So a better approach here is not to try to make too much of the rationality/reasons contrast nor of the justification/confirmation contrast, focusing instead on the holism/atomism distinction itself, treating the other contrasts as stylistic variants for referring to this fundamental distinction.

Once we attend to the holism/atomism distinction, there is an easy tale to tell about how and why atomistic elements take priority over holistic features. For the holistic features are a function of the atomistic ones, and one can't read off the inputs to a function from its outputs. If your function is addition and its output is 12, that output doesn't give sufficient information for characterizing the inputs. They could be 8 and 4, 7 and 5, or something else. So if holistic elements are a function of atomistic ones, the direction of explanation should go from the inputs to the outputs, yielding priority for the atomistic elements over the holistic. In slogan form, the theory of incremental confirmation is prior to the theory of justification. The overall holistic picture of justification arises from the matrix of dot-like atomistic details concerning specific states of information and the epistemic support they generate for other specific states of information.

This point is worth commenting on a bit further, given the history of epistemology over the past century. Somewhere around the mid-twentieth century, coherentist sensibilities came to dominate epistemology: think of Sellars, Goodman, and Quine of the 1950s. Chisholm seemed to be the lone foundationalist left standing, but my point isn't about the foundationalism/coherentism distinction but the way in which the rise of coherentism focused epistemology on the holistic character of justification or rationality (conceived to be a constituent or necessary condition for knowledge). In the process of this rise of coherentism, certain historically dominant concerns, most notably the atomistic ones involved in the theory of reasons and confirmation, were no longer the focus of discussion. The theory of confirmation continued to flourish in the philosophy of science, but in a way generally divorced from work by those working in the theory of knowledge. This bifurcation is both historically important and disconcerting, since a broader understanding of the domain of epistemology makes it relatively easy to see why the atomistic aspects cannot be ignored in a complete epistemology.

So even if we found a completely adequate theory of justification or rationality or warrant, our initial inclination should be to think that such a theory will not give us a decent atomistic account of confirmation, reasons, or reasoning. If the former is a (non-bijective) function of the latter, attempts to reverse engineer the latter from the former are bound to fail.

One may hold out hope for this turn to holism by insisting that the holistic notion of justification is all that is needed in epistemology. One way to do this would be to maintain that of atomistic elements is best put in the arena of logic as part of its theory of reasoning. An alternative would be to express skepticism about the existence of the atomistic relations in question, holding instead that all there is to epistemic normativity is holistic. Either route would relieve the pressure of trying to reverse engineer these relations from the holistic character of justification, but neither route is especially promising. The problem for both views concerns the basing relation.

On this score, it is worth reminding ourselves of what I take to be failed objections from John Pollock and Alvin Plantinga against coherentism. Both authors claim that the holistic nature of coherentism renders it incapable of explaining what it is to properly base a belief on something that supports it. Plantinga (1993, p. 77ff.) claims that coherentists view all justified beliefs as properly basic, insisting that at least the pure form of the view resists the idea that warrant (or justification) is ever transmitted from some beliefs to other beliefs: there simply is no such thing as inferential justification for holistic theories such as pure coherentism. Pollock (1986, p. 81) claims that coherentists can't explain the distinction between doxastic and propositional justification because they can only explain the basing relation in terms of basing a belief on the entire system of information that generates justification for that belief, a hopelessly implausible claim. If Pollock is correct, then the only hope for coherentists would be to embrace Plantinga's characterization, but doing so requires that they reject the idea of inferential justification, the idea that some of our beliefs are properly based on other of our beliefs.

In my view, both authors are mistaken in supposing that coherentists have no resources for addressing the nature of the basing relation apart from the holistic character of justification which they emphasize. There is no good reason for thinking so, as I argue in Kvanvig (1995), but the relevance of the issue here doesn't depend on whether coherentists can successfully resist Pollock's criticism or Plantinga's characterization. What is relevant is the dire straits these authors put holistic theories in if they are correct. For if correct, the charges show that holistic theories are incapable of distinguishing between cases where one has good evidence but believes for the wrong reasons and cases where one's believing is properly based on the information that epistemically supports it. In short, the distinction between propositional and doxastic justification shows why there is no future for an epistemology that either eliminates the atomistic domain or tries to make it irrelevant to the central issues in epistemology. Even if the turn to holism is to be lauded, as I think it is, it can't also be a jettisoning of the relevance to epistemology of the atomistic domain.

Coherentists need to tread carefully here, however, for there is a danger that in characterizing the basing relation, their view will embrace claims that entail foundationalism. For holistic coherentism, it is only entire systems of information that impart justification, and yet it would seem that characterizing the basing relation is going to require maintaining that some subparts of such a system impart justification as well. Proper basing, that is, would seem to require basing on something that justifies. In what follows, I will assume that this claim is true, but coherentists shouldn't endorse it and don't need to. What they need is some account of the parts of a system that are crucial for proper basing, even while at the same time denying that those parts are things that justify. In my view, what coherentists need is some relation in the arena of causality or explanation for this purpose. I've suggested in Kvanvig (1995) that J.L. Mackie's notion of an INUS condition, which he uses to characterize his Humean account of causation, as developed in Mackie (1974), might be up to the task. On this approach, a properly based belief is one that is based on something that is an INUS condition for justification: it itself is insufficient for imparting any degree of justification but is also a non-redundant part of a system of information that is unnecessary but sufficient for justification. This is but one idea for how coherentists can approach the basing relation without rejecting holism, and perhaps there are other, more promising ideas that can be gleaned from considerations about the nature of causation and explanation.

In the next section I want to pursue the connection between atomism and propositionalism, with the aim of showing how one gets from this initial case for atomism to an argument on behalf of propositionalism. Before doing so, though, I want to raise a warning for those who will see hope for avoiding propositionalism by defending the priority of the holistic over the atomistic. The arguments against alternatives to propositionalism that I am here shelving in order to focus on the positive case for propositionalism were in the holistic domain of the theory of justification itself (or rationality or warrant). If those arguments are successful, even the priority of holistic notions concerning epistemic normativity will provide no safe haven for avoiding propositionalism. Moreover, even if those arguments could be skirted in some way, the more general case for propositionalism would remain, if propositionalism provides the best approach to atomistic epistemological tasks.

One more cautionary word about terminology before proceeding. I am using the language of propositions here to talk about semantically evaluable elements involved in mentation. Perhaps there remain some who think that propositions exhaust this domain, but even such diehards recognize the problems for such a view. In short, propositions are not fine-grained enough for this purpose, on the best accounts I know of regarding the nature of propositions. On this issue, I endorse the Fregean idea that there is also the need for some mode of presentation in order to get a fine-grained enough picture of mental content to explain its role in action and reasoning. There are reasons for thinking that such modes of presentation have to be semantically evaluable as well, as I argue in Kvanvig (2020), since they play a crucial role in reasoning.

Here, however, we can abstract from these issues, understanding the language of propositions to be a simplifying device for focusing on the semantically evaluable contents of mental states, for nothing regarding the debate between propositionalists and doxasticists turns on the issue of whether propositional content is exhaustive of mental content. What matters is the link between atomism and propositionalism, for I will argue that the former provides a good argument for the latter.

Atomism and Propositionalism

Once we focus on the theories of reasons and confirmation, ignoring for the time being any potential links to the theories of reasoning and inference, we face two options. One is that one of these two is fundamental and the other derivative, or that neither is derivative of the other. There is some temptation toward this latter conclusion, since the theory of confirmation would seem to involve a relation on informational contents, which we might represent as $C(p,q)$ when p confirms (incrementally) q, whereas the language of reasons may seem to advert to some mental state that is a reason for some other mental state. Or perhaps only the target of a reason need be a mental state or attitude (in epistemological discussions), as when Thomas M. Scanlon (2014) proposes that the reasons relation is a four-place relation that obtains between a proposition p, an agent x, a set of circumstances c, and an action or attitude a: $R(p,x,c,a)$. Scanlon also wants to maintain that his account doesn't make reasons relative to persons, but rather holds that "something is a reason for an agent only if it is also a reason for any other agent in similar circumstances" Scanlon (2014, p. 32). This claim doesn't follow from the four-place characterization of reasons, and if we want to maintain the point, we don't need the place for a person at all. Dropping the reference to a person would nicely simplify the view to one on which a reason is properly characterized as a three-place relation between a proposition, a set of circumstances, and an attitude, mirroring what we seem to have learned in the theory of confirmation, to wit, that confirmation is not a two-place relation between informational contents, but at least a three-place relation between an input, a target, and some assumed background system of information.

Regardless of how best to think about Scanlon's view, the point to note is that a first glance suggests a relation on propositions or informational content, and relation on mental states themselves or perhaps a mixed relation between propositional contents and mental states (attitudes). There is also a considerable literature on whether reasons are mental states or facts, but I think we can skirt this issue by treating the language of facts in terms of that of (true) propositions, and the issue of whether one's reasons must be true won't affect the prospects of propositionalism so long as the support generated is generated by informational content alone. We thus have some work to do if we wish to show that the atomistic parts of epistemology are best understood in terms of $C(p,q)$ instead of some more complex R relation involving at least one component that is itself a mental state or attitude.

The Scanlon view is instructive in another way as well. For it shows that the debate between propositionalists and doxasticists in not exhaustive of the options here. A doxasticist holds that the reasons relation is a relation between mental states, and the propositionalist maintains that it is a relation on propositions or informational contents. Scanlon's view is a hybrid of these two views, identifying an input that is propositional and an output that is (in the case of its epistemic application) a mental state. I suppose there is theoretical room here as well for switching places for the propositional elements and the mental elements, but the possibilities are not as important as the fact that neither propositionalism nor doxasticism can succeed merely by resisting the other. The logical space is simply too large for that, as Scanlon's approach shows.

It is instructive here to put a bit of pressure on Scanlon's characterization of the fourth *relatum*, in terms of an act or attitude. Acts and attitudes are subject to a type/token ambiguity: raising one's arm can be done by many different individuals, when thinking about it in terms of a type of act, but only once on a given occasion by a specific person when thinking about it in terms of a tokening of the type in question. So Scanlon's view comes in two different forms, depending on whether the act or attitude is thought of at the type-level or at the token-level.

Suppose the proposal is that reasons relation targets at the token-level. The problem for such a proposal is that reasons for action and belief can be generic and unspecific. You have a reason to obey the speed limit, let us suppose. But obeying the speed limit doesn't delimit any particular token action, as would be needed if reasons always target at the token-level. There are a variety of ways of obeying the speed limit: if it is 35, one could drive 34, or 33, or 34.5, and so on. Similarly for belief: having a reason to think that the President lies leaves open a variety of ways of encoding that content in a token mental state. First, there is the issue of modes of presentation, since the belief type in question can be instanced through a variety of Fregean senses. Second, belief itself is a broad category, compatible with considerable variability in terms of degrees of belief and levels of confidence. In short, appeal to the token-level of mentality requires more specificity than our subject matter involves.

Note as well that it won't help here to change the focus of the reason to some particular degree of belief. First, going Bayesian in this way doesn't help with the first issue concerning degrees of belief. More important, though, is this. There is simply no good explanation as to why or how reasons have to target such precise entities as degrees of belief. For lots of our reasons are reasons on behalf of ranges of values, as when we have statistical reasons for thinking that some political candidate will lose an election. Note the central features here: there are such things as reasons that are statistical in nature, and no statistical reason is ever a reason for some precise degree of belief.

Moreover, if we resort to confidence intervals to replace the notion of degrees of belief, we run into the problem of psychological limitations. For statistical reasons can pick out intervals of any arbitrarily specified sort, but what confidence intervals a person, or humanity in general, is capable of is a matter of contingent fact. So some of the possible confidence intervals will be incapable of being psychologically encoded, and hence once again, the reasons in question will have to be able to be honored by a variety of specific confidence intervals.

Hence going Bayesian will provide no safe haven for the view of reasons that requires targets at the token-level. The moral of the story is that a decent account of reasons must acknowledge the generic character of what a reason is a reason for. The token-level view simply cannot do that.

So perhaps resorting to the type-level is a better idea. On this approach, the generic character of the targets of reasons is honored, for a given belief type can often be tokened in a variety of ways. (This claim is meant to be compatible with the fact that some belief types may be tokenable in only one way, but those cases are unusual even if possible.) Moreover, one could alter this approach to accommodate Bayesian inclinations by talking about degree-of-belief types or confidence interval types in place of belief types themselves, if one prefers fancier and more formal epistemology. What is central here is the type-level itself, not the psychological reality at the type-level.

The problem for the type-level view concerns the issue of individuating states at the type-level. For purposes of discussion, I will assume that we are talking about belief types, though what I say can be easily transposed into Bayesian frameworks as well. The issue of individuation gives us a quick and pleasing argument for why the relation between conferrers and doxastic targets of epistemic support is best explained in terms of the relation between the content of the conferrer and the content of the target.

At the type-level, we individuate mental states in terms of their informational content. The difference between that content and the mental state itself is some type of attitude by a particular individual or group, though there may be other items in the belief relation other than the attitude and its content. Perhaps we should say the same of conferrers:

conferrers are individuated by their contents, under a mode of representation of some sort, typically thought of in terms of belief or experience. This remark about conferrers would need further discussion, however, given the popularity of the idea that reasons are always factive. If so, there is some inclination for thinking that conferrers should simply be construed as facts, thereby undermining the mentalistic view just articulated. Matters are complicated though, since both views can be true if conferrers are always seeming states, for then the seeming state itself would be the reason, and the reason would also be a fact, the fact of the seeming state itself.

Regardless of how these issues play out, the individuation of mental states plays a central role in the argument from atomism to propositionalism. For if belief types are individuated in terms of their propositional content, we get a pleasing explanation of how and why conferrers make rational the beliefs that they support: they do so by providing grounds for thinking that the content in question is true. The existence of such grounds informs us that there is something in the grounds themselves that shows that the propositional content is true, and hence that the believing of that content is warranted by the prior relationship between the grounds and the truth of the propositional content in question.

The basic idea here is that once we move to the type-level and distinguish the attitude from the content, the support for the attitude becomes clearly derivative on the support for the content. When something that counts as a conferrer is present, our theoretical question is what to make of it. The doxasticist tells us that the conferrer supports taking the attitude of belief toward a particular content. We should want to know why that content and not some other. The answer to this why-question generates the argument for propositionalism: this content and not some other because the conferrer *shows* that the content in question is true.

Lest this last remark seem to overstate, note that x can show y without entailing it and without generating an extreme probability for it. The look on your face shows that you are angry, but that remark doesn't require entailment or unsurpassable probability. It is the showing that is central to the idea of epistemic support that is sufficient for rational belief, given the absence of defeaters and underminers.

Propositionalism requires more than that the targets of epistemic support are propositional. It also requires that our account of conferrers bottoms out at the propositional level as well. Here the story is quite simple and similar. If conferrers are facts, we can identify facts with true propositions and simplify our ontology a bit, and we get the other half of propositionalism for free. If conferrers need not be facts, we can still distinguish between the evidence and one's evidence, where the latter reveals to one what is best to conclude, and it does so because the evidence—that which confers justification—supports that which is best to conclude. As before, tracing the explanatory links lands us in the territory of propositionalism, where the fundamental epistemic idea is that there is a confirmation relation between semantic contents that is the bedrock for the story of how any of us come to have rational opinions based on either our experience, our other beliefs, or other facts that might be relevant.

Conclusion

Seen in this light, the idea that mental state types are the conferrers and targets of epistemic support is partially right, if we focus on the typing in question in terms of propositional content. If we focus, however, on the attitude rather than the content, we see why the appeal to mental state types is just a kind of Rube Goldberg machine. It has some stuff that is doing the fundamental work needed (that is, the propositional content in question) and then it has a bizarre multitude of other machinery that contributes nothing to the functioning of the machine but is powered by the parts that are doing all the work. That's the story as to why the appeal to mental state types is only partially right. It is right enough to sustain propositionalism, partial enough to undermine doxasticism.

References

Harman, Gilbert and Sanjeev R. Kulkarni. (2006). "The Problem of Induction." *Philosophy and Phenomenological Research* 72(3): 559–575.

Kvanvig, Jonathan L. (1992). *The Intellectual Virtues and the Life of the Mind: On the Place of the Virtues in Contemporary Epistemology*. Savage, Maryland: Rowman and Littlefield.

Kvanvig, Jonathan L. (1995). "Coherentists' Distractions." *Philosophical Topics* 23: 257–275.

Kvanvig, Jonathan L. (1996). "Plantinga's Proper Function Theory of Warrant." In *Warrant and Contemporary Epistemology*, edited by Jonathan L Kvanvig, pp. 281–306. Savage, Maryland: Rowman and Littlefield.

Kvanvig, Jonathan L. (2000). "Zagzebski on Justification." *Philosophy and Phenomenological Research* 60: 191–196.

Kvanvig, Jonathan L. (2003a). "Propositionalism and the Perspectival Character of Justification." *American Philosophical Quarterly* 40(1): 3–18.

Kvanvig, Jonathan L. (2003b). "Simple Reliabilism and Agent Reliabilism." *Philosophy and Phenomenological Research* 66(2): 451–457.

Kvanvig, Jonathan L. (2003c). *The Value of Knowledge and the Pursuit of Understanding*. Cambridge: Cambridge University Press.

Kvanvig, Jonathan L. (2005). "On Denying a Presupposition of Sellars' Problem: A Defense of Propositionalism." *Veritas* 50: 173–190.

Kvanvig, Jonathan L. (2007a). "Propositionalism and the Metaphysics of Experience." *Philosophical Issues* 17: 165–178.

Kvanvig, Jonathan L. (2007b). "Two Approaches to Epistemic Defeat." In *Alvin Plantinga: Contemporary Philosophy in Focus*, edited by Deane-Peter Baker, pp. 107–124. Cambridge: Cambridge University Press.

Kvanvig, Jonathan L. (2011). "Against Pragmatic Encroachment." *Logos & Episteme* 2(1): 77–85.
Kvanvig, Jonathan L. (2014). *Rationality and Reflection*. Oxford: Oxford University Press.
Kvanvig, Jonathan L. (2020). "Virtue Epistemology, Two Kinds of Internalism, and the Intelligibility Problem." In *Virtue Theoretic Epistemology: New Methods and Approaches*, edited by John Greco and Christoph Kelp, pp. 147–166. Cambridge: Cambridge University Press.
Kvanvig, Jonathan L. and Christopher P. Menzel. (1990). "The Basic Notion of Justification." *Philosophical Studies* 59: 235–261.
Mackie, J. L. (1974). *The Cement of the Universe: A Study of Causation*. Oxford: Oxford University Press.
Plantinga, Alvin. (1993). *Warrant: The Current Debate*. Oxford: Oxford University Press.
Pollock, John. (1986). *Contemporary Theories of Knowledge*. Totowa, NJ: Rowman and Littlefield.
Pritchard, Duncan. (2007). "The Value of Knowledge." In *The Stanford Encyclopedia of Philosophy*, edited by Edward N. Zalta, fall 2007 edn. Metaphysics Research Lab, Stanford University.
Pritchard, Duncan. (2009). "Knowledge, Understanding, and Epistemic Value." *Royal Institute of Philosophy Supplement* 84: 19–43.
Pritchard, Duncan. (2010). "Knowledge and Understanding." In *The Nature and Value of Knowledge: Three Investigations*, edited by Adrian Haddock, Alan Millar, and Duncan Pritchard, pp. 3–90. Oxford: Oxford University Press.
Scanlon, T. M. (2014). *Being Realistic About Reasons*. New York: Oxford University Press.
Sorensen, Roy A. (1988). *Blindspots*. Oxford: Oxford University Press.

3 What Does Logic Have to do With Justified Belief?

Why Doxastic Justification is Fundamental[1]

Hilary Kornblith

As George Boole (1958/1854) saw it, the laws of logic are the laws of thought, and by this he meant not that human thought is actually governed by the laws of logic, but, rather, that it should be. Boole's view that the laws of logic have normative implications for how we ought to think is anything but an outlier. The idea that violating the laws of logic involves epistemic impropriety has seemed to many to be just obvious.

It has seemed especially obvious to those who see propositional justification as more fundamental than doxastic justification. Whatever other principles are required for defining propositional justification, the laws of logic seem indispensable. The idea that violation of the laws of logic involves some sort of epistemic impropriety—whatever the peculiarities of our psychology may be—has served as a fixed point around which defenders of the fundamentality of propositional justification are largely united, whatever their other differences.

In this chapter, I defend the contrary view, that the laws of logic do not, in virtue of being the laws of logic, have implications for a theory of justified belief. Moreover, I defend the view that the notion of doxastic justification is more fundamental than the notion of propositional justification. The connection between these two apparently unrelated claims is an important focus of this chapter.[2]

The Arguments-On-Paper Thesis

Here is one very natural way to think about justified belief. Elsewhere, I have referred to it as the Arguments-On-Paper Thesis (c.f., Kornblith, 1980). On this way of thinking about things, questions about justification

---

1 Thanks to Jonathan Kvanvig and Luis Oliveira for comments on a draft of this chapter. This chapter is dedicated to the memory of Gil Harman.
2 I provided a defense of these claims in my (2017) and (2020). This chapter further develops the arguments of those papers, arguments which are deeply indebted to Goldman (1979). Gilbert Harman (1970) argued early on that the laws of logic have nothing to do with a theory of inference. These ideas are developed in important ways by Malmgren (n.d.) and Talbott (n.d.).

are addressed by thinking about the quality of certain arguments. Imagine for a moment that we were to list all of the propositions which a certain subject believes. We may now say that a subject is propositionally justified in believing a proposition just in case that proposition requires no argument, or, alternatively, there is a good argument for the proposition on the basis of appropriate propositions on the list. A subject is doxastically justified in holding a belief just in case that subject holds the belief and is propositionally justified in holding the belief, and either the proposition believed requires no argument and is held on that basis or the subject holds the belief on the basis of the argument in virtue of which it is propositionally justified.[3]

Clearly, such a view needs to be filled out in a number of ways. Someone who holds such a view needs to say which propositions, if any, require no argument. In addition, the propositions which may serve as justifying premises need to be identified. And, of course, one needs to say what constitutes a good argument. Different theorists will fill out this view in a variety of ways.

Foundationalists will hold that there are certain propositions which require no argument at all. Perhaps such propositions are indubitable, or they are infallible, or they are self-evident, or they have a presumption in their favor, or some such thing. On any foundationalist version of the Arguments-On-Paper Thesis, however, there is some class of propositions which has a special epistemic status in virtue of which they require no argument. We can put a star next to each such proposition on the list of propositions which a subject believes. A good argument, on this view, will then be one which takes only starred propositions as premises. But of course, there will be additional constraints on good arguments specifying the favored relationship or relationships between premises and conclusions. I will come back to this issue.

Coherentists will hold that there are no propositions which require no argument. No proposition, on this view, has the special epistemic status which foundationalists claim for their favored premises. But far from being more selective about the premises of good arguments, coherentists will allow every proposition on the list of propositions believed to serve as a premise; every proposition on the list gets a star. A good argument, for a coherentist, will have a very long list of premises; it must include every proposition a subject believes. And here too, additional constraints are needed specifying the relationship between premises and conclusions in good arguments.

---

3 Richard Foley (2012) and Paul Silva (2015) have offered interesting and important arguments against the basing requirement on doxastic justification, but this is definitely a minority view. Unfortunately, I cannot engage with these arguments here because they would take me too far afield from the concerns of this chapter, but see Oliveira (2015) for discussion.

What then is the proper relationship between premises and conclusion in a good argument? This, it seems, is the subject matter of logic. Were we to limit the notion of logic here to deductive logic, however, our account of justified belief would be extremely impoverished. We should thus acknowledge that the relevant notion of "good argument" at issue here is broader than deductive validity. What is needed to fill out this view is an inductive logic as well, or an account of inference to the best explanation, or abductive inference, or some such thing. Some will wish to appeal to probabilistic notions as well. Although the details here matter, and they vary significantly among different theorists, the big picture is quite straightforward: propositionally justified belief is explained in terms of the notion of a good argument, and goodness of argument is explained by the laws of logic, both deductive and non-deductive, together, perhaps, with a theory of probability.

Questions about justified belief are thus addressed in apsychological terms. This crucial feature of the Arguments-On-Paper Thesis is obscured by a familiar bit of terminology: We speak of rules of inference within a logical system, thereby eliding the important distinction between a certain psychological process, namely, inference, on the one hand, and logical and probabilistic relations among propositions, on the other. This terminology both hides the transition from claims about the logical realm to claims about the psychological, and it thereby makes the Arguments-On-Paper Thesis seem entirely innocuous when, instead, it involves a very powerful substantive claim. The Arguments-On-Paper Thesis endows the laws of logic with fundamental normative significance. Such significance cannot, of course, be provided by terminological fiat. It will therefore be important to bring the transition from the psychological to the logical out from its hiding place in a convenient bit of terminology into the light.[4]

Justification as an Empirical Phenomena

Let me present a motivation for looking at justified belief in a different way. I begin with an anti-skeptical assumption: we have a great deal of knowledge and justified belief. Some, no doubt, will see this as cheating. The rejection of skepticism must be earned, they will say, rather than simply assumed. I certainly understand this sentiment, but I will proceed with my working anti-skeptical assumption nonetheless. Indeed, it seems to me virtually undeniable that we have a great deal of knowledge and justified belief. From the most modest epistemic achievements of everyday life—our knowledge of our whereabouts, the objects in front of us, the likely consequences of various actions which we might undertake, and so on—to the very substantial epistemic achievements of the sciences, our

---

4 The points of this paragraph are, of course, due to Harman (1970). See also Quilty-Dunn and Mandelbaum (2018).

lives are permeated by knowledge and justified belief and our thoughts and our actions are incomprehensible without supposing that knowledge and justified belief are widespread. In what follows, I will simply focus on justified belief.

What I suggest is that we view justified belief as an epistemic phenomenon to be examined, in much the same manner as various physical phenomena, such as heat, or motion, or lightning may be viewed as phenomena worthy of examination and elucidation. Such an examination can only begin if we embark on our study with at least a rough capacity to recognize many instances of the phenomenon at issue. Thus, for example, when Galileo set out to measure temperature for the first time, he took himself to have a very rough recognitional capacity for temperature differences. He knew that a summer's day in Genoa was warmer than a winter's day at the top of the Matterhorn, even if he was in no position to quantify that difference. He knew that steam was hotter than water which, in turn, was warmer than ice. He could recognize gross differences in temperature, or at least many such differences, and this was a necessary condition for so much as beginning to study temperature. If he had no capacity for making any judgments about temperature at all, then he would have been in no position to undertake, or even conceive of, a study of such a phenomenon.

So too, I shall assume, with justified belief. We have a first-pass recognitional capacity for justified belief, and it is this recognitional capacity which affords us epistemic access to the phenomenon we wish to examine. Just as with Galileo's study of temperature, we may have a good many beliefs about the phenomenon at the beginning of our study, but many of these pretheoretical beliefs will need to be modified or abandoned as our study progresses. We make use of our recognitional capacity to get our study going, and then we examine the instances of the phenomenon to see what features those instances share, what it is that provides the theoretical unity to the phenomenon, what it is that makes the phenomenon a fit object of theoretical investigation.

This sort of assumption is certainly not unique to me, or to philosophers who share my view about the Arguments-On-Paper Thesis or the relationship between propositional and doxastic justification. Roderick Chisholm, for example, makes a similar assumption about the phenomenon of knowledge. We presuppose, first, that there *is* something that we know and we adopt the working hypothesis that *what* we know is pretty much that which, on reflection, we think we know (cf., Chisholm, 1977, p. 16).

Chisholm here adopts the very assumption about knowledge that I make about justified belief: he assumes, although he does not make use of this terminology, that we have a good first-pass recognitional capacity for instances of knowledge. And this, as he sees it, is absolutely necessary for embarking on a study of the nature of knowledge. Indeed, he makes the very same assumption about justified belief.

This is a working hypothesis, as Chisholm puts it, and it is one which, at least in principle, we might be forced to give up as our study proceeds. Like Chisholm, I see such a failure, at the outset, as exceptionally unlikely. Nevertheless, as our theoretical investigation progresses, we could fail to find any real unity in the phenomenon we set out to study. We might, in short, come to the view that there really is no such phenomenon at all. Scientific studies sometimes come to an end in just this way. It is especially common in medicine, for example, to set out to investigate what one takes to be a certain disease or illness on the basis of a characteristic set of symptoms, only to find that there is no such underlying condition, but only some symptoms in a collection of cases with heterogeneous causes. What seemed like a genuine phenomenon, a fit object of theoretical investigation, turned out to lack the requisite theoretical unity. Were this sad end to be the case with knowledge or justified belief, we would be forced to a certain sort of skepticism: not the view that a well-defined phenomenon had, as it turns out, no actual instances, but instead, the conclusion that there was no well-defined phenomenon there in the first place.[5] With Chisholm, however, I not only begin my study of justified belief with the optimistic view that this is unlikely to be the case; I also share his view, at the end of the day, that the phenomenon of justified belief is genuine, much as we disagree about the nature of that phenomenon.

In viewing justified belief as a phenomenon worthy of investigation, we are led to see the Arguments-On-Paper Thesis for the substantive empirical claim it is. If the Arguments-On-Paper Thesis is correct, then when we examine the phenomenon of justified belief, we should find that such beliefs are based on arguments of the sort elucidated in section I above: they are either ultimately based on premises which need no argument by way of good deductive and non-deductive arguments, or they are based on good deductive and non-deductive arguments which take as premises the entire body of our beliefs at an earlier moment. We have, at present, a well-developed account of the nature of good deductive argument, and there are various approaches available, both probabilistic and otherwise, to an account of the goodness of non-deductive argument. Although there are some who hold that basing requires the self-conscious endorsement of the arguments at issue (e.g., BonJour, 1985), others endorse a looser "taking" requirement on inference (e.g., Boghossian, 2014) or, more commonly, still weaker causal requirements. What all of these accounts entail, however, is that the logic of good argument be reflected in our belief acquisition and revision. The Arguments-On-Paper which define good argumentation must, in short, be psychologically real. While many epistemologists who have defended versions of the Arguments-On-Paper Thesis have been attracted to it because they viewed it as a way of

---

5 This skeptical conclusion is exactly the way Michael Williams (1996) views the matter in rejecting what he revealingly terms "epistemological realism."

depsychologizing epistemology,[6] viewing justified belief as a phenomenon for theoretical investigation forces defenders of that Thesis to come to terms with its psychological implications.

Is There Empirical Support for the Arguments-On-Paper Thesis?

I don't mean to suggest that the psychological implications of the Arguments-On-Paper Thesis are pretheoretically implausible. Indeed, I think that quite the opposite is true. The suggestion that our justified beliefs are, in fact, psychologically based on good argumentation, where good argumentation is defined by some combination of deductive logic, inductive logic, inference to the best explanation, and/or the kinds of probabilistic transitions elaborated upon by formal epistemologists, has not only informed a variety of research programs in epistemology since Aristotle; it has done so precisely because this suggestion is so attractive on its face.

This approach not only provides a satisfying unification of various formal studies in logic broadly conceived with the normative issues addressed by epistemologists; it also makes sense of a good deal of our normative practice of giving and asking for reasons.[7] Someone who makes a surprising claim will likely find that others press a demand for reasons: What makes you think that? The challenge can be met, of course, by argumentation, but those who cannot respond satisfactorily will not only be pressed to withdraw their claim; they will feel the force of the demand for reasons and, if finally unable to provide a satisfactory argumentative defense, will come, at least typically, to give up their belief. The Arguments-On-Paper Thesis provides a straightforward explanation of this practice. Those whose beliefs are justified will have at their disposal a good argument in favor of their beliefs. If we come to realize that we have no such argument, we are thereby shown that our belief was not justified, and we will therefore give it up. The readiness with which we are able to provide such arguments when challenged, and the readiness to give up our beliefs when we fail to meet the challenge, jointly serve to provide an exceptionally attractive line of support for the Arguments-On-Paper Thesis. The psychological and sociological implications of the Thesis thus should not be ignored, nor should they be seen as a source of embarrassment. These implications should, instead, be embraced by those who subscribe to the Arguments-On-Paper Thesis for they provide a crucial source of its support.

---

6 For an extremely interesting discussion of the history of the debate about psychologism in the German-speaking world during the late nineteenth and early twentieth centuries, see Kusch (1995).

7 The line of thinking in this paragraph has been forcefully pressed by Brandom (2000), especially Chapter 3; Kaplan (1985), Leite (2004), and Williams (1996), among others.

Additional support may be garnered from psychological research, and this support comes, it seems, in two different forms: investigation of our logical capacities, and a very general account, implicit in much research in the cognitive sciences, of how cognition is possible.

There has been a good deal of research on the logical capacities of human beings, even apart from any special training in logic. One research program has it that there are substantial such capacities, and that these capacities play a central role in cognition. Lance Rips (1994) has been a leader in such research, and he has argued that we not only show a striking sensitivity to deductive relations among our beliefs, but that we regularly engage in valid deductive inference. Those who have taught an introductory logic course may approach this work with a good deal of skepticism. How could it be that the very same individuals who regularly show great difficulty in learning the basics of deductive logic, and who regularly make a wide range of errors when confronted with basic deductive problem sets, should nevertheless be credited with substantial deductive capacities and viewed as regularly making use of them?

The work of such mental logicians as Rips are not so easily discredited. The first point to make is that it is one thing to be sensitive to deductive relations among beliefs and to regularly engage in valid deductive reasoning. It is quite another to be able to articulate valid principles of deductive logic and to manipulate a formal system. No one denies, for example, that human beings are sensitive to all manner of perceptual constancies in their environment and that these capacities play a central role in the production of perceptual belief. But allowing that there are such sensitivities in no way commits one to the absurd view that ordinary perceivers are in any position to articulate what these perceptual constancies are. The position of the mental logicians is that our sensitivity to logical relations among beliefs is very much like our sensitivity to perceptual constancies. These capacities play a central role in governing belief acquisition and revision without our having explicit beliefs about them.

But what should we say about the errors that our students make in courses on formal logic? How is this supposed to be compatible with the existence of a mental logic guiding our reasoning? Here, as elsewhere in cognitive science, it is necessary to appeal to a competence/performance distinction. The suggestion that we have a substantial deductive competence is fully compatible with the existence of performance errors. Just as the supposition of a grammatical competence is compatible with a wide range of errors in the production of speech, the existence of a deductive competence is equally compatible with a wide range of errors in deductive reasoning. The competence/performance distinction does not provide the mental logicians with a get out of jail free card, permitting them to simply ignore all evidence of deductive malfeasance and chalk them up, on every occasion, to factors interfering with a perfect underlying deductive competence. Nor do mental logicians treat it in this way. There are sensitive issues here about how best to explain the patterns of good and bad reasoning which we see in ordinary cognizers. My point is simply that there is an active research program ongoing which may serve to provide aid and comfort to defenders of the Arguments-On-Paper Thesis.

Just how much deductive competence is to be credited to ordinary cognizers thus remains to be settled, but even the most ambitious and optimistic researchers in this area have not claimed to find evidence of a full inductive logic of the sort needed to fund the Arguments-On-Paper Thesis. The work of the mental logicians needs to be extended and developed a good deal for a full-fledged empirical defense of the Arguments-On-Paper Thesis to be within reach. The work of the mental logicians, however, provides a non-trivial start on such a defense.

Further grounds for optimism on this score may be thought to be found in very general considerations about how cognition is possible. What I have in mind here is the kind of approach championed by Jerry Fodor (1975, 2008) in support of the language of thought hypothesis. Fodor argues that implicit in an extraordinarily wide range of research in the cognitive sciences is a commitment to viewing cognition as computation over sentences in a language of thought. This hypothesis requires that such computation is sensitive to syntactic features of our mental representations, and what this comes to is nothing more nor less than the postulation of the very sort of mental logic required to fund the Arguments-On-Paper Thesis. Our mental mechanisms, on this view, are sensitive to logical relations among our mental representations, and our inferences are thus simply a matter of drawing out relevant consequences, both deductive and non-deductive, of new information provided by our input systems together with the great fund of information which is stored in memory. If Fodor is right that such a view is implicit in virtually all research in the cognitive sciences, then there is very substantial ground for optimism about an empirical defense of the Arguments-On-Paper Thesis.

There is, however, a fly in the ointment. Fodor distinguishes between the operation of input systems, which, he argues, are modular, and the operation of central cognitive processes, which are not. Modular systems are able to work as smoothly and efficiently as they do precisely because they do not have access to the large body of information stored in memory. They don't need to have access to such information in order to perform the work that they do. This simplifies the cognitive task which input systems are required to perform, and it makes our task of understanding how it is that they perform these tasks that much easier. As Fodor argues, we know a great deal about input systems.

Central cognitive processes, however, are another matter entirely. Such processes can only do their appointed job by drawing extensively on information stored in memory. These processes are global, and this makes their computational task that much more difficult, and, consequently, that much more difficult for us to understand. Accordingly, Fodor is led to endorse what he calls *Fodor's First Law of the Nonexistence of Cognitive Science*: "the more global ... a cognitive process is, the less anybody understands it" (Fodor, 1983, p. 107).

The problem is, I believe, even more severe than Fodor makes it out to be. The kinds of global computational processes which Fodor claims are performed in central processing are ones which directly raise problems of computational complexity.[8] Such processes are not difficult to understand; they simply cannot actually exist. Indeed, it is Fodor's language of thought hypothesis which raises this very problem. While one might seek to circumvent the problem of computational complexity by arguing that global processes should be understood in non-computational terms, explained, perhaps, by the operation of lower-level non-computational processes, Fodor insists that all of cognition is to be explained by syntactic operations over representations in the language of thought, and, at the same time, that such operations must operate globally rather than locally. Problems of computational complexity demonstrate, however, that global computational processes of this sort cannot be carried out in real time.

The kind of support for the Arguments-On-Paper Thesis which is implicit in Fodor's work, then, proves to be illusory. If the Arguments-On-Paper Thesis is to obtain empirical support, it will need to come from further developments in the work of the mental logicians.

Let me summarize the argument of this section and its predecessor. The Arguments-On-Paper Thesis may seem, at first glance, to be innocuous. The identification of propositional justification with good argumentation seems quite trivial and undeniable. But if we are to understand doxastic justification in the usual manner, as belief which is propositionally justified and held on the basis of an argument which propositionally justifies it, and if we are to endorse, in addition, a robust anti-skepticism, then the Arguments-On-Paper Thesis commits us to a substantial empirical claim: that the great majority of our beliefs—the body of our justified beliefs—are held on the basis of good arguments. I have urged that we need to take this empirical commitment seriously. This section has explored some of the ways in which one might try to make good on that empirical commitment.

An Alternative Account

There is, however, very strong reason, I believe, to think that the Arguments-On-Paper Thesis is false: justified belief is not the product of mental mechanisms governed by logical form. The best way to make the case against the Arguments-On-Paper Thesis, however, is not to provide

---

8 On this point, see Cherniak (1986), Harman (1986, pp. 25–7), Kornblith (1989), and Mole (2016).

a direct argument against it. What is needed instead is a different picture of how belief acquisition and revision might work. I provide a sketch of such an account here.

No one thinks that our perceptual systems work by taking sensory input and then constructing arguments for the existence of physical objects, however subconsciously, which would work equally well in any logically possible environment.[9] This is not because inferential accounts of the uptake of perceptual information are universally rejected. Quite the opposite is true: inferential accounts of the workings of our perceptual systems have been exceptionally common at least since Helmholtz. Rather, the perceptual systems could not possibly function effectively without, in effect, making very substantial presuppositions about the nature of the environment in which they operate.

The environment in which we live contains, to a first approximation, three-dimensional objects with fairly stable boundaries which move through space in predictable ways. The task of our perceptual systems is to recover information about such objects on the basis of the input which our senses provide. Consider, for example, what that input involves in a fairly simple case of visual perception: someone tosses a book to me from a short distance away, and I catch it. The book is, very roughly, a rectangular solid. If I am presented with the book at eye level and straight on, my visual system takes in an image of the book which is rectangular. If the book moves so that its lower edge comes somewhat closer to me than its upper edge, but it does not rotate on either of its other axes, then the visual image which my senses pick up is not rectangular, but trapezoidal. If the book rotates along its other axes as well, the visual image may be of an irregular quadrilateral. And if the book is presented to me on its edge, and it is thin enough, the image will approximate a line. Now if the visual system did not make any presuppositions about the environment in which it operates, nothing whatsoever about the book could be extracted from this continuously changing array of shapes. If, for example, the visual system did not take for granted that external objects are three dimensional, rather than two dimensional, or ten dimensional, the task of extracting information about shape would become impossible. If the environment were one in which objects might pop in and out of existence, or constantly change shape as they move, then the sensory input which the visual system provides would be compatible with infinitely many different possibilities, and there would be no reason whatsoever for favoring any one of these over the others. The visual system is able to do its work, providing roughly accurate information about the shape

---

9 Or, more cautiously, any logically possible environment with enough constancies in it to allow, in principle, for the reliable uptake of information. I will not add this qualification in the text in the remainder of the chapter, but it should be understood throughout.

of physical objects in our environment because it is preloaded with very substantial assumptions about that environment, assumptions—such as that physical objects are three dimensional and that they tend to maintain their shape as they move, and that they don't pop in and out of existence—which are typically true in the environments in which we operate. These assumptions constrain the range of possibilities in ways sufficient to allow for the pickup of information about the shape of physical objects. Our perceptual systems would not work in just any logically possible environment, for no information processing system could do that. Perception is possible only because the perceptual systems make presuppositions which are at least approximately true in typical environments in which we live. These presuppositions work below the level of conscious thought and are not available to introspection.

The fact that our perceptual systems work in this way leads to a characteristic pattern of errors—the perceptual illusions—when we are in non-standard environments. The straight stick partially submerged in water looks bent, and even when we are familiar with the illusion, it still looks bent. We can compensate for the illusory appearance once we become aware of this fact; what we can't do is make the illusion go away.

The Arguments-On-Paper Thesis is committed to the view that our reasoning does not work in a similar way. Deductive arguments take us from true premises to true conclusions not just in the environment in which we live, or environments which bear deep similarities to it, but in all logically possible environments. And those who have hankered after an inductive logic have sought to develop formal systems which, even if they don't, and, of course, can't assure true conclusions from true premises, will produce conclusions from such premises which, in some important sense, are likely to be true, not only in our environment, but in any environment that has sufficient structure in it to allow for the reliable pickup of information. Thus, for example, what makes statistical reasoning of a certain sort good reasoning, it will be said, is not any feature of the actual world, or worlds roughly similar to it; what makes statistical reasoning good reasoning makes it good reasoning no matter what the environment is like.

What I want to suggest is that, contrary to the assumptions of the Arguments-On-Paper Thesis, much of human inference should be viewed in a way which parallels the structure of the perceptual systems: we make inferences which achieve their great successes in delivering reliable information about our environment precisely because inference works in ways which make substantive presuppositions about that environment, presuppositions which are not learned, but are built in to our inferential system in a way unavailable to introspection, and which are at least approximately true of the typical environments in which we live. Our inferences thus would not work well in just any logically possible environment, or any such environment in which it is possible to extract information. They work well because they are adapted to contingent but pervasive features of typical environments in which we are found, and they exploit assumptions about those features to allow for the efficient and reliable uptake of information.

Let me provide an illustration of how this can work. Statisticians speak of the *Law of Large Numbers*, the fact that the larger a sample, the more likely it is to reflect features of the population from which it is drawn. Famously, Tversky and Kahneman (1971, p. 25) found that human inductive inference seems to obey a different law:

> The law of large numbers guarantees that very large samples will indeed be highly representative of the population from which they are drawn... People's intuitions about random sampling appear to satisfy the law of small numbers, which asserts that the law of large numbers applies to small numbers as well.

As Tversky and Kahneman (1971, p. 31) argued, this represents a "sin against the logic of statistical inference." In what seemed to be an analogy with visual illusions, they described this as a "cognitive or perceptual bias" (Ibid). But if this is truly analogous to the visual illusions, our errors should be seen as a biproduct of a process which works quite reliably in normal environments, producing errors when it operates outside them.[10] More importantly, the analogy with visual perception, if it holds up, would suggest that this inferential tendency should not be viewed as any sort of cognitive impropriety, but as a cognitive strategy well adapted to the environments in which it tends to operate. So the question for us here is whether these inferences should be viewed as ones which make a presupposition about normal environments that both explains why we get things right when environmental conditions are normal, and produces a characteristic pattern of errors outside of normal conditions. And that is precisely, I believe, what we see.

It would, of course, be a serious cognitive error if, on noticing that one of the coins in my pocket is a penny, I concluded that all of the coins in my pocket are pennies. Other inferences from small samples are far less problematic. If I notice that a particular piece of copper conducts electricity and conclude that all copper conducts electricity, or if I notice that a particular sample of alcohol freezes at a certain temperature and conclude that all alcohol freezes at that temperature, I will not be led astray. Natural kinds have a sort of uniformity that random collections, such as the coins in my pocket, tend to lack. If our tendency to make inductive inferences from small samples is, by and large, applied to natural kinds, and if it is brought to bear on the sorts of properties of those kinds which are essential to them, then inferences in accord with the law of small

---

10 For an exceptional useful discussion of good versus bad biases, see Antony (1993).

numbers will be fairly reliable, although they will lead us into error when they are applied outside of the range to which they are adapted.

In order to make the case that this is, indeed, what one finds, one needs to show that we do not just apply the law of small numbers indiscriminately. For example, the inference about the coins in my pocket is not remotely compelling psychologically, even if other applications of the law of small numbers are. In addition, one must show that the manner in which kinds are conceptualized by us accords a special place to natural kinds.[11] And one must show, in addition, that the properties which we tend to project in the case of natural kinds are ones which have the requisite degree of regularity in the population.[12] With all of these pieces of the puzzle in place, however, a strong case emerges that inductive inference operates in us in a way that is structurally similar to the manner in which perception works (cf., Kornblith, 1993).

Just as in the perceptual case, the suggestion here is not that ordinary cognizers know relevant premises, either about objects in space, in the perceptual case, or about natural kinds, in the case of inductive inference, to make our inferences track the kinds of argumentation which defenders of the Arguments-On-Paper Thesis attribute to us. Rather, the suggestion is that we should be seen as having certain inferential tendencies which track deep regularities in our normal environments which serve to make our inferences reliable, even though the facts which makes those inferential tendencies reliable need not be known, and typically are not known, by ordinary cognizers. A creature which had an innate tendency to conclude that fire is present whenever it sees smoke would be quite reliable, even though it needed no evidence that smoke and fire are typically found together before it made that inference. Such a creature would not have inferences which track good argumentation, but it would be extremely reliable nonetheless. The suggestion here is that inductive inference works in us in much the same way.[13]

A realistic picture of how human inference works, then, does not support the empirical claims needed for a defense of the Arguments-On-Paper Thesis. Successful human inference, or justified belief, or rational belief, just doesn't work that way.

Why Have We Been Led Astray?

If all of this is right, why has the Arguments-On-Paper Thesis seemed so attractive? Why is it that, pretheoretically, the Thesis seems so obviously true? There are, I believe, two different factors which combine to explain this.

---

11 On this point, see especially Gelman (2003).
12 On this point, see especially Billman and Heit (1988).
13 A similar picture is presented in Gigerenzer et al. (1999).

We sometimes stop to reflect on what we believe in order to evaluate whether we should continue to hold some particular belief or, instead, give it up. We may wonder whether we have been hasty in forming a belief, or whether we have engaged in a bit of wishful thinking, or, in some other mood, whether we have formed some belief out of protective pessimism or some other sort of bias. When we do this, we attempt to determine the reasons for which we hold the belief in question and assess whether those reasons are good reasons. When we introspect in this way, it is quite common to have the very vivid impression that we can just directly detect the mental process by which we formed the belief we seek to evaluate; we just know, in short, why we believe as we do. But there is reason to believe that this vivid impression is an illusion. We do not have direct access to our mental processes. Instead, what seems to be the direct apprehension of our reasons for belief is the product of after-the-fact rational reconstruction: although introspection does not reveal this, we are engaging in subconscious inference to an explanation, devising an account of why it is we believe as we do. Such after-the-fact rationalization, or confabulation, need not be inaccurate. But the manner in which this inference proceeds makes it quite unlikely, in a wide range of circumstances, that we should detect any inferential errors we might have been making. In effect, our subconscious reconstruction of our mental process of belief acquisition makes use of a crucial minor premise: I'm a reasonable person, and if I believe this, I must have had good reasons. When we reconstruct our reasons, then, the reasons we find are typically reasons which appear to support the belief we seek to evaluate. The result is that the process of reflection which we undertook in order to provide some additional check on our belief is, unbeknownst to us, performed in a way which is likely to make us more confident of the belief we antecedently held, whether it was in fact formed on the basis of good reasons or not.[14]

In effect, then, the process of reflection provides us with a convincing argument for our beliefs, whether those beliefs were held on the basis of such arguments or not. Reflection thus gives us the illusion that belief acquisition conforms to the Arguments-On-Paper Thesis. The manner in which our beliefs are actually formed, however, is quite different than it seems from the first-person perspective. The actual processes of belief acquisition and revision need not track anything that answers to good argument at all.

This is not to say that we are typically unreliable in believing as we do. We are, indeed, often very reliable. Our reliability, however, is not achieved in the way it seems to be when we stop to reflect. Reliable belief acquisition and revision frequently work, like the perceptual systems, by way of processes which exploit certain deep but contingent regularities in

---

14 See Nisbett and Wilson (1977) and Wilson (2002). For discussion, see Kornblith (2002, ch. 4, 2012, ch. 1).

the environments in which we are typically found. These regularities are not ones we are mindful of; they are not known to most believers, nor need they be. When we stop to theorize about the nature of reasonable belief, however, if we simply engage in reflection on our beliefs rather than examine the experimental evidence about how our beliefs are actually formed, the Arguments-On-Paper Thesis will seem obviously true.

There is, however, another reason why the Arguments-On-Paper Thesis has appeared so attractive, and here, I believe, there is an important grain of truth to be found in the ideas which serve to support the Thesis. The Arguments-On-Paper Thesis presents our justified beliefs as the product of arguments licensed by rules of inference which do the good epistemic work they do in ways that would be equally epistemically good in any logically possible environment. I have argued that just as our perceptual processes work in ways which are adapted to contingent features of our environment, rational inferences producing justified beliefs may be similarly adapted to such deep but contingent features of environments we regularly inhabit. This does not make our capacity to arrive at true beliefs a matter of luck. It is not as if any slight change in our circumstance would have our belief-producing processes misfire, producing horribly mistaken beliefs. The features of our environments to which these processes are adapted provide those processes with a good deal of modal robustness. They work well, tending to produce true beliefs, in a wide range of counterfactual circumstances. They would not, however, work well throughout all of logical space; they would not work well in just any logically possible environment.

One may reasonably wonder, however, whether all of our inferential tendencies could possibly be of this sort. Even if not all of our justified beliefs are produced in ways which conform to the standards of the Arguments-On-Paper Thesis, the idea that none of our inferences are of that sort does seem especially implausible. We are capable, quite clearly, of drawing out at least some of the logical consequences of things we believe. It is hard to imagine how a system of nothing but merely ecologically adapted inference could provide us with this capacity. Moreover, it is for this reason that even those who reject the Arguments-On-Paper Thesis, as I do, should not be surprised that the research of the mental logicians has seemed to uncover some basic logical capacities operating within the human mind. Defenders of the Arguments-On-Paper Thesis are right, I believe, in thinking that it is overwhelmingly plausible that we have some such logical capacities. It is one thing to think, however, that such logical capacities inform some of our inferential behavior; it is quite another to think, as defenders of the Arguments-On-Paper Thesis do, that all of our justified beliefs are the product of inferences which are more than just ecologically valid, and would do good epistemic work across all of logical space. It is only this latter Thesis which I have been arguing against.

The Fundamentality of Doxastic Justification

What has all of this to do with whether we should see propositional or doxastic justification as the more fundamental notion? A great deal, I believe.

The standard way of viewing the distinction between propositional and doxastic justification has it that propositional justification is the more basic notion: a proposition is propositionally justified if one has good reason to believe it; a proposition is doxastically justified if one has propositional justification for it and one believes it on the basis of that justification (see, e.g., Firth 1978; Conee and Feldman 2004). This way of viewing things encourages one to view the issue of propositional justification in ways independent of the psychological issues that inevitably arise in considering questions about basing. And once one thinks about propositional justification in this apsychological manner, the assimilation of questions about justification to questions about good argument that defines the Arguments-On-Paper Thesis looks utterly natural.

More than this, such a view comports well with a very traditional notion of the nature of philosophy itself. On this view, philosophical questions are to be addressed by *a priori* means, and the nature of epistemic justification, when viewed in this way, will inevitably involve principles of inference which do their good epistemic work across all of logical space. Epistemology, and philosophy generally, on this view, do not deal in the sort of merely contingent truths uncovered by an investigation of human psychology.

In addition, if one views one of the most fundamental tasks of a theory of justified belief to involve providing an answer to the skeptic, as traditional epistemologists tend to do, then the epistemic principles which define propositionally justified belief must have this *a priori* status in order to be able to play their skeptic-fighting role: anything less than this merely begs the question against the skeptic, on this view. So taking propositional justification as the more fundamental notion comports well with traditional views about the purity of philosophy as an *a priori* discipline.

If instead we begin thinking about the notion of justification by thinking about doxastically justified belief, the question of what our beliefs are actually based upon is immediately brought to center stage, with all of the psychological complications that entails. The rich phenomenon of justified belief may now be seen as one which does not answer to our pretheoretical conceptions of how our epistemic successes are achieved. And this, in turn forces us to give a psychologized account of propositional justification: a proposition is propositionally justified for a person just in case that person has available psychological processes which could reliably produce belief in that proposition absent any additional sensory input (cf., e.g., Goldman, 1979; Kornblith, 2017, 2020). The key to understanding the phenomenon of justified belief, as I see it, thus lies in taking the notion of doxastic justification to be the more fundamental notion.

Conclusion

I have argued that the question of whether we should view propositional or doxastic justification as the more fundamental notion is tied up with questions about the very nature of philosophy itself: whether philosophy is an *a priori* discipline, and the extent to which psychological questions enter in to epistemological theorizing. I have defended a naturalistic picture of the epistemological enterprise according to which the notions of both doxastically justified belief and propositionally justified belief as well are defined in frankly psychological terms. Finally, I have argued that this picture has implications for the normative status of logic.

References

Antony, L. (1993). Quine as feminist: the radical import of naturalistic epistemology. In L. Antony, & C. Witt, (Eds.), *A Mind of One's Own: Feminist Essays on Reason and Objectivity* (pp. 185–225). Boulder, CO: Westview Press.

Billman, D., & Heit, E. (1988). Observational learning from internal feedback: a simulation of an adaptive learning method. *Cognitive Science, 12*, 587–625.

Boghossian, P. (2014). What is inference? *Philosophical Studies, 169*, 1–18.

BonJour, Laurence (1985). *The Structure of Empirical Knowledge*. Harvard University Press.

Boole, G. (1958/1854). *An Investigation of the Laws of Thought on Which Are Founded the Mathematical Theories of Logic and Probabilities*. New York, NY: Dover Publications.

Brandom, R. (2000). *Articulating Reasons: An Introduction to Inferentialism*. Cambridge, MA: Harvard University Press.

Cherniak, C. (1986). *Minimal Rationality*. Cambridge, MA: MIT Press.

Chisholm, R. (1977). *Theory of Knowledge*, 2nd edition. Englewood Cliffs, NJ: Prentice-Hall.

Conee, E., & Feldman, R. (2004). *Evidentialism: Essays in Epistemology*. Oxford: Oxford University Press.

Firth, R. (1978). Are epistemic concepts reducible to ethical concepts? In A. Goldman, & J. Kim (Eds.) *Values and Morals: Essays in Honor of William Frankena, Charles Stevenson, and Richard Brandt* (pp. 215–229). Dordrecht, Holland: Reidel.

Fodor, J. (1975). *The Language of Thought*. New York, NY: Thomas Y. Crowell Company.

Fodor, J. (1983). *The Modularity of Mind: An Essay on Faculty Psychology*. Cambridge, MA: MIT Press.

Fodor, J. (2008). *LOT 2: The Language of Thought Revisited*. Oxford: Oxford University Press.

Foley, R. (2012). *When is True Belief Knowledge?* Princeton, NJ: Princeton University Press.
Gelman, S. (2003). *The Essential Child: Origins of Essentialism in Everyday Thought.* Oxford: Oxford University Press.
Gigerenzer, G., Todd, P., & the ABC Research Group. (1999). *Simple Heuristics that Make Us Smart.* Oxford: Oxford University Press.
Goldman, A. (1979). What is justified belief? In George Pappas (Ed.) *Justification and Knowledge* (pp. 1–23). Dordrecht, Holland: Reidel.
Harman, G. (1970). Induction: a discussion of the relevance of the theory of knowledge to the theory of induction (with a digression to the effect that neither deductive logic nor the probability calculus has anything to do with inference). In M. Swain (Ed.) *Induction, Acceptance, and Rational Belief* (pp. 83–99). Dordrecht, Holland: Reidel.
Harman, G. (1986). *Change in View: Principles of Reasoning.* Cambridge, MA: MIT Press.
Kaplan, M. (1985). It's not what you know that counts. *Journal of Philosophy,* 82, 350–363.
Kornblith, H. (1980). Beyond foundationalism and the coherence theory. *Journal of Philosophy, LXXVII,* 597–612; reprinted in Kornblith, H. (2014). *A Naturalistic Epistemology: Selected Papers* (pp. 17–31). Oxford: Oxford University Press, 2014.
Kornblith, H. (1989). The unattainability of coherence. In J. Bender (Ed.) *The Current State of the Coherence Theory* (pp. 207–214). Dordrecht, Holland: Kluwer, 207–214; reprinted in Kornblith, H. (2014). *A naturalistic epistemology: selected papers* (pp. 60–70). Oxford: Oxford University Press.
Kornblith, H. (1993). *Inductive Inference and Its Natural Ground.* Cambridge, MA: MIT Press.
Kornblith, H. (2002). *Knowledge and Its Place in Nature.* Oxford: Oxford University Press.
Kornblith, H. (2012). *On Reflection.* Oxford: Oxford University Press.
Kornblith, H. (2017). Doxastic justification is fundamental. *Philosophical Topics,* 45, 63–80; reprinted in Kornblith, H. (2019). *Second Thoughts and the Epistemological Enterprise* (pp. 201–220). Cambridge, UK: Cambridge University Press.
Kornblith, H. (2020). Naturalism, psychologism, relativism. In N. Ashton, M. Kusch, R. McKenna, & K. Sodoma (Eds.), *Social Epistemology and Epistemic Relativism* (pp. 66–84). New York, NY: Routledge.
Kusch, M. (1995). *Psychologism: A Case Study in the Sociology of Philosophical Knowledge.* New York: Routledge.
Leite, A. (2004). On justifying and being justified. *Philosophical Issues,* 14, 219–253.
Malmgren, A.-S. *Understanding Inference.* Manuscript.
Mole, C. (2016). *The Unexplained Intellect: Complexity, Time, and the Metaphysics of Embodied Thought.* New York, NY: Routledge.
Nisbett, R., & Wilson, T. (1977). Telling more than we can know: verbal reports on mental processes. *Psychological Review,* 84, 231–259.
Oliveira, L. (2015). Non-agential permissibility in epistemology. *Australasian Journal of Philosophy,* 93, 389–394.

Quilty-Dunn, J., & Mandelbaum, E. (2018). Inferential transitions. *Australasian Journal of Philosophy*, 96, 532–547.

Rips, L. (1994). *The Psychology of Proof: Deductive Reasoning in Human Thinking*. Cambridge, MA: MIT Press.

Silva, P. (2015). Does doxastic justification have a basing requirement? *Australasian Journal of Philosophy*, 93, 371–387.

Talbott, W. *Learning from Our Mistakes: Epistemology for the Real World*. Manuscript.

Tversky, A., & Kahneman, D. (1971). Belief in the law of small numbers. *Psychological Bulletin*, 2, 105–110; reprinted in Kahneman, D., Slovic, P., & Tversky, A. (Eds.), (1982). *Judgment Under Uncertainty: Heuristics and Biases* (pp. 23–31). Cambridge, UK: Cambridge University Press.

Williams, M. (1996). *Unnatural Doubts: Epistemological Realism and the Basis of Skepticism*. Princeton, NJ: Princeton University Press.

Wilson, T. (2002). *Strangers to Ourselves: Discovering the Adaptive Unconscious*. Cambridge, MA: Harvard University Press.

4 Justification *Ex Ante* and *Ex Post*
Why We Need Both Notions, and Why Neither is Reducible to the Other

Ram Neta

Some of us have an impressive ability to speak impromptu in sentences that are syntactically complicated and yet still well-formed. Occasionally, however, our efforts fail: we lose track of our syntax mid-sentence and end up saying something that is not well-formed. Even when we lose track of our syntax mid-sentence, though, we can still end up uttering a well-formed sentence anyway, if only by lucky accident. More commonly, though, when we utter a well-formed sentence, our doing so is not just a lucky accident, but is instead a competent exercise of a general ability that we have to utter well-formed sentences. Rarely does a sentence come out well-formed just by accident.

To the extent that you've understood what I've said in the last paragraph, you've also understood a distinction between the well-formedness of a sentence, on the one hand, and the competent exercise of a general ability that we have to utter well-formed sentences, on the other. Maybe you don't understand this distinction with any precision, and you don't understand what the metaphysical basis of the distinction is, and you don't know what conceptual resources are necessary to draw the distinction, and you're not sure how to go about applying the distinction to cases—but even so, you've still understood the distinction to some extent if you can understand the possibility that I described as that of uttering a well-formed sentence "by lucky accident."

I want to use this distinction between well-formedness, on the one hand, and the competent exercise of an ability, on the other, to help us understand a distinction that's significant to theorists of normativity. Such theorists always assume, commonly mention, and sometimes attempt to understand, a distinction analogous to the one that I've just described. Ethicists, for instance, distinguish between whether a course of action is one that an agent ought to perform, on the one hand, from whether the agent's performance of that action is the competent exercise of a good will or character, on the other. Moral psychologists distinguish between whether an attitude is one that is fitting for an agent to have with respect to some person or prospect, on the one hand, from whether the agent's having of that attitude is the competent exercise of virtue, on the other.

DOI: 10.4324/9781003008101-6

And epistemologists distinguish between whether a belief or credal state is one that an agent ought to have, on the one hand, from whether the agent's having that belief or credal state is the competent exercise of a reliable or appropriate belief-forming capacity, on the other. Epistemologists typically mark this latter distinction with the terms "propositional justification" and "doxastic justification."[1] But since the epistemological distinction between propositional and doxastic justification is just one species of a genus of distinction that is drawn across all normative theories, and since it is the genus that I want to investigate here, I will use the more general but less standard terms "*ex ante* justification" and "*ex post* justification" to draw the more general distinction.[2] To say that an agent has "*ex ante* justification" to perform some action or to have some attitude or to hold some belief is to say that there is something about the agent and her situation that makes it the case that the relevant action or attitude or belief is one that the agent *ought* to perform or have or hold—whether or not she actually does perform or have or hold it. In contrast, to say that an agent is "*ex post* justified" in performing some action or having some attitude or holding some belief is to say, at least, that there is something about the way in which the agent actually performs the action or has the attitude or holds the belief that makes it *not just a lucky accident* that the agent's performance or having or holding is as it ought to be.

I hope it is clear how closely analogous this distinction between *ex ante* justification and *ex post* justification is to the distinction between the well-formedness of a sentence, on the one hand, and the competent utterance of that sentence, on the other. But how, precisely, should we understand the distinction between *ex ante* justification and *ex post* justification?

This chapter attempts to answer that question. I provide my answer in Section 4.1. But my answer entails something that many philosophers will find hard to swallow, viz., that justificatory status can both *guide* and *explain* our beliefs, attitudes, and intentional actions. Most of this chapter, therefore, is devoted to rebutting the widely accepted philosophical views that will impede the acceptance of my account.

What Does the Distinction Amount to?

Ex ante justification is the standard to which one appeals to in *regulating* one's attitudes and actions. To say that one is *ex ante* justified in thinking

---

1 The literature on this distinction in contemporary epistemology begins with Firth (1978), who marked the distinction by means of the terms "propositional warrant" and "doxastic warrant."
2 Goldman (1979) coined the terms "*ex ante* justification" and "*ex post* justification," but he used these terms to mark not the generic distinction mentioned here, but only the epistemological species of the generic distinction.

or acting a certain way is to say that one's so thinking or acting *complies with the standard for so thinking or acting*.

Of course, there is only one fully responsible agent whose thoughts and actions I generally have both the ability and the responsibility to regulate: namely, me. Thus, it is practically important for me to recognize what attitudes and actions are *ex ante* justified *for me*, and to recognize it in a way that allows me to respond in light of the recognized facts about *ex ante* justification. There may also be reasons for me to recognize what attitudes and actions are *ex ante* justified for others, but of course these reasons (if any) aren't the same as my reasons for recognizing what is *ex ante* justified for me.

I've said what *ex ante* justificatory status is and given at least one important reason why it's important for us to recognize when a thought or action has that status. But what is *ex post* justificatory status, and why is it important for us to recognize when a thought or action has that status? *Ex post* justification is a standard to which one appeals in *explaining why* certain people have certain attitudes or perform certain actions. *Ex post* justification is not merely a normative notion, but it is also an explanatory one. To say that someone's attitude or action is *ex post* justified is to say that their attitude or action is *caused in a way that satisfies a particular norm, or standard*. It's tempting to read this as saying that the notion of *ex post* justification is a composite of two independent notions—one explanatory, and the other normative. But this is wrong: *ex post* justification is, to use Williamson's expression, "prime."[3] If two conditions are causally explained in precisely the same way, then they necessarily enjoy the same *ex post* justificatory status.

In short: it's important for us to recognize cases of *ex ante* justification as such in order to regulate our own exercises of agency, whereas it's important for us to recognize cases of *ex post* justification as such in order to understand why agents, including ourselves, think or do whatever they think or do. The notions of *ex ante* justification and of *ex post* justification are notions that ordinary agents ordinarily apply to themselves and to one another, and they do so almost all the time, even if they don't employ the relevant vocabulary. That is my thesis.

If you're like most philosophers, you are committed to thinking that this thesis can't possibly be right. Why not? First, because (as is commonly thought) *ex ante* justificatory status cannot, in general, be regulative: for it to be regulative, we would have to be able to regulate the attitudes and actions that are subject to assessment as *ex ante* justified, and we are generally not able to do this. Second, because (as is often thought) the explanatory dimension of *ex post* justificatory status cannot itself be normative: the explanatory dimension concerns how a particular belief, feeling, or action was caused, but *causes alone* have no normative

3 See Williamson (2000).

implications—it's only causes together with some independent normative factors which, in conjunction, have normative implications. The next two sections of this chapter are devoted to rebutting each of these two objections to my thesis: it turns out that the objections are related, for both of them rest on a confusion about the kind of agency distinctive of creatures who can reason.

Ex Ante Justification, and Regulating Our Attitudes and Actions

I've said that we are supposed to regulate our attitudes and actions according to whether they are *ex ante* justified. But this claim provokes several questions. The first (but certainly not the only) question is, what is it to "regulate our attitudes and actions"? In trying to answer this first question, I confront the following dilemma.

On the one hand, I might be using the quoted phrase to signify a particular kind of voluntary action that you can perform with respect to anything over which you can have some regular impact. You might regulate the temperature in your house, or you might regulate how frequently your course website is updated, or you might regulate the content of the discussion boards on that site. In each case, *regulating* is a voluntary action that you can perform with respect to some object in order to modify the condition of that object or achieve some further aim. But this kind of voluntary action is not one that anybody typically performs with respect to their own attitudes or actions. The relatively rare cases in which one does perform such a voluntary action with respect to one's own attitudes or actions are what we might describe as cases of self-manipulation: in such cases, one *gets oneself* to think or act a certain way by dint of some psychological effort, much as one might get the temperature of one's house to go down by turning the knob on the thermostat. Of course, such psychological self-regulation is possible, and sometimes actual (e.g., Pascal's wager is one alleged example, and reciting a mantra in order to put oneself in a certain frame of mind is another), but it is hardly the typical case, and most of our attitudes and actions do not directly result from such self-manipulation. If *ex ante* justification is just the standard that I'm supposed to follow when I engage in such self-manipulation, then that standard governs too minuscule a portion of my psychological life.

On the other hand, I might be using the phrase "regulate our attitudes and actions" to signify whatever is involved in our simply *having* those attitudes and *performing* those actions. Since we cannot normally be said to perform our attitudes or to have our actions, perhaps the verb "regulate" is just being stretched in the quoted phrase above to indicate whatever relation it is that an agent bears to the attitudes that she has and the actions that she performs. In this way, terminology is being adjusted to accommodate the needs of efficient communication. The problem with this view is that it leaves it completely mysterious why "regulation" covers the relationship that we bear to our attitudes and actions, but not, say, to our toothaches, mental images, or proprioceptive sensations. Of course, if "regulation" also covers the latter relations, then, according to the current proposal, *ex ante* justification is a standard that's supposed to govern toothaches, mental images, and proprioceptive sensations. But of course this is not the case. If the norms of *ex ante* justification are simply the norms governing those conditions that are, in some sense, my own, then those norms govern too extensive a portion of my psychological life.

To defend my claim that *ex ante* justification is the standard by which we are supposed to regulate our beliefs, feelings, and actions, I must find a way between the horns of this dilemma. And to do that, I must find a non-ad hoc way to demarcate all and only the conditions that are subject to assessment as *ex ante* justified, or not. These conditions will include more than just our voluntary actions, but will not include all of our psychological conditions (e.g., toothaches, mental images, etc.). How can I demarcate such a category?

In a series of recent papers, I've demarcated a category of conditions that I've sometimes called "rationally determinable conditions" and sometimes called "rationally assessable conditions."[4] Let me now explain what these labels mean, explain how I've demarcated the category at issue, and, finally, argue that this category is precisely the category of conditions that are subject to norms of *ex ante* justification.

First, the labels. I use the term "condition" as a generic term intended to cover events, processes, and states. To say that a condition is "rationally determinable" is to say that it is a condition that an agent can have, and which is such that there can be a *reason for which* the agent has that condition. A reason for which the agent has that condition is not just any old reason *why* the agent has that condition. A reason for which is a reason that not only explains why the agent has that condition but explains it by appeal to the agent's possession and appreciation of some reason for her to have that condition, and not by means of any deviant causal chain. (Exactly how to understand this exclusion of deviant causal chains is an issue we will discuss below.) Thus, intentional actions are rationally determinable conditions, because an agent's intentional action can be explained by appeal to the agent's possession and appreciation of some reason for her to perform that intentional action. Beliefs are rationally determinable conditions, because an agent's belief can be explained by appeal to the agent's possession and appreciation of some reason for her to have that belief. Some feelings are rationally determinable conditions,

---

4 On "rationally determinable conditions," see Neta (2018, 2019). On "rationally assessable conditions," see Neta (forthcoming). A unified account of such conditions is provided in Marcus (2021).

because those feelings can be explained by appeal to the agent's possession and appreciation of some reason to harbor that feeling. But itchiness is not a rationally determinable condition, because an agent's feeling itchy cannot be explained by appeal to her possession and appreciation of some reason to feel that itch, unless the explanation proceeds by means of a deviant causal chain. Of course, an agent may attempt to form a vivid mental image of feeling itchy, and this attempt is itself a rationally determinable condition, for it may be explained by appeal to the agent's possession and appreciation of some reason to make that attempt, and this appeal needn't involve any deviant causal chain. But even if the attempt is a rationally determinable condition, the mental image itself is not, and neither is the feeling of itchiness.

Now, what about "rationally assessable conditions"? These are just those conditions (i.e., states, processes, events, etc.) that can be assessed as rational or irrational. Beliefs are rationally assessable conditions, because they can be assessed as rational or irrational. The same is true of reactive attitudes such as resentment, anger, gratitude, and so on. And, of course, the same is true of intentions, plans, resolutions, and intentional actions. But the same is not true, say, of feeling itchy: the feeling of itchiness may be pleasant or unpleasant, helpful or unhelpful, healthy or unhealthy, but it cannot be rational or irrational.

In sum, rationally determinable conditions are conditions that an agent can occupy for a reason, while rationally assessable conditions are conditions that can be occupied rationally or irrationally. Are the rationally determinable conditions all and only the rationally assessable conditions? It's commonly agreed that all rationally determinable conditions are rationally assessable: if a condition is one than an agent can occupy for a reason, then it's one that the agent can occupy rationally or irrationally. But is it also true that only rationally determinable conditions are rationally assessable? Couldn't an agent think or do something rational, even if for no reason at all? I'm happy to grant (at least for the sake of argument) that the answer to this last question is "yes," but that doesn't show that there are rationally assessable conditions that are not rationally determinable. The most it shows is that there are rationally assessable conditions that are not rationally *determined*. But that is consistent with the claim that only rationally determinable conditions are rationally assessable. And indeed, the latter claim seems plausible, since, for any attitude or action you might choose, it's at least possible to hold that attitude or perform that action for a reason, whether or not one actually does so. So, I conclude, all and only rationally determinable conditions are rationally assessable conditions. We can henceforth think of these terms as denoting a single category, even if under different modes of presentation.

But how to demarcate this category of conditions? What makes it the case that a particular kind of condition is rationally assessable, or rationally determinable? Here's my guiding thought: when an agent occupies some condition for a particular reason, that agent is thereby *committed to* that particular reason being a good reason for occupying that condition. To say that an agent is committed to its being a good reason is just to say that the agent makes herself subject to the charge of incoherence if, say, she criticizes another relevantly similar agent for occupying the very same condition for the very same reason, or if she believes propositions that jointly entail that it is not a good reason for occupying that condition, or if she refuses to admit that it is a good reason for occupying that condition, and so on. The notion of commitment that I'm using here is one that we use when we say that, if you accept various premises, then you are "committed to" the conclusion that follows from them: to describe such a thing as a "commitment" is in no way to compare it to a promise or a pledge, but rather to say what coherence demands of such an agent. When an agent occupies some rationally determinable condition for no reason at all, she is thereby committed to that condition being one that is permissible to occupy for no reason at all. Thus, she would open herself to the charge of incoherence if, say, she criticizes a relevantly similar agent for occupying a relevantly similar condition for no reason at all, or if she believes propositions that jointly entail that it is not permissible to occupy that condition for no reason, and so on. In contrast, when an agent feels itchy, she does not thereby commit herself to doing or thinking anything. The category of rationally determinable conditions is the same as the category of rationally assessable conditions, which is the same as the category of conditions one's occupying of which involves commitments of the sort mentioned above.

But how can one's merely occupying some condition involve commitments of the sort just described? There are all sorts of conditions an agent can occupy without thereby committing herself to anything at all. What is it about these conditions that explains why, in occupying them, an agent commits herself to various things? Here's my proposal: occupying any such condition is partly *constituted by* one's own representation of one's occupying that condition on that occasion as appropriate. To say that a condition C is *constituted by* one's representation of it as appropriate is to say that, whatever condition one occupies, it is not the condition C unless one represents *that very condition itself (de re) as appropriate*. To occupy the relevant kind of condition is, in part, to endorse one's occupying that condition as appropriate. And, of course, if you endorse something as appropriate, then you are guilty of incoherence if you go on to deny that it's appropriate, or to believe things incompatible with it's being appropriate, and so on.

In short, it is both necessary and sufficient for occupying any particular rationally determinable condition that you have a *de re* representation of your occupying that condition on that occasion as appropriate. Without the representation, the condition that you're occupying is not rationally determinable. Without your occupying that condition on that occasion, the representation is empty—there's no "*res*" for it to be "*de*." Thus, rationally determinable conditions are rationally assessable conditions, which, in turn, are just any conditions that an agent occupies exactly when she represents *de re* her occupancy of that very condition itself as appropriate. These are the conditions in occupying which we undertake commitments. Of course, these commitments, like all commitments, can be commitments that one is *ex ante* justified, or *ex ante* unjustified, in making. Thus, I can now begin to make my way between the horns of the dilemma sketched above by saying: these are the conditions that are subject to norms of *ex ante* justification.

So far, all I've attempted to do is to demarcate the category of conditions that are subject to norms of *ex ante* justification. But what I have not yet done is to show that we *regulate* these conditions in accordance with those norms. Of course, as I admitted above, the use of the verb "regulate" here is at best awkward: our "regulation" of our own attitudes or actions is not generally like our regulation of our energy consumption or our bank balance. For instance, it is not something that we do at will. Still, if my thesis is correct, there must be some not completely stipulative sense in which our attitudes and actions are *regulated* by norms of *ex ante* justification. But what sense can we make of this claim?

To answer this question, let's compare the norms of *ex ante* justification, on the one hand, and norms of syntactic well-formedness, on the other. Both sets of norms are constrained by various natural facts about humans: for instance, the norms of *ex ante* justification cannot render impermissible such things as breathing, drinking water, walking, ingesting nutrition, and so forth, and the norms of syntactic well-formedness cannot render ill-formed any sentence shorter than 1,000 words, or any sentence formed without the use of semaphores, and so on. Also, both sets of norms interact with the conventions of a community to generate norms specific to the members of that community: for instance, the norms of *ex ante* justification interact with the driving laws in the United States to make it impermissible for me to drive on the right side of the road, and the norms of syntactic well-formedness interact with the conventions of my dialect to make ill-formed a sentence such as "They too eager be." But, despite these similarities, there is an important difference. To bring out this difference, let's try to imagine a community whose norms of syntactic well-formedness are not just superficially, but fundamentally, different from ours, and a community whose norms of *ex ante* justification are not just superficially, but fundamentally, different from ours.

If there were a community whose norms of syntactic well-formedness were *fundamentally* different from ours, then any effort to understand their syntax and our syntax as two different specifications of some universal grammar would necessarily fail. But perhaps such efforts will fail anyway: even if every natural language is learnable by every normal human child, it doesn't follow that every natural language is a variant of some universal grammar implicit in the brain of every normal human child. From the fact that there are constraints on the syntax of every natural language, it doesn't follow that those constraints take the form of a universal grammar. But whether those constraints do or do not take that form, we can imagine a linguistic community whose language doesn't satisfy those constraints. Its language would not be one that we could learn, and perhaps for this reason we could never know that the behavior of its members was linguistic. But, even if such a scenario is not one that we could ever know to obtain—and even if it is one that we know *not* to obtain—it is at least one that we can coherently imagine to obtain. And, when we imagine it obtaining, we imagine a community whose linguistic practices are radically different from ours, but whose practices need not thereby be defective or wrong in any way.

Now let's try to imagine a community whose norms of *ex ante* justification are *fundamentally* different from ours. What could such a fundamental difference amount to? Could their norms render permissible such things as believing what they know to be false, or intentionally acting against what they know to be best? Some philosophers would say that this is not coherent: for any mental state to qualify as a belief, it must be governed by a norm of *ex ante* justification against believing what one knows to be false, or for any bit of behavior to qualify as an intentional action, it must be governed by a norm of *ex ante* justification against intentional acting against what one knows to be best. Although I have some sympathy with this "constitutivist" view of our attitudes and actions, I need not commit to any such view here, since the point I want to make now doesn't depend on it. For the point I want to make is this: to the extent that their norms of *ex ante* justification differ fundamentally from ours—that is to say, to the extent that the difference cannot be understood simply as the application of the same fundamental norms to different circumstances with different conventions—we are committed to regarding their attitudes and actions as defective or wrong. It might be permissible for Brits to drive on the opposite side of the road, given the difference between their road conventions and ours. But it cannot be permissible for the members of any community anywhere to form their beliefs about the world in complete disregard of all of their evidence, or to demand compliance with policies that they know to be inconsistent, or to practice a form of punishment consistently directed not against perpetrators but against their randomly chosen children, and so on. Any (putative) norms of *ex ante* justification that pronounced such things permissible would be a system of "norms" that had no normative authority: they would be normatively defective, or wrong. Or at least, so we are committed to thinking.

There is, therefore, a sense in which we can recognize the norms of syntactic well-formedness as *normatively arbitrary*, but we cannot recognize the norms of *ex ante* justification as normatively arbitrary. A community with fundamentally different syntactic norms is coherently imaginable, whether or not it is possible given the constraints of the human brain. When we imagine such a community, we are not committed to thinking of it as in any way defective. In contrast, a community with fundamentally different norms of *ex ante* justification might or might not be coherently imaginable—but even if it is coherently imaginable, we are committed to thinking of it as very seriously defective. Nothing about our linguistic practices commits us to thinking of the norms of syntactic well-formedness as non-arbitrary. In contrast, something about our attitudes and actions commits us to thinking of the norms of *ex ante* justification as fundamentally non-arbitrary. We are committed to the normative authority of the latter norms in a way that we are *not* committed to the normative authority of the former. We are committed to thinking of our most fundamental norms of *ex ante* justification as not merely *our* norms of *ex ante* justification, but as *the* norms of *ex ante* justification. In contrast, we are not committed to thinking of our most fundamental norms of syntactic well-formedness as anything more than *our* norms.

This contrast enables me to explain the sense in which we "regulate" our attitudes and actions in accordance with the norms of *ex ante* justification—but we don't do so at will. In thinking and acting as we do, we are (at least implicitly) committed to the authority of the norms of *ex ante* justification to which our attitudes and actions are answerable. But that is just to say that, if our attitudes or actions run afoul of those norms, their doing so is something that we ourselves are committed to fixing. Of course, we might fail to recognize that our attitudes and actions run afoul of those norms, and even if we recognize it, we might fail to fix it. But the crucial point is that, when our attitudes or actions run afoul of those, we are, by virtue of those very norms, *committed to* recognizing that, and *committed to* fixing it. Simply in thinking and acting as we do, we are committed to recognizing and fixing failures of our thinking and acting to comply with norms of *ex ante* justification. In contrast, in speaking as we do, we are not thereby committed to recognizing and fixing failures of our utterances to comply with norms of syntactic well-formedness. (If we happen to be so committed, that commitment arises from something else.) We could put this point by saying that our thoughts and deeds are *autonomous* in a way that our grammar is not.

If what I've said so far is correct, then it imposes a condition of adequacy on any account of the norms of *ex ante* justification: such an account should help us to understand why it is that, in thinking and acting, we are thereby committed to the authority of those norms. Our thoughts and deeds are answerable to those norms only because, in having those thoughts and performing those deeds, we commit ourselves to their being answerable to those norms. In thinking and acting, we commit ourselves to norms for thinking and acting, but to commit ourselves to those norms involves committing ourselves to abiding by those norms for thinking and acting: it is to commit ourselves to thinking and acting in accordance with those norms. It is in this (admittedly extended) sense of "regulate" that we can be said to regulate our thoughts and deeds in accordance with those norms.

Ex Post Justification, and Explaining Attitudes and Actions

In the preceding section I argued that, in thinking and acting, we commit ourselves to thinking and acting in accordance with certain norms of thinking and acting—these are the norms of *ex ante* justification.

In this section, I want to examine the notion of *ex post* justification. In particular, I claim that this notion is designed to serve an explanatory purpose: to describe an act or attitude as *ex post* justified is to explain the performance of that act, or the holding of that attitude, in a certain kind of way that I will specify more fully in this section. But, as I said in Section 4.1, my claim confronts a popular objection. To say that an act or attitude is *ex post* justified is to say (at least) that the act or attitude satisfies some norm. Of course, the norm in question may demand that acts or attitudes be explicable in a certain way, and so satisfying the norm might thereby imply that the act or attitude is explicable in a certain way. But—according to the envisaged objection—the fact that the act or attitude is explicable in a certain way cannot *by itself* imply anything about the normative status of that act or attitude. The normative status of the act or attitude must, according to this objection, be a further fact—perhaps involving its being explicable in a certain way, but necessarily involving something over and above that as well. Explanatory factors *alone* cannot determine normative status. To think otherwise is to commit some version of the naturalistic fallacy—or so says the present objection.

This objector's central contention is that explanatory factors *alone* cannot determine normative status. This is certainly true for many explanatory factors. For example, one of the many factors explaining why I am typing this paragraph at this very moment (shortly after noon) is that my noon appointment today was canceled. Although the cancellation of my Noon appointment is one of the factors explaining why I am performing this specific action at this moment, nothing about the normative status of this action follows from its being explained by appeal to this factor. Or, take another example: one of the many factors explaining why I expect it to be sunny this afternoon is that I happened to catch a glimpse of the weather channel at a particular moment this morning. (As it happens, that was just the moment that it was predicting sunshine for this afternoon.) But nothing follows about the normative status of my expectation of sunshine from that expectation's being explained by appeal to the fact that I happened to catch a glimpse of the weather channel at that very moment. Can't we generalize this point to other examples, and say that explanatory factors alone never fix normative status? Can't we conclude that something else, over and above explanatory factors, is required to fix normative status—perhaps our social practices of normative appraisal, or our conventions, or the greatest good of the greatest number, or God's commands, and so on?

Before succumbing to the common temptation to answer that last question in the affirmative, let's first examine more closely the explanatory factors that are relevant to the *ex post* justification of an action or an attitude. For an action or an attitude to be *ex post* justified, it must be *the exercise of a competence*, and so be explained by appeal to that competence. Competences are individuated in part by what they are competences to do. A competence to speak English and a competence to speak French are distinct at least *partly* in virtue of their being competences to do different things. I stress the word "partly" in order to make clear that this point is consistent with their being other factors that individuate competences as well. But what matters for the present point is that competences are individuated *at least* by appeal to distinctions in what they are competences to do.

Of course, any particular action or attitude can be understood as the exercise of many different competences. For example, in typing this very sentence, I am exercising my competence at expressing myself in English, exercising my competence at expressing myself in written English, and exercising many specific pragmatic, semantic, syntactic, and morphological competences. I am also exercising my competence to type, my competence to use Microsoft Word, my competence to move my fingers intentionally, and so on. Of course, this is not to suggest that *any* feature of my action is the exercise of a competence to perform an action with that feature. For instance, if my action (of typing this very sentence) were, by a series of unforeseen events, to initiate a causal sequence that produces a mass extinction, this does not show that my action is the exercise of a competence to produce a mass extinction. I have no such competence. And even if I did have such a competence—for instance, if I were in possession of biological weapons and the skill necessary to use them to produce a mass extinction—my action of typing this very sentence still would not be an exercise of that competence, not even if it happened, through a series of unforeseen events, to produce a mass extinction. Even if an action *happens* to produce a certain result, it doesn't follow that the action is the exercise of a competence to produce that result. Exercising a competence to F involves exercising a skill at F-ing, and the mere fact that one might happen to F on some occasion does not imply that one has a skill at F-ing, let alone that one exercised that skill on that particular occasion of one's F-ing.

I've said that acts and attitudes are *ex post* justified only if they are exercises of a certain kind of competence. What kind of competence is that?

To answer this question, let's first review a few points. It's built into our distinction between *ex ante* and *ex post* justification that acts and attitudes can be *ex post* justified only if the agent is *ex ante* justified in performing those acts or having those attitudes. And we said, back in Section 4.2, that an agent is *ex ante* justified in performing acts or having attitudes only if those acts or attitudes are ones that the agent can regulate in accordance with norms of *ex ante* justification—or, to use the vocabulary mentioned above, only if those acts or attitudes are rationally determinable (or assessable) conditions. And, finally, we've said that acts or attitudes are conditions that we can regulate in accordance with norms of *ex ante* justification only if those acts or attitudes are partly individuated by our *de re* representations of those very same acts or attitudes as normatively appropriate. Putting all these points together, I now propose the following answer to the question of what kind of competence is exercised in those acts and attitudes that are *ex post* justified.

An act or attitude is *ex post* justified only if it is the exercise of a competence to perform acts, or to hold attitudes, that are individuated by the agent's *de re* representations of each such exercise as *ex post* justified.

Of course, an agent can represent something as *ex post* justified even without the use of that particular phrase, or any translation of it into another language: to represent a particular exercise as *ex post* justified is simply to represent it in a functionally distinctive way—but what is functionally distinctive about this kind of representation is more or less similar to what is functionally distinctive of our concept of *ex post* justification. Before elaborating on this point, let me try to ward off some potential misunderstandings.

An act or attitude is *ex post* justified only if it is the exercise of a certain kind of competence. But will just *any* exercise of the relevant kind of competence be *ex post* justified? Or must the exercise in question be of a particular kind? Before we can answer these questions, we must first get clearer on what it is for something to be the "exercise" of a particular competence. Suppose, for instance, that I walk in my sleep: am I thereby exercising my competence at walking? Or suppose I am an actor on the stage, playing the role of a racist character telling racist jokes: am I thereby exercising a competence at telling racist jokes? It may seem that an affirmative answer to both of these questions is recommended by the following consideration: if I lacked the competence in question, I would not be able to perform the specified action. If, say, I couldn't walk, then I also couldn't walk in my sleep. And if I had no competence at telling racist jokes, then I also couldn't play the role of the racist in the stage play. But, although these considerations may *seem* to recommend an affirmative answer to the questions raised above, this appearance may be misleading. The most that follows from the considerations just mentioned is that possession of the relevant competence is a *necessary condition* of the specified performance. We might even concede that *exercise* of the relevant competence is a necessary condition of the specified performance. But none of this implies that the specified performance *is* an exercise of the corresponding competence.

Indeed, to expand on a point made above, we can see that some performances cannot be exercises of competences to make performances of that kind. Consider the lucky 3-pointer that a beginner miraculously manages to shoot. On this occasion, the shot went in the basket, but that was lucky: the beginner might have the competence to shoot an easy free throw, but she certainly does not have the competence to shoot 3-pointers. The fact that an agent F's does not in general imply that the agent exercises, or even possesses, a competence to F.

Conversely, the fact that an agent has and exercises a competence to F does not in general imply that the agent F's. LeBron James has the capacity to shoot a 3-pointer, and he may exercise that capacity on some occasion. But if, just as his attempt at a 3-pointer is about to go into the basket, his ball is struck by another ball and knocked far off its trajectory, then he will have failed to make the 3-point shot, even though he exercised his competence to make 3-point shots. In general, then, exercises of a competence to F are neither necessary nor sufficient for actually F'ing. Perhaps there are some particular values of F for which the exercise of a competence to F is necessary, or is sufficient, for F'ing. But that's not relevant to our present point, which is simply that exercising a competence to F is *not always* either necessary or sufficient for F'ing.

Nonetheless, we can evaluate exercises of a competence to F according to how likely those exercises are to result in F'ing. Of course, when we evaluate this likelihood, we can do so relative to different features of the exercise. For instance, relative to the fact that LeBron James exercised his capacity to shoot a 3-pointer, it's 34% likely that he will shoot a 3-pointer. Relative to the fact that LeBron exercised his capacity to shoot a 3-pointer without being guarded, it's 45% likely that he will shoot a 3-pointer. Relative to the fact that LeBron exercised his capacity to shoot a 3-pointer during solo practice, it's 52% likely that he will shoot a 3-pointer, and so on. How likely it is that his exercise of competence will result in an actual 3-pointer depends upon lots of different factors.

In general, we can separate those various factors into two broad categories: the skillfulness of that particular exercise, on the one hand, and the conduciveness of the surroundings, on the other. LeBron might take the most skillful shot he's ever taken, but if the ball is blown up by a hand grenade half-way to the basket, then of course the ball won't actually make it into the basket. Or, the surroundings might be just perfect for a 3-pointer: no interference at all. But if LeBron is having trouble concentrating and he just lets go of the ball too early, then the ball almost certainly won't make it into the basket either. The distinction just illustrated between internal and external factors is a distinction that mirrors a difference in who can typically regulate those factors. Internal factors are those that the agent herself is typically positioned to regulate (in the extended sense of "regulate" we discussed in the preceding section), whereas external factors are those that the agent is not typically positioned to regulate—in different cases, those factors might be regulated by anybody, or by nobody. Thus, how well the agent is concentrating on this occasion is a factor internal to the exercise of her competence, but how many distractions there are around the agent on this occasion is a factor external to the exercise of her competence: the agent is typically positioned to regulate the former, though not typically positioned to regulate the latter.[5]

In so far as we can distinguish these internal and external factors in any particular exercise of a competence, we can also distinguish how likely that exercise is to succeed relative to the factors internal to the agent from how likely that exercise is to succeed relative to the factors external to the agent, and we can distinguish both of those from how likely that exercise is to succeed given both the internal and the external factors.

Against the background of these remarks, I can now provide my full account of *ex post* justification, as follows:

An act or attitude is *ex post* justified just in case it is

(a) The exercise of a competence to perform acts, or to hold attitudes, that are individuated by the agent's *de re* representations of those acts or attitudes as *ex post* justified, and
(b) That exercise is sufficiently likely to succeed, *relative to the factors internal to the agent*.

Of course, the phrase "sufficiently likely" is vague, but I take this vagueness to capture the vagueness in the notion of *ex post* justification itself. An act or attitude is *ex post* justified if it is the exercise of the appropriate competence, and relative to the factors internal to that exercise (i.e., the factors that the agent herself is typically positioned to regulate), the exercise is sufficiently likely to succeed. Thus, to say that an act or attitude is *ex post* justified is to explain that act or attitude as arising in a distinctive way: as an exercise of a certain kind of competence, where the features of that exercise which the agent is typically positioned to regulate are features that make the success of that exercise sufficiently likely.

---

5 Although he does not commit to my particular way of distinguishing the factors internal to the exercise of a competence from those external to the exercise of a competence, a distinction of this sort, along with an account of *ex post* justification built on its basis, is famously developed in Sosa (2007). Anyone who knows that book will recognize its vast influence on the present chapter.

With this account of *ex post* justification in the background, let's now reconsider the objection that explanatory factors alone cannot determine normative status. We conceded that some explanatory factors cannot determine normative status. But what about the explanatory factors involved in *ex post* justification? Do those explanatory factors determine normative status, or must there be a way to regard the notion of *ex post* justification as a composite of two independent factors—the explanatory and the normative?

Let's see what would happen if we tried to follow the latter route, and separate the explanatory dimension of *ex post* justification from the normative dimension. How could we characterize the explanatory dimension without appeal to any normative notion? In characterizing an act or attitude as *ex post* justified, we are explaining it as the exercise of a particular competence. But which competence? A competence to perform acts or hold attitudes that are individuated by the agent's de re representations of them as *ex post* justified. In other words, it is essential to the competence at issue that each exercise of that capacity involve the application of a normative notion to that very exercise. To separate the explanatory dimension of the present account of *ex post* justification from the normative dimension, we would need to find a way to characterize this very same competence without describing it as a competence to think or do things under the guise of the *ex post* justified, or under any normative guise whatsoever. But what reason do we have to think that this very same competence can be characterized in a way that neither employs nor presupposes those descriptions? Without an answer to this question, I see no prospect of progress in separating the two dimensions of *ex post* justification. Trying to characterize the explanatory dimension of *ex post* justification without appeal to the normative dimension is not, so far as I can see, a viable project.[6] Some causal explanations are inherently normative.

Conclusion

This chapter has defended the view that we track *ex ante* justification in order to regulate our own exercises of agency, whereas we track *ex post* justification in order to understand why agents (including ourselves) think or do whatever they think or do. Along the way, I've offered more specificity about the sense in which agents regulate those conditions with respect to which they are *ex ante* justified, and also about the sense in which causal explanations of an act or attitude can themselves fix their *ex post* justificatory status.

---

6 Sylvan and Lord (2019) argue that it is not possible.

References

Firth, Roderick. (1978). "Are Epistemic Concepts Reducible to Ethical Concepts?" in *Values and Morals*, edited by Alvin Goldman and Jaegwon Kim. D. Reidel: 215–229.

Goldman, Alvin. (1979). "What is Justification?" in *Justification and Knowledge*, edited by Gregory Pappas. D. Reidel: 1–23.

Marcus, Eric. (2021). *Belief, Inference, and the Self-Conscious Mind*. Oxford University Press.

Neta, Ram. (2018). "Rationally Determinable Conditions," *Philosophical Issues: A Supplement to Nous* 28: 289–299.

Neta, Ram. (2019). "The Basing Relation," *The Philosophical Review* 128: 179–217.

Neta, Ram. (Forthcoming). "Rationality, Success, and Luck," *Acta Analytica*.

Sosa, Ernest. (2007). *A Virtue Epistemology: Apt Belief and Reflective Knowledge*. Oxford University Press.

Sylvan, Kurt and Lord, Errol. (2019). "Prime Time for the Basing Relation," in *Well-Founded: New Essays on the Basing Relation*, edited by J. Adam Carter and Patrick Bondy. Routledge: 141–173.

Williamson, Timothy (2000). *Knowledge and Its Limits*. OUP.

Part II
Reasons, Basing, and Justification

5 Factive Reasons and Propositional Justification[1]

Duncan Pritchard

My interest is in the internalist conception of propositional justification, where by this I mean an account of propositional justification that goes hand-in-hand with an internalist conception of doxastic justification. I take this to be any account of doxastic justification that is essentially concerned with reflectively accessible epistemic reasons. In addition, I will follow orthodoxy in treating propositional justification as fundamental in this regard, such that one defines doxastic justification in terms of propositional justification plus appropriate basing.[2] This commitment is significant because it is common to understand the internalist conception of doxastic justification in terms of the subject's non-factive mental states. Accordingly, if doxastic justification is just propositional justification plus appropriate basing, then it follows that the constituents of propositional justification are also restricted to the subject's non-factive mental states. It is precisely this conception of propositional justification that I will be objecting to. In particular, I will be arguing that a better account of propositional justification, and thus doxastic justification, is available that allows a subject's factive mental states to be part of a

---

1 Thanks to Paul Silva and Mona Simion for detailed comments on an earlier version of this chapter.
2 Orthodoxy among epistemic internalists at any rate, as there is an influential tradition in epistemic externalism that follows Goldman (1979) in treating doxastic justification (reliabilistically understood) as the fundamental notion (though he expresses the propositional/doxastic justification distinction in different terminology—viz., *ex ante/ex post* justification). See, for example, Kornblith (2017). For a dissenting voice regarding this orthodoxy within epistemic internalism, see Turri (2010b). See also Melis (2018). Note that I won't be commentating on the basing relation here, but rather taking this notion as understood. For what it is worth, I defend a causal explanatory account of the basing relation—see Pritchard (2019). For two helpful surveys of recent work on the basing relation in epistemology, see Neta (2019) and Sylvan (2016b). See also the comprehensive account of the basing relation offered in Neta (2019). For further discussion of the distinction between propositional and doxastic justification, see Silva and Oliveira (forthcoming).

DOI: 10.4324/9781003008101-8

subject's propositional justification. This is an account of propositional justification that goes hand-in-hand with *epistemological disjunctivism*.[3]

The Classical Internalist Account of Justification

Standard forms of epistemic internalism about doxastic justification understand the rational support that constitutes a subject's justification in terms of that subject's non-factive mental states, such as her beliefs and her experiences. We find this thesis in both mentalist and accessibilist versions of epistemic internalism. The former endorses this thesis directly by claiming that doxastic justification supervenes on the subject's non-factive mental states, while the latter endorses this thesis indirectly by claiming that subjects only have the special epistemic access that is relevant to doxastic justification with regard to their non-factive mental states.[4] In both cases, the contrast is with epistemic externalist accounts of doxastic justification, such as process reliabilism, which allow facts about the world, such as whether a belief was formed via a reliable process, to have a bearing on the justification of the target belief.[5]

There are various rationales offered for why epistemic internalism incorporates this demand, but I want to focus on one overarching consideration in this regard, which is the so-called *new evil demon intuition*.[6] This is the intuition that a subject and her envatted counterpart are equally justified in the beliefs that they form. The experiences had by the unenvatted subject are, *ex hypothesi*, indistinguishable from the experiences had by the envatted counterpart. Accordingly, as counterparts, both subjects will respond to these experiences in the same way, and hence form identical beliefs as a result on the very same basis. It seems to follow that these two subjects must share a justification for their beliefs, in the sense that if one of these subject's beliefs is justified, then the other subject's corresponding belief is also justified, and to the same degree. Moreover, if doxastic justification is just propositional justification plus appropriate

---

3 I have defended epistemological disjunctivism in a number of works, but see especially Pritchard (2008, 2012, 2015). I claim that such a view is rooted in the work of McDowell (1995). See also Neta and Pritchard (2007).
4 The dominant version of mentalism in the literature is that defended in Conee and Feldman (2004). See also Wedgwood (2002). For some key defences of accessibilism, see Chisholm (1977) and Bonjour (1985, ch. 2).
5 See, for example, the process reliabilist account of epistemic justification (both doxastic and propositional) offered by Goldman (1979). For further discussion of the epistemic externalism/internalism distinction more generally, see Pryor (2001), Vahid (2011), and Pappas (2014). For my own recent take on these issues, see Pritchard (forthcoming-a).
6 The *loci classici* for discussion of the new evil genius intuition are Lehrer and Cohen (1983) and Cohen (1984). For discussion, see Littlejohn (2009).

basing, then sameness of doxastic justification appears to entail sameness of propositional justification too. After all, given that both subjects seem to be forming their beliefs on the very same basis, it is hard to see how a difference in propositional justification could possibly arise.

Epistemic internalism is held to be uniquely well-placed to accommodate the new evil demon intuition. Indeed, the new evil demon intuition was originally presented as an objection to epistemic externalism (and hence in support of epistemic internalism).[7] A process reliabilist account of doxastic justification, for example, seems to be in direct conflict with this intuition, given that the beliefs held by the subject and her envatted counterpart clearly differ quite dramatically in terms of whether they are reliably formed. Proponents of such a view are thus faced with the dilemma of either rejecting the intuition or finding some way of modifying the view so as to accommodate it.[8]

When it comes to epistemic internalism, in contrast, there doesn't seem to be any *prima facie* tension in play. In particular, epistemic internalism can accept this intuition as being straightforwardly true. Since the subject and her envatted counterpart share the same non-factive mental states, and form their beliefs in identical ways, it follows that they ought to be counterparts in terms of the doxastic justification that their beliefs enjoy.

Notice that it is crucial to epistemic internalism that it is the non-factive mental states that are relevant here, as clearly the subject and her counterpart do not share their factive mental states. Take a factive mental state like *seeing that p*, or *remembering that p*, where the mental state entails the target proposition. There will clearly be many factive mental states of this kind that will be possessed by the subject and not her envatted counterpart. For example, while the unenvatted subject, who has veridical perceptual experiences of the world around her, can count as seeing that such-and-such is the case, her envatted counterpart clearly cannot exhibit the same mental state, given that her perceptual experiences are not at all veridical. Nonetheless, the subjects will share their non-factive mental states, and in particular will share their experiences and beliefs about the nature of the world around them, and that is all that matters with regard to capturing the new evil demon intuition.[9]

Accordingly, epistemic internalism about doxastic justification is standardly thought to be solely concerned with the subject's non-factive

---

7 See, especially, Lehrer and Cohen (1983) and Cohen (1984).
8 For a prominent example of a view that takes the first horn, see Bach (1985). See also Engel (1992). With regard to the second horn, see Goldman's (1986, 1988) influential proposals in this regard (normal worlds reliabilism and the distinction between strong and weak justification, respectively).
9 For our purposes we can set aside complications that might arise concerning content externalism in this regard. If you like, stipulate that the mental states in question are not only non-factive, but also more specifically concern narrow contents.

mental states.[10] Moreover, as we've already noted, sameness of doxastic justification in this case implies sameness of propositional justification too, and so we get the further claim that propositional justification is also to be understood in terms of non-factive mental states. This is a plausible way of thinking about propositional justification. Propositional justification is meant to be a kind of justification that is available to the subject to believe the target proposition, regardless of whether she in fact believes it, such that if she appropriately forms a belief on this basis then that belief is doxastically justified. If the subject's propositional justification concerns her non-factive mental states, then that would ensure that it is suitably available to the subject, given that we are held to have special epistemic access to our mental states.

We will call the thesis that doxastic and propositional justification are to be understood in terms of non-factive mental states in the manner just described the *classical internalist account of justification*. While the classical internalist account of justification, and the new evil demon intuition that motivates it, is usually expressed directly at the level of justification, we can also express the view (and the new evil demon intuition too) at the level of the reasons that comprise this justification.[11] Call the reasons that are the actual reasons for which a subject believes that p the subject's *motivational reasons*.[12] The upshot of the new evil demon intuition seems to be that the subject and her envatted counterpart form their beliefs on the basis of the very same reasons, but since they only share their non-factive mental states, this suggests that the motivational reasons must be concerned with such states. In any case, when one's motivational reasons are sufficiently good reasons (and whatever conditions required for appropriate basing are met), then one's belief will be doxastically justified.

---

10 Note that I am setting aside here the potential complication posed by normative defeaters, and in particular whether a normative defeater of which the subject is currently unaware might nonetheless be relevant to the doxastic justification of her belief even by epistemic internalist lights. On this point, see the exchange between Greco (2005) and Fumerton (2005). I am grateful to Paul Silva for pressing me on this issue.

11 See Turri (2009) for a presentation of the new evil demon intuition that is expressed at the level of reasons rather than justification. Note that in what follows we will take it as given that reasons are to be understood epistemically, as reasons for belief, rather than, say, as reasons for action.

12 The terminology is relatively common in the literature, though Sylvan (2016b) refers to motivational reasons as "operative reasons", on account of what he regards as the awkwardness of talking of motivation in the context of doxastic attitudes. Note that for motivational reasons it is the subject's *actual* reason for believing that *p* that is important, which might not be the same as the subject's *perceived* reason for believing that *p*. In what follows we will focus on cases where no such conflict arises. I discuss motivational reasons, and in particular their relation to normative and explanatory reasons, in more detail in Pritchard (2019, forthcoming-b). For further discussion of epistemic reasons, see Turri (2009) and Sylvan (2016a, 2016b).

Whereas a subject's motivational reasons are the reasons for which she believes, regardless of whether those reasons are of good epistemic pedigree, *normative reasons* are facts that constitute good epistemic reasons to believe a proposition, independently of whether anyone actually believes that proposition (*a fortiori*, whether anyone actually believes that proposition on this rational basis). Propositional justification is concerned with normative reasons. In particular, it is concerned with those normative reasons that are available to the subject, such that she could form a belief in the target proposition on this basis (which would in turn ensure that the very same reason is the subject's motivational reason).

Expressed in terms of the classical internalist account of justification, we thus get the idea of there being a sub-class of normative reasons that concern the subject's non-factive mental states. These are accessible to the subject, and so can constitute the subject's propositional justification for believing a target proposition. That the obtaining of such states can be normative reasons looks credible, since a subject's beliefs and experiences (non-factively understood) are often thought to provide good reasons for belief. Accordingly, if the subject appropriately forms her belief on the basis of the non-factive mental states that constitute the normative reasons, such that the normative reason is also her motivational reason, then her belief will be doxastically justified.

A Non-Classical Internalist Account of Justification

I want to take issue with the classical internalist account of justification. My concern with the proposal is not the commitment to epistemic internalism that it incorporates, however. Accordingly, I won't be defending an epistemic externalist account of propositional and doxastic justification instead. Rather, I will be arguing that there is a more plausible non-classical internalist account of propositional justification available, one that isn't bound by the new evil demon intuition into thinking of the constituent normative reasons that propositional justification involves as being restricted to non-factive mental states. In particular, I will be arguing for a non-classical internalist account of justification that allows one's *factive* mental states to play the relevant rational role.

Defending such a position means accommodating the new evil demon intuition in such a way that it doesn't entail the classical internalist account of justification. In particular, it involves arguing that the subject and her envatted counterpart are not equally doxastically justified in their beliefs (though I will be claiming that there is a sense in which both beliefs are justified nonetheless). I will be suggesting, however, that there are independent grounds for not taking this intuition at face value. Moreover, I will be maintaining that one can motivate this alternative accommodation of the new evil demon intuition from *within* epistemic internalism.

We noted earlier that those who defend the new evil demon intuition can do so at the level of reasons, and that this involves claiming that the subject and her envatted counterpart share the same motivational reason. I think that it is entirely right that these subjects do share this motivational reason, but I don't think that the classical internalist account of justification correctly identifies what this is, and that this has a bearing on the question of whether the subjects are alike in terms of doxastic justification. Recall that one's motivational reason is the reason for which one actually believes the target proposition. The classical internalist account of justification takes it as a given that this reason is a non-factive mental state. This is certainly how they understand the doxastic justification that the subjects have in this case, as we noted above.

But notice how theory-driven this claim is. In particular, our everyday conception of reasons is not limited to non-factive mental states at all. In fact, we are normally only prompted to appeal to non-factive mental states as reasons when we have grounds to doubt the target proposition. Imagine, for example, that we have a subject in conditions that are entirely normal who believes that there is a computer in the room because that's what she sees, and who has no grounds to doubt what she sees. If this subject is asked why she believes that this is the case, wouldn't she naturally respond by appealing to a factive mental state, such as that she can see that there is a computer in the room? In contrast, if she did only appeal to a non-factive reason, such as by saying that it seems to her as if there is a computer in the room, wouldn't we take this to indicate that she has some grounds to doubt what she is seeing (which would thus be puzzling, given that the subject has been given no grounds for doubt)?[13]

This point is important since it indicates that the subject's motivational reason in normal circumstances is usually not a non-factive reason at all (i.e., a reason that concerns a non-factive mental state), but rather a factive reason (i.e., a reason that concerns a factive mental state). This is problematic for the classical internalist account of justification since doxastic justification was meant to consist of the subject appropriately forming a belief in the target proposition on the basis of an accessible normative reason that consisted of a non-factive mental state, and hence a non-factive reason. But it seems that subjects do not normally form their beliefs on this basis at all, in which case it is not clear how, on the classical account, they are to form justified beliefs, given that doxastic justification is essentially concerned with the subject's motivational reasons.

With the foregoing in mind, suppose that instead of treating the subject's motivational reason—in normal conditions, where the subject is offered no grounds for doubt in this regard—as being a non-factive mental state we instead follow our everyday epistemic practices and appeal

---

13 For further defence of this point about our everyday usage of factive reasons, see McDowell (1995) and Pritchard (2012, part one).

to a factive mental state instead. So our subject's motivational reason for believing that p, where p is some claim about her environment, is not that (say) it seems to her that p, but rather that she sees that p. Since seeing that p is evidently a good reason for believing that p (since it entails it), there can't be any dispute that this would constitute a normative reason in this regard. It is certainly a normative reason if the corresponding nonfactive state is a normative reason. Given that the subject appropriately forms her belief that p on this basis, then, such that it is also her motivational reason, then we can capture her doxastic justification in terms of the possession of this factive reason. This way of thinking about doxastic justification, whereby one's factive mental states can function as the rational support for one's beliefs, is central to *epistemological disjunctivism*, though we are here extending this non-classical internalist account of justification to propositional justification as well.[14]

We noted earlier that the proponent of the classical internalist account of justification claims in response to the new evil demon intuition that the counterpart subjects believe what they do on the basis of the same motivational reasons. I agree that this is so, except that I would claim, for the reasons just noted, that the motivational reason common to both subjects is the factive reason concerned with the subject's factive mental state. In particular, since the two counterpart subjects have indistinguishable experiences, the envatted counterpart will also form her belief that p on the same factive basis. Of course, the envatted subject doesn't in fact see that p, but that needn't prevent this from being her motivational reason for believing that p. Moreover, she has been given no grounds for doubting the veracity of her experiences in this regard. Accordingly, if the motivational reason for the unenvatted subject's belief is that she sees that p, then that is also the motivational reason for the corresponding belief held by her envatted counterpart.

We've previously noted that motivational reasons can be good or bad from an epistemic point of view, as this is simply the name of the reason for which one believes as one does, and that might have no epistemic status whatsoever. What makes a motivational reason a good reason from an epistemic point of view is whether it is also a normative reason with regard to the target proposition. If it is, and the subject appropriately forms her belief in the target proposition on the basis of this normative reason, such that it is also their motivational reason, then this can generate doxastic justification. This is why the unenvatted subject has a justified belief that p. But what should we say about her envatted counterpart whose motivational reason is also the factive mental state that she sees that p?

Clearly the justificatory story just offered with regard to the unenvatted subject's belief is not applicable to her envatted counterpart, as the normative reason in question simply doesn't obtain. In particular, one

---

14 For some key defences of epistemological disjunctivism, see footnote 3.

cannot see that p if p is false. But even if by some quirk p happened to be true, it would still be the case that this normative reason doesn't obtain. As many commentators have noted, seeing that p involves more than just the truth of p, or even that one genuinely sees the objects at issue in p, as it captures an epistemic relationship that one stands in with respect to p, one that wouldn't be available to the subject in conditions where one is massively in error regarding one's perceptual environment.[15] If the normative reason doesn't obtain, however, then it cannot be the source of doxastic justification for the subject. Accordingly, we are obliged on this proposal to deny that our counterparts are identical in terms of the doxastic justification they have for their beliefs, even though they are identical in terms of the motivational reasons that underpin these beliefs.

Explanatory Justification as a Positive Epistemic Standing

Does this mean that allowing that our motivational reasons in good epistemic conditions can be factive mental states entails that we must completely reject the new evil demon intuition? I think that this would be too quick, for while epistemological disjunctivism, as a non-classical internalist account of justification, is committed to maintaining that the beliefs of the two subjects in this case are not alike in terms of doxastic justification, this is not the only way of accommodating this intuition (even if it is the most direct way of accommodating it). In particular, there is a justificatory story that the proponent of epistemological disjunctivism justification can offer with regard to the envatted subject's belief.

Compare motivational reasons with *explanatory reasons*. Whereas the former concerns the reason for which the subject believes as she does, the latter concerns the reason that we would offer to explain why she believes as she does. Often, the two will coincide, and I think it is common as a result for epistemologists to treat them as the same thing. Indeed, in normal conditions, the distinction between a motivational and an explanatory reason simply will not arise. But there are important differences, and they come to light precisely in the kinds of cases that interest us, where agents are unbeknownst to them forming erroneous beliefs. In terms of our pairing of an envatted and unenvatted subject, for example, while they both share their motivational reasons for belief (since the envatted subject is unaware of their epistemic situation), they are distinct in terms of the explanatory reasons that apply in each case. In particular, we would not explain why the envatted subject believes that p by appealing to her

---

15 Indeed, a number of commentators have argued that seeing that p entails knowing that p. See, for example, Dretske (1969), Williamson (2000), and Cassam (2007). I have argued elsewhere that this entailment doesn't hold—see Pritchard (2011, 2012, part 1)—though it is still true on my view that seeing that p and knowing that p are closely related. See also Turri (2010a) for a distinct critique of the thesis that seeing that p entails knowing that p.

motivational reason that she sees that p, since of course she doesn't see that p, and hence this wouldn't explain anything about why she believes as she does. The applicable explanatory reason would rather be the non-factive mental state that it *seems to her that p*. That is a fact, and it also explains why she would believe that p even though p isn't the case. It is not, however, her reason for believing that p. Explanatory and motivational reasons thus come apart.

This point is significant for our purposes as it enables us to offer a justificatory story regarding our envatted subject's belief, albeit not one that involves doxastic justification. For notice that the fact that it seems to a subject that p is a normative reason for believing that p. Moreover, we have already granted that a subject's non-factive mental states can be accessible normative reasons that can comprise that subject's propositional justification. It follows that in the kind of case where the distinction between motivational and explanatory reasons arises, which will essentially be cases where doxastic justification is lacking, it is nonetheless possible to appeal to a normative reason that is part of that subject's propositional justification to account for why an explanatory reason can confer a positive epistemic status on the target belief. Call this positive epistemic standing *explanatory justification*, as distinct from the doxastic justification that is applicable to the non-envatted counterpart (whose motivational reason aligns with a normative reason).

We can think of explanatory justification as a kind of epistemic charity. It is a mode of epistemic evaluation that only becomes relevant when doxastic justification is lacking. The idea is that we take a further step back in our epistemic evaluation of the subject's belief and consider whether there is an explanatory story available that accounts for why the subject believes as she does which aligns with an accessible normative reason. Explanatory justification is thus a secondary notion of justification, albeit one which mirrors in crucial respects the structure of doxastic justification.

Recall that doxastic justification involves a belief based on the propositional justification provided by the accessible normative reason. The motivational and accessible normative reasons thus need to align. Similarly, explanatory justification also appeals to the propositional justification provided by an accessible normative reason, albeit by appealing to the subject's explanatory reason rather than her motivational reason in this regard. For this secondary notion of justification, only applicable when doxastic justification is lacking, what is important is that the explanatory reason and the accessible normative reason aligns.[16]

---

16 Notice that this proposal is subtly different from that offered by Bach (1985) and Engel (1992). While they deny that the subjects in the new evil demon case share doxastic justification, they maintain that the envatted subject is nonetheless "personally justified", where this means that as a belief-forming subject she is justified in believing as she does (even if she lacks doxastic justification). Explanatory justification, however, is still a form of justification that applies to the target belief.

In this way, we can accommodate the intuition that both agents in the new evil demon case are justified in their beliefs, while also denying that they are alike in terms of doxastic justification. In particular, the two agents are not on an epistemic par with regard to their beliefs in the target proposition, as only the secondary, explanatory, notion of justification is applicable to the envatted subject's beliefs (and which, moreover, concerns a non-factive normative reason, as opposed to a factive one). Furthermore, as we have seen, what is crucial to recognizing that there is this secondary notion of justification in play is to realize that while the subjects in the new evil demon case do share the same motivational reason, since that reason concerns a factive mental state, only the unenvatted subject has a belief that is in the market for doxastic justification.

That the subject's explanatory reason aligns with an accessible normative reason that comprises her propositional justification is thus one way of motivating the claim that explanatory justification is a *bona fide* positive epistemic standing, even if it is not a form of doxastic justification. We can further motivate this claim by contrasting cases of explanatory justification with cases where we aren't at all inclined to treat the subject's belief as justified. Such cases emphasize the point that while explanatory justification is not on a par with doxastic justification, it is a positive epistemic standing that contrasts with cases where justification is altogether lacking.

Suppose our subject's reason for believing that p is that this was predicted in the tealeaves. Now the motivational and explanatory reasons for this subject's belief don't line up at all with any normative reason, since the tealeaves don't offer any rational basis for the truth of the target proposition. In such a case, doxastic justification is lacking, in virtue of the motivational reason failing to be a normative reason. But there is also no explanatory justification either, as the explanatory reason and the motivational reason are identical. In particular, we would explain why the subject believes that p by appealing to the prediction of the tealeaves.

We can also run a case of envatment to illustrate this point. We tend to imagine the subjects who are envatted as otherwise rational (just like their unenvatted counterparts), but this is obviously not at all necessary.[17] Suppose our envatted subject's belief that p does not appeal to a factive mental state as a motivational reason, but rather something altogether dubious, such as the "evidence" of the tealeaves. Not only is this subject lacking in doxastic justification, but also explanatory justification, as we would explain why she believed as she does by appeal to the same motivational reason, and neither the motivational nor the explanatory reason aligns with a normative reason.

---

17 See Pryor (2001, §4.3) for further discussion of cases involving agents who are both envatted and irrational.

We noted earlier that an envatted subject, while lacking lots of doxastic justification, can nonetheless have explanatory justification for their beliefs so long as their explanatory reasons align with accessible normative reasons. But our current point is that this is far from guaranteed, as the envatted subject could lack even explanatory justification for their beliefs. This further reinforces the idea that explanatory justification, while falling short of doxastic justification, is nonetheless an authentic positive epistemic status, one that is absent from beliefs that we have no temptation to regard as justified.

Defending Non-Classical Epistemic Internalism

We have thus offered a conception of propositional and doxastic justification, albeit one that rejects the new evil demon intuition and, with it, the classical internalist account of justification. Recall that it was meant to be crucial to this alternative conception of justification that it was also squarely an internalist account of justification. But how plausible is it that an account of justification which allows non-factive mental states to function as normative and motivational reasons is genuinely a form of epistemic internalism?

The first point we can make on this score is to highlight the contrast between this proposal and what a traditional epistemic externalist denial of the new evil demon intuition would look like. The epistemic externalist will appeal to differences in the environmental facts concerning the two agents in the new evil demon case, such as regarding the reliability of their belief-forming processes. In contrast, the proposal offered here appeals to facts about the mental states of the two subjects. Aren't a subject's mental states central to our understanding of epistemic internalism? In particular, aren't a subject's mental states, including her factive mental states, epistemically accessible to the subject in a way that environmental facts are not?

The objector will no doubt respond by arguing that even if environmental facts are not being appealed to directly in this regard, they are being appealed to indirectly in virtue of how factive mental states entail such environmental facts. But why, exactly, is that problematic? Our mental states are paradigmatically "internal," after all, so what is the basis for thinking that it is only our non-factive mental states that are relevant in this regard? This question is particularly pressing once we notice how our ordinary epistemic practices are shot-through with appeals to factive mental states as reasons—indeed, as we noted above, we paradigmatically appeal to them, in that we are usually only led to appeal to non-factive mental states as reasons when we have some reason to doubt that we are in normal epistemic conditions.

Moreover, it would obviously be dialectically problematic to fallback on an appeal to the new evil demon intuition in this regard, and thereby argue that only non-factive mental states can be constituent parts of a subject's propositional justification. After all, we have offered an alternative way of thinking about justification that accommodates this intuition in such a way that allows that our factive mental states can be the source of propositional justification. It would thus be important to offer an independent basis for thinking that factive mental states cannot function as normative and motivational reasons.

One consideration that might be invoked in this regard is that factive mental states are not reflectively accessible, unlike non-factive mental states, or at least that they aren't as reflectively accessible anyway. If so, then that would distinguish them from non-factive mental states in the relevant respect, and thereby put them in the camp with the kind of environmental facts that epistemic externalists appeal to in this regard. So expressed, however, this claim is rather implausible, at least to the extent that we take our ordinary epistemic practices seriously as I have suggested we should. For in those practices the factive reasons that one paradigmatically offers in support of one's beliefs are clearly treated as reflectively accessible. The subject can, for example, cite such reasons without having to undertake any further empirical inquiry (of a kind that could well be required of the environmental facts at issue with epistemic externalism).

I take it, however, that the real issue that faces the claim that factive mental states are reflectively accessible is not so much the idea that such states are reflective accessible itself, but rather what is thought to be a troubling consequence of this claim. We can delineate two core concerns on this front. The first is that in having reflective access to one's factive mental states one thereby has reflective access to specific facts about one's environment. After all, since such factive mental states entail specific empirical propositions, and one can know *a priori* that this entailment holds, then why doesn't one have an exclusively reflective route available to one to know the entailed empirical proposition? Elsewhere I have called this the *access problem* for epistemological disjunctivism.[18]

The second concern is that in having reflective access to one's factive mental states one is thereby in a position to come to know that one is not radically deceived about one's environment. It is built into cases of envatment as they are usually understood that the subject cannot distinguish between being the unenvatted agent and being the envatted counterpart. After all, how could the subject possibly discriminate between the two, given that the experiences in each case are *ex hypothesi* indistinguishable? And yet, if one can know that one's belief is supported by factive reasons, then given that one can also know that only an unenvatted agent can be in possession of such reasons, then can't one thereby conclude that one is the unenvatted agent rather than the envatted counterpart?

---

18 See, especially, Pritchard (2012, part 1).

In short, it seems that one is able to come to know something simply by reflecting on the nature of the rational support that one's beliefs enjoys that it ought not to be possible to know. I have previously called this the *distinguishability problem* for epistemological disjunctivism.[19]

I've written about both problems extensively elsewhere, and it would take us too far afield to rehearse my responses to each problem at length here, so let me instead offer a summary. As regards the access problem, it simply doesn't follow from the fact that one has reflective access to one's factive mental states that one is thereby able to know, by reflection alone, the specific empirical proposition entailed by that factive mental state. What we have to remember here is that the factive mental state itself is the result of an empirical process. Take seeing that p as an example. One acquires such a mental state by standing in an appropriate perceptual relationship to the world. Thus although it is a mental state, it is also an empirical reason, in virtue of how it is acquired. It follows that in having reflective access to such a factive mental state, and knowing that this entails the target proposition, one doesn't thereby possess a purely *a priori* route to knowing that proposition, as the resulting belief would be based on an empirical reason.[20]

Notice that in responding to the access problem I wasn't denying that one could infer the proposition that is entailed by the factive mental state, and thereby come to know that proposition. My claim was only that such knowledge would not be *a priori*. Such a claim suffices to block to the access problem, but one might nonetheless think that it is puzzling enough that one can come to know a specific empirical fact about the world in this way, even if such knowledge is not *a priori*. The source of the worry here, I take it, is that there is something problematic about how one's reflective access to factive reasons provides one with a means to know facts about the world.

I think this latter problem is in essence the distinguishability problem. In particular, the distinguishability problem brings out just why it might be problematic to know facts about the world on this basis, in that it seems to enable one to know facts about the world that ought not to be able to know, such as that one is not envatted. This highlights an important point about the distinguishability problem, however, which is that it is not specifically about one's *reflective* access to factive reasons at all. After all, this issue would arise even if one's way of knowing that one's reasons are factive was straightforwardly empirical, such as via testimony, since it would still be puzzling that such knowledge could be used as way of coming to know something such as that one is not envatted.

I think the distinguishability problem raises deep epistemological issues, of a kind that extend well beyond our current concern with

---

19 See, especially, Pritchard (2012, part 1).
20 For my full response to the access problem, see Pritchard (2012, part 1).

epistemological disjunctivism. Accordingly, a complete response would demand a self-standing article in its own right. But at the heart of my response to this problem is a distinction that I have drawn elsewhere and which I think is of general import to epistemology.[21] In essence, this is that the rational support our beliefs enjoy can fall into two distinct categories. The first consists of reasons to think that one has a relevant discriminative capacity. So, in the perceptual case, this might be reasons to think that one has the perceptual discriminative capacity to tell, say, goldfinches apart from other birds that could feasibly be in the vicinity, such as chaffinches. Call this *discriminative rational support*. Discriminative rational support does not exhaust the rational support one's beliefs might enjoy, however, for we can have reasons that are completely independent of a discriminative capacity. For example, one might have an excellent testimonial basis for thinking that the bird before one is a goldfinch, and thus a goldfinch rather than chaffinch, even though one wouldn't be able to tell goldfinches apart from any other bird (including a chaffinch). Call this *favoring rational support*.

The significance of this distinction is that it entails that there is a way of knowing the difference which is not thereby a way of telling the difference. For example, one can know that the bird before one is a goldfinch rather than a chaffinch, in virtue of the possession of favoring rational support, even though one lacks a perceptual capacity to discriminate between goldfinches and chaffinches. It follows that one's inability to discriminate between two alternatives does not entail that one cannot know that one alternative obtains rather than the other. In particular, one's lack of discriminating rational support (i.e., reason to think that one has the target discriminative ability) doesn't entail that one can't know that a particular alternative obtains.

I think this distinction is of general relevance to epistemology; indeed, I claim that it is a distinction that all epistemologists should accept (i.e., and not just those attracted to epistemological disjunctivism). The distinction is nonetheless of particular import to the distinguishability problem, and thus to epistemological disjunctivism. This is because the nub of that problem is that being in possession of factive reasons seems to allow subjects to distinguish between scenarios that, *ex hypothesi*, are indistinguishable. But this claim is ambiguous.

In particular, it has a strong and a weak reading. On the strong reading, what is being suggested is that the subject has a reason for believing that she a discriminative capacity that would enable her to distinguish between the two scenarios. That would clearly be implausible, since it is built into the envatment case that one lacks a discriminative capacity to tell one's ordinary experiences apart from the experiences had by one's envatted counterpart. The subject thus lacks any rational basis for

---

21 See especially Pritchard (2010).

thinking that she has such a discriminative power. On the weak reading, in contrast, all that is being claimed is that the subject can know that she is in the one scenario rather than the other. Crucially, this claim can be satisfied by the subject having appropriate favoring rational support; it needn't imply that the subject has any reason for believing that she has a special discriminative power, something that would not be credible in this case.

It is clearly the weak reading that is relevant to epistemological disjunctivism. In particular, there is no suggestion on this view that subjects have a special discriminative power to tell ordinary experiences apart from the experiences of the envatted counterpart. What is being suggested is that subjects can reflect on their factive reasons and draw appropriate consequences. These reasons are thus favoring reasons, albeit of a special kind, in that they actually entail the target proposition, rather than merely tipping the rational scales in its favor. So construed, the teeth are removed from the distinguishability problem, in that what epistemological disjunctivism is committed to is not an implausible claim about special discriminative powers, but rather a point about how one can possess decisive favoring reasons.[22]

Finally, notice that the claim that our factive mental states can be as reflectively accessible as our non-factive mental states is also important to treating them as relevant to a subject's propositional justification. Recall that we noted earlier that for a normative reason to be part of a subject's propositional justification it was important that it was available to the subject. We didn't dwell on what such availability amounted to, except to note that being reflectively accessible to the subject should suffice in this regard, and hence that a subject's propositional justification can be concerned with her non-factive mental states. If factive mental states are no less reflectively accessible in this regard, however, then it follows that the relevant class of normative reasons which concern these states will also satisfy the rubric for propositional justification.

Conclusion

We've argued against the classical internalist account of justification, and in particular against the new evil demon intuition that is held to motivate it. As we've seen, once this proposal, and also the intuition that drives it, is expressed at the level of reasons, then a key issue emerges. This is that

22 For my full response to the distinguishability problem, see Pritchard (2012, part 3, 2015, part 3). Note that the full response also considers how the distinguishability problem relates to the challenge posed by radical scepticism, whereas I have set aside this challenge for our purposes here. In particular, it does not follow from what we've just argued that such decisive favouring rational support is applicable in terms of responding to radical scepticism. As it happens, I think it is applicable, but that requires further argumentation, as I explain in my full response to this problem.

the most natural way to understand a subject's motivational reasons in ordinary circumstances is often as concerning that subject's factive mental states, as opposed to her non-factive mental states. Accordingly, while the proponent of the new evil demon intuition is right that a subject and her envatted counterpart will share motivational reasons for their beliefs, it won't follow that both subjects have beliefs that are equally doxastically justified. In particular, where the envatted subject's motivational reason for belief concerns a factive mental state, then the subject's motivational reason cannot align with a normative reason, as of course that factive mental state doesn't obtain.

That said, we have contended that the new evil demon intuition can nonetheless be accommodated. Moreover, this accommodation becomes apparent precisely because we have cast these issues at the level of reasons rather than exclusively at the level of justification. For there is a secondary notion of justification available that concerns a subject's explanatory reasons and whether they align with a normative reason. While explanatory justification is not on a par with doxastic justification—indeed, it is kind of justification that becomes relevant when doxastic justification is lacking—it is nonetheless a bona fide positive epistemic standing, in that one's beliefs could be so poorly formed from a rational point of view as to lack it. It follows that there is a sense in which the subject and her envatted counterpart are both justified in their beliefs, just as the new evil demon intuition maintains, albeit not in a fashion that would underwrite the classical internalist account of justification.

Finally, we have seen that the alternative, non-classical, account of justification that we have offered –epistemological disjunctivism, as it is known—can plausibly lay claim to being a form of internalism about justification (and not only because it can accommodate the new evil demon intuition). In particular, unlike epistemic externalism, it appeals to the subject's reflectively mental states rather than to purely environmental factors. Moreover, we have argued that while the idea that one's factive mental states can be reflectively accessible could be viewed as having problematic ramifications, there are grounds to resist these putative counterintuitive consequences. I conclude that one can best capture internalist insights about justification by allowing that one's factive mental states can play a justificatory role. In particular, their obtaining can constitute the accessible normative reasons that comprise a subject's propositional justification, such that if the motivational reason for the subject's belief aligns with this normative reason, then the belief is thereby doxastically justified.

References

Bach, K. (1985). A rationale for reliabilism. *Monist* 68, 246–63.
BonJour, L. (1985). *The Structure of Empirical Knowledge*. Cambridge, MA: Harvard University Press.

Cassam, Q. (2007). Ways of knowing. *Proceedings of the Aristotelian Society* 107, 339–58.
Chisholm, R. M. (1977). *Theory of Knowledge* (2nd edn.). Englewood Cliffs, NJ: Prentice-Hall.
Cohen, S. (1984). Justification and truth. *Philosophical Studies* 46, 279–96.
Conee, E., & Feldman, R. (2004). *Evidentialism: Essays in Epistemology*. Oxford: Oxford University Press.
Dretske, F. (1969). *Seeing and Knowing*. London: Routledge & Kegan Paul.
Engel, M. (1992). Personal and doxastic justification. *Philosophical Studies* 67, 133–51.
Fumerton, R. (2005). Justification is internal. In E. Sosa & M. Steup (Eds.), 270–84. *Contemporary Debates in Epistemology*. Oxford: Blackwell.
Goldman, A. (1979). What is justified belief? In G. S. Pappas (Ed.), *Justification and Knowledge*, 1–23. Dordrecht, Holland: Springer.
Goldman, A. (1986). *Epistemology and Cognition*. Cambridge, MA: Harvard University Press.
Goldman, Alvin (1988). Strong and weak justification. *Philosophical Perspectives* 2, 51–69.
Greco, J. (2005). Justification is not internal. In E. Sosa & M. Steup (Eds.), 257–69. *Contemporary Debates in Epistemology*. Oxford: Blackwell.
Kornblith, H. (2017). Doxastic justification is fundamental. *Philosophical Topics* 45, 63–80.
Melis, G. (2018). The intertwinement of propositional and doxastic justification. *Australasian Journal of Philosophy* 96, 367–79.
McDowell, J. (1995). Knowledge and the internal. *Philosophy and Phenomenological Research* 55, 877–93.
Lehrer, K., & Cohen, S. (1983). Justification, truth, and coherence. *Synthese* 55, 191–207.
Littlejohn, C. (2009). The new evil demon problem. In B. Dowden & J. Fieser (Eds.), *Internet Encyclopaedia of Philosophy*. www.iep.utm.edu/evil-new/.
Neta, R. (2019). The basing relation. *Philosophical Review* 128, 179–217.
Neta, R., & Pritchard, D. H. (2007). McDowell and the new evil genius. *Philosophy and Phenomenological Research* 74, 381–96.
Pappas, G. (2014). Internalist vs. externalist conceptions of epistemic justification. In E. Zalta (Ed.), *Stanford Encyclopedia of Philosophy*. https://plato.stanford.edu/entries/justep-intext/.
Pritchard, D. H. (2008). McDowellian neo-Mooreanism. In A. Haddock & F. Macpherson (Eds.), *Disjunctivism: Perception, Action, Knowledge*, 283–310. Oxford: Oxford University Press.
Pritchard, D. H. (2010). Relevant alternatives, perceptual knowledge, and discrimination. *Noûs* 44, 245–68.
Pritchard, D. H. (2011). Epistemological disjunctivism and the basis problem. *Philosophical Issues* 21, 434–55.
Pritchard, D. H. (2012). *Epistemological Disjunctivism*. Oxford: Oxford University Press.
Pritchard, D. H. (2015). *Epistemic Angst: Radical Skepticism and the Groundlessness of Our Believing*. Princeton, NJ: Princeton University Press.
Pritchard, D. H. (2019). Epistemological disjunctivism and factive bases for belief. In P. Bondy & J. A. Carter (Eds.), *Well-Founded Belief: New Essays on the Epistemic Basing Relation*, 235–50. London: Routledge.

Pritchard, D. H. (Forthcoming-a). Moderate knowledge externalism. In L. R. G. Oliveira (Ed.), *Externalism about Knowledge*, Oxford: Oxford University Press.

Pritchard, D. H. (Forthcoming-b). Shadowlands. In J. Dutant (Ed.), *The New Evil Demon: New Essays on Knowledge, Justification and Rationality*. Oxford: Oxford University Press.

Pryor, J. (2001). Highlights of recent epistemology. *British Journal for the Philosophy of Science* 52, 95–124.

Silva, P., & Oliveira, L. R. G. (Forthcoming). Propositional justification and doxastic justification. In M. Lasonen-Aarnio & C. Littlejohn (Eds.), *Routledge Handbook of Evidence*. London: Routledge.

Sylvan, K. (2016a). Epistemic reasons I: normativity. *Philosophy Compass* 11, 364–76.

Sylvan, K. (2016b). Epistemic reasons II: basing. *Philosophy Compass* 11, 377–89.

Turri, J. (2009). The ontology of epistemic reasons. *Noûs* 43, 490–512.

Turri, J. (2010a). Does perceiving entail knowing? *Theoria* 76, 197–206.

Turri, J. (2010b). On the relationship between propositional and doxastic justification. *Philosophy and Phenomenological Research* 80, 312–26.

Vahid, H. (2011). Externalism/internalism. In S. Bernecker & D. H. Pritchard (Eds.), *Routledge Companion to Epistemology*, 144–54. London: Routledge.

Wedgwood, R. (2002). Internalism explained. *Philosophy and Phenomenological Research* 65, 349–69.

Williamson, T. (2000). *Knowledge and its Limits*. Oxford: Oxford University Press.

6 The Epistemic Function of Higher-Order Evidence[1]

Declan Smithies

Imagine you're a solo pilot flying a small plane in Arizona.[2] You're wondering whether to take a scenic detour via the Grand Canyon en route to your final destination. You know how far you can travel on a full tank and how much fuel remains in the tank. You also know the distance from here to the Grand Canyon and from there to your final destination. But you need to do some mental arithmetic in order to calculate whether you have enough fuel to safely complete the journey. You perform the calculation correctly and deduce that you have enough fuel. On that basis, you decide to take the detour. So far, so good.

Moments later, however, you acquire worrying new evidence that you are suffering from *hypoxia*—an oxygen deficit that impairs cognitive functioning in ways that tend to remain undetectable to the victim. You know about the dangers of hypoxia: pilots have crashed and died because of bad decisions made under its influence. You know there is a serious risk of hypoxia when the altitude is high enough and the cabin pressure is low enough. Moreover, your control panel says you're now in the danger zone. As it happens, this evidence is misleading, since there is a malfunction in the barometer that measures cabin pressure. The truth is that you're at no risk of hypoxia, although there's no way you can know this.

Should you now reconsider your decision to take the scenic detour once you acquire this new evidence? Intuitively, you should. Consider the *steadfast pilot* who decides to stick with his original plan. This decision seems grossly irrational. After all, the pilot has no way of knowing the evidence for hypoxia is misleading. This evidence indicates that he is cognitively impaired in ways that dispose him to make basic errors in calculation. It seems reckless for him to ignore the possibility that he has miscalculated in deciding to stick with his original plan. Of course, we know there is no risk of hypoxia and so we can rest assured that the pilot will arrive safely. But the pilot himself doesn't know this. Anyone who

---

1 Many thanks to David Barnett, David Christensen, Maria Lasonen-Aarnio, Ram Neta, Paul Silva, and Michael Titelbaum for valuable feedback.
2 This example is adapted from Elga (2008, 2013) and Christensen (2010a).

DOI: 10.4324/9781003008101-9

routinely ignores evidence of hypoxia in this way is putting their own life in serious danger.

The irrationality of the decision reflects the irrationality of the belief on which it is based. In general: if it's rationally permissible to believe that p, then it's rationally permissible to use p as a premise in reasoning.[3] When you acquire the new evidence that you're hypoxic, it's rationally impermissible to reason from the premise that you have enough fuel because it's rationally impermissible to believe you have enough fuel. Moreover, this means you cannot *know* you have enough fuel, since it's rationally permissible to believe that p, and hence to reason from the premise that p, whenever you know that p.[4] Previously, however, you did know that you had enough fuel by competently deducing this conclusion from known premises. Therefore, you must lose this knowledge when you acquire the new evidence that you are hypoxic.

This much is intuitively compelling but theoretically puzzling. Why should the evidence that you are hypoxic destroy your knowledge that you have enough fuel? It is plausible *that* it does, but it is not easy to explain *how* it does. After all, the evidence that you are hypoxic doesn't bear directly on the question of whether you have enough fuel: it isn't evidence that you *don't* have enough fuel. But then how exactly does this new evidence undermine the rationality of believing that you have enough fuel and thereby destroy your knowledge?

This is one instance of a more general question about the epistemic function of higher-order evidence. In this context, *higher-order evidence* is defined as evidence about whether your beliefs are appropriately responsive to your evidence.[5] Suppose you know that p on the basis of evidence e, but you subsequently acquire misleading higher-order evidence h that your belief is unresponsive to your evidence. How does this higher-order evidence h destroy your knowledge that p? And why is it now rationally impermissible for you to retain your belief that p on the basis of your first-order evidence e?

This chapter provides a critical overview of several influential proposals in the literature on higher-order evidence. I start by criticizing explanations that appeal to evidential defeat (Section 6.1), epistemic conflicts (Section 6.2), and unreasonable knowledge (Section 6.3). Next, I propose

---

3 Some (e.g., Jackson 2019) reject this principle for high-stakes cases, but this feature of the example is incidental, since the same intuitive reactions are plausible in low-stakes cases too, including Christensen's (2010a, pp. 186–7) cases of peer disagreement and reason-distorting drugs.
4 See Fantl and McGrath (2009, p. 66). Hawthorne and Stanley (2008, p. 578) endorse the biconditional that it's rationally permissible to reason from the premise that p if and only if you know that p, but this is more controversial.
5 I reject the usual definition of higher-order evidence as evidence about what your evidence supports, since I deny that you can have misleading evidence about what your evidence is or what it supports (see Section 6.2).

an alternative explanation that appeals to a combination of improper basing (Section 6.4) and non-ideal rationality (Section 6.5). I conclude by summarizing my reasons for preferring this explanation to the alternatives (Section 6.6).

Evidential Defeat

Richard Feldman (2005) argues that higher-order evidence functions as an *evidential defeater*: it undermines knowledge by defeating evidence. For example, the higher-order evidence that you are hypoxic undermines your knowledge that you have enough fuel by defeating your first-order evidence for this conclusion. You lose your knowledge because your total evidence no longer supports the conclusion that you have enough fuel.

The challenge is to explain why the higher-order evidence that you are hypoxic defeats your first-order evidence that you have enough fuel. After all, your higher-order evidence doesn't provide evidence *against* this conclusion, since hypoxia by itself makes it no more or less probable that you have enough fuel. But then how can it defeat your evidence for this conclusion?

John Pollock (1986) draws an influential distinction between two kinds of defeaters. First, and most obviously, there are *rebutting defeaters*, which reduce the overall degree of evidential support for a conclusion by giving you evidence against the conclusion. Crucially, though, not all defeaters work this way. There are also *undercutting* defeaters, which reduce the overall degree of evidential support for a conclusion without giving you evidence against the conclusion. As Pollock writes, "Such defeaters attack the connection between the reason and the conclusion rather than attacking the conclusion itself" (1986, p. 196).

Consider a textbook example: the fact that the wall looks red is evidence that it is red, although this evidential connection can be undercut by background evidence that the wall is bathed in red light. Of course, this is no evidence *against* the conclusion that the wall is red, since the lighting alone makes it no more or less probable that the wall is red. As I'll explain, however, the background evidence reduces the degree to which your sensory evidence supports the conclusion.

Under normal circumstances, the most probable explanation of why the wall looks red is that it is red. Hence, the evidence that the wall looks red makes it highly probable that the wall is red. Given the background evidence that the wall is bathed in red lighting, however, this is no longer the most probable explanation. In these abnormal lighting conditions, the wall looks red whatever color it is. Hence, the evidence that the wall looks red under red lighting does not make it at all probable that the wall is red. Putting these points together, the probability that the wall is red given that it looks red under red lighting is much lower than the probability that the wall is red given only that it looks red. In this way, the background evidence about the lighting reduces the degree to which your sensory evidence supports the conclusion that the wall is red. This is one way to interpret Pollock's claim that undercutting defeaters "attack the connection" between the evidence and the conclusion, rather than attacking the conclusion itself.

Now let's revisit the hypoxia example: how does the evidence that you are hypoxic defeat your evidence for the conclusion that you have enough fuel? It's not a rebutting defeater, of course, but not all defeaters are rebutting defeaters. Is it perhaps an undercutting defeater that reduces the degree to which your evidence supports the conclusion? I'll argue that it's not, since the evidence that you're hypoxic makes no impact on your degree of evidential support for the conclusion. There is no sense in which this higher-order evidence defeats the evidential support provided by your first-order evidence.

The key point is that the conclusion that you have enough fuel is *entailed* by known premises about the distance of the journey and the amount of fuel in the tank. Entailment is *monotonic*: we cannot undermine an entailment from premises to conclusion by adding new premises. In particular, we cannot undermine the entailment by adding the premise that hypoxia caused you to botch the deduction from premises to conclusion. This expanded set of premises continues to entail the conclusion that you have enough fuel.

Moreover, entailment is the strongest kind of evidential link between premises and conclusion. Arguments come in varying degrees of strength: the stronger an argument, the higher the probability that its conclusion is true given that all its premises are true.[6] A deductively valid argument is the strongest kind of argument, since it is not merely *improbable* but *impossible* that the conclusion is false when the premises are true. This is the limiting case in which the probability of the conclusion given the premises is 1. Since the premises of a deductively valid argument entail its conclusion, the probability of the conclusion can be no less than the probability of the conjunction of the premises. Thus, deductively valid arguments preserve not only *truth* from premises to conclusion, but also *degrees of evidential support*.[7]

Before you acquire the evidence of hypoxia, your premises about the distance of the journey and the amount of fuel in the tank are highly probable given your evidence. Indeed, the probability of the conjunction of these premises is high enough that you can know the conclusion that you have enough fuel by deduction from these premises. Since your

---

6 Here, I'm following Skyrms (1966, ch. 2), who proposes that the strength of an argument is measured by the conditional probability that its conclusion is true given that all its premises are true. This is what he calls "inductive probability."

7 On a probabilistic conception of evidential support, probabilities are used to model degrees of evidential support. In this context, I have in mind an absolute rather than an incremental conception of evidential support.

premises entail the conclusion, the probability of the conclusion can be no less than the probability of the conjunction of the premises.

What changes when you acquire the new evidence that you are hypoxic? You now have evidence that you are cognitively impaired in ways that dispose you to botch the reasoning from your premises to your conclusion. As we've seen, however, this doesn't undermine the entailment from premises to conclusion. Moreover, it doesn't affect the evidential probability of the premises themselves. The strength of your evidence for these premises remains unchanged. After all, hypoxia doesn't impair your eyesight or your ability to read the control panel. Rather, the point of the example is that hypoxia impairs your capacity to acquire new knowledge by deduction. Since the evidence of hypoxia doesn't change the evidential probability of the premises, and it doesn't undermine the entailment, it doesn't change the evidential probability of the conclusion.

I conclude that evidence of hypoxia is no evidential defeater at all, since it does nothing to reduce the evidential probability of your conclusion. All evidential defeaters, whether or not they provide evidence against a conclusion, reduce the degree to which your total evidence supports a conclusion. Given a probabilistic conception of evidential support, we can articulate this constraint as follows:

A Probabilistic Constraint on Evidential Defeat: If d defeats the evidential support that e provides for h, then the probability that h given e and d is less than the probability that h given e alone.[8]

The higher-order evidence that you are hypoxic doesn't satisfy this probabilistic constraint on evidential defeat, since it doesn't reduce the evidential probability that you have enough fuel.

Some epistemologists may respond to this objection by rejecting the probabilistic conception of evidential support on which it depends. In reply, however, the probability calculus is no more than a convenient framework for articulating the intuitive idea that entailment preserves strength of evidential support from premises to conclusion. Of course, someone might reject this claim too, but this comes at the cost of obscuring an important epistemic distinction between deduction and induction. Deductive entailment is the strongest kind of evidential link between premises and conclusion, since it preserves not only truth, but also degrees of evidential support.

I conclude that the higher-order evidence that you are hypoxic doesn't destroy your knowledge that you have enough fuel by defeating your first-order evidence for this conclusion. This is not to deny the intuitive datum that it destroys your knowledge in some other way. Moreover, I have no

---

8 Compare Kotzen's (2019, p. 15) thesis that defeaters are *credence lowering*: "D is a defeater for the evidence that E provides for H just in case $p(H \mid E \wedge D) < p(H \mid E)$."

complaint about the common practice of articulating this datum using the language of "defeat" just so long as we recognize that this is not an explanation of the datum but merely a restatement of the datum to be explained. The challenge that remains is to explain *how* higher-order evidence of hypoxia destroys your knowledge that you have enough fuel. In this section, I've argued that it doesn't destroy your knowledge by reducing your degree of evidential support for the conclusion that you have enough fuel. Some other explanation is needed.

Epistemic Conflicts

David Christensen (2007, 2010a) argues that higher-order evidence destroys knowledge by creating *epistemic conflicts*. On this view, higher-order evidence can be "rationally toxic" in the sense that it forces you to violate one of the following epistemic ideals:

Respecting your first-order evidence.
Respecting your higher-order evidence.
Meta-coherence: that is, coherently integrating your first-order beliefs with your higher-order beliefs.

In the hypoxia case, for example, you cannot respect all your evidence while coherently integrating your first-order and higher-order beliefs. Your first-order evidence supports believing that you have enough fuel, while your higher-order evidence supports believing that this first-order belief is probably based on bad reasoning. And yet this combination of beliefs seems dubiously coherent. As Christensen writes, "the rationality of first-order beliefs cannot in general be divorced from the rationality of certain second-order beliefs that bear on the epistemic status of those first-order beliefs" (2007, p. 18).

Christensen argues that the rationally optimal way of resolving this conflict is to violate the epistemic ideal of respecting your evidence. Rather than believing what your evidence supports—namely, that you have enough fuel—you should instead remain agnostic. Hence, epistemic rationality requires that you "bracket" your first-order evidence in the sense that you refrain from believing what it supports. On this view, your knowledge that you have enough fuel is destroyed when you acquire the evidence that you are hypoxic because it is no longer epistemically rational to believe what your evidence supports.

There is something puzzling about this proposal. How can epistemic rationality require you to refrain from believing what your evidence supports? According to *evidentialism* in epistemology, epistemic rationality is simply a matter of proportioning your beliefs to your evidence.[9]

---

9 See Feldman and Conee (1985) for a classic statement of evidentialism.

On this view, epistemic rationality never requires or even permits you to "bracket" any of your evidence. On the contrary, it imposes a requirement of *total evidence*, according to which you should believe whatever is supported strongly enough by your total evidence.

Christensen's proposal can be understood as a form of *bifurcationism* about epistemic rationality.[10] On this view, the structural requirements of coherence, including meta-coherence, are distinct from and irreducible to the substantive requirement of respecting your evidence. Moreover, these requirements can come into conflict when you have misleading higher-order evidence about your response to your first-order evidence, since your total evidence supports meta-incoherent beliefs. Christensen's proposal is that the rationally optimal way of resolving these conflicting requirements is to maintain meta-coherence in response to your higher-order evidence by disrespecting your first-order evidence.

I argue elsewhere that we should prefer a *unified* conception of epistemic rationality, according to which the structural requirements of coherence are built into the structure of the evidential support relation (Smithies, Forthcoming). For example, we can build in requirements of logical or probabilistic coherence by endorsing a probabilistic conception of the evidential support relation, according to which degrees of evidential support are evidential probabilities. Similarly, we can build in a meta-coherence requirement by endorsing structural constraints on higher-order probabilities, such as the following:

Probabilistic Accessibilism: Necessarily, if the evidential probability that p is n, then it is evidentially certain that the evidential probability that p is n.[11]

On this unified conception of epistemic rationality, there is no distinction to be drawn between the substantive requirement to respect your evidence and the structural requirement to be coherent. There is just one evidentialist requirement that incorporates both substantive and structural dimensions—that is, to proportion your beliefs to your evidence in the sense that your beliefs cohere with substantive facts about your evidence in accordance with structural facts about the evidential support relation. These structural constraints on the evidential support relation guarantee that your evidence never supports an incoherent set of beliefs.

---

10 See Smithies (Forthcoming) for criticisms of bifurcationism, including Christensen's version, and a defense of unificationism.
11 See Smithies (2019, Chs. 7–11) in defense of probabilistic accessibilism. Christensen (2010b) and Elga (2013) reject probabilistic accessibilism in favor of rational reflection principles, but these higher-order constraints are too weak to prohibit forms of epistemic akrasia in which you are certain that your credence is irrational, although you are agnostic about whether it is too high or too low.

Occam's razor prohibits multiplying requirements of epistemic rationality beyond necessity. Why then might someone endorse bifurcationism? The usual answer is that bifurcationism is supported by reflection on examples. In the hypoxia case, for example, your evidence seems to support the following beliefs:

(1) I have enough fuel.
(2) But my belief that I have enough fuel is probably based on bad reasoning, since I am cognitively impaired as a result of hypoxia.
(3) Therefore, my belief that I have enough fuel is probably not supported by good evidence.

And yet this combination of beliefs violates the meta-coherence requirement, since it is always irrational to hold a belief while also believing that it is probably neither based on nor supported by good evidence. Hence, the substantive requirement to respect your evidence seems to conflict in this case with the structural requirement of meta-coherence.

As we've seen, however, we can build the requirement of meta-coherence into the structure of the evidential support relation. Given probabilistic accessibilism, for example, you cannot have misleading higher-order evidence about what your evidence supports, since the facts about what your evidence supports are always made certain by your evidence. On this view, your evidence never supports meta-incoherent beliefs of the form, "p and my evidence probably doesn't support p." Hence, respecting your evidence guarantees meta-coherence.

On this view, you can have misleading higher-order evidence about your *response* to your evidence, although you can never have misleading higher-order evidence about what your evidence *supports*. This is because facts about your response to your evidence, unlike facts about what your evidence supports, are not made certain by your evidence. In general, the argument from (2) to (3) is inductively strong, since beliefs based on bad reasoning are not usually supported by good evidence. In the hypoxia case, however, the inference from (2) to (3) is blocked. When you have misleading higher-order evidence about your response to your evidence, your total evidence supports believing (1) and (2) but not (3).

Moreover, believing (1) and (2) is not incoherent in the same way as believing (1) and (3). It's always irrational to believe that p while believing that your evidence doesn't support p. This combination of beliefs is self-defeating: by your own lights, you should abandon your belief that p, since you think it is unsupported by your evidence. In contrast, it's not always irrational to believe that p while believing that your belief is not properly based on supporting evidence. Indeed, this can be a perfectly rational response to misleading evidence that you believe the right thing for the wrong reasons. It is not self-defeating in such cases to conclude that your belief is supported by good evidence, although it is not properly based on good evidence.

To illustrate the point, consider an analogy from the practical domain. Suppose a wealthy philanthropist receives public acclaim for donating large sums of money to charity. He knows he is doing the right thing, but he suspects he is doing it for the wrong reasons, since he has evidence that his motivation is selfish. In fact, however, this evidence is misleading, and his action is motivated by altruistic moral reasons. This is not an example of akratic action. There need be no incoherence in doubting your own motivation for action. The philanthropist can coherently think to himself, "Perhaps I'm doing this for the wrong reasons, but there's not much I can do about that, and it's still the right thing to do."

The same point applies in the epistemic domain. Suppose a loving mother is convinced that her son is innocent of a crime for which he has been charged. She knows her belief is supported by good evidence, but she suspects her belief is based on bad reasons, since she has evidence that she is motivated by wishful thinking. In fact, however, this evidence is misleading, and her belief is rationally responsive to good evidence. This is not an example of akratic belief. There need be no incoherence in maintaining your beliefs while doubting their motivation so long as you know they are supported by good evidence. The mother can coherently think to herself, "Perhaps I believe this for the wrong reasons, but there's not much I can do about that, and it's still the right thing to believe."

Admittedly, there is something unusual about an evidential situation that supports the following line of argument:

(a) It's certain that my evidence supports believing that I have enough fuel.
(b) But my belief that I have enough fuel is probably based on bad reasoning.
(c) So, I probably got lucky because bad reasoning led me to form a belief that is supported by the evidence.[12]

In the absence of strong evidence, it's irrational to believe in a lucky coincidence. After all, the prior probability of a coincidence is very low. Even so, coincidences do sometimes happen. And we sometimes have strong evidence that they happen. Given strong enough evidence, the posterior probability of a coincidence may be extremely high. There is nothing in principle to rule out the possibility that your evidence supports the conclusion that you got lucky by believing the right thing for the wrong reasons. As we've seen, these cases do happen. In my view, the hypoxia example is another case in point.

---

12 Horowitz (2014, pp. 9–10) makes a related point, although her objection targets views on which your total evidence supports believing, "I probably got lucky because my true belief is based on misleading evidence."

Does this mean dogmatism is a rational response to misleading higher-order evidence? I don't think so. Consider our steadfast pilot who maintains his belief that he has enough fuel in the face of the evidence that he is hypoxic. Suppose he concludes that he must have got lucky, since his belief is supported by evidence although it is based on bad reasoning. Intuitively, this merely compounds his irrationality. It was already irrational for him to retain his first-order belief that he has enough fuel, and this problem is exacerbated when he doubles down by retaining the higher-order belief that his evidence supports this conclusion. Our steadfast pilot maintains meta-coherence at the cost of adding irrationally dogmatic higher-order beliefs to his irrationally dogmatic first-order beliefs.

This just goes to show that our original problem arises at multiple levels. At level one, the problem is to explain why the pilot cannot rationally believe that he has enough fuel when his evidence supports this conclusion. At level two, the problem is to explain why the pilot cannot rationally believe that his evidence supports this conclusion when his evidence also supports this higher-order conclusion. And so, the problem iterates as we ascend the hierarchy.

I'll propose my own solution to this problem in due course. My goal in this section is merely to argue that we cannot solve it by arguing that the pilot's evidence supports incoherent beliefs. There are general theoretical reasons to doubt that your evidence can ever support incoherent beliefs and more specific reasons to doubt that the pilot's evidence supports meta-incoherent beliefs. We must look elsewhere to explain why it is irrational for the steadfast pilot to retain beliefs that are nevertheless supported by his evidence.

Unreasonable Knowledge

Maria Lasonen-Aarnio (2010, forthcoming) argues that the steadfast pilot has *unreasonable knowledge*.[13] On this view, the pilot retains his knowledge that he has enough fuel when he acquires the misleading higher-order evidence that he is hypoxic. The only problem is that his belief is unreasonable because it manifests a more general disposition to be unresponsive to evidence in other cases. And yet this needn't undermine his knowledge so long as he responds appropriately to the evidence he actually has. Thus, reasonable belief is not necessary for knowledge.

What is it for a belief to be reasonable? Lasonen-Aarnio writes:

> Reasonableness is at least largely a matter of managing one's beliefs through the adoption of policies that are generally knowledge

---

13 Lasonen-Aarnio (2010) focuses on standard cases of undercutting defeat, but she extends her proposal to higher-order evidence in Lasonen-Aarnio (Forthcoming).

conducive, thereby manifesting dispositions to know and avoid false belief across a wide range of normal cases.

(2010, p. 2)

The steadfast pilot is unreasonable because he fails to manifest dispositions that are generally conducive to knowledge—that is, dispositions to know and avoid false belief across a wide range of normal cases. In particular, he is disposed to ignore higher-order evidence that his beliefs are based on bad reasoning not only in the "good case" in which his higher-order evidence is misleading but in the "bad case" in which it is accurate. Since he is actually in a good case, his belief is not only true, but also supported by his evidence. Nevertheless, it is held dogmatically in a way that disposes him to retain beliefs in bad cases that are both false and unsupported by evidence.

In short, the steadfast pilot is unreasonable because he manifests a general disposition that leads him astray in other cases. And yet this leaves his knowledge intact so long as the disposition doesn't lead him astray in this case. He retains his knowledge because his true belief remains as safe from error, and as responsive to his first-order evidence, as it was before he acquired the higher-order evidence. Since he had knowledge beforehand, he retains his knowledge in the face of his new higher-order evidence, despite the fact that his belief is now unreasonable.

It's worth noting that the same proposal applies at multiple levels. Presumably, the steadfast pilot can retain not only his first-order knowledge that he has enough fuel, but also his higher-order knowledge that his evidence supports this conclusion. Moreover, given the misleading evidence that he is hypoxic, he can rationally conclude from these known premises that he probably got lucky, since his cognitive impairment didn't lead him astray on this occasion. The problem with these first-order and higher-order beliefs is that they are unreasonable because they manifest more general dispositions to go awry in bad cases in which his higher-order evidence is accurate. But this has no tendency to undermine either the pilot's first-order knowledge or his higher-order knowledge.

I'll now raise three objections to this proposal. First, it fails to vindicate all our intuitions about the hypoxia case. It vindicates the intuition that the steadfast pilot is unreasonable, but not the intuition that he loses knowledge. It is counterintuitive to suppose that the steadfast pilot retains both his first-order knowledge that he has enough fuel and his higher-order knowledge that his evidence supports this conclusion. And it is even more counterintuitive that he can use this knowledge, together with the misleading evidence that he is hypoxic, to rationally conclude that he probably got lucky on this occasion.

Lasonen-Aarnio explains away conflicting intuitions by appealing to the error theory that we tend to conflate reasonableness and knowledge. I agree that our intuitions in this case, and many others, are guided by the implicit assumption that only reasonable beliefs can be knowledge. This explains why we find it so natural to infer from the premise that someone's belief is unreasonable to the conclusion that they lack knowledge. Given the intuitive plausibility of this assumption, however, why think it is mistaken? To my mind, the error theory should be regarded as a last resort: all else being equal, we should prefer an epistemological theory that vindicates our intuitive reactions.

Second, there are general theoretical grounds for doubting that you can acquire knowledge by manifesting unreasonable dispositions. To have knowledge, it's not enough that your belief is true: it must be *reliable* in the sense that it manifests a more general disposition to have true beliefs. Similarly, to be justified or rational, it's not enough that your belief is supported by good evidence; it must be *properly based* on good evidence in the sense that it manifests a more general disposition to have beliefs that are supported by good evidence. Hence, knowledge requires manifesting good dispositions that are reliably responsive to evidence and truth. When your beliefs manifest unreasonable dispositions, however, they are not reliable enough to constitute knowledge. Presumably, this is why it remains so plausible that only reasonable beliefs can be knowledge. This is not just a brute intuition with no theoretical support. It is supported by the theoretical consideration that knowledge must be reliably responsive to evidence and truth.

Lasonen-Aarnio expresses some sympathy for the simple externalist view that knowledge is true belief that is *safe from error* in the sense that it couldn't easily have been false. And yet the case of mathematical knowledge suggests that this simple view needs refinement. I cannot know that Fermat's Last Theorem is true just by wishful thinking, but there is no danger that my belief is false, since its content is necessarily true. Arguably, this is because my safe belief has an unsafe basis: it is based on exercising an unreliable disposition that could easily yield false beliefs in other propositions. As Sosa (2003, pp. 137–40) puts the point, a belief is knowledge only if it is not only safe from error but also *virtuous* in the sense that it manifests a more generally reliable disposition to form safe beliefs.[14]

Third, there are theoretical costs involved in rejecting the principle that only reasonable beliefs can be knowledge. Knowledge is valuable. If we allow that knowledge can be unreasonable, however, then we risk devaluing knowledge. For example, knowledge is often thought to set normative standards for belief and action: if you know that p, then it is rationally permissible to believe that p, and to act on the premise that p, and so you cannot legitimately be blamed for doing so. And yet the steadfast pilot is blameworthy for acting on the premise that he has

---

14 Elsewhere, I extend this point from knowledge to justified belief by considering the problem of the speckled hen (Smithies 2019, pp. 349–60).

enough fuel: his loved ones can be justly angry that he acted so recklessly. As Lasonen-Aarnio acknowledges: "Subjects who retain knowledge in defeat cases are genuinely criticisable" (2010, p. 15).

We cannot explain the pilot's culpability, while also maintaining that he retains knowledge, without abandoning a plausible theoretical connection between knowledge and blameworthiness. It is plausible that you can be blameless for your beliefs despite lacking knowledge, but it is not so plausible that you can be blameworthy for your beliefs despite having knowledge. This devalues knowledge in ways that should be unattractive to anyone and perhaps especially to proponents of knowledge-first epistemology.

To conclude, we need to explain how higher-order evidence can not only make your beliefs unreasonable but can also destroy your knowledge. Although Lasonen-Aarnio's proposal fails to explain this datum, it nevertheless contains an important insight about the importance of dispositions in epistemic evaluation.[15] This point figures prominently in the discussion to follow, since I argue that we need to invoke facts about the reliability of your doxastic dispositions in order to explain how higher-order evidence destroys knowledge.

The Proper Basing Relation

My own explanation of how higher-order evidence destroys first-order knowledge appeals to *the proper basing relation*.[16] On this view, the higher-order evidence that you are hypoxic doesn't defeat your first-order evidence that you have enough fuel, but merely prevents you from properly basing your beliefs on this evidence. This explains why you lose your knowledge that you have enough fuel when you acquire the higher-order evidence that you are hypoxic. A belief is justified only if it is properly based on good evidence and only justified beliefs can be knowledge.

We can articulate the point in terms of the familiar distinction between propositional and doxastic justification.[17] A belief is *propositionally justified* when its propositional content is supported by good evidence, whereas a belief is *doxastically justified* when the belief is held in a way that is properly based on good evidence. Hence, *proper basing* is the relation between a belief and a body of evidence that converts propositional justification into doxastic justification.

---

15 See Lasonen-Aarnio (Forthcoming) for her current views on dispositional evaluations.
16 Compare Smithies (2015, 2019, Ch. 10). Similar views are defended by van Wietmarschen (2013) and Silva (2017), but I give a different explanation of how higher-order evidence undermines proper basing.
17 This distinction is usually traced back to Firth (1978), although it is now ubiquitous in the literature on epistemic justification.

The higher-order evidence that you are hypoxic doesn't undermine your propositional justification to believe that you have enough fuel by defeating your evidence for this conclusion. Rather, it undermines your doxastic justification by preventing you from properly basing your belief on this evidence. Elsewhere, I put this by saying that this higher-order evidence is a *doxastic defeater*, rather than a *propositional defeater* (Smithies 2015, p. 2786).

When is a belief properly based on supporting evidence? It's not enough that my belief is based on evidence that happens to support the belief. My belief must manifest a more general disposition that is reliably sensitive to differences in what my evidence supports. If I'm disposed to retain my belief even if my evidence changes in ways that no longer support the belief, then it is not properly based on the evidence. My belief is properly based on the evidence only if it manifests a more general disposition to believe what the evidence supports.[18]

Dogmatic beliefs violate this condition. Consider my belief that drinking red wine in moderation is good for my health. Let's assume that while the evidence for this claim is somewhat mixed, the evidence in its favor outweighs the evidence against, and that the supporting evidence is strong enough to justify belief. Although I'm aware of all this evidence, the problem is that I hold my belief dogmatically in a way that makes me insensitive to changes in what my evidence supports. I am not disposed to respond to changes in what my evidence supports with corresponding changes in what I believe. I will remain unmoved, for example, if I discover new studies casting doubt on the health benefits of drinking red wine. Moreover, this is something that could easily happen. Intuitively, I don't know that drinking wine is good for me, even if my belief is true and based on good evidence. This is because my belief is not *properly based* on my evidence, since it manifests a disposition that is not sensitive enough to changes in what my evidence supports.

I propose that the same is true of the steadfast pilot. He doesn't know that he has enough fuel, despite the fact that his belief is true and based on good evidence, because it is not *properly based* on his evidence. The problem is that his belief is held dogmatically, which means it is not sufficiently sensitive to changes in what his evidence supports. We can see this by comparing the "good case" in which his higher-order evidence is misleading with the "bad case" in which it is accurate because he really has made a mistake in reasoning.

---

18 In other work, I use the problem of the speckled hen to motivate this constraint on proper basing (Smithies 2015, 2019, Ch. 11). More specifically, I propose that a belief is properly based on supporting evidence only if it manifests a more general disposition to form beliefs that are safe from the absence of evidential support. On this view, doxastic justification requires safety from the absence of propositional justification just as knowledge requires safety from error.

We can set aside modally remote cases in which the steadfast pilot is actually suffering from hypoxia, since this dramatically changes his capacity for reasoning. Instead, let's consider more quotidian cases in which his reasoning capacities are held constant. Since his capacity for reasoning is fallible, there are bad cases in which he makes routine errors in calculation through a defective exercise of the very same capacities he employs in the good case. Let's consider a bad case in which he makes a routine error, and his co-pilot points out the mistake. Again, this is something that could easily happen. If he is disposed to remain steadfast in the face of evidence that he is hypoxic, then he will be equally disposed to ignore his co-pilot and stick to his guns. Moreover, both cases manifest the same disposition to dogmatically retain beliefs in spite of higher-order evidence that those beliefs are based on bad reasoning.

As we saw in Section 6.3, Lasonen-Aarnio makes similar points in arguing that the steadfast pilot is unreasonable despite retaining his knowledge that he has enough fuel. In contrast, my goal here is to argue that his belief is doxastically unjustified, and so fails to be knowledge, since it is not properly based on supporting evidence. In the good case, his belief is true and supported by evidence, whereas in the bad case, it is false and unsupported by evidence. So, even in the good case, the steadfast pilot lacks knowledge, since his belief manifests a disposition that is insufficiently sensitive to changes in what his evidence supports. After all, there are close cases in which exercising the same disposition leads him to hold false beliefs in the absence of evidential support.[19]

We can apply the same reasoning one level up to explain why the steadfast pilot lacks *higher-order* knowledge about his own epistemic situation. Suppose he believes not just that he has enough fuel but also that his evidence supports this conclusion. Although this higher-order belief is true and entailed by his evidence, it is not properly based on this evidence. After all, the steadfast pilot is disposed to believe exactly the same thing in the bad case in which his higher-order belief is false and unsupported by his evidence. So, even in the good case, he doesn't know that his evidence supports his conclusion, since his belief manifests a disposition that is not sufficiently sensitive to changes in what his evidence supports.

To be clear, I am not saying that that the steadfast pilot *loses* his knowledge when he acquires the higher-order evidence that he is hypoxic. As Lasonen-Aarnio (2010, pp. 3–8) explains, this claim is hard to sustain. How exactly is his knowledge destroyed when he acquires this higher-order evidence? There is no relevant change in what his evidence supports, since his new evidence continues to support the conclusion that he has

---

19 To undermine knowledge, there has to be a close enough case in which the agent ignores accurate higher-order evidence that she has made a mistake, but I doubt we can specify in non-epistemic terms what counts as a close enough case.

enough fuel. Moreover, there is no relevant change in his response to his evidence, since he is steadfast enough that acquiring this new higher-order evidence makes no difference to the basis on which his belief is held. So how can this new higher-order evidence destroy his knowledge?

My response is that the steadfast pilot doesn't *lose* his knowledge, since he never had knowledge to begin with. You cannot acquire knowledge by manifesting dogmatic dispositions that are insensitive to changes in what your evidence supports. In contrast, the *conciliatory pilot* loses knowledge when he acquires the new higher-order evidence that he is hypoxic because he responds by abandoning his belief that he has enough fuel. There is no knowledge without belief.

The key point is that knowledge sometimes requires being disposed to abandon belief in response to new evidence. The steadfast pilot doesn't have knowledge because he is disposed to retain his belief in the face of higher-order evidence whether it is misleading or accurate. In contrast, the conciliatory pilot has knowledge only because he is disposed to respond to such higher-order evidence by abandoning his belief. The conciliatory pilot is more reliable than the steadfast pilot in responding to evidence because he is not disposed in bad cases to ignore accurate higher-order evidence that he has made a mistake.

I don't claim that it's impossible in principle for anyone to retain knowledge in the hypoxia case, but only that it's impossible in practice for creatures like us. I see no reason to rule out the metaphysical possibility of ideally rational agents who have misleading evidence that they are suffering from hypoxia. Because ideally rational agents are perfectly sensitive to what their evidence supports, they can remain steadfast in good cases without thereby manifesting any disposition to remain steadfast in bad cases where their reasoning dispositions are held constant. And yet this is beyond our limited human capacities, since we are only imperfectly sensitive to our evidence. Any human who remains steadfast in the good case thereby manifests some disposition to remain steadfast in the bad case too.

We can now draw a more general conclusion about the relationship between propositional and doxastic justification. There are cases where your evidence gives you propositional justification to believe a conclusion, although you are unable to form a doxastically justified belief that is properly based on your evidence. We should therefore reject the doxastic constraint on propositional justification stated below:

The Doxastic Constraint: Necessarily, you have propositional justification to believe that p only if you have the psychological capacity to believe that p in a way that is doxastically justified.[20]

---

20 Proponents include Goldman (1979) and Turri (2010).

There are independent reasons to reject the doxastic constraint. Suppose you ingest a reason-distorting drug that temporarily impairs your ability to form beliefs and other doxastic attitudes that are properly based on your evidence. Whatever doxastic attitudes you adopt, they are guaranteed to be doxastically unjustified. It is implausible that ingesting this drug undermines your propositional justification to adopt any doxastic attitude at all. There is always some doxastic attitude that you have propositional justification to hold toward any given proposition. If your evidence is not strong enough to justify either belief or disbelief, then by default you have justification to remain agnostic. Even so, there is no guarantee that you can always form a doxastic attitude that is properly based on what your evidence supports. After all, you might have ingested a reason-distorting drug.

The natural thing to say about the reason-distorting drug is that it impairs your epistemic rationality. It prevents you from properly basing your beliefs on your evidence and thereby converting propositional justification into doxastic justification. If there are doxastic constraints on propositional justification, however, then we cannot say this. We must say instead that ingesting the drug somehow changes what you have propositional justification to believe. But this is hard to square with the evidentialist thesis that you have propositional justification to believe whatever is sufficiently supported by your evidence, since ingesting the drug doesn't change what your evidence supports. It is more plausible that ingesting the drug compromises your epistemic rationality by disabling you from responding appropriately to your evidence and thereby converting propositional justification into doxastic justification.

On a plausible version of evidentialism, there are no doxastic constraints on propositional justification. What your evidence supports is one question, but it's another question whether you can form beliefs that are supported by and properly based on your evidence. One theoretical cost of conflating these questions is to obscure the epistemic function of higher-order evidence.

Ideal and Non-Ideal Rationality

Any plausible account of the epistemic function of higher-order evidence must explain two intuitive data points about the hypoxia example:

(1) *The Negative Datum*: You cannot know or rationally believe that you have enough fuel given higher-order evidence that you're hypoxic.
(2) *The Positive Datum*: You are rationally required to withhold belief that you have enough fuel given higher-order evidence that you're hypoxic.

The negative datum was explained in Section 6.4, but this is not yet to explain the positive datum. After all, a reason-distorting drug might prevent you from rationally believing what your evidence supports without thereby imposing any rational requirement to refrain from believing what your evidence supports. Indeed, there is something rather puzzling in the very idea of such a requirement. According to evidentialism, epistemic rationality is simply a matter of proportioning your beliefs to your evidence. So how can epistemic rationality ever require you to refrain from believing what your evidence supports?

To answer this question, we need a distinction between *ideal* and *non-ideal* standards of epistemic rationality.[21] By ideal standards, epistemic rationality always requires respecting your evidence. This ideal sometimes outstrips our limited human capacities: we are not always capable of responding rationally to our evidence. Moreover, we know this; or we should know this, since we all have compelling evidence of our own cognitive limitations. By non-ideal standards, in contrast, epistemic rationality sometimes permits (indeed, requires) responding to such higher-order evidence by adopting policies that diverge from the ideal. In particular, we are sometimes required by non-ideal standards to "bracket" our first-order evidence when we have higher-order evidence that we cannot reliably follow our first-order evidence where it leads.

This is what happens in the hypoxia example. When you acquire the higher-order evidence that you cannot respond rationally to your first-order evidence, you are required to "bracket" this evidence and refrain from believing what it supports—namely, that you have enough fuel. Given evidence of cognitive impairment, the sensible strategy is to become agnostic, rather than trying to believe what your evidence supports. On this view, the epistemic function of higher-order evidence is not to defeat your first-order evidence and thereby to change which conclusions are supported by your total evidence. Rather, it determines which response to your total evidence is required by non-ideal standards of epistemic rationality.

This is an instance of a more general point. It doesn't always make sense to try to achieve what you know would be best if only you were to succeed. This is because you sometimes know—or have good evidence—that your attempt to achieve the optimal outcome may fail. In such cases, trying to do the best thing sometimes risks a worse outcome than would be achieved by settling for second best. Hence, what is best by ideal standards is not always what is best by non-ideal standards that take into account your evidence about your own limitations.

We can articulate this general point more precisely within the framework of *rule consequentialism*, which evaluates rules by their expected consequences.[22] We can evaluate rules in a way that is sensitive to the

---

21 Compare Smithies (2015, 2019, Ch. 10).
22 Here, I follow Lasonen-Aarnio (2010, pp. 14–15) and Schoenfield (2015, pp. 650–3), who both use rule consequentialism to draw normative distinctions, but see below for some important strategic differences.

distinction between *following* a rule and merely *trying* to follow a rule. Following a rule is a kind of achievement: merely trying to the follow the rule doesn't guarantee that you will succeed. When you have evidence that you may fail in your attempt to follow a rule, the expected consequences of trying to follow the rule can diverge from the expected consequences of successfully following the rule. In such cases, the best rule to follow is not always the best rule to try to follow.

Consider the case of Professor Procrastinate (Jackson and Pargetter, 1986). When he is invited to review a book, he has three options available to him, which are listed below in rank order from best to worst:

R1. Accept the invitation and complete the review on time.
R2. Decline the invitation.
R3. Accept the invitation and fail to complete the review on time.

Which option should he take? There is no single answer to this question, since deontic modals in ordinary language are notoriously context-sensitive. Intuitively, there is a sense in which he should accept the invitation and complete the review on time, since he knows this is the best possible outcome. But there is also a sense in which he should decline the invitation, since he knows (or perhaps has misleading evidence) that he is unlikely to complete the review on time: if he tries to achieve the best outcome, then he is more likely to bring about the worst outcome. Instead of trying to do what is best, it makes more sense to settle for second best. By ideal standards, he should accept the invitation and complete the review on time, whereas by non-ideal standards, he should decline.

We can capture this distinction in the framework of rule consequentialism. R1 is the best rule to *follow*, but it is not the best rule to *try* to follow. After all, the expected consequence of trying to follow R1 is that he will end up following R3 instead. The expected consequence of trying to follow R2, in contrast, is that he will succeed. And there is greater expected value in following R2 than following R3. Hence, the expected value of trying to follow R2 is greater than R1, although the expected value of successfully following R1 is greater than R2. This is why ideal standards require following R1, although non-ideal standards require following R2.

We can extend the same framework to *epistemic rules*: that is, rules for forming and revising beliefs. In epistemic evaluation, we're concerned solely with the *epistemic value* of the expected consequences of following (or trying to follow) a rule. And when we evaluate rules for *epistemic rationality*, we're concerned with a specific dimension of epistemic value: namely, how well you succeed in proportioning your beliefs to your evidence. Finally, we're concerned only with the *direct* consequences that are expected to result from following (or trying a follow) an epistemic rule. As Sophie Horowitz (2019, p. 116) observes, it's not epistemically rational for an agent with severe arachnophobia to follow the rule, "Never believe there is a spider nearby," just because this indirect strategy helps him to remain calm and follow other epistemically rational rules.

By ideal standards, epistemic rationality requires following the evidentialist rule: "Always proportion your beliefs to your evidence!" Assuming evidentialism, this is the best rule to follow, since the expected outcome of following the rule is perfect epistemic rationality. Since we are not perfectly rational agents, however, we are not always capable of following the evidentialist rule. Moreover, this is not always the best rule to try to follow when we have evidence that we are likely to fail. There is sometimes greater expected epistemic value in trying to follow an alternative rule when you have evidence that adopting this strategy increases your responsiveness to evidence. In such cases, trying to follow the evidentialist rule is a kind of epistemic self-sabotage: it's a counterproductive strategy for maximizing your responsiveness to evidence. This is why non-ideal standards of epistemic rationality sometimes prohibit believing what your evidence supports.

Now let's apply this distinction to the hypoxia example. When you receive the higher-order evidence that you are hypoxic, you have three options:

Steadfastness: Maintain your first-order belief that you have enough fuel and your higher-order belief that your evidence supports this conclusion.

Level Splitting: Maintain your first-order belief that you have enough fuel, while abandoning your higher-order belief that your evidence supports this conclusion.

Conciliation: Abandon your first-order belief that you have enough fuel and your higher-order belief that your evidence supports this conclusion.

Which option should you take? Once again, there is no single answer to this question. By ideal standards, you should opt for Steadfastness, since this is the best rule to follow: the expected consequence of successfully following this rule is that your beliefs are perfectly proportioned to your evidence. By non-ideal standards, however, you should opt for Conciliation, since this is the best rule to try to follow. As I'll explain, trying to follow Conciliation has greater expected epistemic value in the hypoxia case than either Steadfastness or Level Splitting.

It's clear enough that the *expected pragmatic value* of trying to follow Conciliation in the hypoxia case is greater than the alternatives. After all, the expected outcome of trying to follow either Steadfastness or Level Splitting is that you run the risk of an early demise, which is not worth taking for a scenic detour. But why think there is any discrepancy in *expected epistemic value*?

Miriam Schoenfield (2015, p. 652) and Maria Lasonen-Aarnio (Forthcoming, §5) argue that trying to follow Conciliation has greater expected epistemic value than the alternatives because they run the risk of false belief in bad cases where your higher-order evidence is accurate. But this strategy faces a problem. Why isn't the risk of false belief in bad cases neutralized by the chance of knowledge or true belief in good cases where your higher-order evidence is accurate? And why is this neutral outcome any worse than a consistent policy of agnosticism? Of course, we might assume that the value of knowledge or true belief in good cases is outweighed by the disvalue of false belief in bad cases, but I see no compelling basis for this assumption. My own strategy is different: it appeals to the disvalue of unjustified belief in good cases, rather than false belief in bad cases.[23]

The expected consequence of trying to follow Steadfastness in the hypoxia case is that you are like the *steadfast pilot*. As we saw in §4, the steadfast pilot cannot know or rationally believe that he has enough fuel. This is because his belief is held dogmatically in a way that is insensitive to changes in what his evidence supports. He is disposed to maintain his belief when he acquires the higher-order evidence that it is based on bad reasoning. And he is disposed to maintain his belief not only in the good case in which his higher-order evidence is misleading, but also in the bad case in which his higher-order evidence is accurate. Dogmatic beliefs of this kind are not rational enough to constitute knowledge.

In contrast, the expected consequence of trying to follow Conciliation is that you are like the *conciliatory pilot*. The conciliatory pilot rationally believes and knows that he has enough fuel so long as he is disposed to become agnostic when he acquires the higher-order evidence that he is hypoxic. Hence, there is greater expected epistemic value in trying to follow Conciliation than Steadfastness: this strategy increases your expected degree of epistemic rationality by making your beliefs more sensitive to changes in what your evidence supports.

What about Level Splitting? The expected consequence of trying to follow this rule is that your first-order belief is like the steadfast pilot's, while your higher-order belief is like the conciliatory pilot's. Like the conciliatory pilot, you have higher-order knowledge that your evidence supports the conclusion that you have enough fuel so long as you are disposed to become agnostic when you acquire the evidence that you are hypoxic. Like the steadfast pilot, however, you lack the first-order knowledge that you have enough fuel, since your first-order belief is held dogmatically in a way that is insensitive to changes in your evidence.

---

23 Lasonen-Aarnio (2010, forthcoming) disagrees, of course, since she maintains that the steadfast pilot has knowledge in the good case. Schoenfield's (2015) strategy is different too, since she evaluates epistemic rules in terms of expected accuracy, rather than expected epistemic rationality.

As we have seen, trying to follow Conciliation has greater expected value than the alternatives because it yields knowledge and justified belief in the good case so long as you are disposed to become agnostic when you acquire the evidence of hypoxia. This is why you are required by non-ideal standards of epistemic rationality to become agnostic in response to this higher-order evidence, rather than believing what your evidence supports. Thus, we can explain the positive datum as well as the negative datum.

In summary, the epistemic function of higher-order evidence is twofold. First, it prevents you from responding properly to your evidence in the way that is required by ideal standards of epistemic rationality. And second, it affects which response to your evidence is required by non-ideal standards of epistemic rationality that are sensitive to evidence about your cognitive limitations.

Conclusion

Why prefer my account of the epistemic function of higher-order evidence to the more familiar alternatives discussed in Sections 6.1–6.3?

First, my view explains the intuitive datum that you lose knowledge when you acquire the higher-order evidence that you are hypoxic. In this respect, it is preferable to the *unreasonable knowledge* view. The grain of truth in this view is that the steadfast pilot manifests bad dispositions when he retains his belief in the face of misleading higher-order evidence. But the problem is that manifesting these bad dispositions is incompatible with knowledge. The steadfast pilot doesn't have knowledge because his dispositions are not sufficiently sensitive to changes in what his evidence supports. It's possible in principle for ideally rational agents to retain knowledge in the face of misleading higher-order evidence, but it's impossible in practice for non-ideal agents like us.

Second, my view explains this intuitive datum without distorting the structure of the evidential support relation in ways that compromise the objective constraints imposed by logic and probability theory. In this respect, it is preferable to the *evidential defeat* view. The grain of truth in this view is that your knowledge is destroyed when you acquire the higher-order evidence that you are hypoxic. The problem is that this is not plausibly explained by a change in what your evidence supports. My view explains how you can lose your knowledge of a conclusion without losing your evidential support for that conclusion. Misleading higher-order evidence can prevent you from properly basing your beliefs on what your total evidence supports.

Third, my view explains this intuitive datum without any bifurcation between substantive and structural requirements of epistemic rationality. In this respect, it is preferable to the *epistemic conflict* view. The grain of truth in this view is that epistemic rationality somehow requires "bracketing" your first-order evidence when you have misleading higher-order evidence. The problem is that this is not because your total evidence supports incoherent beliefs. On the contrary, it is because misleading higher-order evidence prevents non-ideal agents from properly basing their beliefs on their evidence. As a result, they are required by non-ideal standards of epistemic rationality to manage their cognitive limitations by adopting policies that deviate from the epistemic ideal of respecting the evidence. The "rationally toxic" nature of higher-order evidence is best explained in terms of a distinction between ideal and non-ideal requirements of epistemic rationality, rather than a distinction between substantive and structural requirements of epistemic rationality.

In conclusion, my proposal accommodates the intuitive data about the epistemic function of higher-order evidence with minimal theoretical mutilation. We can explain why you should conciliate in response to misleading higher-order evidence without abandoning evidentialism or compromising the objective logical and probabilistic constraints on the evidential support relation. The key point is that we are not always capable of rationally believing what our evidence supports. Moreover, we sometimes know or have misleading evidence that we are in this unfortunate predicament. In such cases, we should adopt strategies for managing our epistemic limitations that deviate from the epistemic ideal of believing what our evidence supports. This is one instance of the more general point that you shouldn't always try to do what is best when your efforts are likely to backfire. Sometimes, you should settle for second best.

References

Christensen, D. (2007). Does Murphy's Law apply in epistemology? Self-doubt and rational ideals. *Oxford Studies in Epistemology*, 2, 3–31.

Christensen, D. (2010a). Higher-order evidence. *Philosophy and Phenomenological Research*, 81(1), 185–215.

Christensen, D. (2010b). Rational reflection. *Philosophical Perspectives*, 24, 121–140.

Elga, A. (2008). Lucky to be rational. *Bellingham Summer Philosophy Conference*, unpublished manuscript.

Elga, A. (2013). The puzzle of the unmarked clock and the new rational reflection principle. *Philosophical Studies*, 164(1), 127–139.

Fantl, Jeremy & McGrath, Matthew (2009). *Knowledge in an Uncertain World*. New York: OUP.

Feldman, R. (2005). Respecting the evidence. *Philosophical Perspectives*, 19, 95–119.

Feldman, R., & Conee, E. (1985). Evidentialism. *Philosophical Studies*, 48(1), 15–34.

Firth, R. (1978). Are epistemic concepts reducible to ethical concepts? In A. Goldman & J. Kim (Eds)., *Values and Morals* (pp. 215–229). Dordrecht: Kluwer.

Goldman, A. (1979). What is justified belief? In G. Pappas (Ed.), *Justification and Knowledge* (pp. 1–25). Dordrecht: Reidel.

Hawthorne, J., & Stanley, J. (2008). Knowledge and action. *Journal of Philosophy*, 105(10), 571–590.

Horowitz, S. (2014). Epistemic akrasia. *Noûs*, 48(4), 718–744.

Horowitz, S. (2019). Predictably misleading evidence. In M. Skipper (Ed.), *Higher-Order Evidence: New Essays* (pp. 105–123). New York, NY: Oxford University Press.

Jackson, F., and Pargetter, R. (1986). Oughts, options, and actualism. *Philosophical Review*, 95(2), 233–255.

Jackson, L. (2019). How belief-credence dualism explains away pragmatic encroachment. *Philosophical Quarterly*, 69, 511–533.

Kotzen, M. (2019). A formal account of evidential defeat. In B. Fitelsen, R. Borges, & C. Braden (Eds.), *Themes from Klein: Knowledge, Justification, and Skepticism* (pp. 213–234). Cham: Synthese Library.

Lasonen-Aarnio, M. (2010). Unreasonable knowledge. *Philosophical Perspectives*, 24, 1–21.

Lasonen-Aarnio, M. (Forthcoming). Dispositional evaluations and defeat. In J. Brown & M. Simion (Eds.), *Reasons, Justification, and Defeat*. New York, NY: Oxford University Press.

Pollock, J. (1986). *Contemporary Theories of Knowledge*. London: Hutchinson.

Schoenfield, M. (2015). Bridging rationality and accuracy. *Journal of Philosophy*, 112 (12), 633–657.

Silva, P. (2017). How doxastic justification helps us solve the puzzle of misleading higher-order evidence. *Pacific Philosophical Quarterly* 98: 308–328.

Skyrms, B. (1966). *Choice and Chance: An Introduction to Inductive Logic*. Belmont, CA: Dickenson.

Smithies, D. (2015). Ideal rationality and logical omniscience. *Synthese*, 192(9), 2769–2793.

Smithies, D. (2019). *The Epistemic Role of Consciousness*. New York, NY: Oxford University Press.

Smithies, D. (Forthcoming). The unity of evidence and coherence. In N. Hughes (Ed.), *Epistemic Dilemmas*, New York, NY: Oxford University Press.

Sosa, E. (2003). Beyond internal foundations to external virtues. In L. BonJour & E. Sosa (Eds.), *Epistemic Justification: Internalism vs. Externalism, Foundations vs. Virtues*. Oxford: Blackwell.

Turri, J. (2010). On the relationship between propositional and doxastic justification. *Philosophy and Phenomenological Research*, 80(2), 312–326.

van Wietmarschen, H. (2013). Peer disagreement, evidence, and well-foundedness. *Philosophical Review*, 122(3), 395–425.

7 Doxastic Justification and Creditworthiness

Anne Meylan

Philosophers traditionally distinguish between having justification for believing a certain proposition and believing this proposition with justification (Silva and Oliveira, forthcoming). They call the former *propositional justification* and the latter *doxastic justification*. The relevance of this distinction is beyond doubt. The difficulty arises when we attempt to describe the relationship between propositional and doxastic justification.

The simplest way of connecting propositional to doxastic justification is as follows:

> **SIMPLE:** A subject S is doxastically justified in believing that p at some time t iff:
>
> (i) S believes that p at t;
> (ii) S has propositional justification to believe that p at t.

As has often been emphasized, SIMPLE is deficient. I presently have propositional justification to believe that the extinction of the Neanderthals was not just due to climate change (this is a something that is supported by recent studies). But suppose that I believe this because I have deceived myself about the impact of climatic changes in the past (suppose that the present climate change makes me extremely anxious and believing that the extinction of the Neanderthals was not just due to climate change helps me minimize the importance of present climatic variation). Given the self-deceptive origin of my belief, I am not doxastically justified in believing that the extinction of the Neanderthals was not just due to climate change. But, as I have just said, it is something that I have propositional justification to believe. Therefore, SIMPLE is not correct.

Clearly, the difficulty in this example comes from the fact that my belief is not held on the right basis. There is something —for example the fact that recent studies corroborate this—that means that I have propositional justification to believe that the extinction of the Neanderthals was not just due to climate change. Let us call the fact that makes a subject propositionally justified in believing something "the existing justifier." In

DOI: 10.4324/9781003008101-10

the example, my belief about the extinction of the Neanderthals is not propositionally justified because I do not base it on the existing justifier.

At first sight, then, a way of fixing this problem would be to make clear that, in order to hold a doxastically justified belief, the subject must hold her belief on the basis of an existing justifier:

BASING: A subject S is doxastically justified in believing that p at some time t iff:

(i) S has propositional justification to believe that p at t in virtue of some existing justifier J, and;
(ii) S believes that p on the basis of J.

BASING is a popular conception of the connection between propositional and doxastic justification, one that has been employed in several different influential arguments (see Silva and Oliveira, forthcoming). However, as has forcefully been shown by Turri (2010), BASING does not pass muster either. Turri's (2010, 316) counterexample to BASING includes two jurors—Miss Proper and Miss Improper—who at the end of the trial know the following things:

(P1) Mansour had a motive to kill the victim.
(P2) Mansour had previously threatened to kill the victim.
(P3) Multiple eyewitnesses place Mansour at the crime scene.
(P4) Mansour's fingerprints were all over the murder weapon.

In virtue of P1–P4 Miss Proper and Miss Improper have propositional justification to believe that Mansour is guilty. And, in fact, both believe that this is the case on the basis of P1–P4. However, the reason why Miss Improper takes P1–P4 to make it probable that Mansour is guilty is that the tealeaves say that P1–P4 make this probable. In contrast, the reason why Miss Proper takes P1–P4 to make it probable that Mansour is guilty is that she recognizes that P1–P4 provide excellent inductive grounds for thinking that Mansour is guilty. While Miss Proper and Miss Improper both have propositional justification and both base their beliefs on a propositional justifier (a piece of reasoning that relies on P1–P4), intuitively, only Miss Proper is doxastically justified in believing that Mansour is guilty. Therefore, BASIS is unsatisfactory.

Here is another counterexample in which the existing justifier of the belief is not a piece of inductive reasoning. Suppose instead that my belief that the extinction of the Neanderthals was not just due to climate change is based on a serious study in prehistoric archaeology that I have read. Importantly, however, the reason why I base my belief on this study is that the leader of the sect to which I belong urged his disciples to believe everything that he claims himself as well as everything that is stated in the journals that his library contains. Since his library contains many books that are full of forgeries and fabrications, the consequence of his demand is that I have a huge amount of false and unsound beliefs. Now, it happens that his library includes one single serious study in prehistoric archaeology and my belief about the extinction of the Neanderthals is based on this one. This belief is (i) propositionally justified and (ii) based on an existing justifier. The fact that a serious study corroborates my belief about the extinction of the Neanderthals means my belief is propositionally justified and, as I just said, I hold this belief on the basis of this study. But, intuitively, I am not, in this case, doxastically justified in believing that the extinction of the Neanderthals was not just due to climate change. The fact that I believe the content of this study in archaeology because the sect's leader requires me to do so makes it incorrect to say that I am doxastically justified in believing this. So, again, BASING does not seem to tell us the whole story about the relationship between propositional and doxastic justification.

This worry leads Silva (2015) to suggest that a doxastically justified belief must be *properly* based on an existing justifier:

> **PROPER:** A subject S is doxastically justified in believing that p at some time t iff:
>
> (i) S has propositional justification to believe that p at t in virtue of some existing justifier J and;
> (ii) S's belief that p is *properly* based on J.

Hence, what the counterexamples to BASIS show is that, even when a belief is based on a good ground—that is to say, when the belief is based on an existing justifier—*there is a proper and an improper way to base it*. The upshot of Turri's objection to BASIS is that one needs to distinguish between:

(a) a belief being based on a good ground, and;
(b) a belief being based on a good ground in a proper way.

Henceforth, I shall call a belief that is based on a good ground "a well-based or well-grounded belief" and a belief that is based on a good ground in a proper way "a properly based belief." A properly based belief is a well-based belief, but it is one which is well-based in a proper way.

What is required for a belief to be based on a good ground in a proper way? In his 2015 paper Silva sets this question aside "given that the question of what properly basing a belief requires is bound to be tied up with broader epistemological issues (reliabilism, dogmatism, etc.)" (Silva, 2015, 954). I agree with Silva that answering this question is tied to larger epistemological issues. But this does not, I think, make it illegitimate to want to know more about what a properly based belief is. The objective of the next section is to make some progresses in this regard.

What is a Properly Based Belief?

At the risk of spoiling the ending, let me start by stating the view for which I argue in detail in this section:

> **The Credit View:** A properly based belief is a well-based belief for which the believer can be credited.

According to the Credit View, a properly based belief is not a belief whose ground displays some superior intrinsic quality in comparison to a mere well-based belief. What differentiates PROPER from BASIS is not that PROPER is more demanding as far as the intrinsic goodness of the belief's basis is concerned. According to the Credit View, what differentiates PROPER from BASIS is that PROPER requires something additional regarding the involvement of the believer: the believer must be creditable for her holding a well-based belief.

Here is the argument that I intend to defend in order to support the Credit View:

1. It is better to hold a properly based belief than a mere well-based belief (*Betterness*).[1]
2. If it is better to hold a properly based belief than a mere well-based belief, there must be a normative difference between holding a properly based belief and holding a mere well-based belief that explains why holding a properly based belief is better.
3. The best explanation is that to hold a properly based belief is to hold a well-based belief for which the believer can be credited or is creditworthy. (*The Credit Explanation*)
4. *The Credit View*: To hold a properly based belief is to hold a well-based belief for which the believer can be credited or is creditworthy. (Inference to the best explanation)

Let me start my defence of this argument by considering premise 1, *Betterness*.

Betterness seems firmly entrenched. There is something wrong in my believing what a study says as a result of the prescription of a sect's leader and this seems true even when the study is serious and when my belief is based on this study. In absence of the leader's prescription, there is, however, nothing wrong in believing something on the basis of a serious

---

[1] I formulate the argument in terms of betterness, but it would have also been possible to state it in terms of worseness and to start the argument with the following premise: it is worse to hold a mere well-grounded belief than a properly based belief.

study found in a library. Well-based but improperly based beliefs—that is, mere well-based beliefs—are wrong in a way that properly based beliefs are not. For this reason, mere well-based beliefs are worse than properly based beliefs.

The defence of premise 2 is also quite straightforward. When two states of affairs are equally good, neither is better than the other. Therefore, when one is better than the other, there must be a normative difference between the two, for instance, a difference in the degree (or amount?) of goodness exemplified by each state of affairs.

Credit Explanation is the most controversial premise of the argument. I shall argue for it in two steps. I shall, first, explain why a well-based belief that can be credited to the believer is better than a mere well-based belief. Second, I shall try to show why the Credit Explanation seems to be the best explanation of why a properly based belief is better than a mere well-based belief.

The view that a valuable performance or state is even more valuable when it is creditable to a subject has been forcefully defended by virtue-reliabilists (see mainly Greco, 2003, 2010, 2012; Sosa, 2007, 2009, 2011, 2015).[2] Consider—to re-use Sosa's favorite example—two perfectly accurate archery shots. Both superbly hit the target exactly in its center. Now, suppose that, in the first case, the success of the shot is due to a gust of wind. In the first case, the archer would never have hit the target without the lucky intervention of the breeze. In the second case, the successful shot is due to the impressive competences of the archer. In the second case, the success or accuracy of the shot can, therefore, be credited to the archer. Both shots display some form of goodness since both perfectly fulfill the constitutive goal of archery: they hit the target in the center. Yet, there is a strong intuition that the second shot is better than the first one. A subject S's successful performance seems better when it is not due to luck but is creditable to S. To put it differently, when a successful performance—for example an accurate shot in archery—is creditable to a subject, this performance displays two values. The first is the one that a performance possesses when it achieves its purpose. The second one is what I have called elsewhere its *credit value* (Meylan, 2013). Credit value is the value that a successful performance additionally possesses when it is creditable to a subject and not a lucky outcome. As just explained, such a normative claim is strongly supported by intuition.

Let us apply this lesson to properly based beliefs. A well-based belief whose acquisition can be credited to the believer has some additional credit value. This additional credit value makes a properly based belief better than a mere well-based belief, the well-groundedness of which is due to mere luck. Or, to put it another way, the fact that it lacks any

---

2 This view grounds the virtue-reliabilist solution to the problem of the value problem of knowledge.

126 *Anne Meylan*

additional credit value explains why my belief concerning the extinction of the Neanderthals is in some way deficient when it is merely well-based (because it was imposed by a sect's leader).

This concludes the first step in my defence of premise 3. As promised, the second step consists in vindicating the claim that this explanation—that is, the credit explanation—is the best explanation of why it is better to hold a properly based belief than a mere well-grounded belief.

What could be another candidate explanation for the fact that a properly based belief is better than a mere well-based belief? Here is one which, as we will soon so, proves to be unsatisfactory:

> **The Instrumentalist Explanation:** A properly based belief is better than a mere well-based belief because, in normal conditions, the probability that a belief is true is higher when the belief is properly based than when it is merely well-based.

This is an *instrumentalist* explanation because, according to it, the additional value of a properly based belief is derived from the fact that, at least in normal conditions, someone with a properly based belief is more likely to achieve the goal of forming true beliefs than someone with a mere well-based belief.

This instrumentalist explanation fails and this is because, even in normal circumstances, the probability that a properly based belief is true is no higher than the probability that a mere well-based belief is true. Usually, mere well-based beliefs and properly based beliefs do not differ with regards to the respective probability of their truth.[3] For instance, whether I believe the serious study in prehistoric archaeology because the leader of the sect to which I belong urges me to believe it (a mere well-based-belief) or because I rightly consider this study to be a relevant source of information (a properly based belief) does not make any difference to the probability that the belief based on this study be true. A belief based on a serious study in prehistoric archaeology has a certain probability of being true and it is no more (or less) probable in virtue of being properly based rather than merely well-based.

Here is what I think is a more promising instrumentalist explanation.

> **The Instrumentalist Explanation that Regards Future Beliefs:** A properly based belief is better than a mere well-based belief because, in normal circumstances, the probability that future beliefs of the

---

3 It is also possible to conceive of non-normal circumstances in which a properly based belief is less likely to be true than a mere well-based belief. Suppose that an omniscient being tells you: p is true iff you hold a merely well-based belief about p. In such a case $Pr(p|E)$ & I do merely base my belief on E) is 1 and $Pr(p|E)$ & I do properly base my belief on E) is 0. [You need to specify what "E" is here]. Thanks to the editors of this volume for having helped me to see [make?] this point more clearly.

same kind will be true is higher when the belief is properly based than when it is merely well-based.[4]

At first sight, this seems true. Basing my belief on what I read in the library of a sect's leader is a method that may, due to luck, have been successful in the case of my belief regarding the extinction of the Neanderthals but such a method usually leads to forming false beliefs. Similarly, tea leaves will, most often, be poor indicators of what counts as good inductive reasons.

The main problem with this alternative instrumentalist explanation is that a mere well-based belief seems worse than a properly based belief (or a properly based belief seems better than a mere well-based belief) even when the method from which the mere well-based belief results *is used only once*. Suppose that Miss Improper consults the tealeaves only because she is a juror and cannot stand the pressure of having to deliver a verdict and that she will never consult tealeaves again. This does not seem to remove the intuition that there is something wrong with Miss Improper's well-based belief that Mansour is guilty. Her belief remains deficient, not as good as Miss Proper's, even if Miss Improper's method cannot impact the truth of Miss Improper's future beliefs since she won't make use of this method again.

This concludes my defense of premise 3, according to which the credit explanation is the best explanation of why holding a properly based belief is better than holding a mere well-based belief.

The conclusion of the argument, to recall, is the Credit View, that is, the view that a properly based belief is a well-based belief for which the believer is creditworthy. Since being properly based is a necessary condition for being doxastically justified (this is the lesson we took from Turri's objection, to recall) and since a properly based belief is, according to the Credit View, a belief whose well-groundedness can be credited to the believer, the Credit View makes creditworthiness a necessary condition for doxastic justification. Put more straightforwardly, if the above argument withstands scrutiny, doxastic justification depends on the subject being creditable for her well-grounded belief. Here is a re-formulation of PROPER that clarifies this.

RE-PROPER: A subject S is doxastically justified in believing that p at some time t iff:

(i) S has propositional justification to believe that p at t in virtue of some existing justifier J and;
(ii) S's belief that p is *properly* based on J, where a properly based belief is one that is:

---

4 See Goldman and Olsson, 2009 for a similar sort of explanation that concerns the additional value of knowledge in comparison to mere true belief.

based on *J* (i.e. well-based) and;
whose well-groundedness is creditable to *S*.

Importantly, it would be a mistake to think that RE-PROPER is only compatible with an internalist conception of doxastic justification. My being creditable for a well-based belief does not, in fact, require the satisfaction of some internalist condition such as my being aware of the fact that the belief is well-based. Just like the gifted archer is creditable for her splendid shot when this shot is the result of her own talent, I can be creditable for my well-based belief simply because I hold this well-based belief as a result of some cognitive mechanism that is my own (that is a mechanism that is not implemented or manipulated by a crazy scientist, a sect's leader, an evil Demon, etc.). The idea that your belief can be well-based as a result of some cognitive mechanism is perfectly compatible with an externalist picture of doxastic justification. In this sense, the Credit View is neutral as to whether doxastic justification should be understood along internalist or externalist lines.[5]

An Interesting Rapprochement

According to the most popular account of doxastic *responsibility* (that is, of responsibility for believing), a believer is responsible for her belief that *p* when her belief is *responsive to her reasons*, that is, when the believer holds this belief for—what she takes to be—a reason. The contemporary literature contains numerous specifications and improvements of this kind of view (see e.g. Hieronymi, 2006; McHugh, 2014, 2017; Wolf, 1990). These details do not matter here. For my purposes, a rough understanding of this kind of account is sufficient. The general idea is as follows. A believer is responsible for her belief when she holds this belief for—what she takes to be—a reason because the fact that she holds this belief for—what she takes to be—a reason faithfully mirrors the believer's rational take on it. Put differently, a reasons-responsive belief results from the believer's rational capacities and this is why it is also one for which the believer is responsible.

As we saw previously, if a subject *S* has propositional justification to believe that *p* but does not believe that *p* on the basis of the existing justifier but as a result, say, of self-deception, *S*'s belief that *p* is not doxastically justified. One minimal requirement for a belief to be doxastically justified is that it must *be based on* the existing justifier. Let me re-formulate the latter claim by replacing "justifier" with "reason" and by using the preposition "for" to denote the relation that holds between a belief and a reason when the belief is held *on the basis* of the reason. This gives

---

[5] The view I defend has obvious affinities with virtue epistemology, and virtue epistemology can come in internalist and externalist versions.

us one minimal requirement for a belief to be doxastically justified: it must be held for a reason. There is, I believe, nothing contentious in this re-formulation.

Now, let us put side by side the popular account of doxastic responsibility just described and this well-recognized requirement for doxastic justification. Their extensions overlap. More precisely, all the beliefs I have that are doxastically justified are also beliefs for which I am doxastically responsible. This is because doxastic justification requires that I hold a belief for a reason and holding a belief for a reason is sufficient to be responsible for it according to the account of doxastic responsibility in terms of reasons-responsiveness. Note that the reverse does not hold: not all the beliefs for which I am doxastically responsible are necessarily doxastically justified. This is because I am sometimes responsible for a belief that I hold for what I take to be a reason but is not a reason and, in this case, the belief is not doxastically justified since it is not based on an existing justifier.

What interests me here is the overlap. One implication of the account of doxastic responsibility in terms of reasons-responsiveness is that doxastically justified beliefs are also beliefs for which I am doxastically responsible. This is reminiscent of the view that I try to defend in this chapter, the view that a doxastically justified belief is a well-based belief that is creditable to the believer. The purpose of this brief section was to briefly present an independent reason to think that the rapprochement between doxastic justification and responsibility/creditworthiness is promising.

Conclusion

One of the most fruitful upshots of reliabilist virtue epistemology is its emphasis on the normative distinction between a successful performance and a successful performance whose success can be credited to the agent. This distinction plays a crucial role in this article as well. To believe something on the basis of an existing justifier—such as what you hear in a trial or what you read in some serious scientific journals—is to achieve something and so a sort of success. In this sense, a well-based belief is a successful belief. A well-based belief is a successful belief with respect to the quality of its basis. Just like any other successful performance, an additional question is whether the success in question—in this case, the well-groundedness—can be credited to the believer. The view defended in this chapter is that to hold a doxastically justified belief is to hold a well-based belief that can be credited to the believer.[6]

---

6 I am most grateful to the editors of this volume, to Silvia De Toffoli and to Robin McKenna for their very useful comments on an earlier version of this article. Needless to say, the remaining mistakes are my own responsibility.

References

Goldman, A. I., and E. J. Olsson 2009. "Reliabilism and the Value of Knowledge." In *Epistemic Value*, eds. A. Haddock, A. Millar, and D. Pritchard, Oxford University Press: 19–41.

Greco, J. 2003. "Knowledge as Credit for True Belief." In *Intellectual Virtue: Perspectives from Ethics and Epistemology*, eds. M. DePaul, and L. Zagzebski, Oxford University Press: 111–134.

———. 2010. *Achieving Knowledge: A Virtue-Theoretic Account of Epistemic Normativity*, Cambridge University Press.

———. 2012. "A (Different) Virtue Epistemology," *Philosophy and Phenomenological Research* 85: 1–26.

Hieronymi, P. 2006. "Controlling Attitudes," *Pacific Philosophical Quaterly* 87, 1: 45–74.

McHugh, C. 2014. "Exercising Doxastic Freedom," *Philosophy and Phenomenological Research* 88: 1–37.

McHugh, C. 2017. "Attitudinal Control," *Synthese* 194: 2745–2762.

Meylan A. 2013. "The Value Problem of Knowledge: An Axiological Diagnosis of the Credit Solution," *Res Philosophica* 90: 261–275.

Silva, P. 2015. "On Doxastic Justification and Properly Basing One's Beliefs," *Erkenntnis* 80: 945–955.

Silva, P., and L. Oliveira forthcoming. "Propositional Justification and Doxastic Justification." In *The Routledge Handbook of the Philosophy of Evidence*, eds. M. Laarsonen-Aarnio, and C. Littlejohn, Routledge.

Sosa, E. 2007. *A Virtue Epistemology*, Oxford University Press.

———. 2009. "Knowing Full Well: The Normativity of Beliefs as Performances," *Philosophical Studies* 142, 1: 5–15

———. 2011. *Knowing Full Well*, Princeton University Press.

———. 2015. *Judgment and Agency*, Oxford University Press.

Turri, J. 2010. "On the Relationship between Propositional and Doxastic Justification," *Philosophy and Phenomenological Research* 80: 312–326.

Wolf, S. 1990. *Freedom Within Reason*, Oxford University Press.

8 Does the Basing Demand on Doxastic Justification Have Any Dialectical Force?
A Response to Oliveira

Paul Silva Jr

The distinction between propositional and doxastic justification is typically characterized as the distinction between *having justification to believe that p* (=propositional justification) versus *having a justified belief that p* (=doxastic justification). When characterized in this way the distinction between propositional and doxastic justification appears to highlight the obvious difference between having justification *to be* in a state versus *being in* a justified state.

Virtually all epistemologists reject the idea that doxastic justification is simply belief that *p* together with having justification to believe that *p*. Rather, epistemologists tend to hold that at least part of what makes the difference between these two kinds of justification has to do with what one's belief is based on. For example, Alston (1989, p. 108) claims that:

> (it is) conceptually true that one is justified in believing that *p* iff one's belief that *p* is based on an adequate ground.

And Huemer (2007, pp. 40–41) says:

> *justification for believing* that *p* is not to be confused with *justified belief* that *p*... a justified belief must be held because of what provides adequate justification for it.

We will capture this idea in the following way:

> **The Basing Demand (TBD):** Necessarily, S has a (doxastically) justified belief that *p* only if S believes that *p* on the basis of an epistemically appropriate reason to believe that *p*.[1]

---

1 See Silva (2015) for further citations. Some epistemologists prefer a qualified version of TBD since, arguably, there can be some instances of reason-free justified beliefs. The point here is that there are a wide range of cases where one's justification *is* dependent on one's epistemic reasons (e.g. inferential and paradigmatic perceptual beliefs) and in *those* cases most epistemologists think a suitably qualified version of TBD holds.

TBD is of particular interest because it is an intuition with bite because it facilitates powerful arguments in support of heavy-weight epistemological doctrines. Here are just a few examples: Pollock and Cruz (1999) use TBD to undermine coherentism, and if they are right about that then they cast a shadow over subjective bayesian epistemology as well; Silins (2008) and Neta (2010) both rely on TBD in their justification of liberalism about perceptual justification; Huemer (2007) uses TBD to justify phenomenal conservatism; and Comesaña and McGrath (2014) use TBD to justify non-factualist views about reasons. TBD is able to do this work because it asserts a link—that is, the basing relation—between the bases of one's justified beliefs and the source of one's justification to believe. If such a link exists, TBD threatens epistemological views that drive a wedge between one's source of justification and the basis of one's justified beliefs, for example coherentism and anti-liberal views of perceptual justification. Similarly, epistemological views that are consistent with such a link are views that are supported to some extent by TBD, for example phenomenal conservatism and non-factualist views of reasons. Accordingly, TBD has seemed to many to have the dialectical power to help resolve, or at least advance, various disputes in epistemology since TBD is typically taken to be a fixed-point.[2]

Silva (2015) suggested a reassessment of TBD. He motivated this reassessment in part by considering how TBD's counterpart would fare in the moral domain. The answer: it would fare quite badly since dominant moral theories entail that one can act in a morally justified way even if one's reasons for acting (i.e. the basis of one's action) are not morally appropriate. Just consider someone who saves a drowning child but their reason for doing so is to enslave that child when they reach adulthood: if one saves the child, that act is morally justified even if one's reasons for acting are morally reprehensible. But if one's reasons for acting are irrelevant to the moral justification of an action, why should one's reasons for believing be important for the epistemic justification of a belief?

Oliveira (2015) sought to undermine this concern with TBD by undermining the following argument:

The Parity Argument

(1) When the term "doxastic justification" is used in epistemic theory it expresses the same concept that "moral justification" does in moral theory, namely, the concept of permissibility within a certain domain.
(2) An action can be morally justified (=permitted) even if it is not performed for morally appropriate reasons.
(3) What is true of the structure of moral justification is true of the structure of epistemic justification.

---

2 Silva and Oliveira (forthcoming).

(4) So, a belief can be doxastically justified (=permitted) even if it is not held for epistemically appropriate reasons. (from 1–3)

If (4) is true, then TBD is false.[3]

As a matter of book-keeping, it is worth noting that Oliveira's summary does not accurately represent Silva's (2015) argument or conclusion. Silva (2015, p. 374) *explicitly* refrained from invoking any commitment to (3) as a premise. Rather, he used the moral case as an *analogy* to motivate rethinking what support there could be for TBD in the epistemic case. Moreover, his conclusion is *not* that TBD is false. Rather, Silva (2015, Section 3) surveyed a wide range of ways of justifying TBD and shows that they either fail *or* they depend on assumptions that are theory-dependent in a way that makes certain appeals to TBD by prominent epistemologists question-begging.

Now, Oliveira's (2015, pp. 391–392) primary move in defense of TBD is to draw attention to an important difference between agents' *actions* and their *beliefs*. For when it comes to states (like belief) that are not voluntarily brought about (and hence "non-agential" in some important sense) Oliveira presupposes that it is always infelicitous to read claims of the form "S's φ-ing is permitted" in a way that involves relating an *agent* to a *norm* which the agent conforms to. Rather, such claims are best understood as positive assessments of a *state of affairs* that involve agents conforming to an ideal to a sufficient degree. So, for example, a claim like "S's believing that p is epistemically permitted" should be understood as a claim about the epistemic *goodness* of a state of affairs: "it is epistemically good that S believes that p." If belief is non-agential in the way that Oliveira asserts, then (3) is arguably false. Further, if belief is deeply non-agential then Silva (2015, pp. 377–78) appears wrong in his appeal to concepts like blameworthiness in his alternative explanation of what is intuitively problematic in cases of bad basing.

There are, however, various problems with Oliveira's defense of TBD. First, consider Oliveira's assumption that a belief's responsiveness to evidence should be understood in a *completely non-agential* way (like the swinging of a clock-hand). When one surveys the epistemological literature on belief and agency virtually all epistemologists agree that belief is not agential in the very same way that paradigmatically free actions are, for example actions like raising one's arm that are directly responsive to an agent's intentions in normal conditions. But even so, most (or at least *very many*) epistemologists also think that beliefs are *sufficiently agential* (and thus sufficiently unlike the movements of a clock-hand) to ground true ascriptions of responsibility, praiseworthiness, and blameworthiness to agents for holding their beliefs. The literature here is vast and undiscussed by Oliveira. So at the very least there is a significant range of

---

3 (1)–(4) is not Oliveira's phrasing of the argument, but it is a faithful representation of it.

epistemologists who have to deal with the Parity Argument if they wish to leverage TBD in a dialectically fruitful way.[4]

There is a further pressing issue for Oliveira's attempted refutation of (3). It concerns the relevant disanalogy that he sought to highlight. For suppose Oliveira were correct that the only coherent way to understand statements of the form "S is permitted to believe that p" is in terms of "it being epistemically good that S believes that p." Even then, there exists a disanalogy between the moral assessment of action and the epistemological assessment of belief. This is because moral theories often have something to say about which states of affairs are good. Indeed, it is arguable that a complete and coherent moral theory will come with an axiology that implies not only that some *actions are permitted* but also imply that the corresponding *states of affairs involving permitted action* are good! From this it will follow that circumstances where people act in morally permitted ways but for morally inappropriate reasons are circumstances where there is a morally *good* state of affairs (the state of affairs *just* involving S's φ-ing) nested within a *more inclusive* state of affairs that is morally *suboptimal* (the state of affairs involving S's φ-ing *on the basis of morally inappropriate reasons*). This motivates the very same question that Silva (2015) raised but in a way that is immune to Oliveira's worries about doxastic agency. Moreover, it identifies a positive epistemic property that is absent in cases where agents fail to base their beliefs appropriately: there is a *good* state of affairs nested within a larger *suboptimal* state of affairs.

Given Oliveira's preferred evaluative interpretation of deontic language when assessing beliefs, this is equivalent to saying that one can have a doxastically justified belief even if it is badly based. And, as far as I can tell, Oliveira has offered no new reason to reject such a possibility that Silva (2015) didn't already address. Accordingly, considerations of

---

4 For example, some have argued that beliefs can be volitional in a way that allows them to be assessed on the same level as actions. See Weatherson (2008); Peels (2015); and Roeber (2019). Oliveira does note this. But there's more. For others think that it makes fine sense to assess both *actions and beliefs* in terms of *responsiveness to reasons* even if the responsiveness in the case of belief is not directly voluntary. See Schroeder (2015); Lord (2018); and Kiesewetter (2017). This is related to the deliberative "ought" (and the deliberative sense of "justified"), of which Schroeder (2011: 24) says: "The sense of 'action' on which I claim that the deliberative 'ought' relates agents to actions *is very broad*. It can be the case that *Max ought to believe that p*, or that Max ought to be saddened by recent events, but believing that p and being saddened by recent events are not commonly thought of as actions." See also Wedgwood (2017); Way and Whiting (2016); Kiesewetter (2017); and Lord (2018) for further discussion and endorsement. Notice too that there are very well explored theories of responsible belief that do not make doxastic responsibility (and hence the fittingness of praise and blame) turn upon the extent to which belief mirrors actions in terms of voluntariness. See Oshana (1997); Scanlon (1998); Heller (2000); Hieronymi (2008); McHugh (2014, 2013); Peels (2015); Rettler (2018); and Smith (2008). See also Sosa's *Judgement and Agency* (2015).

doxastic agency seem almost entirely irrelevant to the question of whether or not TBD is true; at most, doxastic agency concerns our interpretation of the deontic language we employ when talking about TBD.

There is an alternative way to undermine the Parity Argument that Silva failed to consider. It has to do with an ambiguity in ascriptions of doxastic justification. On the one hand, when epistemologists characterize "doxastic justification" they do so in a way that seems to make the object of assessment a *belief state*. (See the citations in the introduction.) Call this *the stative conception* of doxastic justification. On the other hand, when epistemologists provide substantive conditions for doxastic justification, like TBD, what they are offering is a procedural norm, that is, a norm that places limits on *the permissible ways of arriving at* a certain state. Call this *the procedural conception* of doxastic justification.

It is this procedural issue that John Turri (2010: 315) drew attention to when he wrote that:

> we should ask ourselves whether it is plausible to think that *the way in which a subject makes use of his reasons* matters not to whether his belief is well founded (=doxastically justified).... In evaluating beliefs we are evaluating a kind of *performance*, the performance of a cognitive agent in representing the world as being a certain way, and when performing with materials (which, in cognitive affairs, will include reasons or evidence), the success, or lack thereof, of one's performance will depend crucially on *the way in which one makes use of those materials*.

Turri is asking about the epistemic successes of having a doxastically justified belief, and we can tell that even Turri is thinking of "doxastic justification" in the stative sense when asking about procedural norms for doxastic justification. For otherwise his comment would be trivially true. That is, it is trivially true that having a procedurally justified belief—that is, having a belief that one arrived at via a justified procedure—depends on the way in which one arrived at one's belief. That's just what it means to talk about procedural justification.

The non-trivial question that Turri is asking is whether or not having a statively justified belief depends on whether or not that belief is also procedurally justified. This is a substantive question all normative theories must address. For in practical reasoning, politics, and morality we can ask wether (practically, politically, morally) justified *processes* are processes that *always and only* lead to justified *outcomes*. Consider the process of having carefully selected juries decide whether a person is guilty. Many view this process as justified in some important normative sense even if it sometimes yields unjustified verdicts. Similarly, we can imagine unjustified processes that sometimes lead to justified verdicts.

Turri is, quite insightfully, raising these questions for our thinking about the epistemic domain.

These reflections draw attention to two readings of TBD:

> (TBD-Procedural) Necessarily, S has *a procedurally justified belief* that p (=a belief that S arrived at via a justified procedure) only if S believes that p on the basis of an epistemically appropriate reason to believe that p.

> (TBD-Stative) Necessarily, S has *a statively justified belief* (=a justified belief) that p only if S believes that p on the basis of an epistemically appropriate reason to believe that p.

This distinction gives rise to a reconciliatory response to Silva (2015) and the Parity Argument. For if the term "doxastic justification" is ambiguous between stative and procedural readings, then two things are likely to occur. First, TBD will *seem* like the obvious truth that all epistemologists have treated it as. For it seems like the set of justified belief-forming procedures can only include belief-forming processes that are responsive to one's epistemic reasons; after all, procedures that are unresponsive (or improperly responsive) to epistemic reasons will be regarded as epistemically reckless. Second, if "doxastic justification" is ambiguous between stative and procedural readings we should expect exactly the kind of disanalogy that Silva (2015) drew attention to. For TBD-Stative is about states that one is permitted to be in. And when talking about permitted states/actions, dominant moral theories entail that morally permissible states/actions can be arrived at in morally impermissible and blameworthy ways.

It is easy to see that this highly tentative "reconciliation" favors Silva's primary conclusion about the limited dialectical value of TBD. For, as noted above, the dialectical power of TBD lies with its linking one's *bases* for being in a justified state and *what justifies* being in that state. This is what TBD-Stative does.[5] TBD-Procedural asserts no such link, it is just about justified belief-forming *procedures*. Accordingly, Silva was likely correct to (implicitly) assess TBD-Stative in his (2015) since that is the disambiguation of TBD that is in play in the aforementioned discussions of coherentism, liberalism, phenomenal conservatism, and factivity about reasons.

---

5 See Silva (2015: Section 3, Reason#6) for a discussion of the following way of bridging the procedural and stative principles: S's belief state is justified only if S arrived at S's belief in reliable way. This links the justification of states to reliable procedures, and it is a way of justifying TBD-Stative. However, as Silva (2015) explains, it is not a way of justifying TBD-Stative that is fit for the dialectical purposes that it is standardly put to.

References

Alston, William (1989). *Epistemic Justification*. Cornell University Press.
Comesaña, Juan & McGrath, Matthew (2014). Having False Reasons. In Clayton Littlejohn & John Turri (eds.), *Epistemic Norms*. Oxford University Press. pp. 59–80.
Heller, Mark (2000). Hobartian Voluntarism: Grounding a Deontological Conception of Epistemic Justification. *Pacific Philosophical Quarterly*, 81(2), 130–141.
Huemer, Michael (2007). Compassionate Phenomenal Conservatism. *Philosophy and Phenomenological Research*, 74(1), 30–55.
Hieronymi, Pamela (2008). Responsibility for Believing. *Synthese*, 161(3), 357–373.
Kiesewetter, Benjamin (2017). *The Normativity of Rationality*. Oxford University Press.
Lord, Errol (2018). *The Importance of Being Rational*. Oxford University Press.
McHugh, Conor (2014). Exercising Doxastic Freedom. *Philosophy and Phenomenological Research*, 88(1), 1–37.
McHugh, Conor (2013). Epistemic Responsibility and Doxastic Agency. *Philosophical Issues*, 23(1), 132–157.
Neta, Ram (2010). Liberalism and Conservatism in the Epistemology of Perceptual Belief. *Australasian Journal of Philosophy*, 88(4), 685–705.
Oliveira, Luis R. G. (2015). Non-Agential Permissibility in Epistemology. *Australasian Journal of Philosophy*, 93(2), 389–394.
Oshana, Marina A. L. (1997). Ascriptions of Responsibility. *American Philosophical Quarterly*, 34(1), 71–83.
Peels, Rik (2015). Believing at Will is Possible. *Australasian Journal of Philosophy*, 93(3), 1–18.
Pollock, John & Cruz, Joe (1999). *Contemporary Theories of Knowledge*, 2nd Edition. Rowman & Littlefield.
Rettler, Lindsay (2018). In defense of Doxastic Blame. *Synthese*, 195(5), 2205–2226.
Roeber, Blake (2019). Evidence, Judgment, and Belief at Will. *Mind*, 128(511), 837–859.
Scanlon, Thomas (1998). *What We Owe to Each Other*. Belknap Press of Harvard University Press.
Schroeder, M. (2011). Ought, Agents, and Actions. *Philosophical Review*, 120(1), 1–41.
Schroeder, Mark (2015). Knowledge is Belief for Sufficient (Objective and Subjective) Reason. *Oxford Studies in Epistemology*, 5. doi: 10.1093/acprof:oso/9780198722762.003.0008
Silins, Nicholas (2008). Basic Justification and the Moorean Response to the Skeptic. In Tamar Gendler & John Hawthorne (eds.), *Oxford Studies in Epistemology* Volume 2. Oxford University Press. p. 108.
Silva, Paul (2015). Does Doxastic Justification Have a Basing Requirement? *Australasian Journal of Philosophy*, 93(2), 371–387.
Silva, Paul and Oliveira, Luis (forthcoming). Propositional Justification and Doxastic Justification. In *The Routledge Handbook of the Philosophy of Evidence*, eds. M. Laarsonen-Aarnio, and C. Littlejohn, Routledge.

Smith, Angela M. (2008). Control, Responsibility, and Moral Assessment. *Philosophical Studies*, 138(3), 367–392.
Sosa, Ernest (2015). *Judgment and Agency*. OUP.
Turri, John (2010). On the Relationship between Propositional and Doxastic Justification. *Philosophy and Phenomenological Research*, 80(2), 312–326.
Weatherson, Brian (2008). Deontology and Descartes's Demon. *Journal of Philosophy*, 105(9), 540–569.
Way, Jonathan & Whiting, Daniel (2016). If You Justifiably Believe that You Ought to Φ, You Ought to Φ. *Philosophical Studies*, 173(7), 1873–1895.
Wedgwood, Ralph (2017). *The Value of Rationality*. Oxford University Press.

Part III
Other Attitudes and Justification

9 On Suspending Properly

Errol Lord and Kurt Sylvan

Until recently, work on the nature of epistemic justification tended to treat suspension of judgment as an afterthought. This tendency has sedimented itself in the common names for the two main varieties of epistemic justification, 'doxastic' and 'propositional' justification, which are the concern of this volume. 'Doxastic' justification is supposed to cover the property of justifiedness that attaches to doxastic attitudes that one holds, but 'doxastic' (from the Greek for belief, *doxa*) suggests pride of place for belief. Similarly, 'propositional' justification is meant to encompass justification to hold any of the doxastic attitudes, but propositions are better candidates for being objects of belief; suspension is more naturally understood as a question-oriented attitude (i.e., one suspends about *whether p*).

These habits in the theory of epistemic justification reflect a long-standing treatment of suspension as a lack of belief, qualifying nominally as a doxastic attitude only by courtesy of the fact that lacking belief is the alternative to believing and disbelieving. But thanks to the pathbreaking work of Jane Friedman (2013, 2019), and to a concurrent revival of the topic by Ernest Sosa (2010, 2015, 2019) and Lisa Miracchi (2019), suspension has lately received more attention. The consequences of better understanding suspension for the theory of epistemic justification remain underexplored, however. In particular, it remains unclear to what extent the theory of epistemic justification must be restructured in light of a better understanding of suspension. On this question, recent theorists have mainly considered two kinds of views. On the one hand, Friedman's (2017) exploration of reasons for suspending judgment suggested the need for a significant restructuring of traditional epistemology. Since suspension for Friedman is an inquiring attitude and the normative profile of inquiry seems different from the normative profile of belief, one might expect that reasons for suspending will be fundamentally different from reasons for belief. If this were true, theories of epistemic justification could no longer treat suspension as an afterthought: they must be reworked to take reasons for suspension into account. Coming to terms

DOI: 10.4324/9781003008101-13

with this expansion might require rethinking the scope and priorities of epistemology and taking what Friedman (Forthcoming) calls the *zetetic turn*.

Not all new work on suspension recommends a break with the standard conception of epistemology as the theory of knowledge. Instead of restructuring epistemology to make room for suspension, some have sought new ways of relegating suspension of judgment to a subordinate role within established approaches like virtue epistemology and knowledge-first epistemology. Sosa and Miracchi have suggested in importantly different ways that we should continue to accept a teleological virtue epistemology that regards either true belief or knowledge as the epistemic goal, and treat suspending as having a different relationship to this aim than believing and disbelieving. We should, both suggest, regard suspension as manifesting a subordinate kind of epistemic competence, with the competence manifested by believing and knowing given primacy.

We think that these two approaches—call them the *restructuring* and *relegation* approaches—have their attractions. But we ultimately think that a third approach is needed to avoid some unattractive features of each. We will argue that a Kantian reasons-based approach can provide a unified account of justification that neither requires restructuring epistemology nor relegating suspension of judgment to a second-class or spandrel status. More specifically, we will be using this approach to show (1) that suspension of judgment is justified in fundamentally the same way as belief and disbelief, and (2) that justified suspension of judgment has the same kind of epistemic worth relative to the fundamental epistemic value of truth as justified belief (viz., non-instrumental value derived from respect for truth). In line with our earlier work, we will also maintain that properly accounting for suspension requires acknowledging that some epistemic reasons are non-evidential. But we will suggest that this position is compatible with (1) and (2). For, as we'll argue, non-evidential considerations qualify as epistemic in the same way in which evidence qualifies as epistemic. Hence a radical zetetic turn is not needed.

Suspension and the Theory of Epistemic Justification: The Challenge and the Relegation Approach

Illustrations of the Challenge: Evidentialism and Early Virtue Epistemology

Taking suspension of judgment seriously presents a challenge to traditional theories of propositional and doxastic justification (henceforth we will use Goldman's (1979) broader terms *ex ante* and *ex post* justification). The challenge is usefully illustrated by considering some unseemly features of two otherwise appealing views: evidentialism and virtue epistemology.

Evidentialism, Reasons for Suspending, and Ex Ante Justification

Let's reflect on why evidentialism might seem an attractive account of *ex ante* justification. The appeal rests on the attraction of two thoughts:

> **Reasons-First about *Ex Ante* Justification:** What it is for doxastic reaction D to be *ex ante* justified for A is for A's epistemic reasons to sufficiently support D.
> **Epistemic Reasons = Evidence:** Epistemic reasons = evidence.

The first claim is a near-truism. The second claim is sometimes treated even by opponents of evidentialism as an analytic truth. After all, one might think that reasons qualify as *epistemic* in virtue of a logical or probabilistic relation to truth, and what bears a logical or probabilistic epistemic relation to truth is evidence.[1]

There is, however, a simple-minded complaint about the conjunction of these two theses, which we take to reveal a deeper problem for evidentialist epistemology that Conee and Feldman's (2004) presentation of the view papers over. The evidence-for relation just isn't the right kind of thing to relate evidence and suspension. There cannot, after all, be evidence for suspending. Evidence is always evidence for belief or disbelief.

Of course, one might insist that it doesn't sound so bad to speak of the evidence as *supporting* suspension of judgment. But if this doesn't mean that the evidence is evidence for suspending, it seems most natural to take it to mean that the evidence provides sufficient epistemic reason for suspending. And—here is the deeper problem—it remains difficult to understand from an evidentialist perspective how the evidence can support suspending judgment in the way that it can support belief and disbelief. Consider simple cases in which suspending is the right attitude:

> **Even Split:** Barry is given the chance to pull a ball out of a bag of balls. He is informed that the bag has 100 balls and 50 of them are red and 50 of them are black. He considers the question of whether he will draw a red ball. He ponders for a moment before suspending.

Barry's evidence doesn't by itself speak in favor of suspension. One piece of evidence he has—the fact that 50 balls are red—speaks in favor of believing, and another piece of evidence he has—the fact that 50 balls are black—speaks in favor of disbelieving. Neither speaks in favor of suspending. Why, then, does the evidence support suspending?

---

1 We needn't put the point in Veritist manner, however, since there is also a more knowledge-first friendly version of this idea: sufficient epistemic reasons are sufficient for attaining the level of rational support required for knowledge ('knowledge-level justification', as Fantl and McGrath 2010 put it).

Of course, there is a reason for Barry to suspend here, and it is a fact about the evidence: it is split. But facts about the evidence are not always evidence, nor do they support suspension by bearing the evidence-for relation to suspension. Furthermore, we need to know more about why there is decisive epistemic reason to suspend judgment when the evidence is split. Evidentialism does not help here. Epistemic Reasons = Evidence suggests that the property of decisiveness that attaches to epistemic reasons should be the same property as the property of decisiveness that attaches to evidence. But these properties are distinct, since decisiveness in evidence is a matter of its decisively establishing some truth.

We recognize that Conee and Feldman are unlikely to be moved by these concerns. One reason why is that they haven't thought that any positive account of reasons for suspension is needed. The right conclusions about suspension follow, they think, from the proper evidentialist account of *ex ante* justified belief and disbelief. In particular, they will suggest that suspension is justified whenever belief and disbelief are not justified. Hence, if the evidence supports p, there is *ex ante* justification for believing p, if the evidence supports ~p, there is *ex ante* justification for disbelieving p, and there is otherwise *ex ante* justification for suspending.[2]

The trouble with this suggestion is that the fact that the evidence supports p does not guarantee that there is sufficient epistemic reason for believing p, since there may yet be sufficient epistemic reasons for suspending judgment. As we suggested in Lord and Sylvan (2021), some

---

2 See Conee and Feldman (2004: 83, 102, 179) and Conee and Feldman (2005: 106) for a hint of this angle. Feldman (2005: 282–83) elsewhere suggests that one of the three options must always be reasonable. This helps to explain why Conee and Feldman (2004) gave the following quick treatment of ties:

The first, and easiest to dispose of, are cases in which the evidence for and against a proposition is equally weighty. In that case, evidentialism implies that the sole acceptable attitude is suspending judgment. *Neither belief nor disbelief is permitted* (179; italics ours).

The reasoning hence seems to be the following: it follows from the necessary conditions for rational belief and rational disbelief and the fact that at least one doxastic attitude must be permissible that suspension is permissible when belief and disbelief couldn't be rational. Since the overall evidence does not support belief and does not support disbelief in tie cases, it follows that suspension is the sole justified attitude.

It is worth noting that Conee and Feldman (2018: 75) draw attention to this feature of their view and also admit that they had previously been thinking of suspension as including taking no attitude. While they now don't treat suspension of judgment as a mere absence, they continue to accept the 'extreme implication of (EC). that belief or disbelief is the fitting attitude whenever the evidence is not counterbalanced' (76), and indeed think that belief is fitting even when the evidence only slightly favors p over ~p. This continues to seem wrong to us, and we aren't persuaded by their argument for it on (76–78), which doesn't engage with views on which higher-order evidence provides reasons for suspension, a view which is especially compelling given an understanding of evidence as an indication of truth (which they accept on p. 77).

cases of higher-order defeat (e.g., Christensen (2010)'s Drugs case) are best understood as cases in which there is conclusive evidence for p, but in which suspension remains rational owing to reasons for suspension that derive from the higher-order evidence.

Here it is important not to be misled by the fact that the reasons for suspension derive from something called 'higher-order evidence': For it remains deeply unclear why conclusive evidence for p shouldn't always generate at least a sufficient epistemic reason for believing p. As we've already suggested in previous work, a better approach is to take the intuitions at face value and accept that reasons for suspension are directly given by higher-order evidence. We can then seek a deeper theory, such as either epistemic Kantianism or epistemic consequentialism, to unify reasons for belief given by first-order evidence and reasons for suspension given by higher-order evidence.

Let's take stock of the main points, which give us some initial desiderata on a better account. The first point is that the evidence-for relation doesn't seem to be the right kind of thing to relate reasons for suspension and suspension. The second related point is that we don't have a compelling evidentialist account of higher-order defeat. The final point is that we don't have a sufficiently fundamental and unified view about what makes certain reasons for belief and certain reasons for suspending both qualify as epistemic. A better account should provide such a view and explain higher-order defeat in doing so.

Early Virtue Epistemology, Reasons for Suspension, and Ex Post Justification

So much on *ex ante* justification. Let's now consider how suspension creates a problem for attractive theories of *ex post* justification. For narrative unity and simplicity, we'll focus on reliabilist virtue epistemology in its early form in Sosa (2007). Parallel points arise for process reliabilism, Conee and Feldman (2004: 106), and Tang (2015).

Let's first back up again and reflect on what is promising about virtue epistemology in comparison with evidentialism. As we (Lord and Sylvan 2020) and others (Turri 2010 and Goldman 2012) have noted, evidentialism doesn't provide an attractive account of *ex post* justification without helping itself to tools from other theories. Beliefs can be based on sufficient evidence, but remain unjustified because they are based on it in the wrong way. Evidentialism doesn't tell us about how to discriminate between good and bad ways of basing beliefs on evidence. Here Conee and Feldman have long been unconcerned (as have other internalists, like Fumerton 1995: 92). They doubt that cases of irresponsible belief-formation should be addressed by a theory of epistemic justification rather than an ethics of belief. It is, however, hard to believe that we can ignore the goodness or badness of inferences in an account of *ex post* justification. As we've suggested in Lord and Sylvan (2020), it is wise at this stage for reasons-based epistemologists in general to consider invoking a tool from virtue epistemology—that is, competence—and to hold that *ex post* justification be understood in terms of competent basing on good epistemic reasons.

Although we think that a notion of competence will play some important role in the theory of *ex post* justification, we do not think that existing non-hybrid versions of virtue epistemology provide a satisfactory account of justified suspending. The core problem is simple. The main point can be seen by considering the barest version of teleological virtue theory (although it applies more generally). A *simple veritist* virtue theorist maintains that *true belief* is the fundamental epistemic value and that epistemic activities *aim* at this value. The proper *method* for achieving this aim is the manifestation of *epistemic competences to believe truly*. Since we are focusing on justification, we just need to focus on cases where such competences are manifested.

This account does a nice job with beliefs. Consider Colin and Harry. Both believe that *Bake Off* is on tomorrow. Harry believes this because he infers it competently from his knowledge that today is Monday and *Bake Off* is on Tuesdays. Colin, on the other hand, believes *Bake Off* is on tomorrow because he inferred it from his unjustified belief that starting tomorrow there will be a new episode of *Bake Off* every day for 10 years.

Colin doesn't manifest a competence to believe truly, whereas Harry does. This gives a nice explanation of why Harry is *ex post* justified and Colin is not. But, unfortunately for teleological virtue theory, this view can't explain justified suspension in a straightforward way. The problem is very simple: Competences to *believe* truly essentially produce beliefs. So if *ex post* justified reactions are always the products of competences to believe truly, it looks like suspension will never be *ex post* justified. But this is clearly false.

In response, the teleological virtue epistemologist has a few options:

1. Invoke some other kind of competence to explain justified suspension.
2. Abandon the view that the fundamental epistemic aim is truth and find an aim that can be commonly advanced by believing and suspending.
3. Distinguish between proper and degenerate or offshoot manifestations of a disposition to X and say that suspension involves this kind of manifestation.
4. Hold that it is possible for both believing and suspending to be equally direct manifestations of a competence to believe truly (... or to know).

Option (1) seems ad hoc, and to abandon the project of giving a unified account of epistemic justification. Some teleological virtue epistemologists (e.g., Miracchi 2015) have already applied (3) to cases in which one tries but fails to achieve the aim (e.g., cases of justified false belief). But while (3) may be a plausible move in such cases, it will need to be stretched and applied in a very different way to explain cases of justified suspending, since one is not trying but failing to achieve the aim in these cases. Option (4) strikes us as inconsistent with a simple general thought in the metaphysics of dispositions, on which the direct manifestation of a disposition to X must be X-ing in appropriate conditions. Since one refrains from X-ing precisely when the appropriate conditions for manifesting the disposition to X do not obtain, the manifestation conditions for X-ing and refraining from X-ing are surely different. But a disposition to X just is a disposition to X in the manifestation conditions appropriate for X-ing. So it is hard to see how it could be possible for X-ing and refraining from X-ing to equally be manifestations of the disposition to X.[3] Finally, (2) will not help if one accepts the most plausible alternative views about what the fundamental epistemic aim might be. The most plausible candidates are truth, knowledge, and understanding. Suspending advances none of these aims.[4] Having justified doxastic attitudes is epistemically valuable, but it seems to be derivatively so. And if it were a fundamental epistemic value, one could not give a non-circular and informative account of epistemic justification by understanding it as a manifestation of a competence to achieve epistemic justification.

This problem is known to teleological virtue theorists, and is the basis of the recent exchange between Sosa (2019) and Miracchi (2019), who are both concerned by it. Miracchi focuses her discussion on what she calls Rational Parity:

> **Rational Parity:** The features that make epistemic rational assessment applicable to suspension are the very same features that make such assessment applicable to beliefs.

A simple veritist who wants to vindicate the possibility of justified suspension must give up on Rational Parity. That is, they must embrace option (1) above. Suspension cannot be the product of a competence to believe truly. Simple veritists explain the justification of beliefs in terms of manifesting competences to believe truly. So they must explain the

---

3 Might one claim that there is some other multi-track disposition, not itself the disposition to X, which has X-ing whenever the conditions are appropriate for X-ing and refraining from X-ing whenever the conditions are appropriate for refraining from X-ing as its manifestations? Yes, but the relevant multi-track disposition in the epistemic case is a disposition to form doxastic attitudes in accordance with the reasons. So this view would appear to converge with the kind of view we suggest below.
4 This problem thus plagues virtue-theoretic views that appeal to understanding as well (e.g., Schafer 2018, 2019).

justification of suspension in a different way than they explain the justification of belief.

Sosa (2019) wants to hold on to Rational Parity, which pushes him to amend the relevant aim and go for option (2) above. A full discussion of Sosa's views is beyond our scope. We agree with Miracchi that (i) Sosa's view doesn't explain all cases of justified suspension and (ii) the aim he appeals to overintellectualizes.

Miracchi responds by rejecting Rational Parity. She provides differing explanations of the justification of suspension and belief (thus going with option (1)). According to Miracchi, epistemic virtue not only includes aiming to get what is fundamentally valuable (knowledge, in her view), but also includes *respecting* the aim of getting what is fundamentally valuable. This respecting, she claims, is 'derivative' from the fundamental aim. Miracchi's view about *ex post* justification is thus disjunctive. One is *ex post* justified just in case (i) one manifests a disposition to believe knowledgeably or (ii) manifests respect for the aim of knowing by suspending.

Disjunctive views are always disunified. While Miracchi has something to say about the connection between the disjuncts, it is still worth asking whether more unity can be found. We think that Miracchi goes wrong by holding onto a teleological virtue theory. We can hold on to Rational Parity and its unity by adopting a Kantian virtue theory. Explicating such a theory is the task for the next section.

Before we get to that, though, it is worth taking stock about what we want from an epistemology of suspension. First of all, an ideal theory of justified suspension should possess the following unity desiderata:

(U1) It should illuminate how reasons for suspending can be epistemic in the same way in which evidence-provided reasons for belief are epistemic.
(U2) It should illuminate how justified suspending and justified believing manifest fundamentally the same kind of epistemic competence.
(U3) It should be compatible with a unified and plausible account of epistemic value and the relationship between epistemic value and epistemic norms.
(U4) It should be able to explain the epistemic standing of all varieties of suspending.

We haven't yet seen an account that satisfies all these desiderata. Evidentialism primarily stumbles on U1 and U3. Sosa's virtue epistemology primarily stumbles on U4. Miracchi's virtue epistemology mainly has trouble with U2 and U3.

There are more specific desiderata that emerge from the discussion of higher-order evidence. A theory of justified suspension should ideally be able to explain how suspending on the basis of higher-order evidence could be justified even if the first-order evidence is conclusive. This task has two parts. On the one hand, a story needs to be told about how there could be a sufficient epistemic reason for suspending even in a case of misleading higher-order evidence; this story concerns *ex ante* justification for suspending. On the other hand, a story needs to be told about what competence is employed in responding to this reason for suspending; this story concerns *ex post* justification for suspending. So far we haven't seen an account that captures these desiderata without flouting the unity desiderata.

Suspension of Judgment, Evidence, and Respecting Reality

While both of our animating problems are simple to state, adequately solving them requires comprehensive views of the nature of suspension of judgment and, more grandiosely, the structure of epistemic normativity. Our strategy will be to first sketch our view about the nature of suspension and reasons for suspension. This will allow us to defend a view about *ex ante* justification that avoids the problems for evidentialism and vindicates the proper place for higher-order evidence.

After this, we will turn to *ex post* justification. We will argue that a certain Kantian virtue-theoretic view about epistemic normativity does a much better job with U1-U4 than teleological views.

The Nature and Rational Profile of Suspension

Suspension of judgment is a *reaction*. Merely lacking belief is not sufficient for suspension of judgment. But it is importantly different from belief insofar as it is, to use Sturgeon's (2010) apt phrase, a type of *committed neutrality*. When you suspend about whether p, you stand in some rationally evaluable relation toward p, but *not* because you have a commitment about the *truth-value* of p. Belief and disbelief are the reactions which involve that sort of commitment.

Crucially, there are several different types of committed neutrality. On our view, all of them have has their objects the *question* <whether p?>. What differentiates them is how they relate the subject to the question. There is a spectrum of forms of suspension. What the spectrum measures is how *open-minded* the subject is about the question.

This allows us to distinguish two different families of suspension (see Lord and Sylvan (forthcoming) for the full details). The first family contains *open-minded* forms of suspension. We think that there are two forms of open-minded suspension worth theorizing about. First, there is strong open-minded suspension. When one is strongly open-minded about <whether p?>, one *merely* wonders about whether p. When one is in this state, one is disposed to respond to reasons to take a more committed stand on the question, although whether one ends up being more committed is determined by other factors—most pressingly, whether there are sufficient reasons to be in a more committal state. Since this state is the most non-committal form of suspension, we think there is strong reason to think it is the foundational attitude of inquiry.[5]

Next we have weak open-minded suspension. When one is weakly open-minded about <whether p?>, one is in an inquisitive state of mind that disposes one to *settle* the question. This is the form of suspension one adopts when one is *investigating* the question.[6] This is the way in which Barry ought to suspend judgment in Even Split. He should adopt an inquisitive attitude that attunes him to evidence that settles the question of what color ball will come out. In his case this is not difficult since he himself will be the one pulling the ball. As any researcher will tell you, other cases present further difficulties.

Open-minded suspension is one family. That family involves *inquisitive* attitudes. Close-minded suspension is the other family. It involves *agnostic* attitudes. Once again there are two forms worth investigating. Weak close-minded suspension involves mere agnositicism, which is a state of mind that disposes you to treat both your evidence for p and your evidence for ¬p as insufficient. In contrast, strong close-minded suspension involves these dispositions *plus* dispositions to *ignore* evidence that bears on <whether p?>. The reason why it is important to differentiate between these two mental states is that sometimes one can know (or be very confident) that no future evidence will be able to settle the question. In these cases, it makes sense to *insulate* oneself from the question by being strongly close-minded. But these cases are fairly extreme, and more often one should have a more unsettled form of agnosticism. This weaker form doesn't insulate one from the question. In contrast with the weaker form of open-minded suspension, it also doesn't dispose one to settle the question. It leaves one merely neutral between belief and disbelief (which is why, historically, it has been the main competitor with weak open-minded suspension in debates that presuppose there is only one kind of suspension (see Lord and Sylvan (forthcoming, Section 3.1) for more on the history)).

So, on one end of the spectrum you have full open-mindedness toward the question—mere wondering. On the other you have full close-mindedness toward the question—a state that insulates you from the question. In the middle you have two types of moderate state. One involves

---

5 The basic reason why is that all of the other attitudes (the other forms of suspension and belief/disbelief) rule each other out. Strong open-minded suspension is the only attitude that is completely neutral when it comes to the others. It seems like we need an attitude like this at the beginning of inquiry otherwise inquiries will always be prejudiced against some of the options. See Lord and Sylvan (forthcoming).

6 For this reason, Jane Friedman (2017, 2019) maintains that it is something like weak open-minded neutrality that is at the foundation of inquiry. For reasons stated in the previous note, we don't think this is quite right.

dispositions to investigate the question; the other involves a sort of mere neutrality between belief and disbelief.

Given that these states have very different functional profiles, they also have quite different rational profiles. Thus, the sorts of considerations that provide reasons to be in these states are diverse. To wit: Reasons to be strongly open-minded are considerations that favor wondering <whether p?>; reasons to be weakly open-minded are considerations that favor investigating <whether p?>; reasons to be weakly close-minded are considerations that favor being merely neutral between belief and disbelief; and reasons to be strongly close-minded are considerations that favor insulating oneself from the question <whether p?>.

A helpful way of thinking of this spectrum is to think of it from the perspective of inquiry. Strong open-minded suspension is the only option completely neutral with respect to the others, and thus lays claim to being the fundamental inquisitive state. The others, by contrast, are all states that can be the *result* of wondering—that is, of being strongly open-minded—at least temporarily. In other words, when you are strongly open-minded, you open yourself up to responding to the reasons to be in a more committal state. These are the reasons to suspend in one of the other three ways, the reasons to believe, and the reasons to disbelieve.

The Diversity of Epistemic Reasons

First things first, the preceding view easily allows us to solve the problem plaguing Reasons=Evidence. The fact that the evidence is evenly split comes out directly as a reason to suspend, on our view. As we said in the previous section, Barry ought to be weakly open-minded about whether the ball picked is red. The fact that the evidence is evenly split provides a decisive reason to be weakly open-minded, in his case.

More generally, many non-evidential facts will provide reasons to suspend judgment in each variety. This allows us to explain the rational impact of higher-order evidence. Higher-order evidence provides reasons to suspend judgment. These reasons compete with the reasons to believe provided by the evidence. The reasons to suspend can outweigh these reasons to believe, even if they are misleading. This is no more strange than misleading reasons for belief beating out weaker reasons that happen to point to the truth. This discharges the burden of explaining how misleading higher-order evidence can make suspension *ex ante* justified. (Again, we'll discuss *ex post* rationality in the next section.)

This does not exhaust the importance of non-evidential reasons to suspend. To see a stark example, consider some cases of justified strongly close-minded suspension. Consider the question of whether Julius Caesar had to go to the bathroom when he was murdered. This is a good candidate for a question we ought to be strongly close-minded about. This is partly because it is very, very unlikely any evidence will ever surface that settles the question. But it is also because it is *unimportant*. It is not something it is worth having a view about. Now, of course, things might be different if there was decisive evidence staring you in the face—if a reliable chronicle was at your disposal, say. In that case the reasons to believe would be sufficient. But given that the evidence is unlikely to ever come in, it is not worth one's resources to be open to the question.

A similar, albeit less drastic choice comes up more often. Imagine Beth and Bea are both students in this semester's metaphysics course. They both read the assigned papers on mereology. Let's suppose that, given the papers they read, the evidence fails to sufficiently support any view about unrestricted composition. They both are strongly open-minded about it at the moment—they're in the class after all. We can also stipulate that strong close-minded suspension is irrational for each of them. Their initial investigation through the course is coming to an end and it is time to become more committal. Should they be weakly open-minded or weakly close-minded? We need more information, it seems. Here's some: Beth plans to be a metaphysician and Bea plans to be a philosopher of psychiatry. This, it seems to us, makes a difference. Given these facts, it makes most sense for Beth to be weakly *open*-minded and Bea to be weakly *close*-minded. This is because qua metaphysician it makes sense for Beth to be more inquisitive about unrestricted composition than Bea. Bea's weak close-minded suspension doesn't rule out coming to form other commitments about mereology later; it doesn't even push against that, but given her interests it makes most sense for her to be merely agnostic at the moment.

While this complicates the epistemic calculus, we think that the evidentialist is right about something important. They are right that reasons for *belief* are only provided by the evidence. So Weak Evidentialism about Epistemic Reasons is true:

> **Weak Evidentialism about Epistemic Reasons:** Epistemic reasons for belief are only provided by the evidence.

The mistake made by strong evidentialists was to think that what goes for belief goes for all of the epistemic. Suspending judgment competes with belief and disbelief, and there is a diversity of reasons for suspension. This is why facts about the evidence and higher-order evidence can make it rational to suspend.

Basing and Respect for Reality

The problem accounting for non-evidential reasons for suspension was, first and foremost, a problem in the theory of *ex ante* justification. This is because it is problem for accounting for the variety of considerations that can provide *ex ante* justification for suspension. It is not directly a problem for the notion that is distinctive to *ex post* justification—viz., basing. As we saw in the last section, one of the most promising ways of understanding basing does run into a problem with suspension. This is teleological virtue theory. Since we think that a virtue-theoretic account of basing is the most promising, we must face up to this problem.

The problem, recall, is simple. Teleological virtue theorists maintain that epistemic normativity is structured around a value that is to be aimed at. Simple veritism maintains that the value is true belief. The proper way to get this value is by exercising competences to believe truly. These competences provide a resource for understanding basing. This is for two reasons. First, it looks like competences to believe truly will be sensitive to evidence in the way properly based beliefs are sensitive to the evidence. Second, exercises of competences are achievements, and proper basing is an achievement. The problem, though, is that suspension cannot be the product of a competence to *believe* truly. Only beliefs are the products of such competences.

This is a problem for teleological virtue theory. Suspension is one of the doxastic options. It can be *ex post* justified. Thus, it can be based on sufficient epistemic reasons. It is implausible that we can understand such basing in terms of the competences at the heart of teleological virtue theory. As we saw, Miracchi opted for a disjunctive view that appeals both to competences to know and respect for the aim of knowing. This view lacks a certain sort of unity we think is worth striving to preserve. Fortunately, we can preserve it. We can also preserve virtue theory more generally and a virtue-theoretic account of basing.

This is because one needn't be a teleological virtue theorist. There is also *Kantian* virtue theory. Whereas teleological virtue theory maintains that there is a fundamental epistemic value *to be promoted*, Kantian virtue theory maintains there is a fundamental epistemic value *to be respected*.

A veritist Kantian holds that the fundamental epistemic demand is that truth is to be respected. The competences involved in achieving various specific epistemic statuses are thus analyzed in terms of what it takes to respect the truth. We maintain that normative reasons are central to understanding what it takes to respect the truth. In short, respecting the truth coincides with competently responding to epistemic normative reasons.

This is all the Kantian needs to solve the structural problem for teleological views. This is because reasons for suspension are epistemic normative reasons, since competently responding to them is a way of respecting the truth. This is to the Kantian view what promoting the truth is to the teleological theorist—viz., the fundamental requirement of epistemic normativity. Thus, the Kantian view can easily account for the epistemology of suspension.

This gets us a better virtue-theoretic account of basing:

Competent Basing: A doxastic reaction D's being based on sufficient epistemic reasons R is D's being the output of an exercise of a competence to D for the reasons provided by R.

Competent Basing is true because Respecting and Respect are true, in turn.

Respecting: A doxastic reaction D's respecting the truth coincides with D's being the output of a competence to react for normative epistemic reasons.
Respect: 'The value of [truth] is fundamentally to be respected'
(Sylvan 2020, p. 14)

These views, if true, obviously explain at least two of our four desiderata:

(U2) It should illuminate how (*ex post*) justified suspending and (*ex post*) justified believing manifest fundamentally the same kind of epistemic competence.
(U3) It should be compatible with a unified and plausible account of epistemic value and the relationship between epistemic value and epistemic norms.

Start with (U2). The Kantian maintains that *ex post* justified suspenders and *ex post* justified believers manifest the same kind of epistemic competence. They manifest the competence of believing for sufficient epistemic reasons.

This, in turn, is a manifestation of a respect for the truth. And this allows the (veritist) Kantian to explain (U3). For the veritist Kantian, truth is the fundamental epistemic value. Epistemic norms are related to this value by articulating what it takes to respect it. To respect it coincides with correctly responding to epistemic reasons. So the account is compatible with a unified and plausible account of epistemic value—veritism— and it gives a plausible account of the relationship between that value and epistemic norms.

This leaves two desiderata that demand more explanation:

(U1) It should illuminate how reasons for suspending can be epistemic in the same way in which evidence-provided reasons for belief are epistemic.
(U4) It should be able to explain the epistemic standing of all varieties of suspending.

To be clear, if everything we have said is true, the Kantian view does easily explain these two desiderata. This is because we've claimed that

(i) reasons for suspension are epistemic reasons, (ii) what it is to respect the truth is to respond to epistemic reasons, and (iii) the fundamental epistemic duty is to respect the truth. If these are all right, then (U1) is vindicated because reasons for suspension and reasons for belief are both epistemic in virtue of standing in the same relation to respecting the truth. Further, all varieties of suspension have epistemic standing because they are all ways to appropriately respect the truth in some circumstances.

What needs more discussion is the claim that correctly responding to all of the reasons for suspension we have posited is a way of respecting the truth. Let's start with (U4). A vindication of (U1) will follow from our story about (U4).

Note, first, that a ubiquitous feature of cases where suspension is epistemically permitted is that the evidence is insufficient.[7] Next notice that weak close-minded suspension *merely* tracks this. It does this by disposing you to treat the evidence as insufficient. Because of this, it is natural to see weak close-minded suspension as being the default reaction to insufficient evidence. Further, it is no mystery that respect for the truth sometimes demands weak close-minded suspension. Because of this, it is no mystery that weak close-minded suspension has epistemic standing and that reasons for it are epistemic.

Nevertheless, in some cases it is plausible that one of our other suspensive attitudes is called for. The vast majority of us should be strongly close-minded about whether Caesar had to go to the bathroom when he was murdered. Not only should we be disposed to treat the evidence as insufficient, we should also be disposed to ignore this question. One explanation of this appeals just to facts about the evidence. Perhaps strong close-minded suspension is called for solely because no sufficient evidence will ever be unearthed. Sometimes this will explain why close-minded suspension is required. Other times, though, the fact that the question is *unimportant* might also explain why one should be strongly close-minded. This demands an explanation from the Kantian. What role does tracking such importance play in respecting the truth?

A similar question arises for weak open-minded suspension. Take Beth and Bea from above. Beth should be weakly open-minded about whether unrestricted composition is true, whereas Bea should be weakly close-minded about whether unrestricted composition is true. Their evidence is the same. What makes the difference, it seems, is that Beth is a budding metaphysician whereas Bea is a budding philosopher of psychiatry. Once again, it seems like a question being important is playing a role in

---

7 We don't think this is always the case because we think there is a standing entitlement to be strongly open-minded—i.e., to wonder. We think one can rationally wonder about whether p even if one knows p—see Lord and Sylvan (forthcoming). For all the others, though, we think they are justified only if the evidence is insufficient.

explaining why one form of suspension is required. What role does tracking such importance play in respecting the truth?

Note that one way of understanding the demands of respect is that they merely impose a negative constraint: Respecting truth is a matter of not disrespecting it, by never forming attitudes in ways that are negligent or reckless relative to the norm of truth. This form of Kantianism might seem to resemble non-consequentialist moral theories that treat respect as imposing side-constraints, but not as generating positive duties. Respect for persons cannot, one might think, require universal beneficence: It is not disrespectful of personhood to refrain from devoting as much energy to others' projects as to one's own. But this fact only shows that respect yields no perfect duty to help others wherever possible. It could still generate imperfect positive duties, as Kant thought, which allow some leeway. The leeway for particular agents could then be restricted by special features of their circumstances, such as their relationships and commitments.

By analogy, then, we suggest that respect for truth generates an imperfect duty to do justice to reality by forming a sufficiently complete view of it. To remain clueless about reality is to be cognitively unhinged. There is a duty, not just an enticing reason, to have a clue. To be sure, one cannot be expected to settle every question, just as one cannot be expected to come to the aid of everyone in need. Which facts one must be settle will depend on one's circumstances. Just as one's relationships can serve to direct the standing imperfect duty to help others in need to specific others, by requiring one to assist those to whom one has commitments, so too can one's inquisitive commitments direct the standing imperfect duty to have a clue, by requiring one to settle the questions one has taken up (insofar as they are answerable).

This explains Beth and Bea. Their wider intellectual projects make a difference to which questions they have reason to pursue. For Beth, her wider intellectual project helps explain why she has reason to be disposed to settle whether unrestricted composition is true. Pursuing this question is one way in which she seeks to do justice to reality and thus discharge her positive duty generated by the duty to respect the truth. This explains why weak open-mindedness has epistemic standing. (It also explains why strong open-mindedness has epistemic standing, since that state is the most fundamental inquisitive attitude and inquiry is at the base of pursuing reality and thus discharging one's positive imperfect duty.)

The explanation of the epistemic standing of strong closed-minded suspension is parasitic on this. We do not have unlimited resources for inquiry. Pursuing a certain set of questions prevents us from pursuing others. Thus, how well we do discharging our imperfect duty to pursue reality will partly depend on how we use these resources. Pursuing unimportant or unanswerable questions will usually be a bad way of using these resources and thus a bad way of pursuing reality. Given that respecting the truth partly consists in pursuing reality, we can now see how tracking importance and answerability is epistemically important. This explains why strong close-minded suspension has epistemic standing.

This explains (U4)—why all forms of suspension have epistemic standing. With this in hand, we can explain (U1)—why reasons for suspension are epistemic in the same way the evidence is. They are epistemic because they are reasons for states that are constitutively tied to respecting the truth. It is natural to see weak close-minded suspension as being constitutively tied to our negative duty to respect the truth by not being negligent and to see the other three as being constitutively tied to our positive duty to respect the truth by pursuing reality.

Putting Things Together

We know from experience that it doesn't ruffle many feathers to say that *ex ante* justification is determined by epistemic reasons and that *ex post* justification is a matter of competently responding to epistemic reasons. This can sound close to textbook. One lesson of this chapter is that in order to plausibly maintain these views, one needs to reject some very popular views. This is because suspension of judgment cannot be handled in exactly the same way as beliefs. Evidentialists run into trouble with *ex ante* justification, whereas teleological virtue theorists run into trouble with *ex post* justification.

These problems are not insurmountable, though. The problem with taking evidentialism too seriously is that it causes us to be blind to non-evidential reasons to suspend. Once we understand more about the nature of suspension, it is not costly to expand our notion of an epistemic reason. The problem for teleology runs deeper. Epistemic goods are not *promoted* by suspension. So anyone who thinks of epistemic goods as to be promoted is going to have serious troubles with suspension. As we've seen, this leads some to a sort of gerrymandered hybrid view that involves both promotion and respect.

Rather than go for the gerrymandered, we advocate rejecting teleology altogether. Epistemic value is not to be promoted, it is to be respected. It is plausible that proper suspension involves respecting the truth. So the Kantian view not only lacks the problem that plagues teleological views, it elegantly explains suspension's role in the epistemic.

One of our main conclusions is that accounting for the epistemology of suspension requires the rejection of well-entrenched views. Even if you are not ready to deny those views, one lesson of this chapter is that epistemologists shouldn't treat suspension as a side act; it needs to be accounted for in the very foundations of one's epistemology.

We've now achieved our main objective: Spelling out a precise view of the justification of suspension of judgment. Here is a recap in reverse order.

At the bottom we have the main tenets of our Kantian epistemology:

Respect: The value of [truth] is fundamentally to be respected.
(Sylvan 2020: 14)

Respecting: What it is for A's doxastic reaction D to respect the truth is for D to be the output of an exercise of a competence to react for normative epistemic reasons.

Respect is a rockbottom truth about the epistemic. Respecting is an analysis of what it takes to do what Respect demands.

From here we can get an analysis of *ex post* justification. *Ex post* justification results when one exercises one's competences to react for (sufficient) normative epistemic reasons. This is to say that one bases one's epistemic reactions on normative epistemic reasons when one exercises the competences that constitute respect for the truth. This gets us Reasons-First about *ex post* Justification:

Reasons-First about *ex post* Justification: What it is for doxastic reaction D to be *ex post* justified for A is for A to exercise a competence to D for epistemic reasons that sufficiently support D.

Finally, we can state an account of *ex ante* justification:

Reasons-First about *ex ante* Justification: What it is for doxastic reaction D to be *ex ante* justified for A is for A's epistemic reasons to sufficiently support D.

The Epistemic and the Zetetic: A Reappraisal

To close, we draw the frame out to consider some consequences of the view just sketched for the relationship between the epistemic and the zetetic—the domain of normativity that governs inquiry. Friedman (2020) argues that traditional analytic epistemology does not sit well with zetetic considerations that one might think are naturally within the domain of the epistemic. Her discussion is organized around a particular case, which we've slightly modified:

Chrysler Count: Martha is in the window business, and it has become important for her to know how many windows the Chrysler Building has. Given her close proximity to the building, she decides the best method of finding out is going to Grand Central Station and counting. This task takes a full 90 minutes of her time and concentration, during which she fails to extend her knowledge about other matters.

What's of interest to Friedman are the norms that govern Martha during this time. On the one hand, it seems like the zetetic norms permit and perhaps even require that she stay focused on the counting task. The question that concerns Martha qua inquirer during this time is the question of how many windows there are, and her taking up this question explains the zetetic facts.

There are several tensions between the epistemic and the zetetic that this sort of case can bring out. We'll focus on this one: It seems like it should always be epistemically permitted to know what one is in a position to know, but it often seems zetetically forbidden. After all, Martha will not come to know how many windows there are unless she *ignores* the evidence available to her about hot dog vendors and shipping details. Her inquiry into the windows demands that she ignore some evidence that bears on other questions for the time being. This, thinks Friedman, should give traditional analytic epistemologists the heebie-jeebies. Her instinct is to expand the epistemic to include at least some of the zetetic.

We share her instinct; and the views presented in this chapter provide an explanation of what is going on in Chrysler Count. Martha has decisive reason to be weakly open-minded about how many windows the Chrysler building has. Given the specifics of her situation, the dispositions involved in this open-mindedness will manifest in counting the windows. These dispositions *cannot manifest* if she attends to the question of how many hot dog vendors there are or to the question of how many trucks are needed. Thus, her reasons to be weakly open-minded about the one question provide her reasons *against* being open-minded about these further questions. Thus, at least for a certain period of time, she is at least indirectly epistemically required to be closed-minded about the questions that are irrelevant to her window inquiry, since she is zetetically required to complete her thinking on the question she's taken up, and satisfying this requirement entails not opening her mind to the question of how many hot dog vendors there are.

We agree with Friedman that this implication is unexpected by the lights of the post-Gettier conception of epistemology, and she is right that this will rub some the wrong way. But what is important is that our view about the epistemology of suspension of judgment provides an elegant explanation of this implication that is not far from traditional epistemology. This is because it provides the resources for explaining both when inquisitiveness is called for and when it is not. These resources are epistemic all the way down. Not only are they epistemic because suspension competes with belief and disbelief, but also because we have a view about how suspension and its reasons are related to the foundational norm of the epistemic—to respect the truth. We are required to ignore certain questions on occasion because respecting the truth demands that we sometimes pursue the truth. What these cases bring out is that for agents like us, successfully pursuing reality demands that we focus our attention in ways that are incompatible with the arbitrary pursuit of knowledge.

Our goal in this section hasn't been to fully defend these claims. Rather, it has been to show how the views defended here can be fruitfully applied to Friedman's puzzle. Our view is attractive partly because it can pull the zetetic and epistemic together in cases where it looks like they might need to come apart. Thus, the zetetic turn in epistemology doesn't need to be as extreme as Friedman suggests.

References

Christensen, D. (2010). Higher-order evidence. *Philosophy and Phenomenological Research*, 81(1), 185–215.
Conee, E. Feldman, R. (2004). Evidentialism: Essays in Epistemology. Oxford University Press.
Conee, E. Feldman, R. (2005). Some Virtues of Evidentialism. Veritas.
Conee, E. Feldman, R. (2018). Between belief and disbelief. In K. McCain (Ed.), Believing in Accordance with the Evidence: New Essays on Evidentialism (71–89). Springer.
Fantl, J. McGrath, M. (2010). Knowledge in an Uncertain World. Oxford University Press.
Feldman, R. (2005). Justification is internal. In M. Steup (Ed.), Contemporary Debates in Epistemology (pp. 270–284). Blackwell.
Friedman, J. (2013). Suspended judgment. Philosophical Studies, 162(2), 165–181.
Friedman, J. (2017). Why suspend judging? Noûs, 50(4), 302–326.
Friedman, J. (2019). Inquiry and belief. Noûs, 53(2), 296–315.
Friedman, J. (2020). The epistemic and the zetetic. Philosophical Review, 129(4), 501–536.
Friedman, J. (Forthcoming). Zetetic epistemology. In Baron Reed and A. K. Flowerree (Eds.), Towards an Expansive Epistemology: Norms, Action, and the Social Sphere. Routledge.
Fumerton, R. (1995). Metaepistemology and Skepticism. Rowman Littlefield.
Goldman, A. (1979). What is justified belief? In G. Pappas (Ed.), Justification and Knowledge (pp. 1–25). D. Reidel.
Goldman, A. (2012). Reliabilism and Contemporary Epistemology. Oxford University Press.
Lord, E. Sylvan, K. (2020). Prime time (for the Basing Relation). In P. Bondy J. A. Carter (Eds.), Well-Founded Belief: New Essays on the Basing Relation (pp. 141–174). Routledge.
Lord, E. Sylvan, K. (2021). Reasons to suspend, higher-order evidence, and defeat. In J. Brown M. Simion (Eds.), Reasons, Justification, and Defeat. Oxford University Press.
Lord, E. Sylvan, K. (forthcoming). Beginning in wonder: Suspensive attitudes and epistemic dilemmas. In N. Hughes (Ed.), Epistemic Dilemmas. Oxford University Press.
Miracchi, L. (2015). Knowledge is all you need. Philosophical Issues, 25(1), 353–378.

Miracchi, L. (2019). When evidence isn't enough: Suspension, evidentialism, and knowledge-first virtue epistemology. Episteme, 16, 413–437.
Schafer, K. (2018). A kantian virtue epistemology: Rational capacities and transcendental arguments. Synthese, 198, 3113–3136.
Schafer, K. (2019). Rationality as the capacity for understanding. Noûs, 53(3), 639–663.
Sosa, E. (2007). A Virtue Epistemology. Oxford University Press.
Sosa, E. (2010). Knowing Full Well. Princeton University Press.
Sosa, E. (2015). Judgment and Agency. Oxford University Press.
Sosa, E. (2019). Suspension as spandrel. Episteme, 16(4), 357–368.
Sturgeon, S. (2010). Confidence and coarse-grained attitudes. In T. S. Gendler J. Hawthorne (Eds.), Oxford Studies in Epistemology (pp. 3–126). Oxford University Press.
Sylvan, K. (2020). An epistemic non-consequentialism. The Philosophical Review, 129, 1–51.
Tang, W. (2015). Reliabilism and suspension of belief. Australasian Journal of Philosophy, 94, 362–377.
Turri, J. (2010). On the relationship between propositional and doxastic justification. Philosophy and Phenomenological Research, 80(2), 312–326.

10 Propositional and Doxastic Hinge Assumptions[1]

Annalisa Coliva

In *Extended Rationality. A Hinge Epistemology*, I put forward a moderate account of perceptual justification, according to which a belief about specific material objects that P is perceptually justified iff, absent defeaters, one has the appropriate course of experience (typically an experience with content that P), and it is *assumed* that H "there is an external world" (and possibly other general propositions, like "My sense organs work mostly reliably", "I am not the victim of massive cognitive deception", etc.).[2]

Since, in my view, "There is an external world" is a "hinge" proposition—for it makes the acquisition of perceptual justification possible—the crucial issue is to determine the nature of hinge assumptions. Do they have to be doxastically assumed by a subject in the process of offering a justification for her belief that P, or can we think of these assumptions as being operative at the propositional level? And what would that mean?

In this chapter, I defend various interlocking claims. First, that there is a legitimate sense in which hinge assumptions are to be cashed out, first and foremost, at the propositional level, or "in the abstract space

---

1 I would like to thank the editors of the volume and Robert Audi for very useful comments on a previous version of this chapter. As always, any remaining mistakes are my sole responsibility.
2 One word of caution about my terminology. Like in Coliva (2015), I will be talking about assumptions in the following. Now, in ordinary parlance, we may also refer to them as beliefs. I have no qualms with that, provided one didn't build into the notion of belief the fact that it must be based on some kind of evidence that would make it suitable for knowledge (as Wright 2004 and Pritchard 2015 do, for instance). If one did, then the terms "assumption" and "belief" would no longer be interchangeable, for reasons that will become apparent in the following. Furthermore, Robert Audi has suggested that I should call them "presuppositions", since this would better fit the case, I will consider in the following, of a child who does not have the conceptual resources to entertain their contents but behaves in conformity with them. I think the terms are largely interchangeable and by "assumption" I certainly don't mean anything that would be incompatible with Audi's suggestion. Should a reader find that terminology more perspicuous, they could substitute "presupposition" for "assumption" (and their cognates).

DOI: 10.4324/9781003008101-14

of reasons". Second, that this does not pre-empt the possibility that they also obtain at the doxastic level (§1). To such an end, I spell out what assuming a hinge proposition at the doxastic level amounts to, in such a way that even subjects who do not have the conceptual resources to entertain its content may be granted with such an assumption.

I then distinguish three possible senses of assuming doxastically that H (§2): one hypothetical, one categorical, and one factual. I claim that while both the second and the third sense are compatible with the moderate account of perceptual justification, only the second is compatible with the development of a non-dogmatic response to skepticism and is therefore preferable.

Along the way, I compare and contrast my account of hinge assumptions with Gilbert Harman's and, in closing I defend it from objections raised by Crispin Wright (§3).

Propositional and Doxastic Hinge Assumptions

The moderate account of perceptual justification consists in the following:

> **Moderate account of perceptual justification**: a belief about specific material objects that P is perceptually justified iff, absent defeaters, one has the appropriate course of experience (typically an experience with content that P) and it is assumed that (H) there is an external world (and possibly other general propositions, e.g. "My sense organs work mostly reliably", "I am not the victim of massive cognitive deception", etc.)

Moderates, like liberals, such as Pryor (2000, 2004), and conservatives, such as Wright (1985, 2004), are concerned, foremost, with propositional justifications. Propositional justifications are those justifications there are, in the abstract space of reasons, for propositions which may become the content a subject's belief. When that happens and the belief is held based on those justifications, then the belief is doxastically justified. Hence, it is not required that subjects be able to entertain the proposition that there is an external world. Even less is it required, were they able to entertain it, that they had to do so explicitly any time they go about forming a perceptual justification for their ordinary empirical beliefs. The basic idea, therefore, is that the information that there is an external world figures as one of the constitutive ingredients of perceptual justification "in the abstract space of reasons". What this metaphor means, in my view, is simply that *qua* theorists is incumbent upon us to specify the constitutive conditions of perceptual justification for propositions which may be the object of subjects' beliefs. In this respect, our activity is no different from the one of mathematicians producing a proof of a given theorem. The steps in the proof need not be believed or even grasped by ordinary folks, who may nonetheless appeal to the theorem and take it to be justified.[3] Nor do they need to be believed by mathematicians as they develop the proof, although most of the times they are. Rather, they are propositions appropriately related to one another, such that the theorem, which is in fact another proposition, turns out thereby to be justified. Thus, the propositions which enter any step of the proof constitute the justification of the conclusion, irrespective of being believed either by ordinary folks or theorists. Similarly, the conditions, which we, *qua* theorists, identify as constitutive of propositional justification for empirical beliefs based on perception, need not be believed or grasped by ordinary folks who may nonetheless be justified in believing those empirical propositions, once the constitutive conditions for perceptual justification are satisfied and those beliefs are formed on appropriate bases.

Within such an abstract specification of the conditions that need to obtain for perceptual justification to be possible, the proposition that there is an external world needs to be posited. For, only by doing so it is possible for a subject's perceptual evidence—for example as of a hand—to be legitimately taken to bear onto the truth of a proposition about a material object—for example "Here is my hand"—which may in turn be the content of a subject's belief. Absent such an assumption, that experience would equally speak in favor of the skeptical counterpart of the latter proposition—for example "I am a handless brain in a vat hallucinating having a hand" (see White 2006). This way, moderatism can overcome the crucial problem of liberalism.

Contrary to conservatives, however, moderates do not further require that such an assumption be justified—evidentially or otherwise (*contra* Wright 2004, but also Wedgwood 2013 and Sosa 2013). Its positing is either considered a- or only pragmatically rational (see Strawson 1985, Wittgenstein 1969, Pritchard 2015, James 1986), or else as epistemically rational because constitutive of epistemic rationality itself (Coliva 2015).

Pursuing the analogy with mathematical proofs, the assumption of a hinge proposition is comparable to the positing, within the proof, of one or more of the theory's axioms, which are typically considered to be true, at least within the theory, and, once fixed, aren't (non-circularly) provable within the theory.[4]

Like liberals and conservatives, moderates too are internalist with respect to justification. Nonetheless, all that is required to that end is that the hinge assumption be graspable and articulable *at least in principle*

---

3 On the assumption that the theorem is actually proved.
4 Of course, they would be (non-circularly) provable if different propositions within the theory were selected to play an axiom role. Yet, once fixed, axioms are the starting points of any proof and thus cannot be non-circularly derived within the theory.

by subjects endowed with the relevant conceptual repertoire. That is, the minimal condition that needs to be satisfied in order for the moderate account to fall within the internalist camp is that of not positing assumptions that would be beyond subjects' intellectual grasp, because the concepts necessary to grasp them would be unattainable at least for subjects relevantly similar to human beings with respect to their cognitive capacities. It is not required of every subject to have them. Compare again with mathematics: many concepts involved in mathematical reasoning are clearly not possessed by every subject. All it is required is simply that such concepts be attainable by at least some of them. Clearly, the concept of an external world fulfills such a condition.

Yet, there is also a sense in which those subjects who do have the relevant conceptual repertoire could be able to entertain it and take it as a datum, which they could, on occasion, make explicit, and from which they could proceed in order to *claim* perceptual justification, thanks to concomitant appropriate sense experiences.

Therefore, there are in fact two, equally legitimate senses in which we can say that the assumption that there is an external world is one of the constitutive ingredients of perceptual justification. The first sense may be called "propositional" and means simply that the proposition that there is an external world does figure as a constitutive ingredient of perceptual justification in the abstract space of reasons. That is, it is a crucial piece of information that we, *qua* theorists, need to posit for perceptual experience to have a bearing onto the truth of a proposition about specific material objects. Add to that that it must be graspable and articulable, at least in principle, for the ensuing justification to be of an internalist fashion. The second, call it the "doxastic" sense, has it, instead, that such a proposition should actually be entertained by subjects endowed with the relevant conceptual repertoire and be part of what they would offer were they requested to make explicit their own justifications for holding that there is a red table in front of them, say. In this doxastic sense, what I call "assumptions" are relevantly similar to Gilbert Harman's "implicit commitments" (Harman 1986, p. 44). I do not, however, subscribe to Harman's "conservativism", according to which "one is justified in continuing fully to accept something in the absence of a special reason not to" (Harman 1986, p. 46). For the absence of defeaters is not enough for me, like for any moderate, to produce a justification for a given proposition one is implicitly committed to.

Given such a distinction, the problem sometimes raised against both conservatives and moderates—that is, that an assumption such as H figures as part of the justification for one's belief that P seems to preclude the possibility that young children and the unsophisticated could have a perceptual justification for their beliefs about specific material objects—is preempted. For their beliefs can be propositionally justified.

At most, what the moderate view would entail is that such a propositional justification would be rationally unavailable to children and the unsophisticated, since they would not possess the concepts necessary to entertain it.

Yet, I contend that they can be granted with a doxastic justification for their beliefs even in the absence of the ability to entertain such an assumption (or presupposition, see fn. 1), let alone to articulate it. Consider a child who was unable to entertain the proposition that there is an external world, or that there are physical, mind-independent objects, and who would thus be unable to offer it as part of her grounds for her perceptually-based beliefs. One could still grant her with that assumption, provided she were able to take part in a practice which has that very assumption as its rational precondition. Hence, suppose the child said things such as "The red table is in the kitchen. I saw it a moment ago", while she is not there seeing it, or "Someone has removed the red table from the kitchen", while she is in the kitchen and realizes that the red table she saw not long ago isn't there anymore. We could then say that, at least implicitly (or tacitly), she is considering the table as a mind-independent object and is taking her experiences to bear onto a belief about such a kind of entity. Hence, even if she does not have the concept of an external world (or of a physical object) as such and is in no position to make explicit her assumption to that effect, she should be granted with a conception of physical objects as mind-independent entities, as implicitly (or tacitly) as that might be.

Hence, the assumption that there is an external world or at least that there are mind-independent objects can be granted, in the doxastic sense, also to children and unsophisticated creatures, if they meet the previously mentioned requirements. Furthermore, it can certainly be granted to those subjects who, while having the necessary conceptual repertoire, do not explicitly consider it each time they form a belief based on the deliverances of their perceptual experiences, so long as they themselves meet the same requirements imposed on children and the unsophisticated.[5]

---

5 Mikkel Gerken raised the following objection. Suppose that a person had just opened her eyes for the first time and made no assumption about the existence of an external world. By the lights of the moderate position, she could not justifiably believe that she has a hand in front of her (supposing for the sake of argument she had those concepts). Now contrast her with a subject, who assumes that there is an external world and could then justifiably believe that there is a hand in front of her, given the moderate conception of perceptual justification. Clearly, however, the two seem to be epistemically on a par, while moderatism predicts they are not. I think this objection is useful because answering it allows me to further clarify the moderate view. If we are concerned with propositional justification, both are equally justified. If we are concerned with doxastic justification, so long as the first subject has the concept of a hand as a mind-independent entity, she could be granted with the relevant assumption, even if she had never entertained the proposition that there is an external world.

To summarize the distinctions introduced thus far:

To assume H propositionally: in the abstract space of reasons, a proposition H is posited (as a constitutive element of the propositional justification for a specific class of propositions C).

To assume H doxastically: a proposition H (which is a constitutive element of the propositional justification for a specific class of propositions C) is either grasped and possibly appealed to in the course of claiming one's justification for a proposition P, belonging to C; or else, it is such that a subject can participate in an epistemic practice that has H as one of its rational preconditions.[6]

Assuming Doxastically – Three Varieties

Another issue worth considering at this stage is what it means to assume that there is an external world in this doxastic sense. In particular, we have to distinguish three possible species of "assuming" doxastically. First, there is a hypothetical (or suppositional) kind of assuming that merely entails acting *as if* a proposition were true. This would be the sense in which one may entertain an assumption in thought and see what would follow from it, without any special commitment to its truth, or even while thinking (or knowing) that it is in fact false.

In this sense "assuming" would be similar to Harman's "tentative assumptions" (1986, pp. 46–47), which he thinks may be corroborated by future investigations and later on turned into full acceptances. Full acceptances for Harman, however, are attitudes for which one has collated enough evidence to stop inquiring into them. According to him, this is enough to enable a subject to *take* oneself to *know* that a given proposition is true (cf. p. 47). I do not follow Harman's latter suggestion though, for, in my view, hinge assumptions are not knowable, properly speaking. For the putative justifications we could have for them would depend on already taking them for granted. As I have argued at length in Coliva (2015, Chapter 3), this form of bootstrapping justification involves us in a vicious circle. Hence, in my view, whatever evidence we may have for them (i.e. everything we do know does in fact speak in favor of them) does not actually play a justificatory role with respect to them.

Secondly, there is a categorical kind of assuming that involves the *commitment* to the truth of what figures as its content, without thereby entailing that one's assumption is correct because it is a fact that things are thus and so. Finally, there is a factual kind of assuming that holds a given proposition for a *fact*. The second and third sense of "assuming"

---

6 The term "doxastic" is typically taken to involve belief. In the present use of the term, that is not entailed. We are in fact talking about contents of assumptions, which, as we have seen, are not beliefs, at least not if belief is taken to involve having reasons in support of its content (cf. fn. 1).

differ insofar as it is one thing to be committed to the truth of a given proposition, while it is a different thing to hold it for a fact. This terminology may not be entirely transparent, since one could give deflationary readings of "holding for a fact". So, a profitable way of thinking about the distinction is to reflect on the direction of fit. In the former case, it is because the subject holds the target proposition true that things are taken to be as the proposition describes them. In the latter case instead, it is because things are as the proposition describes them that the subject holds that proposition true. To sum up:

> **Hypothetical assuming$_D$**: to act or judge as if a given proposition were true, even if one is uncommittal with respect to its truth or even if one believes or knows that it is in fact false.
>
> **Categorical assuming$_D$**: to be committed in one's acts and judgments to the truth of a given proposition.
>
> **Factual assuming$_D$**: to hold a given proposition for a fact.

Now, I think the second and the third option are both consistent with the moderate position, while the first is not, because it is merely suppositional. However, my own preferences go to the second one. Hence, the mode of assumption characteristic of the moderate position, *as I am characterizing it*, has it that the truth of "There is an external world" is not dogmatically posited, even if it is a tenet of the theory that in our actions and thoughts we are committed to it. In the usual terms of the Euthyphro contrast, the mode of assumption I have in mind is metaphysically anti-realist. This does not mean to say that it is irrealist or idealist—for there is a commitment to the truth of "There is an external world"—but it is not realist either, for no claim is made that it is because it is a *fact* that there is an external world that one is making the corresponding assumption.

Externalist theories of knowledge and justification, in contrast, ultimately do that. For consider: externalist theorists typically say, "given that it is in fact the case that there is an external world, with which we causally interact, thus-and-thus follows". Hence, they hold the existence of the external world for a fact and then start building their respective theories from there. However, if one's epistemology is ultimately driven by the idea of taking skepticism seriously, this casts doubts on the prospects of any externalist account, including disjunctivist accounts,[7] or virtue-theoretic ones *à la* Sosa.[8] For it is simply question-begging to

---

7 Disjunctivist accounts, like McDowell (1982, 1986, 1995) and Pritchard (2015), take it for a fact that, at least in good case scenarios, when we are actually perceiving, there is an external world with which we are causally interacting. Yet they are quite impotent to assuage the skeptical worry concerning how we can know of being perceiving (as opposed to hallucinating) and thus of being causally interacting with an external world.
8 See Sosa (2021), who embraces an externalist moderate position.

assume for a fact that there is an external world in the face of skeptical worries, which challenge the rational legitimacy of such an assumption.

Still, one might think that this way of characterizing the moderate position makes it immediately unsuitable to meet any skeptical challenge. For it seems that a skeptic is precisely inviting us to provide a justification to believe that it is indeed a fact that there is an external world, while the moderate position is not committed to that H being a fact.

As I have argued at length elsewhere (Coliva 2018, 2021), this is not true. For, first, the most powerful antidote to any argument based on radically skeptical scenarios, which raise the possibility that, in ways that are totally unknowable to us, there is no external world (or we are BIVs, etc.), is to avoid thinking of truth as mind-transcendent. That is, as a correspondence between our representations and mind-independent facts, whose obtaining is in principle unknowable to us. Furthermore, the most interesting kind of skeptical challenge, which is one of Humean descent, can be met by redeeming the rationality of the basic assumptions on which perceptual justifications rest. Since on the extended notion of rationality I have been proposing since Coliva (2015) that is not a matter of having justifications that bear on the truth of such assumptions, that skeptical challenge can in fact be met.[9]

Let us recap the main features of the moderate position as I have been characterizing it so far. According to such a view, our perceptual justifications depend on a certain course of experience, absent defeaters, together with some very general assumptions, viz. that there is an external world (but also that we are not victims of lucid and sustained dreams, or even that our sense organs are mostly reliable). These have to be understood, in the first instance, as propositions that figure as constitutive ingredients of our perceptual justifications in the abstract space of reasons, together with appropriate kinds of experiences and absent defeaters. This way, contrary to the liberal view, we can actually surpass our "cognitive locality"—that is, we can take our experiences to bear on a realm of mind-independent entities. This is of course compatible with the fact that our specific justifications are defeasible and that we may be mistaken about the identity, the properties and even the existence, on a given occasion, of an object. Since no justification for these general assumptions is required, the fact that it is difficult to see how there could be any does not make the justifications based on them impossible to obtain, contrary to what would happen on the conservative view.[10]

Furthermore, the moderate position, as I have been characterizing it, has a story to tell about what it means doxastically to assume that there

---

9 "See..." Coliva (2015, chapter 4).
10 For criticism of Wright's notion of entitlement, see Pritchard (2005), Jenkins (2007), Williams (2012), Coliva (2015, 2020b).

is an external world. It consists in being committed, in our thoughts and actions, to the existence of an external world. Moreover, to assume doxastically that H does not entail that subjects ought to explicitly entertain its content, or even be able to do it. Rather, it is enough for them to comply with a practice that has as its rational precondition the commitment to the existence of an external world. Of course, this is entirely compatible with the fact that those subjects who do have the necessary conceptual apparatus ought to be able, on occasion and if requested to offer their grounds for their perceptually-based specific empirical beliefs, to mention such an assumption.

In sum, the moderate position holds that we do have perceptual justifications for our ordinary empirical beliefs, but these arise only within a system of assumptions—or "hinges"—which, while not being in turn justified, or even justifiable, make it possible for us to transcend our cognitive locality and therefore take our *experiences* to bear onto a world populated by mind-*independent* entities. Obviously, the most serious challenge the moderate position has to face is the one posed by a kind of skepticism, of Humean descent, that challenges the claim that such an assumption is after all rational, and non-arbitrary, as no justification for it can be provided. I have already taken it up in several writings (Coliva 2015, 2020a, b, 2021) and here I won't go over its details once again. Rather, I will consider it in the context of answering some objections recently leveled by Crispin Wright against the moderate account of perceptual justification and the constitutive account of epistemic rationality.

Wright's Objections

In light of the preceding, in this section I consider a few objections raised by Crispin Wright (2012) against the moderate account as I have been developing it. According to Wright, moderatism is "a genuine additional possibility" (Wright 2012, p. 476) besides the liberal and the conservative account of perceptual justification. Wright proposes an interpretation of my position and explicitly acknowledges that "it may be that the interpretation I will consider is not exactly what Coliva has in mind" (ibid.). As part of his interpretation, Wright writs: "For one thing, it seems to me that Coliva's suggestion is very much more easily received at second level than at first level" (ibid.) According to Wright, that is, the moderate account is more plausible when taken as a view about *claims* regarding the justifiedness of our empirical beliefs, than if taken as an account of the architecture of perceptual justifications. The reason he offers is the following:

> That an unreflective thinker may acquire a perceptual warrant for a particular belief just in virtue of the course of her perceptual experience, without any consideration of authenticity-conditions and defeaters, is common ground both for the dogmatist [i.e. liberal]

and for the conservative who regards the satisfaction of the relevant authenticity-conditions as a matter of entitlement. ... Their disagreement is about the supporting architecture of perceptual justification thereby obtained: the dogmatist holds that the warrant is conferred purely by the occurrence of the relevant perceptual experience; the conservative holds that the perceptual experience confers warrant only in a context in which there is either independent reason to believe that a given authenticity-condition is satisfied, or a right to take it for granted ... even if ... the thinker concerned is in no position to consider it. In other words: although the entitlement-conservative augments his conception of the justificational architecture of a perceptual belief with the thesis that thinkers are rationally entitled to trust in satisfaction of the relevant authenticity-condition, what he requires of the thinker if she justifiably forms a belief on the basis of her experience is exactly what the dogmatist requires.
(Wright 2012, pp. 476–477)

Here Wright is adamant that, as remarked in §1, his conservative position is primarily an account of propositional justification (or warrant, as he prefers to call it). Moreover, it does not require subjects consciously to entertain, let alone be able to grasp the non-evidential justification (the entitlement, in Wright's terminology) there is for the relevant "authenticity-conditions"—that is, in this case, that there is an external world. In this respect the conservative view is on par with the liberal one. They diverge only with respect to the conditions they think should obtain to have propositional perceptual justification.

Yet, Wright goes on to claim that, for this very reason, the moderate account cannot be considered an alternative to either. Here is his argument:

[O]n Coliva's proposal, at least on the natural understanding of "assume" as denoting a propositional attitude, something more would seem to be needed: the thinker will also have to make some assumptions, whatever exactly 'assuming' is taken to consist in. Thus when presented at first level, Coliva's proposal cam seem *more* demanding of the thinker than either entitlement-conservativism or dogmatism—and consequently open to the children-and-intelligent-animals kind of objection that moves the dogmatist in the first place.
(Wright 1992, p. 477)

The problem, however, is that moderatism, as I have construed it in Coliva (2015) and explained in §1, does not require subjects to assume anything, at the level of propositional justification. Yet this fact does not make it collapse onto the liberal position. For the difference is precisely that for a liberal it is enough, for perceptual justification for an empirical proposition P to obtain, that one had the appropriate course of experience, absent defeaters. For a moderate, in contrast, just like a conservative, that is not enough. The hinge proposition H—or in Wright's terminology, the authenticity-condition H—needs to be posited as part of the informational setting which makes perceptual justifications possible. In other words, at the level of propositional justification, the moderate account is more like the conservative than the liberal one. They differ merely in the further requirement that for such a positing to be rational it should be justified (evidentially or otherwise). Whereas the conservative imposes such a requirement—whence also its labeling a "skeptical" account[11]—the moderate denies it. Since I take it, at least for Wright, the conservative account of the structure of perceptual justification is perfectly intelligible, so should the moderate one. Or else, neither is.

Taking himself to have shown that the only level at which the moderate account is plausible is at the level of claims, Wright cashes it out as follows:

> [A] fully reflective, explicit thinker does need to take ownership of anything she recognizes as an authenticity-condition and, if she can muster no evidence on its behalf, to acknowledge that she is taking its satisfaction on trust. ... What sets the 'third way' apart is rather ... that—apart of course from the thinker's having the relevant perceptual experiences – that is *all* that needs to be in place .... In particular, there is no call for some ... non-evidential warrant for the assumption concerned.
>
> (Wright 2012, pp. 477–478)

The problem here is that, as explained in §2, I don't require subjects to take ownership of the authenticity-condition, while lacking a justification for it, in order for them to count as *doxastically* assuming H. Of course, they might do so, but they don't have to, as the second disjunct in the definition clearly states:

> **To assume H doxastically**: a proposition H (which is a constitutive element of the propositional justification for a specific class of propositions C) is either grasped and possibly appealed to in the course of claiming one's justification for a proposition P, belonging to C; or else, it is such that a subject can participate in an epistemic practice that has H as one of its rational preconditions.

---

11 Wright follows skeptics in holding that, unless H is justified (or warranted), it is not rationally. Contrary to skeptics, however, he believes that H *can be* justified, albeit non-evidentially.

Yet, according to Wright, it would be problematical for subjects to claim a justification for P, based merely on assuming H, while having no justification for it. Of course, I can see the worry here—it is the typically skeptical worry that, absent such a justification, that assumption is no more epistemically rational than any other one incompatible with it. Yet notice, first, that this worry is not in the least assuaged by embracing Wright's notion of entitlement. For Wright-style entitlements are not justifications (or warrants) that speak to the truth of the proposition they are meant to justify (Wright 2004, p. 206). Second, the worry can indeed be assuaged by providing a story, like the constitutive one we will review momentarily, which explains why, despite not being justified, H is epistemically rational.

And here comes Wright's third objection, against the plausibility of the constitutive view, based on his own interpretation of it

> [Coliva] suggests [that] there are certain assumptions that are *constitutive* of rational empirical enquiry. It is not that making them is sustained by certain special considerations that serve to explain why it is rational so to do. Rather, rational empirical enquiry simply *is* an activity in which these assumptions are made and allowed to govern the enquirer's conception of the evidential significance of various types of occurrence. To ask *why* they are rational—Coliva doesn't say exactly this, but it would seem to be in keeping with what she does say—is to ask a question incorporating a mistake very similar to that made by someone who asks what it is in the nature of Chess that mandates playing it on a board of 64 squares, 8x8, alternating black and white.
>
> If this interpretation is broadly correct, then Coliva's third way is a … "paradigm case" response to scepticism.… [I]f it really were constitutive of our conception of rational empirical enquiry to assume that there is an external material world, then there should be a kind of unintelligibility about a sceptical challenge to the rationality of this assumption which would be at odds with the sense of paradox created by the best sceptical arguments that challenge it. … How can a thesis about what is primitively constitutive of a concept be controversial? And how, if it can, might it be recognized to be correct?
>
> (Wright 2012, pp. 478–479)

I find this objection quite perplexing. First, my account is an account of epistemic rationality itself. In fact, it is in large part a standard account of it, as evidenced by the following definition.

> **Epistemic Rationality Extended**: For a subject S, it can be epistemically rational both to believe perceptually justified propositions and

to assume those unjustifiable propositions that make the acquisition of perceptual justifications possible in the first place and are therefore constitutive of them.

That is, no skeptic disputes that epistemic rationality consists in providing epistemic justification for or against specific empirical beliefs.[12] What I add to that is simply making it explicit that the production of such justifications constitutively depends on taking for granted certain assumptions (or "authenticity-conditions", in Wright's terminology). Just like constitutive rules are essential to the games they constitute because otherwise moves within them would either be impossible or lose their point, so there are basic assumptions that are essential to epistemic rationality because without them the moves within it—that is, justifications for (or against) ordinary empirical propositions—would either be impossible, or lose their point (i.e. their epistemic significance). Thus, I take myself to be providing an explanation primarily of what epistemic rationality *is*, like other theorists before me have taken themselves to be providing accounts of what knowledge is, or of what warrant is (including Wright). It is not required, to such an end, that ordinary folks, or even theorists of different persuasions, should find those accounts intuitive, or that they should spontaneously assent to them, in a fashion similar to what, according to generative linguists, native speakers of a language should do when presented with a well-formed sentences of their language, say.

Indeed, any so-called "over-riding" solution to skeptical paradoxes depends on proposing accounts of the central notions involved that somewhat depart from their typical, or pre-theoretical understanding.[13] Of course, in order not to sound *ad hoc*, these solutions need to make a case that the typical understanding is somewhat misleading. And indeed I do claim, based on the reasons we have just rehearsed (however briefly), that sticking to a narrow conception of epistemic rationality is wrong. To be sure, it is understandable to some extent, since we typically dispute the rationality of *ordinary* empirical beliefs, and do not discuss the status of the hinge assumptions that are constitutive of their justification. Yet, it is mistaken nonetheless.

Now, it is true that I am no Platonist, and that I think that (at least many) concepts are grounded in practices—or in use, as Wittgenstein would have put it—and that if an account of a given practice is constitutive of a concept it should be eventually recognized as such by conceptually

---

12 A cautionary note: for the purposes of this chapter, which is centered on the notion of perceptual justification, I am not adding the adjective "perceptual" to qualify the form of epistemic rationality considered here.
13 Other prominent examples of over-riding solutions to skeptical paradoxes are semantic contextualist accounts of knowledge claims, and Wright's own account of non-evidential warrants (or entitlements).

endowed and reflective creatures. Yet, this is inessential to the proposal, from an epistemological point of view. That is, the epistemological proposal I am making does not stand or fall with the correctness of this account of concepts. For example, one could have a purely externalist account of concepts, which typically severs the connection between the identity conditions of concepts and their recognition from the first person point of view (think of "water"/"twater" and H_2O/XYZ) and still hold that epistemic rationality extends to its constitutive assumptions.

Yet, I do think that skeptics—and theorists like Wright who follow them in their request for justification (or warrant) of assumptions constitutive of epistemic justification—are actually blind to an essential feature of the practice they engage in and, to the extent that that practice is constitutive of the concept of epistemic rationality, also to one of the constitutive inferences of that concept. This is not as unusual as Wright thinks. Take any concept we have: it typically takes some doing to individuate its constitutive inferences and it is certainly not required that ordinary folks should be able to individuate them or even spontaneously assent to them, once they are presented with them. What counts, rather, is how they actually go on inferring and judging. If those actions are carried out in conformity with the inference rules individuated by theorists, that is all that is required to grant subjects with some implicit (or tacit) acceptance of those constitutive inferences.

Notice, moreover, that Wright's own claim that we should recognize non-evidential warrants—"entitlements" as he calls them—alongside evidential ones is certainly not any better off in this regard. First because it entails that the term "warrant"—and the corresponding concept—is ambiguous between earned (evidence-based) and unearned (non-evidence-based) warrants in a way that would typically escape ordinary folks and theorists of a different persuasion, like skeptics. Second because unearned warrants, contrary to earned ones, do not speak to the truth of the proposition they warrant (Wright 2004, p. 206). Therefore, they are not just different in provenance from earned one, but also in their fundamental properties. This makes it suspect to consider them as a subspecies of ordinary warrants (or justifications). It would be a bit like noting that chairs are those objects we can sit on, irrespective on the number of legs, and then say that a pole is a chair even if we cannot sit on it, maybe because it has a leg.

What is more, it should be noted that skeptics of a Humean descent, *qua* human beings, do carry out their activities and make judgments, even about the justifiedness of ordinary empirical beliefs, in conformity with the assumption that there is an external world. As I have argued in other writings (Coliva 2015, 2020a), Humeans can actually be moderates with respect to perceptual justifications and admit that, once the relevant conditions are met, we are justified in believing that there are specific physical objects in our surroundings, while simply insisting that the basic assumption that there is an external world is a-rational, because it isn't supported by any epistemic reason, either a priori or a posteriori, nor can it be. Rather, that assumption comes natural to us because of our psychological make-up (Hume), or because of our upbringing within a community that takes it for granted (Strawson, as an interpreter of Wittgenstein). More importantly, I do not think that skeptics should really object to my constitutive account, once presented with it. That is, they could perfectly well agree, after some prompting and consideration, that the notion of epistemic rationality is extended:

> **Epistemic Rationality Extended**: For a subject S, it can be epistemically rational both to believe perceptually justified propositions and to assume those unjustifiable propositions that make the acquisition of perceptual justifications possible in the first place and are therefore constitutive of perceptual justifications.

Rather than

> **Epistemic Rationality Narrow**: For a subject S, it is epistemically rational to believe only perceptually justified propositions.

Yet, they could raise another kind of objection—namely, the typically epistemic realist worry that if we have no epistemic justification for assumptions such as "There is an external world", then our practice would not be objective—that is, somewhat tracking a mind-independent reality—and would thus be arbitrary—that is, epistemically on par with other practices that have as their constitutive assumptions propositions incompatible with it. This is a worry that neither I nor Wright with his notion of entitlement propose to address head-on. For, to repeat, his entitlements do not speak to the likely truth of "authenticity-conditions". (I have taken up this kind of objection in detail in Coliva 2015 (Chapter 4), 2018, 2021 and Coliva & Palmira 2020, 2021.)

Let us now turn to Wright's final objection, which again is worth citing in full:

> My second, related reservation has to do with the question of what fixes the *identity* of concepts with the kind of normativity—I take it to be relevantly similar—exhibited both by concepts of epistemic rationality and concepts of morality. It seems to me, as to many, that it is possible in principle for cultures to have enormously divergent moral codes, major discrepancies in the things that they are prepared to classify as good, or obligatory, without raising any significant question whether all are exercising genuine, shared concepts of the *moral good* and the *morally obligatory*. Moral concepts can permit all kinds of divergent and *outré* applications without any questions

being raised, necessarily, whether it is indeed concepts of the morally good and obligatory that are being applied. So my suspicion ... is that such concepts have, in effect, *no* paradigms, no canonical in-rules, as it were. What unifies morally evaluative concepts across communities whose fundamental moral standards are radically different is rather ... a common conception between the communities concerned of the *consequences* of classifying a type of action as moral.

[I]f that is correct, then the sceptical challenge is not to be silenced by the suggestion that the rational can only be what we most fundamentally call 'rational'. The model does not imply that there will always be a good challenge to explain *why* a particular kind of action in particular circumstances is morally good; or why a particular pattern of belief formation is rational. But the challenge is at any rate not to be stifled by the assertion that it enters primitively into our concepts of the good, or the rational, that they respectively embrace that kind of action, and that pattern of belief-formation.

If this is right,... then the basic claim of the third way about the constitution of our concept of epistemic rationality should give way to a thesis about the epistemic value of ... an uncritical acceptance of the existence of an external material world. The argument should be, not that the rationality of such acceptances is part of what we mean by "rational" but, substantively, that they are an essential part of any form of enquiry that is harnessed to the essential goals of enquiry: truth, knowledge, the avoidance of error, understanding, and the construction of an integrated, systematic and powerfully predictive framework of belief.

(Wright 2012, p. 480)

As we saw, the extended rationality claim is about epistemic rationality itself, and it is a claim to the effect that the assumption of the existence of an external world is indeed an essential part of any genuinely epistemic inquiry. Yet, reflecting on concepts, I am not entirely clear about what suggestion is being made here. Is Wright perhaps embracing a form of semantic atomism, whereby inferences are not constitutive of concepts? In that case, radically diverging communities would merely diverge in their applications of the same concept. Yet, the theoretical question remains: what is the concept of epistemic rationality at play? And this question would be hard to answer since no appeal to canonical inferences could be made. Yet it would be necessary to answer it to be in a position to determine which applications of that concept are right or wrong. Now, Fodor (1998) notoriously proposed to think of concepts roughly as labels for properties and of properties, like being a dog, as the property of eliciting the emergence in our minds of a given concept, such as the concept *dog*, upon causal interaction with (typical) dogs. I would find Wright's leaning toward such a view surprising given his anti-realist and Wittgensteinian proclivities,[14] but maybe he has changed his mind as of late. Still, in the case of a theoretical concept like the one of epistemic rationality, it is not clear what kind of properties we could have been in causal contact with such as to become endowed with that concept. All we have ever causally encountered (in this area) are practices of considering certain empirical beliefs rational and others irrational, while taking for granted that they were about mind-independent physical objects. Yet, if no inference is ever constitutive of a concept, even asking the question whether the concept of epistemic rationality that comports with that practice is extended or not would be illicit.

Or maybe the suggestion is that we should forget about the concept of epistemic rationality and talk about epistemic rationality itself. In that case, the claim I should make, according to Wright, is that assumptions such as "There is an external world" "are an essential part of any form of enquiry that is harnessed to the essential goals of enquiry: truth, knowledge, the avoidance of error, understanding, and the construction of an integrated, systematic and powerfully predictive framework of belief" (ibid.). Yet, if this is the suggestion, then I don't see in what way I have not already conformed to it. For it has always been part of my defense of the constitutive account that either skeptics, in a Pyrrhonian vein, are going to live and judge without making the assumption that there is an external world, thereby forsaking knowledge and running incredible risks all the time, since there is no reason to think that they should be worried of crossing a street, say, if they had a visual appearance as of a fast-approaching car; or else, in a Humean vein, they would already live in conformity with it, as we just saw. In this latter case, their skepticism would be merely hypothetical, or, at most, regarding the concept of epistemic rationality itself. Yet, since, as maintained in Coliva & Palmira (2020), only the extended concept would comport with the practice they would abide by, the extended version of it should be preferred. For reflect: if Humeans engage in the practice of providing reasons for or against ordinary empirical beliefs, and consider it rational, how could they account for the rationality of the practice if, by their lights, it would rest on *a*-rational assumptions? Hence, in response to such Humeans, one should insist that the extended rationality view allows one to claim

---

[14] Indeed, for Wittgenstein, the meaning of terms, and *mutatis mutandis* the identity of concepts, is determined by definitions, which often appeal to paradigmatic examples (e.g. "*This* is good/rational" or "*This* is called 'good/rational'"), and by an agreement in judgements about what counts as good/rational. Thus it would be entirely in keeping with his views to hold that if communities radically diverge about either, they would not assign the same meaning to "good"/"rational" and would have different concepts of good and rational.

or preserve harmony between our epistemic practices and the constitutive inferences of the concept of epistemic rationality.

Thus, to conclude, I think there are interesting issues about the concept of epistemic rationality which could have a bearing on how we ultimately want to cash it out, to best account for the harmony between that very concept and our epistemic practices. Yet, my proposal is primarily one about epistemic rationality itself and, as such, it does not stand or fall with any specific claim about the concept of epistemic rationality.

Conclusion

In this chapter, I have clarified what it means for a hinge proposition like "There is an external world" to be propositionally and doxastically assumed, given a moderate account of the structure of perceptual justification, such as the one presented in Coliva (2015) and defended in a number of subsequent writings. Those clarifications have been brought to bear on several objections raised by Wright (2012) against the moderate account of perceptual justification and the constitutive account of epistemic rationality. If I am right, both accounts do not succumb to Wright's criticisms and are worth taking seriously in contemporary debates about the structure of perceptual justifications and the nature of epistemic rationality.

References

Coliva, A. 2015 *Extended Rationality: A Hinge Epistemology*, London, Palgrave.
Coliva, A. 2018 "What anti-realism about hinges could possibly be", in R. McKenna and C. Kyriacou (eds.) *Epistemic Realism and Anti-Realism: Approaches to Metaepistemology*, London, Palgrave, pp. 267–288.
Coliva, A. 2020a "Skepticism unhinged", *Belgrade Philosophical Annual* 33, 7–23.
Coliva, A. 2020b "Against neo-Wittgensteinian entitlements", in N. J. L. L. Pedersen and P. Graham (eds.) *Epistemic Entitlement*, Oxford, Oxford University Press, pp. 327–343.
Coliva, A. 2021 "Hinges, radical skepticism, relativism and alethic pluralism", in N. J. L. L. Pedersen and L. Moretti (eds.) *Non-Evidentialist Epistemology*, Leiden, Brill.
Coliva, A. and Palmira, M. 2020 "Hinge disagreement", in M. Kusch (ed.) *Social Epistemology and Epistemic Relativism*, London, New York, Routledge, pp. 11–29.
Coliva, A. and Palmira, M. 2021 "Disagreement unhinged", Metaphilosophy 52(3–4), 402–415.
Fodor, J. 1998 *Concepts: Where Cognitive Science Went Wrong*, Oxford, Oxford University Press.
Harman, G. 1986 *Change in View: Principles of Reasoning*, Boston, MA, MIT Press.

James, W. 1986 "The will to believe", *The New World* 5, 327–347.
Jenkins, C. 2007 "Entitlement and rationality", *Synthese* 157(1), 25–45.
McDowell, J. 1982 "Criteria, defeasibility and knowledge", *Proceedings of the British Academy* 68, 455–479.
McDowell, J. 1986 "Singular thought and the extent of inner space", in P. Pettit and J. McDowell (eds.) *Subject, Thought and Context*, Oxford, Clarendon Press, pp. 137–168.
McDowell, J. 1995 "Knowledge and the Internal", *Philosophy and Phenomenological Research* 55, 877–893.
Pritchard, D. 2005 "Wittgenstein's *On Certainty* and contemporary anti-skepticism", in D. Moyal-Sharrock and W. H. Brenner (eds.) *Readings of Wittgenstein's on Certainty*, London, Palgrave, pp. 189–224.
Pritchard, D. 2015 *Epistemic Angst: Radical Skepticism and the Groundlessness of Our Believing*, Princeton, NJ, Princeton University Press.
Pryor, J. 2000 "The skeptic and the dogmatist", *Noûs* 34, 517–549.
Pryor, J. 2004 "What's wrong with Moore's argument", *Philosophical Issues* 14, 349–378.
Sosa, E. 2013 "Intuitions and foundations: The relevance of Moore and Wittgenstein", in A. Casullo and J. Thurow (eds.) *The a Priori in Philosophy*, Oxford, Oxford University Press, pp. 186–200.
Sosa, E. 2021 *Epistemic Explanations: A Theory of Telic Normativity, and What It Explains*, Oxford, Oxford University Press.
Strawson, P. 1985 *Scepticism and Naturalism: Some Varieties*, New York, Columbia University Press.
Wedgwood, R. 2013 "A priori bootstrapping", in A. Casullo and J. Thurow (eds.) *The a Priori in Philosophy*, Oxford, Oxford University Press, pp. 226–246.
White, R. 2006 "Problems for dogmatism", *Philosophical Studies* 131, 525–557.
Williams, M. 2012 "Wright against the sceptics", in A. Coliva (ed.) *Mind, Meaning and Knowledge: Themes from the Philosophy of Crispin Wright*, Oxford, Oxford University Press, pp. 352–376.
Wittgenstein, L. 1969 *On Certainty*, Oxford, Blackwell.
Wright, C. 1985 'Facts and certainty', *Proceedings of the British Academy* 71, 429–472.
Wright, C. 1992 *Truth and Objectivity*. Cambridge, MA, Harvard University Press.
Wright, C. 2004 "Warrant for nothing (and foundations for free?)", *Aristotelian Society Supplementary* 78, 167–212.
Wright, C. 2012 "Replies – Warrant, transmission and entitlement", in A. Coliva (ed.) *Mind, Meaning and Knowledge: Themes from the Philosophy of Crispin Wright*, Oxford, Oxford University Press, pp. 451–486.

11 On Behalf of Knowledge-First Collective Epistemology[1]

Mona Simion, J. Adam Carter and Christoph Kelp

There is a growing consensus in epistemology that groups are genuine epistemic agents in the sense that, as far as epistemology is concerned, groups are more than the sum of their members. The reason for this is that it is more and more widely agreed that groups can have epistemic properties that none of their members have (e.g. Lackey 2014b, pp. 282).[2]

Most importantly for present purposes, one key thought here is that groups can have knowledge that *none* of their members have individually. Cases like the following forcefully drive this point home: having responsibly evaluated the evidence in accordance with the highest epistemic standards, a jury comes to know that the accused is innocent. At the same time, each individual member privately, due to prejudice, bias, and so on, does not form the corresponding belief and so fails to know this.[3]

What is the structure of group knowledge? Given that groups are indeed genuine epistemic agents, we may expect that, whatever the right answer turns out to be, it is going to be the same as for individual knowledge. For instance, according to the traditional view in the literature, individual knowledge is justified true individual belief, supplemented by a suitable anti-Gettier condition.[4] Accordingly, the straightforward view of group knowledge is that it is ungettiered justified true group belief.

Unfortunately, trouble is looming for the straightforward view of group knowledge: there has been a growing number of researchers in recent literature who embrace a view we will henceforth refer to as *rejectionism* and according to which groups simply cannot have beliefs (e.g. Hakli 2007; Meijers 1999; Preyer 2003; Wray 2001). If this is right, then since on the straightforward view group knowledge entails group belief,

---

[1] We thank Paul Silva and Duncan Pritchard for their very helpful comments on this work, as well as Alexander Bird and Orestis Palermos for many inspiring conversations on this topic.
[2] For some representative discussions of this kind of view, see for example the essays in Brady and Fricker (2016) and Lackey (2014a).
[3] See, for example, Kallestrup (2020, pp. 7) for such a case.
[4] For discussion see, e. g., Shope (2017) and Ichikawa and Steup (2017).

groups cannot have group knowledge either. The straightforward view of group knowledge threatens to lead straight to group knowledge scepticism. Furthermore, with regard to epistemic justification, two properties have been regularly distinguished and thought to be central to epistemic inquiry: having justification to believe that p (=propositional justification) versus justifiedly believing that p (=doxastic justification). Neither notion, however, is applicable to groups if groups cannot have beliefs. So these two central epistemic properties of such interest and importance in individual epistemology would also have no application whatsoever to group epistemology if groups lack beliefs. In this way, collective epistemology as a whole threatens to fall into disarray.

In this chapter, we do two things. First, we argue that extant collective epistemology faces a dilemma: on the one hand, rejectionism about group belief, unpacking knowledge in terms of group acceptance, remains unsatisfactorily motivated and extensionally inadequate (§2). On the other hand, extant traditional responses to rejectionism, unpacking group knowledge in terms of distributed group belief, conflate belief hosting with belief formation (§3). Second, we argue that a knowledge-first approach to collective epistemology offers us the resources to emerge from the dilemma unscathed and that, as a result, a non-sceptical approach to collective epistemology remains viable (§4 and §5).

Rejectionism

Any viable view of knowledge must account for the mental reality of knowledge.[5] That is to say, it must tell us how knowledge is realized in our minds. According to the traditional view, it is the belief condition on knowledge that does the job. It captures what we will refer to as *the mental realizer* of knowledge.

The most prominent alternative to the traditional view explains the mental reality of knowledge in terms of acceptance, at least in part.

The Acceptance View

Acceptance-based views either take *acceptance* to be *the* mental realizer of knowledge (Lehrer 1990) or *a* mental realizer of knowledge, alongside belief (Cohen 1992). While these views were first developed in

---

5 While in a broad sense, sceptical views, expressivist views (e.g., Ridge 2007), and error-theoretic views (e.g., Olson 2011), of knowledge lack any commitment to the mental reality of knowledge, none of these views presently enjoys any serious defence in contemporary epistemology. To the extent that error theoretic and expressivist views of epistemic discourse have received sympathetic attention, this has been primarily outside epistemology, in metanormative theory. For a metanormative critique of both kinds of proposals from a realist point of view, see, e. g., Cuneo (2007); see also, for discussion, Carter (2016, Ch. 1).

individualist epistemology, an application to collective epistemology naturally suggests itself. And, in fact, an acceptance-based account of group knowledge has been defended in some detail by Raul Hakli (2007).[6]

To see why Hakli thinks that an analysis in terms of acceptance promises to improve on an analysis in terms of group belief, it will be instructive to briefly look at why he thinks that groups cannot have beliefs. In a nutshell, Hakli takes it that beliefs are paradigmatically formed in an automatic and involuntary manner.[7] By way of evidence, consider your perceptual belief that you are currently reading this chapter. You formed this belief automatically and involuntarily. The trouble is that it is hard to see how whatever mental states groups are capable of hosting, they could paradigmatically be formed in this way, especially once we conceive of them as agents over and above their individual members. If this isn't immediately obvious, consider the case of the jury again. When the jury comes to know that the defendant is innocent, the jury members must agree on this view. By the same token, they do not arrive at their view in a likewise automatic and involuntary fashion. Moreover, this point holds for group views in general. That's why, according to Hakli, groups cannot have beliefs.

Crucially, acceptance differs from belief in that, unlike belief, acceptance is non-automatic and voluntary. As a result, even though it's implausible that groups have beliefs, groups may very well accept certain propositions. What exactly does group acceptance amount to? Hakli does not offer a full answer. However, he does suggest that the kind of group acceptance at issue in group knowledge that p "requires that the group members (or perhaps just the operative group members) agree that they, together, take the content p to be the view of their group." (2007, pp. 256) Of course, this is only a necessary condition on group acceptance. But if we assume for a moment that it is also sufficient, we can easily see that, on the resulting view, group acceptance is not only possible but common. For instance, in our jury case, it is clear that the group comes out as accepting that the defendant is innocent. After all, what is going on here is precisely that the (operative) members of the group agree that they jointly adopt as their view that the defendant is innocent. In this way, opting for an account of group knowledge in terms of group acceptance

---

6 The most notable competitor is the joint acceptance account of group belief. According to this view, versions of which have been defended by, e.g., Gilbert (2013), Tuomela (1992), and Tollefsen (2003), the members of a group, P, collectively believe that p if and only if they are jointly committed to believe that p as a body. For our purposes here the debate amongst the defenders of versions of this proposal is largely inconsequential. The arguments that we give here for the implausibility of group acceptance being constitutive of knowledge apply equally to joint acceptance view generally and thus to specific versions of it its proponents have developed.
7 See also Meijers (1999) for a notable defence of this asymmetry.

continues to be promising even if those who think that there cannot be group beliefs are right.

Problems for the Acceptance View

Unfortunately, Hakli's rejectionism remains ultimately unsatisfactory. There are two main reasons for this: first, his justification for the negative claim—that is, that groups cannot have beliefs—fails on closer inspection. Second, his alternative proposal, in terms of acceptance, is too strong to account for all cases of group knowledge.

To see why the former is the case, recall that the main motivation put forth by Hakli (and following in the footsteps of Cohen 1989) for rejecting the idea that groups can have beliefs concerns belief's paradigmatic automaticity. According to Hakli, beliefs are paradigmatically formed in an automatic and involuntary manner, while whatever mental states groups are capable of hosting are not automatic, but rather, the result of careful deliberation—especially once we conceive of them as agents over and above their individual members. Consider the case of the jury again. When the jury comes to know that the defendant is innocent, the jury members must agree on this view. By the same token, they do not arrive at their view in a likewise automatic and involuntary fashion.

Note, however, that even though beliefs are plausibly paradigmatically formed in an automatic fashion—especially beliefs formed for example via perception or memory—it is less than plausible that automaticity is a *necessary* condition on a mental state being a belief. Indeed, beliefs based on inference are paradigmatically sourced in careful deliberation, and often so are beliefs (partially) based on testimony: we often weigh testimonial sources before forming testimonial beliefs. If this is so, however, even if we accept that groups can only come to know via deliberation, it will not follow that group knowledge does not imply group belief.

One way to charitably reformulate the rejectionist argument, in light of this problem, would be as an inference to the best explanation, along the following lines: the vast majority of individual beliefs are automatic; group knowledge is not; the best explanation for these data is that group knowledge is not belief-based. Once again, however, we have reasons to believe this argument fails as well, on two separate grounds. First, it is not plausible that group knowledge is necessarily the result of deliberation: to see this, note that groups, just like individuals, can have implicit knowledge (which, of course, is unlikely to be sourced in active deliberation). To see this, consider the claim: "The government knows the budget will run out before the year ends." This claim can be true, intuitively, even if the members of the government haven't sat down and jointly accepted it, and without any of the individual members having explicit beliefs on the matter. Another kind of case that serves to make this point features simple examples of presupposition. Take, for example, the lexical class of presupposition involving aspectual verbs (e.g., Simons 2001; see also Geurts and Beaver 2012). Suppose the FBI knows that China has stopped stockpiling weapons. This proposition presupposes that China *used to* stock pile weapons. Plausibly, the FBI can know the latter proposition, provided it knows the former, without explicitly coming to a view about the latter through any explicit deliberation or agreement. In this way, it becomes clear that groups can have automatically formed knowledge as well.

If this is so, the rejectionist will have to reformulate their inference to the best explanation as follows: the vast majority of individual beliefs are automatic; the vast majority of group knowledge is not; the best explanation for these data is that group knowledge is not belief-based.

We don't trust that the second claim is correct, even in this weaker form. However, we will not press this any further, and here is why: it's just not clear that, in this shape, the argument will go through to begin with, in virtue of its conclusion not constituting the best explanation of the data in the premises. To see this, note that groups are not the only agents that, when it comes to automaticity, seem to be inclined to mostly form a particular variety of knowledge (i.e., in their case, non-automatic). Non-sophisticated cognizers—such as small children and animals—have the opposite tendency: they tend to mostly form automatic knowledge, in virtue of their impoverished capacity for deliberation.[8] Surely, though, these creatures' knowledge is belief-based.[9] If this is so, however, the best explanation of all these data is that the following picture is correct: tendency to form non-automatic beliefs is directly proportional to cognitive sophistication: non-sophisticated agents have a tendency to form more automatic beliefs—for example children—while more sophisticated agents tend to form more deliberative beliefs, in proportion to their sophistication: that is, groups will do so more than average individual adult agents.

Last but not least: an acceptance-based view of knowledge will have trouble of its own. To see this, consider first cases of distributed cognition that are plausibly cases of group knowledge. For example, consider Edwin Hutchins' (1995) classic case featuring the deliberate and well-informed behavior of a ship crew navigating a ship safely to port. Plausibly, the crew as a whole can know, for instance, that they're traveling north at 80 miles per hour.[10] At the same time, no individual crewmember may

---

8 For discussion on this point, see, e.g., Nagel's (2013) ontogenetic argument from child and developmental psychology for knowledge as a mental state.
9 This is the case, to note, even if Nagel (2013) is right that children acquire the *concept* <knowledge> before acquiring the concept <belief>.
10 See Lackey (2014b, p. 282) for discussion of this case and Bird (2010) and Kallestrup (2020) for alternative cases of group knowledge by distributed cognition that will equally cause trouble for the justified, true acceptance accounts of group knowledge.

have even considered the proposition, as each is occupied just with making their own particular and often very specific contribution to the ship's smooth functioning. By the same token, it's clear that the kind of agreement between group members that Hakli takes to be necessary for group acceptance has not taken place. The group thus knows how fast they are traveling even though they do not jointly host the corresponding acceptance.

It may also be worth noting that there is reason to think that this argument will generalize beyond Hakli's specific view of group acceptance. To see how, note that it's plausible that accepting a proposition is intentional, at least in cases in which the agent doesn't also have the corresponding belief.

As William Alston (2007) captures this line of thinking:

> I find the voluntary character of the act of acceptance to be the best way of giving an initial idea of it. The act of acceptance, unlike a state of belief, is the adoption, the taking on of a positive attitude toward a proposition ... a mental act ... But when we come to saying just what positive attitude to a proposition is adopted when one accepts it, we are back to the pervasive similarity of acceptance and belief ... accepting that p is both a complex dispositional state markedly similar to believing that p, but distinguished from it by the fact that this state is voluntarily adopted by a mental act.
>
> (2007, 133)

For instance, you may not believe that God exists, say, because you find the relevant arguments unconvincing. Compatibly with this, you may accept that he exists. But, in this case, it is hard to see how you could arrive at the point at which you accept this unless you do so intentionally. You cannot take this leap of faith unless you do so intentionally. Since the scenario we are considering is one in which rejectionists are right and groups cannot have beliefs, all group acceptance must be arrived at intentionally. Crucially, however, in cases like Hutchins', no group member even considered the target proposition. For that reason, it is hard to deny that the intention required for group acceptance is not present here.

Last but not least, note that an acceptance-based view of group justification will have difficulties accommodating the plausible thought that groups can have biases: indeed, we often ascribe racism and sexism to groups in everyday talk. Biases, however, are definitionally unjustified implicit beliefs, rather than unjustified conscious acceptances.[11]

---

11 For a detailed recent discussion on this point, see Broncano-Berrocal and Carter (2020, Ch. 6).

Social Distributive Views

Paradigmatic examples of distributed cognition involve relatively tightly integrated groups working together, with scientific research teams being the classic example (e.g., Bird 2010; De Ridder 2014; Palermos 2016). In virtue of the social relations at work, different parts of the system contribute to the generation of the system's collective mental state. Take, as a paradigmatic case, a group of scientists working toward the result p. According to people like Bird (2010) and Palermos (2016), all components of the p-production process constitute the corresponding group belief that p, although no individual component needs to host it. The mathematician contributes her results (e.g., to a centralized database), the physicist contributes hers, and so on, and, as a whole, the group comes to know that p, although individual scientists need not host this belief.[12]

Bird's Account

The distributed model essentially relies on an analogy between groups and individual believers. Bird thinks the best way to see the analogy implicit in the distributed model is in terms of the analogy between social institutions and organisms developed as "structural functionalism" by, most notably, Émile Durkheim (1893). This view sees the whole of society as an organism, with the various institutions (the law, parliament, business, the security services, etc.) performing different functions in order to contribute to social cohesion. The institutions themselves will have a set of roles or goals they pursue. They will do so by giving distinct functions to sub-groups or to individuals. This parallels the different functions of the systems and organs of a biological organism that contribute to its organic unity and stability and to the pursuit of its overall goals. Furthermore, those functions in the social entity may have direct analogues with specific functions in the individual organism. In particular, the pursuit of institutional goals (itself involving the analogue of action) will require social analogues of belief and desire or intention. An institution cannot pursue its goals without institutional beliefs.

It is worth noting that Bird's Durkheimian model (2010) is characterized by quite a radically permissive way of thinking about the subjects of group knowledge. And to the extent that these more radical positions are plausible, we would have further reason to resist a characterization of

---

12 See also Kallestrup (2020) for a similar example case, where individual scientists communicate their own results to an administrator, who simply conjoins the results, generating a group output in a reliable way, despite the administrator not understanding the belief output, nor either contributing scientist being aware of it.

group knowledge in terms of group acceptance, as well as further reason to resist rejectionism. Consider, for example, Bird's case of Dr. N.

> *Case of Dr. N.* Dr. N. is working in mainstream science, but in a field that currently attracts only a little interest. He makes a discovery, writes it up and sends his paper to the Journal of X-ology, which publishes the paper after the normal peer-review process. A few years later, at time t, Dr. N. has died. All the referees of the paper for the journal and its editor have also died or forgotten all about the paper. The same is true of the small handful of people who read the paper when it appeared. A few years later yet, Professor O. is engaged in research that needs to draw on results in Dr. N.'s field. She carries out a search in the indexes and comes across Dr. N.'s discovery in the Journal of X-ology. She cites Dr. N.'s work in her own widely-read research and because of its importance to the new field, Dr. N.'s paper is now read and cited by many more scientists.
>
> (2010, 32)

Bird's take on The Case of Dr. N. is that the (entire) scientific community itself knew the results of Dr. N's paper all along, and that this is so despite there being a period of time where everyone who was aware of Dr. N's result was dead (for critical discussion, see Lackey 2014b).[13]

The main worry we have for Bird's model is that, in virtue of imposing only social constraints on group membership – that is, constraints pertaining to participating in the pursuit of the common goal – membership in the believing group becomes implausibly easy to attain. This, in turn, opens the door to rejectionism about groups' belief once again. To see this, consider the role, *vis-à-vis* a group belief, of the mailperson delivering the correspondence to the group of scientists. Is the mailperson a proper member of the group that believes "*p*", where *p* is a complicated scientific proposition the group arrives at via distribution of labor? According to Bird, this will have to be the case:[14] after all, the mailperson, just like the scientists, contributed to the attainment of the goal of the group – that is, knowledge that *p*. This, intuitively, is highly problematic in more than one way: first, in terms of extensional adequacy: there is a strong intuition that the mailperson is not a proper part of the believing group in this case. Second, the mailperson problem is just one symptom of a more general, theoretical problem for the view: not all contributions to knowledge formation are cognitively relevant contributions, be they in

---

13 For a recent discussion of Bird's case of Dr. N. in connection with epistemic defeat, see, e. g., Lackey (2014b) and Carter (2015).
14 Note, also, that even if the model would survive the mailperson problem, it can become even more counterintuitive once we replace the mailperson with a couple of primary school children (suggested by Alexander Bird, p. c.).

individuals or in groups. Your heart and my stomach contribute to your belief formation via keeping you alive. They are, however, not proper part of your cognitive system. Similarly, the mailperson, the employees of the company delivering electricity to the group of scientists, the workers who repair the Xerox machine and so on are all contributing to forming the group knowledge that *p*. However, not all contributions are such that they render their sources proper parts of the believing group.

Palermos' Account

Orestis Palermos (2016) defends a distributed model of group belief that imposes stronger conditions on membership of the believing group than Bird does. According to Palermos, to produce knowledge, epistemic collaborations rely heavily on the *mutual* interactions of their group members. He takes the following case from Wegner et al. (1985) as paradigmatic of epistemic collaborations:

> Suppose we are spending an evening with Rudy and Lulu, a couple married for several years. Lulu is in another room for the moment, and we happen to ask Rudy where they got that wonderful staffed Canadian goose on the mantle. He says "we were in British Columbia …," and then bellows, "Lulu! What was the name of that place where we got the goose?" Lulu returns to the room to say that it was near Kelowna or Penticton—somewhere along lake Okanogan. Rudy says, "Yes, in that area with all the fruit stands." Lulu finally makes the identification: Peachland.
> (Wegner et al. 1985, p. 257)

Just like in the case above, the thought goes, what is required for membership in the believing group is reciprocal relations of collaboration that function to generate the belief in question. Palermos models his view on Dynamical Systems Theory, which is a mathematical framework for studying the behavior of systems:[15] on this theory, when two (or more) systems engage in continuous, *reciprocal* interactions with each other— such that the effects of each system are continuously fed back to itself — they give rise to an integrated, distributed system. Similarly, on Palermos' view, in collaborative scientific research teams, the completion of the relevant cognitive task involves ongoing reciprocal interactions between the participating individuals. Therefore, in such cases we can talk of an overall distributed cognitive system that consists of all the participating individuals (Palermos 2016).

According to Palermos, then, for a group belief to arise, information must describe a closed feedback loop from each of the group members

---

15 For overviews, see, e. g., Beer (1995) and Abraham et al. (1990).

to the group. This information feedback loop, in Palermos' view, is what delineates group membership: when individuals interact loosely and in a largely unidirectional way they do not give rise to a distributed cognitive system: the mailperson in the case above is not a member of the believing group, because they merely input information, without any feedback loop being described; the relevant causation here is entirely asymmetrical. In contrast, the scientists both input information into the system, and receive information from the system, which they then use in generating further inputs, and so on.

Although Palermos' view seems to do better than Bird's as a way of "ruling out" the mailperson as part of the believing group, it achieves this result at the cost of making group membership *too* hard to attain. To see this, consider a case in which one of the scientists in the group that hosts the belief that *p*—indeed, maybe even the head of the group of scientists—knows that *p* (where p is the content of the group belief at stake) but never communicates that p to any of her colleagues. By stipulation, the informational feedback loop fails to be described in this case. *Mutatis mutandis*, Palermos' model will predict, against intuition, that this scientist is not a member of the believing group.[16]

A Dilemma for Social Distributivism

To sum up: We have considered two distinct models of distributed cognition on which the contributory social relations between the members are taken to circumscribe the margins of the believing group. We have seen that on Bird's model, on which input toward p was all that was needed for membership, group membership was too easy to attain. Conversely, though, we have also seen that a stronger view, on which the traffic of contribution needs to go both ways—both from and to the member, via a closed feedback loop—was too narrow. Thus, a model that delineates believing groups via their social ties—that is, via their contributions toward the formation of the belief in question, is either too weak (if the contribution is unidirectional) or too strong (if the contribution is taken to be bidirectional). This suggests in-principle difficulties for social-first distributed models—that is, distributed models that purport to deal with group individuation via use of the social ties at work: they seem to be bound to run into a strength dilemma.

---

16 Couldn't Palermos slightly modify the view, such that it merely asks for group members to have *a disposition* to contribute to the group knowledge (maybe under reasonably normal conditions), rather than for an actual contribution? While we think a move like this would improve the view, we also think that even a demand for a disposition to contribute is too strong a requirement for group membership. After all, knowledgeable groups often have rogue members, who refuse to contribute to one collective endeavor or another. Rogue members, however, are not non-members. Thanks to Paul Silva for pressing us on this point.

Last but not least, we have one methodological worry for both distributed models under discussion: we worry that they are more plausibly describing the *process* of belief *formation* in groups rather than the group belief itself. Notice, crucially, that in individual cognizers, the respective contributors to the two—that is, belief formation and belief hosting—come apart: my eyes, for instance, contribute to my belief formation, but not to its hosting. If so, we shouldn't conflate belief formation and belief hosting at group level either—at least not if the ambition is to build our model of group belief on the parallel model of the individual belief, as in the case of distributed cognition models.

Note, furthermore, that this conflation explains the difficulties encountered by the models we have been looking at: in the case of Bird's model, the mailman may well be a proper part of the process of group belief formation, while not plausibly a member of the believing group. Conversely, in the case of Palermos' model, the knowledgeable scientist who does not share his knowledge with the rest of the group may well not be part of the process of belief formation—but he surely is a member of the believing group.

Knowledge-First Collective Epistemology

We started off by registering that summativism about group knowledge is widely believed to be mistaken: a group can know a proposition p, that none of its individual members knows. Furthermore, it looks as though a group can know a fact even when none of its members form the corresponding belief.

We have seen, further, that there are two broad reactions to these results in the literature: one places the individual at the center of the analysis of what is going on in cases of group knowledge: according to rejectionism about group belief, group knowledge is individual-acceptance-based: the individuals forming the group in question jointly accept that *p* is the case. When all other epistemic conditions necessary for knowledge are in place (e.g., reliability), this joint acceptance is converted into group knowledge. We have also seen, however, that this individual-first approach suffered from serious problems, both regarding its motivations for belief rejectionism itself, and concerning the extensional adequacy of the acceptance-based model.

We then looked at the alternative, distributivist proposal about group belief. According to the champions of this view, groups are *bona fide* epistemic agents, and they can host beliefs via the distributed contribution of the epistemic labor of their members. This approach places not the individuals in the group, but their social ties at the center of the analysis of group belief: a person is a member of the believing group insofar as she contributes to the group belief (on Bird's model) or exchanges information with the group toward the formation of the group belief (on Palermos' model). We have seen, in turn, that these social-first models suffer from problems of extensional adequacy, in that they either over- or under-generate group membership—and, further, that these proposals also seem to mistakenly conflate group belief with group belief formation.

Overall, the result should be quite worrying for collective epistemology: after all, group knowledge is either based on group belief or it is not. In turn, since there isn't much to groups other than the individuals forming them and the social ties obtaining between them, it would seem that group belief should be a function of the relevant individuals and/or their social ties. However, we have just seen that neither of these models worked well. This result, in turn, threatens to lead straight to an intractable kind of group knowledge scepticism. In this way, collective epistemology as a whole threatens to fall into disarray.

In what follows, we want to argue that things are not as bad as this picture suggests and offer a way out of this dilemma. More specifically, we want to argue that one important social epistemological aspect is omitted by this pessimistic outlook: social epistemological affairs are not mere functions of individual knowers and the social relations obtaining between them. They are also, importantly, characterized by a specifically epistemic output: knowledge. Collective epistemology need not place either individuals or their social ties center stage in philosophical analysis: we can do collective epistemology *knowledge-first*.

Individual-First, Social-First, Knowledge-First

In what follows, then, we will take a cue from the literature on individualist epistemology, where a recent strand of thinking has moved away from the thought that knowledge must itself be analyzed in terms of constituent parts such as belief or acceptance. The most prominent champion of this kind of view is Timothy Williamson (2000), who has pioneered what is called a "knowledge-first" approach to epistemology. One key thought here is that rather than trying to analyze knowledge in terms of various other epistemic phenomena, such as justification, evidence and understanding, other epistemic phenomena are to be analyzed in terms of knowledge. Of course, this raises the question as to whether there is anything of substance to be said about the nature of knowledge. Fortunately, the answer to this question is yes. In particular, Williamson takes knowledge to be a *sui generis* mental state, on a par with more familiar mental states such as belief, desire, fear and regret.

While Williamson's focus is decidedly on individualist epistemology,[17] we believe that his view carries promise for an application to collective

17 See Carter et al. (eds.) (2017) for a recent collection of essays that explore some of the key philosophical questions, in both epistemology and mind, raised by Williamson's knowledge first program. See also the essays by Greenough and Pritchard (eds). (2009) featuring champions and critics of the knowledge-first program in epistemology, specifically.

epistemology, and, in particular, to the problem of group knowledge and group justification. If knowledge in general is a *sui generis* mental state, then so is group knowledge. But if we think of group knowledge as a mental state, we do not need to analyze group knowledge in terms of group belief or group acceptance for that matter. In principle, it may well be that group knowledge does not involve *either* of the two (more on this below). And that will of course immediately sidestep the above problems for belief- and acceptance-based accounts of group knowledge.

What's more, this approach still promises to enable us to do a considerable amount of collective epistemology beyond group knowledge. After all, if we take the knowledge-first program seriously and venture to analyze other epistemic phenomena such as justification, evidence and understanding in terms of knowledge, nothing will prevent us from applying this approach to the collective case to develop accounts of phenomena such as group justification, group evidence, and group understanding. In fact, many of the proposals that have been developed in the individualist literature carry straight over to the collective side. For instance, one might take collective justification to be group knowledge (in line with e.g. Williamson 2000, 2018; Sutton 2007; Littlejohn 2013), possible group knowledge (e.g. Bird 2007; Ichikawa 2014), or one can venture to analyze it in terms of group abilities to know (e.g. Kelp 2016, 2018a, Miracchi 2015, Silva 2018) or group processes that have the function to generate knowledge (Simion 2019). One can also embrace Williamson's "E=K" account of evidence according to which, in the group case, a group's evidence is its knowledge. And one could adopt knowledge-based accounts of understanding such as the view that group understanding, that is understanding why, is group knowledge why (e.g. Lipton 2004; Khalifa 2013; Grimm 2006) or that group objectual understanding, that is understanding of a phenomenon, is best when a group knows everything there is to know about the phenomenon and better as it approximates maximal knowledge more closely (e.g. Kelp 2015).

Compatibly, if one does not like rejectionism about group belief, the knowledge-first program can still deliver the goods: for instance, knowledge-firsters typically also accept a distinctive view of belief, which analyzes belief in terms of knowledge. Roughly, the key thesis here is that belief constitutively aims at knowledge and, as a result, mere belief is tantamount to something like "botched knowledge".[18] Now, it is easy to see that if this view of belief is defensible, then knowledge-firsters can resist on independent grounds the argument that groups simply cannot have beliefs. After all, since groups can have knowledge as well as botched knowledge (see below), if the knowledge-first view of belief is correct, it follows that groups must also be able to have beliefs. Second, even if the knowledge-first view of belief turns out not to be defensible, the claim

---

18 For discussion on this point, see Williamson (2000, pp. 47, 2017, §1–2).

that knowledge entails belief is much less central to the knowledge-first view than it is to the traditional view. After all, the knowledge-first view has an independent account of the mental reality at issue in knowledge, to wit, knowledge is a mental state in its own right. To account for how knowledge is realized in our minds, then, knowledge-firsters simply don't need the thesis that knowledge entails belief. In contrast, according to champions of belief-based views, belief is the mental realizer of knowledge. As such, it is absolutely key to their account of how knowledge is realized in our minds and for that reason much more central to their view.

In previous work (Simion 2020), one of us has defended knowledge-first views of group belief and group justification as part of a broad, integrated knowledge-first social epistemology. In what follows, we will run through the details of the view with an aim at bringing in to sharper focus the excellent resources we have at our disposal as soon as we decided to do collective epistemology knowledge-first.

Knowledge-First Collective Belief Functionalism

On the knowledge-first social epistemological framework defended in (Simion 2019, 2020), we should put not individuals and not social factors, but *epistemic value first* when theorizing about social production and exchange of information. Such an account takes *knowledge* as a primitive in the philosophical analysis of social epistemic phenomena. It starts the investigation with the epistemic function of social epistemic interactions—that of generating knowledge—and asks the question: "How should we proceed in social epistemic interactions in order to generate knowledge?"

Functionalist normative frameworks have been thoroughly researched and developed in the philosophy of biological functions. The etiological theory of proper functions[19] is notably well suited for applications to normative domains more generally. The main idea is that, just like biological functions generate biological functional norms, epistemic functions generate epistemic functional norms: a token process has the etiological epistemic function of producing effect E in system S if and only if (1) tokens of T produced E in the past, (2) producing E resulted in epistemic benefit in S/S's ancestors and (3) producing E's having epistemically benefited S's ancestors contributes to the explanation of why T exists in S.

On this view, social epistemic interactions have produced knowledge in the past, which was epistemically beneficial to us and our ancestors, and this contributes to the explanation of why we continue to engage in social epistemic interactions.

---

19 For defences, see, e.g., David J. Buller (1999), Ruth Millikan (1984), Karen Neander (1991), Peter Godfrey-Smith (1993), and Larry Wright (1973). For applications to epistemology see e. g. Graham (2012), Kelp (2018a, 2018b), and (Simion 2019).

This account predicts there is a difference between a mere social agent and a proper epistemic agent. A group is an epistemic agent rather than a mere social agent insofar as it has an epistemic function: a function to generate knowledge. It is a group that has generated knowledge in the past, which was beneficial and thereby contributes to the explanation of its continuous existence.

Group knowing and believing are analogues of individual knowing and believing: mere group belief that falls short of knowledge is botched knowledge in the sense that it is an instance of failure in epistemic function fulfillment. This account's take on the nature of group belief is strongly committed to multiple realizability: it claims that what makes something a group belief does not depend on either the internal constitution of the group nor on a particular way to realize the mental state in its members. Groups are taken as social epistemic agents; they can have knowledge and beliefs independently of whether any individual member knows or believes the target proposition.

In turn, a subject is a member of a group that hosts a belief that p just in case: (1) she is a member of the corresponding social group (in the sense favored in Bird 2010 and discussed above), and (2) she contributes *cognitively* to the generation of the web of beliefs of the collective epistemic agent. In this, the account predicts that for a given social group "G," the epistemic agent "G" will be a proper subset of the social agent "G." For instance, for the social group "the CIA," the epistemic agent "the CIA" will be a proper subset of the social agent "the CIA."

The model is a distributive belief model insofar as the cognitive contribution in question can be of two sorts: full and partial cognitive contribution. Agents contribute cognitively fully to the group's web of beliefs just in case, for some group belief that p, they host a full belief, an acceptance, or a credence of more than .5 that p is the case. Agents contribute partially to the group's web of beliefs just in case, for some group belief that p, they host a full belief, an acceptance, or a credence that q is the case that stands in a basing relation to the group belief that p.[20]

This account predicts correctly that one can contribute both actively and passively to group web of beliefs. Passive contributors merely host the corresponding the beliefs/acceptances/credences, but don't do any further collaborative cognitive labor. In contrast, active contributors work

---

20 Is this a distributive model proper? After all, traditional distributivism accepts more than agents as proper parts of the belief-holding group: artefacts, for instance, often qualify. Is this model going to allow such liberties when it comes to group parthood attribution? Yes and no. No, it is not the case that any artifact employed in the production of the belief at stake will qualify. However, on an (we take it, extremely plausible) extended mind assumption, many artefacts will be part of the group's mind: for an artifact to be a proper participant in the group holding the belief at stake on this variety of distributivism, then it needs to meet whatever the correct conditions are for extended mind parthood.

collectively to produce the group beliefs by imputing information into the system, on which the output beliefs are based.

The account compares favorably to Bird's account in that it relies on a cognitive rather than a merely social contribution; as such, it does not over-generate group membership. The mailman will not qualify as a member of the knowing group, in virtue of not making cognitive contributions to the output web of beliefs hosted by the group. The account is also more permissive than Palermos', in that it recognizes members who make cognitive contributions to the group belief that p in virtue of merely believing, accepting, or having a credence that is higher than .5 that p.[21]

Knowledge-First Collective Justification

In turn, this knowledge-first functionalist account of group belief affords a corresponding knowledge-first functionalist account of group justification.

The epistemic function of group epistemic processes is generating knowledge. There are two ways a functional device might go right, and two ways it may go wrong. The unhappy cases are: malfunction (my heart beats at an abnormal rate) and failure to fulfill its function (my heart fails to pump blood in my circulatory system). The happy scenarios are proper functioning (my heart beats at a normal rate) and function fulfillment (my heart pumps blood in my circulatory system). Proper functioning can obtain independently of function fulfillment. Just take my heart out of my chest and place it in a vat with orange juice: it will be beating at a normal rate, but it won't pump blood in my circulatory system (Graham 2012).

On the etiological theory of functions, proper functioning obtains when the trait is functioning in the way in which it did back at the moment of function acquisition (my heart is properly functioning when it beats at (roughly) the rate at which it did back when it acquired its function to pump blood in my circulatory system). In turn, when properly functioning and in normal conditions, my heart will reliably pump blood in my circulatory system.

Similarly, when properly functioning and in normal environmental conditions, group epistemic processes reliably generate group knowledge.

---

21 One may worry that the account is too demanding for two reasons:
(1) How about q-contributions that don't stand in the basing relation to q because of overdetermination? Shouldn't their bearers count as members of the believing group? The answer is "no": if one keeps trying to contribute information to group belief formation and fails, one is (alas, blamelessly) not part of the collective belief-producing mechanism. We think this prediction is correct: members of scientific teams can, at times, through no fault of their own, fail to be doxastic contributors due to their contributions not being taken up. This variety of exclusion is a known phenomenon, and it most notably happens to members of historically marginalized groups in scientific practice.

Reliability is not infallibility, however: group epistemic processes can function properly and still fail to generate knowledge (proper functioning without function fulfillment).

On this account, when groups' epistemic processes are functioning properly, even if they fail to fulfill their function of generating knowledge, they generate justified group belief. Epistemic norm compliance supervenes on the proper functioning of group epistemic processes that have generating knowledge as their epistemic function. A group belief is justified if and only if it is generated by a properly functioning group epistemic process that has the etiological function of generating knowledge. The standards for epistemic justification are thus constitutively associated with promoting group knowledge.

The account proposed is inflationist in that group belief justification does not rest on the justifiedness of the beliefs of its members. Inflationism about group justification gets its primary support from *divergence arguments* (Lackey 2016), which purport to show that there can be a divergence between the justificatory status of a group's beliefs and the status of the beliefs of the group's members: a group can justifiedly believe that p, even though not a single one of its members justifiedly believes that p.

It falls beyond the scope of this paper to compare this view of group justification with all of its rivals on the market in order to highlight its comparative strengths. It will be informative, however, to briefly look at how the present proper functionalist inflationist view of group justification compares with its rejectionist inflationist competition, joint acceptance-based accounts of justified belief (Hakli 2011, Schmitt 1994). That is, at how the proposed account deals with what is widely taken to be the main problem for joint acceptance views: cases meant to show that group justification is too easy to come by via manipulation.

Consider a case in which there is overwhelming evidence for p and very little for not-p. The jury, however, because offered a bribe, stubbornly refuses to collectively accept p as well as all the evidence in favor of p, although each of its members justifiably believes that p. Instead, the group jointly accepts that not-p based on the remaining, non-p favoring evidence. Joint acceptance accounts mistakenly predict that, in this case, the jury justifiably believes that not-p (Lackey 2016), since it accepts that not-p based on the evidence it has. Group justification is too easy to come by.

In contrast, Simion's functionalism correctly predicts, in line with intuition, that this is a case of group cognitive fragmentation: since there are cognitive contributions made by the group members for both the belief that p (member's beliefs) and the belief that not-p (members' acceptances), the group believes a contradiction: that p and that not-p. At the same time, the view also explains why the acceptance-based belief is not justified: the process that generates it—that is, deciding to ignore evidence and to accept that p for practical reasons (or being offered a bribe, in this case)—is not a belief formation process that is knowledge-generating.[22]

Conclusion

The rejectionist view that groups cannot have beliefs enjoys a growing degree of popularity in collective philosophy of mind. Rejectionism means trouble for collective epistemology as it threatens to lead straight to a highly unattractive form of scepticism about group knowledge. This chapter has shown a novel way in which this danger can be avoided. In particular, we have argued that a distinctively knowledge-first approach to collective epistemology can allow us to steer clear of group knowledge and justification scepticism even if rejectionists win the day in the philosophy of mind.[23]

---

22 Note that this also gives knowledge-first collective functionalism an edge over truth-first process-based views: after all, we can easily stipulate that as a matter of fact, in the particular case of this jury, this bribe-based process is actually truth-reliable.

23 Mona Simion's contribution to this article was supported by the "Knowledge Lab: Knowledge-First Social Epistemology" project, hosted by Glasgow's COGITO Epistemology Research Centre. This project has received funding from the European Research Council (ERC) under the European Union's Horizon 2020 research and innovation program (grant agreement No 948356). Adam Carter's and Christoph Kelp's contributions to this article were supported by the Leverhulme-funded "A Virtue Epistemology of Trust" (#RPG-2019-302) grant, hosted by the University of Glasgow's COGITO Epistemology Research Centre. The authors are grateful to the funders for supporting this research.

References

Abraham, F. D., Abraham, R. H., and Shaw, C. D. 1990. *A Visual Introduction to Dynamical Systems Theory for Psychology*. Santa Cruz, CA: Aerial Press.

Alston, W. P. 2007. Audi on nondoxastic faith. In M. Timmons (Ed.), *Rationality and the Good: Critical Essays on the Ethics and Epistemology of Robert Audi* (pp. 123–141). Oxford: Oxford University Press.

Beer, R. D. 1995. A dynamical systems perspective on agent-environment interaction. *Artificial Intelligence* 72: 173–215.

Bird, A. 2007. Justified judging. *Philosophy and Phenomenological Research* 74(1): 81–110.

Bird, A. 2010. Social knowing: The social sense of "scientific knowledge". *Philosophical Perspectives* 24(1): 23–56.

Brady, M. S. and Fricker, M. 2016. *The Epistemic Life of Groups: Essays in the Epistemology of Collectives*. Oxford: Oxford University Press.

Broncano-Berrocal, F. and Carter, J.A. 2020. *The Philosophy of Group Polarization*. London: Routledge.

Buller, D. 1999. *Functions*. Albany: SUNY Press.

Carter, J.A. 2016. *Metaepistemology and Relativism*. Basingstoke: Palgrave Macmillan.

Carter, J. A. 2015. Group knowledge and epistemic defeat. *Ergo* 2(28): 711–735.

Carter, J. A., Gordon, E. C., and Jarvis, B. W. (Eds.). 2017. *Knowledge First: Approaches in Epistemology and Mind*. Oxford: Oxford University Press.

Cohen, J. 1989. Belief and acceptance, *Mind* 367–389.
Cohen, L. J. 1992. *An Essay on Belief and Acceptance*. New York: Clarendon Press.
Cuneo, T. 2007. *The Normative Web: An Argument for Moral Realism*. Oxford: Oxford University Press.
De Ridder, J. 2014. Epistemic dependence and collective scientific knowledge. *Synthese* 191(1), 37–53.
Durkheim, E. 1893. *De la division du travail social*. Paris: Alcan. Translated as The Division of Labor in Society, by W. D. Halls, New York, NY: The Free Press, 1984.
Geurts, B., and Beaver, D. 2012. Presupposition. In *The Stanford Encyclopedia of Philosophy*. Stanford: Stanford University. http://plato.stanford.edu/entries/presupposition/.
Gilbert, M. 2013. *Joint Commitment: How We Make the Social World*. New York: OUP.
Godfrey-Smith, P. 1993. Functions: Consensus without unity. *Pacific Philosophical Quarterly* 74: 196–208.
Graham, P. J. (2012). Epistemic entitlement. *Nous* 46(3): 449–482.
Greenough, P., and Pritchard, D. (Eds.). 2009. *Williamson on Knowledge*. Oxford: Oxford University Press.
Grimm, S. R. 2006. Is understanding a species of knowledge? *The British Journal for the Philosophy of Science* 57(3): 515–535.
Hakli R. 2011. On dialectical justification of group beliefs. In Schmid, H. B., Sirtes, D., and Weber, M. (Eds.), *Collective Epistemology* (pp. 119–153). Frankfurt: Ontos Verlag.
Hakli, R. 2007. On the possibility of group knowledge without belief. *Social Epistemology* 21(3): 249–266.
Hutchins, E. 1995. *Cognition in the Wild*. Cambridge, MA: MIT Press.
Ichikawa, J. J. 2014. Justification is potential knowledge. *Canadian Journal of Philosophy* 44(2): 184–206.
Ichikawa, J.J. and Steup, M. 2017. The analysis of knowledge. In Zalta E. N. (Ed.), *The Stanford Encyclopedia of Philosophy* (Summer 2018 Edition). https://plato.stanford.edu/archives/sum2018/entries/knowledge-analysis/.
Kallestrup, J. 2020. Group virtue epistemology. *Synthese* 197: 5233–5251.
Kelp, C. 2015. Understanding phenomena. Synthese 192: 3799–3816.
Kelp, C. 2016. Justified belief: Knowledge first-style. *Philosophy and Phenomenological Research* 93: 79–100.
Kelp, C. 2018a. *Good Thinking: A Knowledge First Virtue Epistemology*. New York: Routledge.
Kelp, C. 2018b. Assertion: A function first account. *Nous* 52: 411–442.
Khalifa, K. 2013. The role of explanation in understanding. *British Journal for the Philosophy of Science* 64(1): 161–187.
Lackey, J. 2014a. *Essays in Collective Epistemology*. Oxford: Oxford University Press.
Lackey, J. 2014b. Socially extended knowledge. *Philosophical Issues* 24(1): 282–298.
Lackey, J. 2016. What is justified group belief?. *The Philosophical Review* 125(3): 341–396.
Lehrer, K. 1990. *Theory of Knowledge*. Boulder and San Francisco: Westview Press.
Lipton, P. 2004. *Inference to the Best Explanation*. London: Routledge.

Littlejohn, C. 2013. The Russellian retreat. *Proceedings of the Aristotelian Society* 113(3): 293–320.
Meijers, A. 1999. Believing and accepting as a group. In Meijers, A. (Ed.), *Belief, Cognition and the Will* (pp. 59–73). Tilburg: Tilburg University Press.
Millikan, R. (1984). *Language, Thought, and Other biological Categories.* Cambridge, MA: The MIT Press.
Miracchi, L. 2015. Competence to know. *Philosophical Studies* 172(1): 29–56.
Nagel, J. 2013. Knowledge as a mental state. *Oxford Studies in Epistemology* 4: 275–310.
Neander, K. (1991). The teleological notion of function. *Australasian Journal of Philosophy* 69: 454–468.
Olson, J. 2011. Error theory and reasons for belief. In Reisner, A. and Steglich-Petersen, A. (Eds.), *Reasons for Belief.* Cambridge: Cambridge University Press.
Palermos, O. 2016. The dynamics of group cognition. *Minds and Machines* 26(4): 409–440.
Preyer, G. 2003. What is wrong with rejectionists? In G. Preyer (Ed.), *Interpretation, Sprache und das Soziale: Philosophische Artikel (Interpretaion, Language and the Social: Philosophical Articles).* Frankfurt, Germany: Humanities Online.
Ridge, M. 2007. Expressivism and epistemology: Epistemology for ecumenical expressivists. *Aristotelian Society Supplementary* 81(1): 83–108.
Schmitt, F. F. 1994. The justification of group beliefs. In Schmitt, F. F. (Ed.), *Socializing Epistemology: The Social Dimensions of Knowledge* (pp. 257–287). Washington, DC: Rowman & Littlefield Publishers.
Shope, R. K. 2017. *The Analysis of Knowing: A Decade of Research.* Princeton, NJ: Princeton University Press.
Silva, P. 2018. Justified group belief is evidentially responsible group belief. *Episteme* 16(3): 262–281.
Simion, M. 2019. Testimonial contractarianism: A knowledge-first social epistemology. *Nous.* Doi: 10.1111/nous.12337.
Simion, M. 2020. *Knowledge First Social Epistemology.*
Simons, M. 2001, On the conversational basis of some presuppositions. In Hastings, R., Jackson, B., and Zvolensky, Z. (Eds.), *Proceedings of Semantics and Linguistics Theory 11* (pp. 431–448). Ithaca, NY: CLC Publications.
Sutton, J. 2007. *Without Justification.* Cambridge, MA: MIT Press.
Tollefsen, D. 2003. Rejecting rejectionism. *Protosociology* 18: 389–405.
Tollefsen, D. 2007. Group testimony. *Social Epistemology* 21(3): 299–311.
Tuomela, R. 1992. Group beliefs, *Synthese* 91: 285–318.
Wegner, M., Giuliano, T., and Hertel, P. (1985). Cognitive interdependence in close relationships. In Ickes, W. J. (Ed.), *Compatible and Incompatible Relationships* (pp. 253–276). New York: Springer.
Williamson, T. 2000. *Knowledge and Its Limits.* Oxford: Oxford University Press.
Williamson, T. (2017). Acting on knowledge. In Carter, J.A., Gordon, E.C., and Jarvis, B.W. (Eds.), *Knowledge-First: Approaches in Epistemology and Mind* (pp. 163–181). Oxford: Oxford University Press.
Williamson, T. 2018. Justification, excuses and sceptical scenarios. In Dutant, J. and Dorsch, F. (Eds.), *The New Evil Demon.* Oxford: Oxford University Press.
Wray, K. B. 2001. Collective belief and acceptance. *Synthese* 129(3): 319–333.
Wright, L. 1973. Functions. *The Philosophical Review* 44: 409–422.

12 Faith, Hope, and Justification[1]

Elizabeth Jackson

Justification comes in many stripes. There's epistemic, practical, and all-things-considered justification. Justification can apply to mental states, like belief, desire, and intention, and to acts, like bodily movements, mental acts, and omissions. And even narrowing in on the *epistemic* justification of *belief* specifically, philosophers make further distinctions. A common one is between *propositional* justification—having justification to believe p—and *doxastic* justification—having a justified belief that p.[2]

Doxastic justification is stronger than propositional justification. Consider two examples of the latter without the former. The first is when one has good reasons to believe p, but for whatever reason, simply doesn't believe p. Suppose I have a justified belief that my paper is due on the 15th, and have a justified belief that today is the 15th, but nevertheless fail to believe that my paper is due today. In this case, I have propositional, but not doxastic, justification to believe that my paper is due today.

The second example of propositional without doxastic justification is when I have good reasons to believe p, but ignore those reasons and instead believe p on a poor basis. Suppose I see that my phone's reliable weather app predicts rain tomorrow. But I distrust the app because I think its creators are a part of a conspiracy. Instead, I grab my magic 8 ball and ask if it will rain tomorrow, and the ball answers "yes," so I believe it will. In this case, I have great reasons to believe it will rain tomorrow, but my belief isn't based on those reasons. Again, I have propositional, but not doxastic, justification to believe that it will rain tomorrow.

While most of the literature on this distinction focuses on the justification of *belief*, beliefs aren't the only attitudes that can enjoy justification.

---

1 Thanks to Luis Oliveira and Ralph Wedgwood for helpful comments on an earlier draft of this paper. Thanks to Justin D'Ambrosio, Chris Tweedt, Peter Finocchiaro, Rebecca Chan, Allison Thornton, Katie Finley, Callie Phillips, Catherine Rioux, Michael Milona, and Andrew Chignell for helpful discussion.
2 The distinction between propositional and doxastic justification was originally introduced by Firth (1978); see Silva and Oliveira (Forthcoming) for an introduction to the distinction.

This chapter focuses on two other mental states: *faith* and *hope*. We'll assume that faith and hope—like belief—are sometimes justified and sometimes unjustified. My faith that my brother will show up to my birthday party may be justified, but my faith that my magic 8 ball is reliable isn't justified. My hope that my paper will eventually be published may be justified, but my hope that our 2-hours-late Uber driver will show up isn't justified.

The primary goal of this chapter is to explore how the propositional and doxastic justification distinction applies to faith and hope. First, in Section 12.2, we'll explore the nature of faith and hope—getting clear on descriptive questions about faith and hope is essential for answering questions about their justification. In Section 12.3, we'll explore general normative questions about faith and hope. Finally, in Section 12.4, we'll apply the propositional and doxastic justification distinction to faith and hope. Throughout this chapter, we'll use belief as a contrast class; there's been a lot of ink spilled over the justification of belief, so it's instructive to start there.

There are a few notable upshots of our discussion. Bringing in faith and hope makes salient additional normative categories, including the way the distinction between epistemic and practical justification interacts with the distinction between propositional and doxastic justification. We will see that there are four ways we can evaluate belief, faith, and hope (and other mental states as well). We'll also see that, while wishful thinking causes a lack of doxastic justification in the belief case, wishful *faith* and wishful *hope* don't as obviously lack doxastic justification. Finally, we'll consider what it might look like for faith and hope to have propositional justification without doxastic justification.

The Nature of Faith and Hope

There are many kinds of faith, and many kinds of hope. Here, we'll focus on faith and hope as *mental states*, as opposed to faith and hope as *actions*. A lost hiker might take an act of faith by attempting to jump a wide crevice, if it's the only way back to civilization (see James 1897). Similarly, some in the hope literature focus on an action-oriented strand of hope, often called *hopefulness* (Martin 2013: 69; Blöser and Stahl 2017a: 367). There are important questions about what justifies faith and hope qua acts, but here we'll restrict our focus to attitudes.

Second, we'll focus on *propositional* versions of faith and hope—as opposed to faith or hope in a person or in an ideal. This again sharpens our focus, and brings the strand of faith and hope of interest in line with belief—which is also a propositional attitude.

Finally, this chapter is about both religious and secular faith and hope. Faith and hope are two of the three theological virtues (alongside love; see 1 Cor. 13:13), but at the same time, they are an important part of our everyday lives and personal relationships (see. e.g. Saran 2014; Preston-Roedder 2018). My remarks in this chapter apply to both strands.

This is a borderline truism: evaluating the rationality of an attitude requires some understanding of the nature of that attitude. For this reason, we'll begin with descriptive questions in this section, then move to normative questions.

Belief, Faith, and Hope

Philosophers often distinguish between two kinds of mental states. *Cognitive* or epistemic states have a mind-to-world direction of fit. They represent the world. They are normally truth-tracking, responsive to evidence, and evaluable from primarily an epistemic point of view. Examples of cognitive mental states include beliefs, credences, and probability-beliefs.

Conative mental states, by contrast, have a world-to-mind direction of fit. They reflect what an agent takes to be desirable or valuable, and are inherently motivating. They needn't involve evidence or epistemic justification for their contents. I can desire that p, even knowing p is false—for example I desire a catastrophe never occurred, but I know it did. Examples of conative mental states include desires, pro-attitudes, and beliefs about the good. Of course, for the belief "p is good" to be justified, one needs evidence that p is good or desirable—but one doesn't need evidence that p is *true*. With this distinction in mind, let's examine the nature of belief, faith, and hope.[3]

Belief is the attitude of taking something to be the case or regarding it as true (Schwitzgebel 2019). Belief generally requires quite a bit epistemically (e.g. fairly strong evidence). We ought not, and often will not, believe p if our evidence strongly favors not-p. In this, belief is primarily sensitive to epistemic factors, like evidence and truth.[4] On the other hand, believing p doesn't have implications for desiring p. I might believe that I failed a test or I missed a flight, even though I have no desire for either of those to be true. Thus, belief has a strong cognitive component but no essential conative component.

What's the relationship between faith and belief? Almost all philosophers think that belief doesn't entail faith. Consider my beliefs that I failed a test or missed a flight—I don't have *faith* that either of these are true. A common explanation for this is that faith that p, but not belief that p, involves a positive conative attitude toward p—for example a desire for p, a positive evaluation of p, and so on.

---

3 For more on the relationship between these three states, see Jackson (2021).
4 I say "primarily" because on some views, practical and moral factors can affect the epistemic justification of a belief (e.g. Fantl & McGrath 2009; Basu & Schroeder 2019). I set these encroachment views aside.

Many also deny that faith entails belief—although this is more controversial.⁵ There are a number of reasons for this, but here is one: faith seems to "go beyond the evidence" in a way that belief doesn't. Similarly, faith is compatible with more doubt than belief. Even if belief is compatible with *some* doubt—as it seems fine to say, "I believe p but there's a chance I'm wrong"—it seems like faith is compatible with *even more* doubt—more counterevidence or lower credences. Both of these observations seem difficult to explain if faith just is, or entails, a kind of believing.

So, if you buy the story about faith from the previous paragraph—which I'll assume is basically correct—this means that faith has (i) a cognitive component (but a moderate one, weaker than belief's) and (ii) a moderate or even strong conative component. I'll expand on each condition in turn.

With respect to (i), faith is *compatible* with believing, but it goes beyond the evidence more than belief. So, if I have very good evidence that God exists, I may both believe and have faith that God exists. But if I lose some of this evidence, I might give up my belief, but nonetheless maintain my faith that God exists. In this case, the epistemic component of faith isn't belief, but might be replaced by, for example a moderately high credence God exists or a belief that God's existence is probable. Nonetheless, it also doesn't seem like faith is compatible with *any* amount of doubt. If I get so much counterevidence that my credence in p is say, 0.1, I should give up my faith—and most would do so. Faith also involves (ii): a desire for, or a pro-attitude toward, its content. So I could also lose my faith that God exists if lose my desire for God to exist, or begin to think that God's existing would be a bad thing.

Faith may include more than the cognitive and the conative states described above. It might also involve the *affective*, so having faith involves, or has implications for, one's emotions (Rettler 2018). Some also maintain that a separate aspect of faith is the fact that it goes beyond the evidence (Buchak 2012). However, I suspect this could be captured in other features of faith (the fact that it is partially grounded in a pro-attitude, and/or that it doesn't require belief). Here, I'll mainly focus on the cognitive and conative components of faith, but my arguments should be consistent with views that include other components as well.

Hope is similar to, but importantly distinct from, faith. On the standard view, hope that p consists of two things: a desire for p to be true and a belief that p is possible (Downie 1963: 248; Day 1969: 89; see Milona 2019 for a recent defense of the standard view). Note that, on this view, the cognitive component of hope—which can be understood as either a belief that p possible or as a non-zero credence in p—is even *weaker* than that of faith. In the case of faith, if one has a very low credence in

---

5 Pojman (1986), Audi (1991), Alston (1996), among others, argue that faith doesn't entail belief. Mugg (2016) and Malcolm and Scott (2016) argue that faith entails belief.

p, one shouldn't—and most wouldn't—continue to have faith. But hope is uncontroversially consistent with very low credences—as long as they are non-zero. Note that hope is consistent with high credences as well, but not maximally high—it seems odd to hope for things in which we are certain. Then, as Martin (2013: 69) notes, hope that p may be consistent with any credence in p between, but excluding, 1 and 0. Even so, hope's cognitive component is weaker than that of faith.

But, like faith, hope has a strong conative component. Hoping for p requires a desire for p to be true. As Born (2018: 107) notes, "Hope is essentially a desire, a pro-attitude …" Almost everyone in the hope literature maintains that a desire for the proposition in question is necessary for hope. Whether the conative component of hope is stronger than the conative component of faith is controversial. In Jackson (2021), I give two reasons to think hope's conative component is stronger than faith's. One, if hope has the same conative component as faith and a weaker epistemic one, hope starts to look like faith's "younger sibling." However, hope seems to have its own power and distinctiveness, apart from faith. It is often considered a virtue in its own right, and something that is important for people to cultivate. Hope's having a stronger conative component than faith can explain its distinctness. Two, there's a puzzle in the hope literature about how hope has such strong motivating power in difficult circumstances, when all it requires is a non-zero credence in p (see Pettit 2004: 154; McGeer 2004: 104; Martin 2013; Calhoun 2018a). One way to help solve this puzzle is to maintain that hope has an *especially* strong conative component. Because the outcome would be *so good*, this motives agents with hope in a unique way.

Some respond to this puzzle—and a related puzzle that involves distinguishing hope from despair—by maintaining that hope has additional components, beyond simply a desire and a possibility-belief (or non-zero credence). For example, Meirav (2009) argues that hope involves "an external factor"—an attitude toward some factor (e.g. nature, fate, God) on which the realization of the hoped-for end causally depends. Calhoun (2018a) argues that hope provides the hopeful a "phenomenological idea of the future." On Martin's (2013) "incorporation" account of hope, the hopeful's cognitive attitudes provide a "justificatory rationale" for related emotions and actions. Finally, Chignell's (2021) "focus theory" of hope entails that hoping involves a special attention to the hoped-for outcome.

Even so, most that supplement "the standard view" of hope nonetheless think that a desire and a non-zero credence/possibility-belief are *necessary* for hope—they just maintain that they aren't jointly sufficient. Again, like the case of faith, I'll mainly focus on the cognitive and conative components of hope picked out by the standard view, but my arguments are consistent with views that include other components as well.

In sum: belief is a cognitive attitude with a mind-to-world direction of fit, that is primarily sensitive to epistemic factors, like evidence. Faith and hope, by contrast, involve both cognitive and conative components, so they consist of states that have a mind-to-world direction of fit, and other states that have a world-to-mind direction of fit. The cognitive and conative components of faith and hope nonetheless differ slightly—for example, most think that hope is consistent with lower credences than faith, but hope may have a stronger conative component than faith.

Mental Fundamentality

Some states are *mentally fundamental*, in the sense that they don't reduce to other states. For example, one debate involves whether beliefs reduce to credences or credences reduce to beliefs, or whether belief and credence are both fundamental attitudes (see Jackson 2020a). Others have argued that knowledge is fundamental (Williamson 2000), that seemings are fundamental (McAllister 2018), or that desires are fundamental (Lewis 1988, 1996). On many of these views, we should understand other mental states in terms of the fundamental states. David Lewis, for example, thought that pretty much all mental states could be traced back to a belief-like state or a desire-like state. Some go even further and reduce desires to beliefs about the good (Price 1989; Gregory forthcoming). Still others reduce beliefs to high credences (Eriksson & Hájek 2007; Lee & Silva 2020). Reducing everything to a small number of attitude-types is challenging, however, because there are many candidate *sui generis* mental states—including imaginings, intentions, and emotions (although some reduce intentions to beliefs and emotions to beliefs; see Marušić & Schwenkler 2018 for the former and Roberts 1998 for the latter).[6]

The point here isn't to settle debates about exactly which mental states are fundamental; I discuss this to shed light on the nature of faith and hope. In my view, faith and hope are *not* good candidates for fundamental mental states. Why? Well, consider our discussion above. Both faith and hope have cognitive components and conative components, which have opposite directions of fit. If faith and hope are *sui generis*, then, for one thing, it's not clear what direction of fit they'd have. Breaking them into smaller components is natural and intuitive, is characteristic of almost all existing philosophical analyses offered thus far, and gives us clearer answers to questions about direction of fit.

Consider faith. The role of the cognitive component of faith can be played by different mental states—including beliefs, credences, probability-beliefs, beliefs in epistemic modals (states that have a mind-to-world

---

[6] If certain mental state(s) are fundamental, this isn't to say that mind-body dualism is true. There's a separate question of whether we can give a satisfactory *physicalist* account of mental states. The mentally fundamental states may or may not reduce to, or supervene on, physical states. These debates about mental fundamentality don't presuppose anything about the dualism/physicalism debate.

direction of fit). The same goes for the conative component—it can be played be a desire, a pro-attitude, or a belief about the good (states that have a world-to-mind direction of fit). Faith may have an affective or emotive component as well. It's thus natural to see faith as a mental state that is "built up" of these more fundamental mental-state parts. The same for hope—many of our hopes may be built up of a probability-belief or non-zero credence (the cognitive component) and a desire or pro-attitude (the conative component).

Because this picture of faith and hope is both natural and orthodox (for faith, see Howard-Snyder 2013; for hope, see Blöser & Stahl 2017b), I'm pretty sanguine about a project that reduces faith and hope to various combinations of more fundamental attitudes. The fact that we've seemed to successfully understand them by breaking them into various components, combined with the theoretical pressure there is to not multiply fundamental entities beyond necessity, suggests there is good reason to go in for a reductionist project.

Before we move to normative questions, note that the idea that faith and hope are non-fundamental states doesn't mean they are invaluable, unimportant, or not worth studying. In fact, as I argue in Jackson (2021), states that have both a conative and a cognitive component have a unique ability to motivate and rationalize action. Further, we'll see in the next sections why evaluating and understanding faith and hope may require more than simply analyzing each of their parts.

Normative Questions

We now turn to normative questions about faith and hope. We'll focus on faith and hope's "justification" or "rationality"—I'm using those terms interchangeably. We'll also focus on rationality as a function of **object-given** reasons—holding an attitude because *its object* is appropriate to hold (e.g. believing something because it is true or desiring something because it is good). Object-given reasons contrast with **state-given** reasons—cases where having *the state itself* brings about certain benefits (e.g. if I offer to pay you $100 to form a certain belief or desire).[7]

So, what makes faith and hope justified? Deriving general principles about faith and hope's justification seems difficult at first blush. Faith and hope are plausibly non-fundamental mental states and include components with opposite directions of fit. This means that accurately representing the world isn't enough to be justified full-stop, and being fitting or conductive to one's flourishing isn't enough to be justified full-stop.

One might think that a token of faith or hope is justified when it is both sufficiently accurate/evidentially supported (fill in your favorite story about rational cognitive attitudes) *and* sufficiently fitting/conductive to

---

7 Thanks to Ralph Wedgwood.

one's flourishing (fill in your favorite story about rational conative attitudes). However, this might not even be enough. Suppose mental state M has parts A, B, and C. Simply because A, B, and C are justified doesn't mean M as a whole is justified—M's justification may depend on how A–C interact. For example, maybe each component is individually justified, but they fail to cohere with each other.[8] So giving a story about the justification of faith and hope seems difficult.

However, "justification" is ambiguous between *practical* and *epistemic* justification; this may help with our problem. First, note that whether we can evaluate *beliefs* for their practical justification is controversial. Several—for example Kelly (2002), Shah (2003, 2006), Way (2012)—argue that evaluating beliefs for practical justification raises wrong-kind-of-reason concerns. On this view, practical reasons don't apply directly to beliefs at all. Others—for example Leary (2017), Rinard (2018, 2019)—argue that there are practical reasons for and against belief. Interestingly, faith and hope are completely different—no one, to my knowledge, has argued that practical evaluations of faith and hope are subject to a wrong-kind-of-reason concern. What's more, many prominent normative accounts of faith and hope *focus primarily* on practical rationality (see Rioux 2021: sec. 2).[9]

This makes sense, given the nature of belief, faith, and hope outlined in the previous section. Since belief is primarily an epistemic or cognitive state, it's natural to think there'd be controversy as to whether it can be practically evaluated. Faith and hope, by contrast, involve both the cognitive and the conative, which makes them natural candidates to be evaluated not just epistemically but also practically—they don't only aim at representing the world, but also involve what is good and valuable.

Thus, it's natural to think that, for each token state of faith or hope that p, there's four possibilities. It could be: both practically and epistemically unjustified, practically justified but not epistemically justified, epistemically justified but not practically justified, and both practically and epistemically justified.

To see how practical and epistemic justification may come apart here, consider some examples. Let's begin with hope. Milona and Stockdale (2018: 209) discuss a case of hoping to get back together with one's abusive ex-partner. This hope might be perfectly *epistemically* justified: given your evidence of your partner's past behavior, it is rational to consider this a live possibility or sufficiently probable. Nonetheless, it is *practically*

---

8 Relevant here is the literature on organic unities and emergent properties; see Moore (1903: 27); O'Connor & Wong (2015).
9 For hope, see Bovens (1999: sec. 3); Pettit (2004: 160); Martin (2013: 48–52); Calhoun (2018b: 86–88). For faith, see Buchak (2012); McKaughan (2013). But others do focus explicitly on epistemic rationality; see Benton (2019, 2021) for an explicit discussion of hope's epistemic rationality, and specifically it's incompatibility with knowledge, and Jackson (2019, 2020b) for a discussion of faith's epistemic rationality.

unjustified: even if you do in some sense desire it, you ought not to desire it; its obtaining would be quite bad for you. Hopes can also be practically justified, but epistemically unjustified. Consider a teenager who hopes his divorced parents will get back together. This hope may be *practically* justified if it would be good for him if they got back together, but it also might be *epistemically* unjustified—if he has strong evidence that essentially guarantees that it would never occur. You can imagine someone telling this teenager, "Why do you still have hope? That isn't going to happen."

Related considerations apply to faith. Consider cases where you ought not desire some outcome, but you desire it anyway, and you have decent evidence the outcome will obtain—for example faith that something will happen that will enable you to satisfy a harmful addiction. Here, faith may be epistemically justified, but not practically justified. And faith can also be practically but not epistemically justified. If you have faith that you are much smarter than you actually are, this might be practically justified if being smarter would be good for you, but it may nonetheless be epistemically unjustified, if it is ill-supported by your evidence. Or consider a case of religious faith in which one has little or no evidence that God exists, but continues to have faith in God anyway, because they think God's existing would be a good thing. This faith may be epistemically unjustified but practically justified. And of course, both faith and hope can be practically and epistemically justified, and practically and epistemically unjustified—compare faith or hope that one's loyal spouse is trustworthy to faith or hope that one's magic 8 ball is reliable.

This distinction between practical and epistemic justification—and the ways that these can come apart—aids us in answering normative questions about faith and hope. It's plausible that faith/hope's *epistemic* normative status derives from the attitude's epistemic/cognitive components, and faith/hope's *practical* normative status derives from the attitude's conative components. This suggests that faith and hope are epistemically unjustified when their cognitive component is unjustified, and practically unjustified when their conative component is unjustified.

More controversially, faith and hope may be epistemically justified when their cognitive component is justified, and practically justified when their conative component is justified. This second claim is more controversial for two reasons. One, it's not clear that we can completely rule out the possibility that a conative state can confer epistemic irrationality, or that a cognitive state can confer practical irrationality. It does seem odd to think that, for example my hoping that p is practically unjustified because my credence in p is practically unjustified. However, this may be possible on some views on which there are practical reasons for belief, or epistemic reasons for desire. Second, it is more controversial because of what was noted above: simply because its components are justified doesn't make a state overall justified, since we then also need to address, among other things, questions about how those components interact. For these reasons, we can conclude that faith and hope are *normally* epistemically justified when their cognitive component is epistemically justified, and *normally* practically justified when their conative component is practically justified.

To close this section, it's worth considering ways that higher-order defeat interacts with faith and hope. Higher-order defeat occurs when you receive evidence that your attitude was formed in a defective way—for instance, if you form a belief that there is a tree in front of you, then find out you just took a drug that causes tree hallucinations.

The standard cases of higher-order defeat of belief are more difficult to apply to faith and hope. For example, debunking arguments for theistic belief may undermine one's belief that God exists, but they may not prevent one from rationally having faith, or rationally hoping, that God exists, since rational faith and hope require moderate to minimal evidential support. Of course, if the higher-order evidence is decisive enough, it can also undermine faith or hope by defeating their cognitive components.

Higher-order defeat can also undermine the *conative* component of faith and hope. If a desire that serves as the conative component of faith/hope is based on a belief, that desire can be defeated if that belief is defeated. For example, if, while at my child's soccer game, I believe my child is on the yellow team, and, on this basis, hope that the yellow team scores. If I get higher-order evidence against my belief that my child's team is yellow, this can undermine my desire and thus my hope that yellow scores. While the specifics will depend on one's theory of rational desire, one explanation for this is because the evidence that undermines my belief *my child's team is yellow* also undermines my belief *the yellow team's scoring is good*, which, in turn, undermines my desire that yellow scores. This evidence may make my belief about goodness *epistemically* irrational, which in turn makes my hope *practically* irrational. Interestingly, then, the epistemic irrationality of some states may cause the practically irrationality of others.

The conative component of faith and hope may also be undermined by non-epistemic factors. Suppose I have faith that God exists, and thus desire for God to exist. However, I also don't want to desire that God exists, because I want to fit in with my non-religious friends. Or maybe I hope that there's a cigarette in my pocket, but I also don't want to desire this since I am trying to quit smoking. Possibly, these higher-order desires could undermine the practical rationality of faith or hope by undermining the conative component of the attitude.[10]

Now, we turn to ways that the propositional/doxastic justification distinction may apply to faith and hope.

---

10 Thanks to Luis Oliveira for helpful discussion about the relationship between faith, hope, and higher order defeat, and for many of these instructive examples.

Propositional and Doxastic Justification

Recall that the distinction between propositional and doxastic justification is the distinction between having justification to have an attitude and having a justified attitude. An attitude is propositionally, but not doxastically, justified in two main sets of cases: when one has good reasons to have attitude but simply hasn't formed it, or when one has the attitude, but on a poor basis.

This distinction is normally applied to *belief*. But it's not clear why we should limit ourselves to the belief case; the distinction seems to apply just as well to faith and hope. One could have justified faith (or hope) that p, or have justification to have faith (or hope) that p.

This distinction also is normally applied *only* to epistemic justification: traditionally, the distinction brings out two ways that *beliefs* can be *epistemically* justified. But when we zoom out to include faith and hope, this raises the question: could this distinction be applied to other kinds of justification, like *practical* justification? It's hard to see why not. For example, one could have a strong practical reason to have faith or hope that p—and thus have practical propositional justification—but not have practical doxastic justification, simply because one hasn't formed the relevant attitude. Further, it may be that one ignores one's strong practical reasons and instead forms faith or hope on a poor basis. As we'll see soon, spelling out the specifics of this case is less straightforward, but it's not at all clear that this is impossible. This brings out at least four ways an attitude might be justified:

> **Epistemic propositional justification for p:** having epistemic justification to have an attitude toward p.
>
> **Epistemic doxastic justification for p:** having an epistemically justified attitude toward p.
>
> **Practical propositional justification for p** having practical justification to have the attitude toward p.
>
> **Practical doxastic justification for p:** having a practically justified attitude toward p.

Faith and hope may be justified in any of the four ways above. And the possibility of practical justification opens up new options even in the belief case: if there are practical reasons for belief, then beliefs may be *practically* doxastically or propositionally justified as well.

What do these possibilities look like, more concretely? First, as noted above, one can have propositional but not doxastic justification in either sense (epistemic or practical) if one simply fails to form the attitude (belief, faith, or hope) in question. This applies across the board: to all three attitudes, and to practical and epistemic justification.

Things get more complex in cases of faith and hope where one lacks doxastic justification because the basing relation isn't met. Let's start with epistemic justification. In the belief case, a common example is *wishful thinking*: Suppose you have a lot of evidence for p, but believe p merely because you think it would be a good thing if p were true. For example, you have good evidence that your favorite sports will win the national championship, but believe they will win merely because you desire that they win. In this case, your belief lacks doxastic (epistemic) justification.

The case of hope and faith is different. Wishful thinking for hope or faith is hoping or having faith that p is true because you think that it would be a good thing if p is true. It's less clear that you'd lack doxastic (epistemic) justification in this case: compare "you only believe that because you want it to be true" with "you only hope for that because you want it to be true." The former seems to accurately point out a problematic way of believing, but the latter doesn't seem problematic. A desire your team wins doesn't seem like a bad basis for hoping they win. Something similar may be said about faith—a desire may not be a bad basis for faith, either (especially if your evidence doesn't decisively count against the proposition of faith). Then, it seems much worse to base a *belief* on a desire than to base *faith* or *hope* on a desire. This is because faith and hope essentially involve the conative, and belief does not. Thus, wishful *thinking* may be irrational, but wishful *hoping* or wishful *faith* may not be.

So, it is at least possible that faith or hope based on a desire for the proposition in question is epistemically, doxastically justified. What might remove doxastic justification, however, is to base the *cognitive* components of faith or hope on desire. So, for example, one hopes one's team will win the championship, but one's only basis for thinking this is possible at all is only one's desire for their team to win. Or, alternatively, one has faith that one's team will win with a credence of 0.6, but one's credence is based merely on the desire for their team to win. In these cases, we can suppose that one has the relevant evidence to justify the cognitive components of each attitude (the possibility-belief and the 0.6 credence, respectively), and thus has propositional justification, but lacks doxastic justification for each cognitive component. We'd then need the further premise linking the justification of an attitude as a whole to the justification of its components—so, for example, if the cognitive component of my faith that p has propositional but not doxastic justification, then my faith that p has propositional but not doxastic justification. Thus, faith or hope might enjoy propositional but not doxastic epistemic justification in cases where their cognitive components have poor bases, for example wishful thinking.

What about practical justification? What would it look like to have practical justification to say, hope that p, without having a practically justified hope that p? Of course, this depends on what practical justification amounts to. At first blush, an attitude is practically, propositionally justified when its object is good for an agent, conductive to their flourishing, or coincides with their goals—recall that we are focusing on object-given reasons. One case where faith and hope might be irrational is when they are based on state-given reasons: that is, we only have the attitude because having it is pleasant or comforting, but it is not held toward an appropriate object. Here, there is belief/faith/hope parity: having faith or hope for merely state-given reasons seems just an irrational as it does in the belief case. If this is irrational, then this might point us to a case of practical propositional justification without practical doxastic justification: I have good object-given reasons to, hope that p or have faith that p. However, I ignore those and instead merely hope that p or have faith that p because having the state itself brings about certain benefits. For example: suppose you'll pay me a large sum of money to hope that it will be sunny tomorrow. I may have practical justification to hope that it will be sunny, if I prefer sun to rain, but suppose I ignore this fact and instead hope for sun just to get the money from you. It seems like I have practical justification to hope that it will be sunny, but lack practically justified hope that it will be sunny.[11]

The chart below summarizes the above discussion. As you can see, many distinctions arise once we have three attitudes and four senses of justification on the table. Further, it also often seems appropriate to treat faith and hope similarly, since the relevant senses of justification often apply in the same way to both attitudes.

	Belief that p	Faith that p	Hope that p
Epistemic propositional justification for p	A function of the epistemic—requires a good amount of evidence for p.	A function of the epistemic—requires a moderate amount of evidence for p.	A function of the epistemic—requires only enough evidence for p to make p a live possibility.
Epistemic doxastic justification for p	Excludes cases where one lacks the attitude and cases where the basing relation isn't met: e.g. wishful thinking.	Excludes cases where one lacks the attitude and cases where the basing relation isn't met. When compared to belief, "wishful faith" or "wishful hope" may not be generally irrational, but only problematic when applied to the cognitive components specifically.	
Practical propositional justification for p	Are there practical reasons for belief? If no, this is empty. If yes, depends on what practically justifies belief; may be similar to faith/hope.	Depends on your theory of practical justification, but may mean an attitude is good for an agent, conductive to their flourishing, or coincides with their goals. May not require epistemic justification.	
Practical doxastic justification for p		Excludes cases where one lacks the attitude and possible cases where one's attitude isn't based on the fact that practically justifies it.	

---

11 Thanks to Ralph Wedgwood.

Conclusion

We've covered the nature of belief, faith, and hope—while belief is an epistemic state, faith and hope have both epistemic and conative components with opposite directions of fit. This sheds light on why it's natural to evaluate faith and hope not just epistemically, but also practically. Bringing in faith and hope to the discussion of propositional and doxastic justification thus highlights additional normative categories, and suggests that practical justification also admits of further precisification.

We've noted that sometimes faith and hope deserve a separate normative treatment than belief: for example, wishful *faith* and wishful *hope* don't lack doxastic justification in the same situations in which wishful *belief* does. The propositional and doxastic *practical* justification of *belief*—if there are practical reasons for belief—also merits further exploration.

In conclusion, faith and hope can enjoy propositional and doxastic justification, in both epistemic and practical senses. Our discussion reinforces the point made in the introduction: justification comes in many forms. Nonetheless, getting clear on the various types of justification enables us to more accurately evaluate in what senses our attitudes are—and are not—justified.

References

Alston, William. (1996). "Belief, Acceptance, and Religious Faith." In J. Jordan and D. Howard-Snyder (eds.), *Faith, Freedom, and Rationality* (pp. 3–27). Lanham, MD: Rowman and Littlefield.

Audi, Robert. (1991). "Faith, Belief, and Rationality." *Philosophical Perspectives* 5: 213–239.

Basu, R. & M. Schroeder. (2019). "Doxastic Wronging." In B. Kim and M. McGrath (eds.), *Pragmatic Encroachment in Epistemology*. New York: Routledge.

Benton, Matthew. (2019). "Epistemological Aspects of Hope." In C. Blöser and T. Stahl (eds), *The Moral Psychology of Hope* (pp. 135–151). Lanham, MD: Rowman and Littlefield.

Benton, Matthew. (2021). "Knowledge, Hope, and Fallibilism." *Synthese* 198: 1673–1689. Doi: https://doi.org/10.1007/s11229-018-1794-8.

Blöser, Claudia & Titus Stahl. (2017a). "Fundamental Hope and Practical Identity." *Philosophical Papers* 46(3): 345–371.

Blöser, Claudia & Titus Stahl. (2017b). "Hope." In E. N. Zalta (ed.), *The Stanford Encyclopedia of Philosophy*. https://plato.stanford.edu/entries/hope/.

Born, Einar Duenger. (2018). "The Logic of Hope: A Defense of the Hopeful." *Religious Studies* 54: 107–116.

Bovens, L. (1999). "The Value of Hope." *Philosophy and Phenomenological Research* 59(3): 667–681.

Buchak, Lara. (2012). "Can It Be Rational to Have Faith?" In J. Chandler and V. S. Harrison (eds.), *Probability in the Philosophy of Religion* (pp. 225–247). Oxford: OUP.

Calhoun, Cheshire. (2018a). "Motivating Hope." In C. Calhoun (ed.), *Doing Valuable Time: The Present, the Future, and Meaningful Living* (pp. 68–90). Oxford: OUP.

Calhoun, C. (2018b). *Doing Valuable Time: The Present, the Future, and Meaningful Living*. New York, NY: Oxford University Press.

Chignell, Andrew. (2021). "The Focus Theory of Hope." In N. Snow (ed.), *Hope*. Oxford: OUP.

Day, J.P. (1969). "Hope." *American Philosophical Quarterly* 6(2): 89–102.

Downie, R.S. (1963). "Hope." *Philosophy and Phenomenological Research* 24(2): 248–251.

Eriksson, L. & A. Hájek. (2007). "What are Degrees of Belief?" *Studia Logica* 86(2): 183–213.

Fantl, J. & M. McGrath. (2009). *Knowledge in an Uncertain World*. Oxford: Oxford University Press.

Firth, Roderick. (1978). "Are Epistemic Concepts Reducible to Ethical Concepts?" In A. Goldman and J. Kim (eds.), *Values and Morals* (pp. 215–299). Dordrecht: D. Reidel.

Gregory, A. (Forthcoming). *Wanting is Believing: A Theory of Human Behaviour and Its Rationality*. Oxford: OUP.

Howard-Snyder, Daniel. (2013). "Propositional Faith: What It Is and What It Is Not." *American Philosophical Quarterly* 50(4): 357–372.

Jackson, Elizabeth. (2019). "Belief, Credence, and Faith." *Religious Studies* 55(2): 153–168.

Jackson, Elizabeth. (2020a). "The Relationship Between Belief and Credence." *Philosophy Compass* 15(6): 1–13.

Jackson, Elizabeth. (2020b). "The Nature and Rationality of Faith." In J. Rasmussen and K. Vallier (eds.), *A New Theist Response to the New Atheists* (pp. 77–92). New York: Routledge.

Jackson, Elizabeth. (2021). "Belief, Faith, and Hope: On the Rationality of Long-Term Commitment." *Mind* 130: 35–57.

James, W. 1897. The Will to Believe. *The New World*, 5: 327–347.

Kelly, T. (2002). "The Rationality of Belief and Some Other Propositional Attitudes." *Philosophical Studies* 110(2): 163–196.

Leary, Stephanie. (2017). "In Defense of Practical Reasons for Belief." *Australasian Journal of Philosophy* 95(3): 529–542.

Lee, Matthew & Paul Silva Jr. (2020). "Toward a Lockean Unification of Formal and Traditional Epistemology." *Episteme*. Doi: https://doi.org/10.1017/epi.2020.11.

Lewis, David. (1988). "Desire as Belief." *Mind* 97(387): 323–332.

Lewis, David. (1996). "Desire as Belief II." *Mind* 105(418): 303–313.

Malcolm, Finlay & Michael Scott (2016). "Faith, Belief, and Fictionalism." *Pacific Philosophical Quarterly* 98: 257–274.

Martin, Adrienne M. (2013). *How We Hope: A Moral Psychology*. Princeton, NJ: Princeton University Press.

Marušić, B. & J. Schwenkler. (2018). "Intending is Believing: A Defense of Strong Cognitivism." *Analytic Philosophy* 59(3): 309–340.

McAllister, B. (2018). "Seemings as sui generis." *Synthese* 195(7): 3079–3096.

McGeer, V. 2004. The art of good hope. *The Annals of the American Academy of Political and Social Science*, 592(1), 100–127.

McKaughan, Daniel. (2013). "Authentic Faith and Acknowledged Risk: Dissolving the Problem of Faith and Reason." *Religious Studies* 49: 101–124.

Meirav, Ariel. (2009). "The Nature of Hope." *Ratio* 22(2): 216–233.
Milona, Michael. (2019). "Finding Hope." *The Canadian Journal of Philosophy* 49(5): 710–729.
Milona, M. & K. Stockdale. (2018). "A Perceptual Theory of Hope." *Ergo* 5(8): 203–222.
Moore, G. E. (1903). *Principia Ethica*. Cambridge: Cambridge University Press.
Mugg, Joshua. (2016). "In Defence of the Belief-Plus Model of Faith." *The European Journal for Philosophy of Religion* 8(2): 201–219.
O'Connor, Timothy & Hong Yu Wong. (2015). "Emergent Properties." In *Stanford Encyclopedia of Philosophy*. https://plato.stanford.edu/archives/sum2020/entries/properties-emergent/.
Pettit, P. (2004). "Hope and Its Place in Mind." *The Annals of the American Academy of Political and Social Science* 592: 152–165.
Pojman, Lewis. (1986). "Faith without Belief." *Faith and Philosophy* 3(2): 157–176.
Preston-Roedder, Ryan. (2018). "Three Varieties of Faith." *Philosophical Topics* 46(1): 173–199.
Price, H. (1989). "Defending Desire-as-Belief." *Mind* 98: 119–127.
Rettler, Bradley. (2018). "Analysis of Faith." *Philosophy Compass* 13(9): 1–10.
Rinard, S. (2018). "Believing for Practical Reasons." *Noûs* 4: 763–784.
Rinard, S. (2019). "Equal Treatment for Belief." *Philosophical Studies* 176 (7) 1923-1950.
Rioux, C. (2021). "Hope: Conceptual and Normative Issues." *Philosophy Compass* 16: e12724.
Roberts, R. C. (1998). "What an Emotion Is: A Sketch." *The Philosophical Review* 97(2): 183–209.
Saran, Kranti. (2014). "Faith and the Structure of the Mind." *Sophia* 53: 467–477.
Schwitzgebel, E. (2019). "Belief." In *Stanford Encyclopedia of Philosophy*. http://plato.stanford.edu/entries/belief/.
Shah, Nishi. (2003). "How Truth Governs Belief." *The Philosophical Review* 112(4): 447–482.
Shah, Nishi. (2006). "A New Argument for Evidentialism." *The Philosophical Quarterly* 56(225): 481–498.
Silva, Paul & Luis R. G. Oliveria. (Forthcoming). "Propositional Justification and Doxastic Justification." In C. Littlejohn and M. Lasonen-Aarnio (eds.), *The Routledge Handbook of Evidence*. New York: Routledge.
Way, J. (2012). "Transmission and the Wrong Kind of Reason." *Ethics* 122(3): 489–515.
Williamson, Timothy. (2000). *Knowledge and Its Limits*. Oxford: OUP.

Part IV
New Horizons for Justification

13 Doxastic Rationality[1]

Ralph Wedgwood

It is widely accepted that the terms "justified" and "rational" can be used to express very closely related concepts. Unsurprisingly, then, it is not hard to find a way of expressing the distinction between "propositional" and "doxastic" justification in terms of "rationality":

(i) There is sufficient *propositional* justification for you to believe a proposition if and only if *it is rational* for you to believe the proposition.
(ii) You believe a proposition in a *doxastically* justified manner if and only if you *rationally believe* the proposition – that is, your belief in the proposition is *rationally held*.

An intuitive explanation of this distinction can be given as follows: The statement that *it is rational* for you to believe a proposition does not entail that you actually do believe the proposition. It entails only that the proposition is, given your cognitive situation, rationally suitable for you to believe. By contrast, the statement that you *rationally believe* the proposition does entail that you believe the proposition—and, moreover, that you believe it in a certain distinctively rational manner.

In most of the existing literature, this distinction between doxastic and propositional justification has been studied only in relation to *belief*. As it seems to me, however, this is far too narrow a view of the matter. The very same distinction applies to attitudes of many kinds. In this discussion, I am particularly interested in applying this distinction to partial *degrees of belief* or *credences*; but in principle the distinction also applies to many other attitudes—including practical attitudes, such as intentions and decisions. My goal here is to give an account of what it is for attitudes of all these kinds to have the property of being, as I shall put it, "rationally held."

---

1 I am grateful to the editors of this volume, and also to Liz Jackson, for extremely helpful comments on an earlier draft.

DOI: 10.4324/9781003008101-18

Previous work on this distinction has been limited in another way as well. It has barely addressed the fact that, intuitively, both propositional and doxastic justification *comes in degrees*. Propositional justification clearly comes in degrees: among the beliefs that it is possible for you to hold now, there are some that it is *perfectly rational* for you to hold, some that it is *slightly* irrational for you to hold, and others that it is *grossly* irrational for you to hold. Similarly, doxastic justification seems also to come in degrees: some of the beliefs or other attitudes that thinkers hold are *more* rationally held than others. I shall also attempt here to show here how any account of these degrees of propositional justification can be used to give a corresponding account of degrees of doxastic justification.

In the first section below, I shall examine the most prominent account of doxastic justification, which appeals to the "basing" relation; as I shall argue, this account faces a series of grave objections. In the second section, I shall argue for an alternative account, which I shall call the "virtue manifestation" account—where the relevant virtue is precisely the virtue of *rationality*. This alternative account will be developed in more detail in the third section, where I shall give an account of how to measure the *degree* to which a particular attitude (such a belief or an intention) is rationally held. In the fourth section, I shall defend the account of the preceding section against some objections that some philosophers may be tempted to raise. Finally, in the fifth section, I shall highlight a further advantage of this account—a further puzzle to which this account can give an illuminating and satisfying solution.

The "Basing" Account

Many epistemologists claim that the crucial factor that differentiates a doxastically justified belief from beliefs that are not doxastically justified concerns the *basis* of the belief—what the belief is *based on*. Indeed, the very first philosopher to use the terms "propositional" and "doxastic" to mark this distinction was Roderick Firth (1978: 217), who claimed that for a belief to be "doxastically warranted," it has to be, as he put it, "psychologically based on or derived from the relevant evidence in a rational way."

A similar view is defended by evidentialists like Earl Conee and Richard Feldman (1985: 24)—although Conee and Feldman use the term "justified" solely for propositional justification, and employ the term "well-founded" to describe beliefs that Firth would call "doxastically warranted." In their view, belief in a proposition p is (propositionally) justified for a thinker at a time t if and only if having the attitude of belief toward p "fits" the "evidence" that the thinker has at t; and for the thinker's belief in p to be "well-founded"—that is, doxastically justified—not only must belief in p be justified, but thinker must also believe p "on the basis of" evidence that the thinker has, where having this attitude "fits" that evidence.[2]

In my opinion, this account of doxastic justification is open to a series of grave objections. However, I shall not attempt to canvas all these objections here. Instead, I shall first argue that a belief's being "based on" evidence that the thinker has for that belief is neither necessary nor sufficient for doxastic justification. Then I shall argue that classical subjective Bayesianism is also extremely hard to reconcile with this "basing" account.

We might wonder at this point: What exactly is this "basing" relation?[3] Fortunately, I do not need to give a full answer to this question here. To some extent, we have a grasp of what the term "based on evidence" means in everyday English. So, to argue that basing is not sufficient, I need only to identify cases where it is intuitively highly plausible that a belief is based on evidence that supports it, but is not doxastically justified; and to argue that basing is not necessary, I need only to identify cases where it is intuitively highly plausible that a belief is not based on evidence, but is nonetheless doxastically justified.

First, then, the mere fact that a thinker holds a belief on the "basis" of evidence that supports that belief is not *sufficient* for the belief's being doxastically justified. This point is clearly shown by an example that is due to John Turri (2010: 317).[4] Consider a thinker whose evidence includes the two propositions p and "If p, then q." Suppose that from these two propositions the thinker infers q, and thereby comes to believe q. This seems to make it plausible that the thinker "bases" her belief in q on her beliefs in those two propositions, which together entail q. Since q is entailed by the thinker's evidence, it also seems that having the attitude of belief toward q "fits" or "is supported by" the thinker's evidence.

On reflection, however, it is clear that this is not sufficient for the thinker's believing q in a doxastically justified manner—because it does not guarantee that she infers q by means of *modus ponens*. Perhaps, as Turri suggests, she just has an insane disposition to infer *any* conclusion from any pair of premises whatsoever. While the particular inference that she accepts is an instance of modus ponens, it is also an instance of countless insane alternative rules as well. If she inferred q by following one of these insane rules, her belief in q would surely not be doxastically

---

2 Strictly, Conee and Feldman (1985: 24) allow that the evidence e on the basis of which the thinker believes p need not be the *total* evidence that the thinker has at the time, but e must be such that there is no more inclusive body of evidence e' that the thinker has at the time such that having the attitude of belief towards p does not "fit" e'. However, this complication will not matter for our purposes.
3 There has been much discussion of the basing relation. For an illuminating recent discussion, see Neta (2019).
4 For an earlier (though less memorable) presentation of this kind of argument, see Wedgwood (2002: 287).

justified—even though it is clearly based on evidence that supports it. Thus, being held on the basis of supporting evidence is not sufficient to make a belief count as doxastically justified.

Admittedly, this is only a counterexample to the formulation that is given by Conee and Feldman. It is not a counterexample to the formulation that is given by Firth, who says that for a belief to doxastically warranted, the belief must be "psychologically based on or derived from the evidence in a rational way"—and a thinker who is following an insane rule of inference is presumably not basing their belief on the evidence in a "rational way". For this reason, some philosophers—such as Neta (2019)—set out to inquire what more is required of an instance of the basing relation if this instance is to be a case of doxastic justification. As I shall argue in the next section, however, the most plausible account of what makes an instance of the basing relation a case of doxastic justification must appeal to a further feature—which turns out *also* to be present in cases in which a belief is not in any obvious sense "based" on evidence at all. On further reflection, it becomes plausible that it is this further feature—and not anything involving the "basing" relation—that is really essential to doxastic justification.

Even if this worry about the *sufficiency* of "basing" can be addressed, it is also doubtful whether being "based" on evidence is *necessary* for doxastic justification. One way to see this point is by coming to appreciate that there are some beliefs that seem not to be based on evidence at all, even though some of these beliefs seem clearly to be doxastically justified. In particular, there are three salient examples of beliefs that seem, at least *prima facie*, not to be based on evidence.

First, there are one's deeply entrenched background beliefs—beliefs that one has held for years, and which have by now just become an entrenched part of one's outlook on the world.[5] For example, I now have a belief about the name that my paternal grandmother was given at birth—specifically, I believe that her name was "Diana Hawkshaw." On what evidence is this belief now "based"? Clearly, I cannot now "base" this belief on any evidence that I do not now *possess*. Presumably, at some time while I was a child, I had an experience as of being told by some family member that my grandmother's name was "Diana Hawkshaw." However, since I now have absolutely no recollection of that experience, it seems that neither that past experience itself nor any recollection of that past experience is part of the evidence that I now possess.

Admittedly, I do now have various beliefs *about* this belief. For example, I now believe that my grandmother's name must have cropped up in conversations with family members on a number of occasions in the

---

5 The significance of these beliefs that are no longer based on evidence or reasons is discussed by Harman (1986, Chap. 4), Peacocke (1986, Chap. 10), and Millar (1991, Chap. 6).

past, and on all those occasions my belief that her name was "Diana Hawkshaw" was confirmed. But it is doubtful whether my belief about my grandmother's name is now "based on" these beliefs that I now have about that belief. It is not particularly plausible to say that the best explanation of why I now hold this belief is because I now believe that I must have had conversations in the past in which this belief was confirmed. It seems more plausible to say that I hold this belief now simply because it has become part of my entrenched system of background beliefs.

Some philosophers—such as J. L. Pollock and Joseph Cruz (1999: 48)—claim that this belief is based on my *seeming to remember that* my grandmother's name was "Diana Hawkshaw." But it is not clear that this state of *seeming to remember that* ... is anything other than the belief itself, stored away and then accessed from long-term memory. So, it seems dubious to look for a "basis" for the belief in such a state. For these reasons, then, it seems more plausible to conclude that this belief is not now "based" on any evidence at all. The same is true of countless entrenched background beliefs about history, geography, language, science, and much more. But it seems plausible that I hold almost all these beliefs in a rational and doxastically justified manner.

A second example of beliefs that cannot be based on evidence would only arise on certain conceptions of "evidence"—namely, conceptions on which there are some propositions that form part of one's evidence precisely because one believes or knows them. This is admittedly not true on all conceptions of evidence, but it is true on some well-known conceptions, such as that of Timothy Williamson (2000, Chap. 9). So, suppose that a proposition p is part of my evidence, and it is part of my evidence in virtue of the fact that I believe p. As I have noted, we are not assuming any complete account of the "basing" relation here; but it seems very odd to suggest that I "base" my belief in p on my belief in p—or even that I base it on a large collection of beliefs that includes my belief in p. In general, then, it seems that no proposition that is part of one's evidence in virtue of one's believing it can itself be believed on the basis of one's evidence.

A third example concerns *logical truths*. On some conceptions of what it is for evidence to "support" believing a proposition, every proposition that is *entailed* by one's evidence is supported by one's evidence. But of course, logical truths are entailed by every body of evidence whatsoever. So, on these conceptions, logical truths are trivially supported by all evidence whatsoever. For this reason, it seems doubtful whether in believing such a logical truth, I believe it because of the *specific* evidence that I have, given that I would have just as much justification for believing this logical truth whatever evidence I had had.

While the proponent of the "basing" account might be able to resist counterexamples of one of these three kinds, the fact that counterexamples arise in so many different areas poses a severe challenge to this account.

In addition, it also seems that classical subjective Bayesianism about rational belief is hard to reconcile with the "basing" account.[6] On this Bayesian view, for every pair of times t_0 and t_1, and for every perfectly rational thinker x, if the conjunction of all the evidence that x has acquired between t_0 and t_1 is e, then at t_0 and t_1 x holds probabilistically coherent systems of credences C_0 and C_1 respectively, such that for every proposition p for which C_0 and C_1 are defined, $C_1(p) = C_0(p|e)$. That is, the thinker's current credences are the result of *conditionalizing* her earlier credences on the conjunction of all the evidence that she has acquired since then. (Strictly speaking, this Bayesian view only applies to thinkers who do not *lose* any evidence over the relevant period of time.)

It is clear on reflection that this classical subjective Bayesian view should be taken as a view of abstract "propositional" rationality. Nothing in the view prevents it from being possible that a thinker might conform to the requirements of this Bayesian theory through a remarkable cosmic accident.[7] First, the thinker might through some lucky accident have a probabilistically coherent system of credences at t_0, and then through a second still more extraordinary accident shift at t_1 to the result of conditionalizing that first system of credences on all the evidence that she has acquired between t_0 and t_1. If the thinker's conformity to these Bayesian requirements is a sheer lucky fluke in this way, then the credences that she has at t_1 may be the credences that it is abstractly or propositionally rational for the agent to have, but they are not rationally held—or, in other words, they are not doxastically justified.

In general, if the "basing account" is the right conception for full or outright beliefs, it is surely also the right conception for credences or partial degrees of belief: it seems much more plausible that a unified account of doxastic rationality can be given—an account that applies both to full beliefs and to partial degrees of belief—than that radically different accounts apply to beliefs of these two different kinds. So, we should consider a "basing account" of the doxastic rationality of systems of credences as well. According to this account, for a system of credences to be rationally held by a thinker at a time is for this system of credences to be "based" on the evidence that the thinker has at the time.[8] However, there is an obvious problem with this account.

It is a crucial feature of this Bayesian view that, for every time, there are *two* factors that explain why it is rational for the thinker to have a particular system of credences at that time: (a) the prior credences that

---

[6] For a classic statement of this kind of subjective Bayesianism, see Jeffrey (2004).
[7] For this point, see Staffel (2019: 129f.). Relatively few epistemologists have discussed in any detail what it is for credences to be doxastically justified; for an interesting exception, see Dogramaci (2018) and Tang (2016).
[8] For an account of doxastically justified credences that is broadly along these lines, see Smithies (2015).

she had in the past, and (b) the evidence that she has acquired since then. The "basing account" mentions that second factor (b), the evidence that the thinker has at a time, but signally omits the other factor (a) that Bayesianism appeals to—the prior credences that the thinker had in the past.

Thus, for these credences to be rationally held, it is not enough that (i) the thinker bases her credences on the evidence that she has, and (ii) it is rational for her to have these credences at that time. It could be that the thinker bases her credences on her evidence, without manifesting any disposition to conform to the principle of conditionalization, and it is simply an extraordinary cosmic fluke that on this occasion the system of credences that she happens to base on the evidence is a system that results from conditionalizing her past credences on the evidence.

The proponents of the "basing" account might try to suggest at this point that what they mean by "evidence" is something *broader* than what the Bayesians normally mean. In particular, they might try to suggest that, in their terminology, the Bayesian view implies precisely that the thinker's past credences constitute part of her current evidence. But this distorts the ordinary meaning of the term "evidence" beyond its breaking point. Specifically, this suggestion implies that on the Bayesian view, a rational thinker always "bases" her present attitude toward p at least in part on the attitude that she had toward p in the past—and, moreover, that she often does so when she has no current memory of what that past attitude was. This is surely not an instance of what we ordinarily mean by phrases of the form "based on one's current evidence for p."

The proponent of the "basing account" might make one final move at this point. They might amend their account, in the following way. According to this amended account, the system of credences that you now have is rationally held if and only if it is based on *both* the evidence that you now have *and* your past credences. However, it is doubtful whether it can really be the same "basing" relation that holds both (a) between your current credences and your current evidence and (b) between your current credences and your past credences. Even if it is the same relation, it is not clear why this "basing relation" cannot hold as a result of an extraordinary cosmic accident. So, it is doubtful whether this attempt to rescue the "basing" account can succeed in avoiding these objections.[9]

For all these reasons, then, it seems to me advisable to abandon the "basing" account, and to look for an alternative approach. Fortunately,

---

9 A second potential problem would arise if Worsnip (2018) is correct, and the credences that fit optimally with the agent's "evidence" might not be ideally coherent. On this view, the credences that are "based" on the agent's evidence might not even be probabilistically coherent—which would clearly prevent them from being perfectly rational by Bayesian standards.

an alternative approach is close to hand—in an idea that I have defended elsewhere, that rationality is a *virtue*.

Rationality as a Virtue

What is the core of the distinction between propositional and doxastic justification—that is, between the beliefs that *it is rational* for me to hold and the beliefs that I *rationally* hold?

Part of the distinction, evidently, is this: if it is rational for me to hold a certain belief, it does not follow that I actually hold the belief—whereas if I rationally hold a certain belief, it trivially follows that I hold the belief. However, even if a thinker *believes* a proposition p at the same time as p's being a proposition that *it is rational* for her to believe, this is still not sufficient for her to count as *rationally believing p*. It might simply be a lucky fluke that both these two conditions hold at the same time. In general, then, for the thinker to count as rationally believing the proposition, it must *not* be lucky fluke that these two conditions hold. It must somehow be *no accident* that the thinker believes the proposition at the same time as its being a proposition that it is rational for her to believe.

As I have argued elsewhere (Wedgwood 2017: 140–2), this distinction is in fact precisely analogous to a distinction that Aristotle drew in the *Nicomachean Ethics* (1105a17–b9). An agent might perform an act of type A at the same time as being in a situation in which *it is just* for her to perform an act of type A—even if it is simply a lucky fluke that both of these conditions hold (perhaps it just so happens that her wickedly unjust plans require her to perform an act of type A in this situation). In this case, the agent might be doing a *just act*, but she would not count as *acting justly*.

If an act is to be a case of the agent's acting justly, the following conditions must hold. First, in performing this act, the agent must be manifesting an *appropriate disposition*—specifically, a disposition that non-accidentally tends to result in the agent's doing just acts. Second, this disposition must manifest itself in its characteristic way—so that the act in question really is just (at least to a significant degree). Some theories of virtue would add further conditions (for example, perhaps the manifestation of this disposition must take the form of the rational pursuit of goals—such that there is a reliable tendency for the rational pursuit of these goals to result in the agent's doing just acts). But we need not worry about these details here. The important point for our purposes is that having such an appropriate disposition is part of what is involved in possessing the *virtue of justice*—that is, part of what is involved in being a just person.

In a similar way, I propose, if a belief is a case of the thinker's rationally believing p, the following conditions must hold. First, in believing p, the thinker must be manifesting an *appropriate disposition*—specifically, a disposition that non-accidentally tends to result in the thinker's believing propositions that it is rational for her to believe.[10] Second, the disposition must manifest itself in its characteristic way—so that the belief in question really is one that it is (to a least a significant degree) rational for the thinker to hold. Such a disposition is an example of a broader genus—namely, dispositions that non-accidentally tend to result in the thinker's having attitudes that it is rational for her to have. Having such dispositions seems to be part of what is involved in being a rational thinker. I shall refer to dispositions of this kind as *rational dispositions*. My central proposal here, then, is that for an attitude to be rationally held is for it to be a characteristic manifestation of a rational disposition.[11]

In this way, there seem to be three features associated with rationality:

(i) Being an attitude that *it is rational* for the thinker to have at the time—a feature exemplified by some of the possible attitudes that are available for the thinker to have at the time.
(ii) *Having a rational disposition*—a feature exemplified by thinkers, which non-accidentally tends to result in the thinkers' having attitudes that have the first feature.
(iii) An attitude's being a case of *the thinker's thinking rationally*—a feature exemplified by an attitude whenever the attitude is the manifestation of a disposition that makes it the case that the thinker has the second feature, and the disposition is manifested in its characteristic way, so that the attitude has the first feature (at least to a significant degree).

As we have seen, there is a parallel trio of features associated with justice:

(i) Being an act that *it is just* for the agent to perform at the time—a feature exemplified by some of the possible acts that are available to the agent at the time.
(ii) Having a *disposition* that non-accidentally tends to result in one's performing such just acts—a feature exemplified by agents.

---

10 What if a belief results from the operation of *two* different dispositions—one of which is rational, and the other irrational? The question here is whether (a) both these dispositions are causally necessary parts of a single sufficient causal explanation, or (b) each of these dispositions is sufficient by itself (so that we have a case of causal overdetermination). I am inclined to think that in the former case, the belief is *not* a case of believing rationally, but in the latter case, it *is* a case of believing rationally. So, more precisely, what is required for believing rationally is that the agent must manifest rational dispositions, and the manifestation of these rational dispositions must be a sufficient explanation of the agent's having the belief. But it is not required that this should be the *only* sufficient explanation of the belief.
11 For a related view, developed within a distinctively externalist framework, see Lasonen-Aarnio (forthcoming).

(iii) An act's being a case of the agent's *acting justly*—a feature exemplified by an act whenever the act is the manifestation of a disposition that makes it the case that the agent has the second feature, and the disposition is manifested in its characteristic way, so that the act has the first feature (to a significant degree).

Each of these three features associated with justice is an evaluatively positive feature—a feature in virtue of which the act or agent in question is good in a certain respect. In the case of rationality too, each of these three features seems to be an evaluatively positive feature—a feature that makes the attitude or thinker in question good in certain respect. Because of these parallels between rationality and a paradigmatic virtue like justice, it seems reasonable to conclude that rationality itself is a virtue. These rational dispositions are at least part of what is involved in possessing the virtue of rationality—or in other words in being a rational thinker.

I have suggested that having rational dispositions of this kind is "part" of what is involved in being a rational thinker. That is, having such dispositions is a constitutively necessary condition, but perhaps not a sufficient condition, for being a rational thinker. This is for two reasons. First, to count as a "rational thinker", it is not enough just to possess a disposition of this kind that covers an extremely narrow range of cases; one has to possess such dispositions covering a sufficiently wide range of cases. Second, in most contexts, it would not be true to describe someone who possessed such rational dispositions as a "rational thinker", unless these dispositions were actually *manifested*, at least much of the time, in the thinker's mental life. As we shall see in Section 13.4 below, it is possible to possess a disposition even if the disposition is blocked or inhibited from being manifested in one's actual thinking by the counteracting influence of some interfering factor.[12]

Exactly how these dispositions operate depends on contingent facts about how the human mind works, or about the particular cognitive skills and abilities that the thinker has acquired. For example, in many cases they may involve what cognitive scientists think of as mental "heuristics", of the sort that are characteristic of quick-and-dirty "System 1" thinking.[13] I am inclined to suspect that for our purposes it does not matter exactly how these dispositions work, so long as these dispositions non-accidentally tend to result in the thinker's having attitudes that it is rational for her to have. Whenever one of your beliefs is the manifestation of rational dispositions of this kind, then in a clear sense it is no accident that it is a belief that it is rational for you to have. In this case,

---

12 For this point about dispositions, see Bird (1998).
13 For a discussion of the distinction between "System 1" and "System 2" thinking, see Kahneman (2011).

this is not just a belief that it is rational for you to have—it is a belief that is actually rationally held.

Moreover, so far as I can see, this conception of what it is for a belief to be rationally held need not presuppose any particular conception of belief. All that is presupposed is that your believing proposition *p* at time *t* can itself count as your manifesting a certain disposition that you now have. This presupposition is compatible with many different conceptions of belief. Even if your believing *p* at *t* consists in the fact that a sentence of your "Language of Thought" that means *p* is tokened in your "Belief Box" at *t*, this fact might itself count as your manifesting an appropriate disposition—specifically, a disposition for sentences of the relevant kind to be tokened in your "Belief Box" in response to stimuli of a certain corresponding kind.

To fix ideas, in what follows I shall assume a more detailed conception of dispositions.[14] Specifically, I shall assume that every disposition can be specified by a *function* that maps *stimulus* conditions onto *response* conditions. For example, the disposition of *fragility* can be specified by a function that maps the stimulus condition *being struck at t* onto the response condition *shattering shortly after t*. The notion of a disposition also presupposes the idea of a *range of normal cases*. These are actual and merely possible cases in which other things are equal—cases in which factors that would interfere with the operation of the disposition are absent. Something possesses the disposition if and only if it has intrinsic properties in virtue of which, in any *normal* case in which it is in one of these stimulus conditions, it goes into the corresponding response condition. For example, something is fragile if and only if it has intrinsic properties in virtue of which, in any normal case in which it is struck, it shatters shortly afterwards.

Each of the rational dispositions that we are interested in is a mental disposition of a certain kind. Specifically, the stimulus conditions for each of these dispositions concern the facts about one's cognitive situation that are beyond the control of one's reasoning capacities at the relevant time—such as facts about one's past attitudes, and facts about the sensory experiences, memories, and emotions that one has at the time. The disposition's response to these facts consists in one's having a certain set of attitudes at the time. The disposition can be specified by a function that maps stimulus conditions of this kind onto corresponding response conditions.

The notion of "manifesting" a disposition is a broadly causal notion. A disposition is triggered by one of the relevant stimulus conditions; and when the disposition is manifested, the response is caused by the stimulus. For example, one rational disposition that a thinker might have

---

14 I am drawing here on some of my earlier discussions of dispositions; see Wedgwood (2007: 27f., and 2017: 76–8).

is what we could call the *modus ponens* disposition. This disposition is triggered by the thinker's considering an argument that is an instance of *modus ponens*, and is manifested in the thinker's accepting that argument (at least in the sense of conditionally believing the argument's conclusion, conditionally on the assumption of the argument's premises). In manifesting this disposition, the response (the thinker's acceptance of the argument) is caused by the stimulus (the thinker's considering the argument).

If this account is along the right lines, there is a *causal* element in an attitude's being doxastically justified or rationally held: whether or not one believes p in a doxastically justified manner depends on the causal explanation of one's believing p—on the dispositions that one manifests in holding this belief.[15] By contrast, there is no such causal condition on propositional justification. Whether or not one has propositional justification for p just depends on how the attitude of believing p "fits" with one's cognitive situation. Even if one does actually believe p, the fact that one has propositional justification for believing p entails nothing about the causal explanation of why one believes p.

It is because of this causally explanatory element that we can also talk about such doxastically justified rational thinking as consisting in having attitudes "for the right kind of reasons." The "reasons" that we are alluding to here are the *motivating reasons* for which one has the attitude in question—that is, the intuitively intelligible psychological explanation of why one has the attitude. (We may assume that these psychological explanations always appeal at least implicitly to the dispositions that the thinker is manifesting in having the attitudes in question.) If the attitude is rationally held, then this psychological explanation is "of the right kind" in the sense that it is the right kind of explanation to make the attitude into a manifestation of rational dispositions of the kind that I have described.

Degrees of Rational Virtue

The account sketched in the previous section is, in an important respect, rough and incomplete. It does not take account of the fact that rationality comes in *degrees*. Indeed, all three of the good features that I distinguished above—the abstract "propositional" rationality of attitudes, the rationality of the relevant dispositions, and the property of being an attitude that is rationally held—seem to come in degrees. Of the various attitudes toward p that are now available to you, some are more rational than others; some mental dispositions of the relevant kind are more rational than others; and some attitudes are more rationally held than others.

---

15 Keith Lehrer (1974: 125) argued against imposing any causal requirement on doxastic justification. For a largely convincing reply to Lehrer, see Audi (1983).

On reflection, it is clearly important to give an account of these degrees of rationality. This is because it is extremely unlikely—if not downright impossible—for creatures like us to have dispositions that are *ideally* rational, in the sense that these dispositions *infallibly* result in *perfectly rational* attitudes in *all* normal cases in which they are manifested. If this sort of ideal rationality is effectively unattainable for us, what we need is some way of comparing which of the actually available dispositions are more rational and which are less rational.

Let us start by investigating the degree of rationality that a mental disposition may have *relative to a range of cases*. This range of cases may consist of *all* normal cases in which the disposition is manifested at all, or it may consist only of some narrower range of cases, all of which are sufficiently similar to some particular case that is under consideration. (We shall later consider how to make sense of statements that characterize dispositions as having some degree of rationality that is not explicitly relativized to a range of cases in this way.)

What is it, then, for one disposition to be more rational than another (relative to to a given range of cases)? The rough idea is that the more rational disposition is more *reliable* at yielding attitudes that it is abstractly or propositionally rational for the thinker to have. This notion of a "more reliable" disposition may be made more precise in the following way.

Crucially, as I noted at the outset, the abstract propositional rationality of attitudes also comes in degrees. Some of the available attitudes "fit" the agent's cognitive situation better than others. For example, given my past beliefs and my current sensory experiences, the attitude of *believing* that I am now sitting in a chair "fits" my cognitive situation much better than the attitude of *doubting* or *disbelieving* that I am now sitting in a chair.

Moreover, I shall assume that the degree to which a set of attitudes is abstractly or propositionally rational can in principle be *measured*. This assumption is especially plausible in the case of credences or partial degrees of belief. According to many probabilistic theories in formal epistemology, for every thinker and every time there is some probability distribution such that the degree to which a set of credences is rational for that thinker and that time is determined by how *closely* those credences *approximate* to that probability distribution.[16] To fix ideas, we may assume that some probabilistic theory of this sort is correct—although strictly all that we need for our purposes is the more general assumption that the degree to which a set of attitudes is rational can in principle be measured.

As I explained, we are investigating the degrees of rationality that dispositions can have relative to a certain "range of cases." This "range of

---

16 For a pioneering discussion of how to measure the propositional rationality of credence assignments, see Staffel (2019).

cases" can be thought of as a *set of possible worlds*—which are all alike in that the thinker manifests the disposition at the relevant time, but differs from each other in the precise cognitive situation of the thinker at the time, and in the response that the manifestation of the disposition yields to that situation. At each of these worlds, the thinker's response has a certain degree of abstract propositional rationality. The facts of the thinker's psychology also fix a certain *chance* function, which assigns a conditional chance to each of these worlds, conditionally on the relevant disposition's being manifested at the relevant time.[17]

Together, these degrees of abstract propositional rationality and this chance function determine the *expected degree of rationality* of the responses that the disposition yields within this range of cases.[18] I propose that for one disposition to be *more rational* than another (relative to a range of cases) is for the first disposition to have a higher expected degree of rationality (within this range of cases).

According to this proposal, then, for a disposition to be *ideally* rational within a given range of cases is for it to be conditionally *certain* that the thinker's attitudes will be *perfectly rational* in all these cases, given that the disposition is manifested at the relevant time. Among the many dispositions that are less than ideally rational, some are more rational than others. For example, it might be conditionally certain that the attitudes resulting from one disposition D_1 will be 80% rational, given that this disposition D_1 is manifested, while there might be a conditional chance of 50% that the attitudes resulting from a second disposition D_2 will be 90% rational and a conditional chance of 50% that these attitudes will be 60% rational. In this case, the expected rationality of the attitudes that result from D_1 is 80% while the expected rationality of the attitudes that result from D_2 is 75%. According to my proposal, then, D_1 is more rational than D_2.

For the rest of this discussion, however, I need not assume the precise details of this account of what it is for one disposition to be more rational than another, relative to a range of cases. These details are given here only as a proof of concept, to make it plausible that there are no insuperable difficulties in developing such an account; I need not deny that other accounts may be worth considering.

---

17 If, as Glynn (2010) has argued, chance functions are relativized to levels of causal structure, these chance functions must be relativized to the *psychological* level. For discussion, see Wedgwood (2017: 80f.).

18 Strictly, this requires that the degrees of propositional rationality of the disposition's outputs in the relevant cases can all be measured on the same scale. On one view of the matter, these degrees of rationality are only comparable between credence assignments that are defined over the *same* set of propositions. If this view is correct, the relevant "range of cases" where the rationality of the disposition is assessed must be restricted to cases where the thinker considers the same set of propositions.

How can this account of the degrees of rationality that dispositions have *relative to a range of cases* make sense of statements that characterize dispositions' degrees of rationality *without* any explicit relativization to ranges of cases? Somehow, the meaning that such a statement has, along with the context in which the statement is made, must determine some particular range of cases as the range that is *relevant* to the statement's truth-conditions in that context. In fact, I do not need to commit myself here to any particular account of how the statement's meaning together with the context determine this. Again, however, it may be useful to gesture in the direction of an account—to make it plausible that no special obstacles stand in the way of developing such an account.

Two possible accounts stand out as particularly promising. According to the first account, if a statement is not explicitly relativized to a range of cases, it is always the *widest* range of cases—including all normal possible cases in which the disposition is manifested at all—that is relevant to the statement's truth-conditions. By contrast, the second account is a form of *contextualism*. On this contextualist account, it is part of the *context* in which the rationality of a disposition is discussed that the participants in the conversation have a certain range of cases at least roughly in mind. In some contexts, they may be focusing on the widest range—all normal possible cases in which the disposition is manifested, but in other contexts, they may be focusing on some *narrower* range of cases that is somehow salient. According to this second account, it is this contextually salient range of cases that is relevant to the truth-conditions of such statements.[19]

At all events, it is straightforward to extend this account of the degrees of rationality that *dispositions* may have, to provide an account of the degrees of rationality of *manifestations* of those dispositions. In saying that one attitude is "more rationally held" than another, we are in effect saying that the first attitude is the manifestation of a more rational disposition than the second.

Finally, we can also use this account of degrees of rationality to give an account of what it means to make the non-comparative statement that a belief is "rationally held" (or that it is "well founded" or "doxastically justified"). I propose that this statement means simply that the belief is the manifestation of a *sufficiently rational* disposition.

Many philosophers of language and semanticists would also accept a contextualist interpretation of this talk of what is "sufficiently rational." On this contextualist interpretation, we can always ask, "The disposition's degree of rationality is sufficient *for what*?"—and an answer to this question must somehow be implicit in the context, if the statement that

---

19 In general, I would argue that disposition ascriptions are typically context-sensitive in this way. For a related claim about the context-sensitivity of explanatory claims, see Wedgwood (2020: Section 5).

the belief is "rationally held" is to have determinate truth-conditions.[20] Again, however, I need not commit myself to this second kind of contextualism here. Perhaps the normal meaning of "rationally held" fixes a certain degree of rationality as "sufficient" independently of the conversational context: for example, perhaps we can say, in general, that a belief counts as "rationally held" if and only if it is the manifestation of a disposition that exemplifies as high a degree of rationality as is feasibly achievable for the majority of human beings. At all events, it seems that there is no difficulty in principle in using this account of degrees of rationality to give an account of what makes it true to say that an attitude such as a belief is rationally held.

Objections and Replies

The account sketched above may seem reminiscent of *reliabilist* approaches to epistemology, such as the approach of Goldman (1979). So, it is natural to inquire whether it is open to the same objections as reliabilism.

First, however, before inquiring into this, we need to see that the account differs from the familiar forms of reliabilism in a crucial way. The most familiar forms of reliabilism focus on reliability at (a) generating *true* beliefs and (b) not generating *false* beliefs. In other words, the relevant kind of "reliability" for these familiar forms of reliabilism is *truth-conduciveness*. This kind of reliability or truth-conduciveness lies at the center both of the older kind of reliabilism that was developed by Goldman (1979), with his emphasis on the idea of "reliable processes," and of the more recent "virtue epistemology" of Sosa (2007).

By contrast, my kind of reliabilism about the virtue of rationality focuses on a different kind of reliability—not truth-conduciveness, but *rationality-conduciveness*. On my account, for an attitude that the thinker holds to be rationally held, the attitude must be the manifestation of an appropriately "reliable" disposition; but the disposition needs to be "reliable," not at resulting in *true* beliefs, but at resulting in the thinker's having credences that it is *rational* for the thinker to have.[21]

For this reason, my account is quite compatible with epistemological *internalism*. This account is thus compatible with the view that the degree

---

20 For a contrary view about "rational," see Siscoe (2021). According to Siscoe, "rational" always strictly means "perfectly rational" (just as "certain" strictly means "fully certain" and "clean" means "completely clean")—although this strict meaning can sometimes be used loosely or imprecisely.
21 It is unclear how to the notion of reliability as truth-conduciveness can even be applied to partial credences or degrees of belief. For an illuminating exploration of this issue, see Tang (2016), although from my internalist point of view, Tang's way of assessing credences' reliability mixes together notions—like truth and evidence—that are best kept more cleanly separated.

to which each of the various available credence assignments is rational for a thinker to have at a time is determined by purely "internal" facts about the thinker's mind at that time. In this way, my account is compatible with internalism about abstract "propositional" rationality.

Indeed, my account is even compatible with a kind of internalism about rationally held (or doxastically justified) attitudes. It is admittedly not plausible that we can infallibly introspect either (a) which dispositions each of our beliefs or other attitudes result from, or (b) how reliable these dispositions are at resulting in our having attitudes that it are rational for us to have. But if internalism about abstract propositional rationality is true, then both of these facts (a) and (b) are, broadly speaking, facts about our minds that are independent of any facts about our environment that could vary while our minds continue to function in the same way.

A further difference from some forms of reliabilism is that my account does not appeal to the notion of a "reliable *process*." The process as a result of which the thinker holds a belief reaches back into the past – sometimes very far back. The account that I have proposed does not focus on this historical process, but on the explanation of why the thinker holds the belief in question at the particular time in question—where I assume that this explanation will be equivalent to one that explicitly cites the dispositions that the thinker manifests in holding this belief at this time.

Nonetheless, some philosophers might object to the appeal to any kind of "reliability." Specifically, these philosophers might object that the "reliability" of a disposition is a matter of its *track record*—whereas it seems that the fact that a particular belief is rationally held at a particular time does not depend on the track record of any of the thinker's traits, but purely on how things are with that belief at that time.

However, this objection misinterprets the kind of "reliability" that my account appeals to. This kind of reliability does not depend on the track record that of any of the thinker's traits have *over time*. It depends on how the disposition performs across a range of *possible worlds*. Talking about the reliability across these possible worlds of the disposition that one manifests in holding a given attitude is really just a way of talking about the *modal* properties that this disposition has in this case; specifically, it is a just of discussing whether in this case the disposition *safely* or *robustly* or *non-accidentally* results in one's holding an attitude that it is rational for one to hold. This is a feature of how the belief is held at the particular time in question—not a feature of any kind of "track record."

Similarly, even the ascription of this mental disposition to a thinker is not a claim about any kind of "track record." There are plenty of dispositions that an item may have without ever manifesting these dispositions. One reason for this is that the item may never be in the relevant stimulus condition: certain poisons may never be ingested; certain fragile objects may never be struck. Moreover, even if the item is sometimes in the relevant stimulus condition, it may never be in such a stimulus condition in a *normal* case: for example, it may be that a certain poison is only ever ingested by someone who has taken the antidote. In other words, it may be that interfering factors always intervene to block the manifestation of the disposition. According to the assumptions about dispositions that I articulated in Section 13.2 above, to ascribe a disposition to a thinker is not to make any claim about the thinker's track record in the actual world, but to make a claim about the modal properties of some of the thinker's traits with respect to normal cases—cases where interfering factors are absent. For these reasons, then, this objection to my account of rationally held attitudes is misplaced.

The best-known objection to reliabilism is the so-called "generality problem," which was pressed by Conee and Feldman (1998). Consider the version of reliabilism that says that a belief is rationally held just in case it results from a belief-forming process that is of a *generally reliable type*. The trouble with this is that every token process that results in a belief is an instance of countlessly many types—and some of these types are much more reliable than others. How are we to tell which, of the countlessly many types that a given token process instantiates, is the type whose degree of reliability determines whether or not the belief is rationally held? The theory as stated seems to have no principled way of answering this question.

However, as I shall now explain, there are several differences between my account and the version of reliabilism that Conee and Feldman criticize, which enable my account to answer this problem.

First, unlike the notion of a "belief-forming process," the very notion of a "disposition" introduces a kind of generality. As explained in Section 13.2 above, the disposition is specified by a *function* from stimulus conditions to response conditions—where both the stimulus conditions and the response conditions are in effect general *types* of condition (not particular conditions). Thus, the very nature of the disposition determines a certain range of cases—namely, the range of normal cases in which the disposition is manifested. These cases are all similar to each other along two dimensions: (a) in the dispositions that are manifested in these cases—and so in the stimulus and response conditions that these dispositions involve, and also (b) in the factors that make these cases count as normal.

Second, as we saw in the previous section, my account makes room for a kind of *contextualism* about what it means to ascribe a degree of rationality to a disposition. It may not always mean that the disposition results in a rational attitude in *every* normal possible case in which it is manifested. It may be that, in the context in which a degree of rationality is ascribed to the disposition, a narrower range of cases is salient. For example, in such contexts, our focus may be on a particular belief that a thinker holds, and on the range of cases that are sufficiently similar to *this* belief on the two relevant dimensions of similarity—namely, (a) the manifestation of the relevant dispositions and (b) the factors in virtue of which these cases count as normal. For it to be true to ascribe a certain degree of rationality-conduciveness to the disposition in a given context, the disposition must yield beliefs with corresponding degrees of rationality in the range of cases that is relevant in this context.

In general, these two elements—the inherent generality of the dispositions that are manifested (along with the two dimensions of similarity associated with these dispositions), and the kind of contextualism that I have described—seem to provide enough material for a successful response to the generality problem.

A Further Advantage of this Account

Probabilism is often thought to be inadequate as an epistemology for mathematics. Presumably, every provable mathematical truth has probability 1. So, the only perfectly rational level of confidence that you can have in a mathematical truth is the highest possible level—that is, credence 1, the attitude of being totally convinced of the mathematical truth. However, consider an extremely complex proposition p that is in fact a mathematical truth. Professional mathematicians may often have a level of confidence in this proposition p that is considerably lower than credence 1. Can it really be right to say that it is not rational for these mathematicians to have such non-maximal levels of confidence in this truth? Considerations like these have often led philosophers—especially philosophers of mathematics—to doubt the correctness of probabilistic approaches to epistemology.[22]

The account given above provides a way of defending probabilism against this objection. Credence 1 is indeed the only attitude that one can take toward this mathematical truth that it is *perfectly* rational for one to have. But it may also be that a lower level of confidence in this truth is the only attitude that would result from any of the mental dispositions that are both (i) sufficiently rational and (ii) genuinely available to the normal human thinker.

So, we can interpret the judgment that it is rational for the mathematician to have a non-maximal degree of belief in the mathematical truth, not as a judgment about abstract "propositional" rationality, but as a judgment about the attitudes that would result from any sufficiently rational available disposition. To interpret the judgment in this second way, we evidently need some way of making sense of what it is for dispositions to

---

22 I have encountered this argument in conversation with both Christopher Peacocke and Ian Rumfitt.

be "sufficiently rational." Fortunately, we can make sense of this by using the account that I sketched in Section 13.3.

Why would it be that the most rational available dispositions would not result in the mathematician's instantly assigning credence 1 to this complex mathematical truth? The reason is just that, if the mathematician were instantly to assign credence 1 to this truth, as soon as she considers it, this could only be through sheer dumb luck; it could not be through the operation of a reliable disposition.

To explore some of the implications of this, let us consider an example that is due to Dogramaci (2018). Before you get a chance to do the math, a credence of 0.1 that the trillionth digit of π is a 2 seems entirely rational. But of course, the probability that the trillionth digit of π is a 2 must be either 0 or 1. So, according to a probabilistic theory of abstract propositional rationality, a credence of 0.1 in this proposition is necessarily irrational: the only perfectly rational attitude to have toward this proposition is either credence 0 (if it is false) or credence 1 (if it is true).

However, consider the disposition that one would be manifesting in having a credence of 0.1 in this proposition. Presumably, this disposition would also yield a credence of 0.1 in each of the nine other propositions of the same form—that the trillionth digit of π is a 3, that it is a 4, and so on. To keep things simple, let us assume that this disposition is *certain* to yield this credence assignment in every relevant case. So, this disposition yields an assignment of credence 0.1 to all ten propositions—where, of these ten propositions, nine have probability 0 and one has probability 1. On plausible measures of degrees of rationality, this credence assignment is at least *more* rational than (say) an assignment of credence 0.5 to all of these ten propositions.[23] Thus, this disposition is more rational than an alternative disposition that is certain to yield an assignment of credence 0.5 to each of these propositions in every relevant case.

In general, it seems that every disposition that is available to us will either assign the *same* credence to all of these ten propositions, or else it will just assign credences to them at random. Thus, the most rational available disposition seems to be the one that assigns a credence of 0.1 to all of these propositions—in spite of the probabilistic incoherence of these credence assignments.

In most discussions of the distinction between propositional and doxastic justification, it is assumed that doxastic justification entails propositional justification. However, the example just discussed shows that this is not true in general. If as a matter of fact the trillionth digit of π is a 2,

---

23 For example, suppose that degrees of irrationality are measured by the expected Brier score (see Staffel 2019: Chap. 4). Then, since it is *certain* that one of these ten propositions is true and the remaining nine are false, the first credence assignment has degree of irrationality 0.9 (= 1 × 0.81 + 9 × 0.01), while the second credence assignment has degree of irrationality 2.5 (= 1 × 0.25 + 9 × 0.25).

then having credence 0.1 in this true proposition does not have a very high degree of abstract propositional rationality; credence 0.1 is quite far from the ideally rational credence of 1. Nonetheless, this may be the credence that is yielded by the most rational available disposition, and in that sense it would be true in many contexts to describe this credence as "rationally held." The reason for this is that having credence 0.1 in this mathematical truth is still, as I put it in Section 13.2 above, a characteristic manifestation of a sufficiently rational disposition.

According to my account, it is only if the disposition manifested by an attitude is *ideally* rational—that is, if the disposition *infallibly* yields a *perfectly* rational attitude in *every* case in which it is manifested—that doxastic rationality guarantees propositional rationality. As I have argued, however, for thinkers like us such ideally rational dispositions are rarely if ever available. It is for this reason that we need an account that recognizes that both doxastic and propositional justification comes in degrees.

The "basing account," as I have argued, cannot provide the sort of account that we need. However, the rival "virtue manifestation" account that I have proposed here looks like a more promising alternative.

References

Audi, Robert (1983). "The Causal Structure of Indirect Justification", *Journal of Philosophy* 80 (7): 398–415.

Bird, Alexander (1998). "Dispositions and Antidotes", *Philosophical Quarterly* 48: 227–34.

Conee, Earl, and Feldman, Richard (1985). "Evidentialism", *Philosophical Studies* 48: 15–34.

——— (1998). "The Generality Problem for Reliabilism", *Philosophical Studies* 89 (1): 1–29.

Dogramaci, Sinan (2018). "Rational Credence Through Reasoning", *Philosophers' Imprint* 18 (11), 1–25.

Firth, Roderick (1978). "Are Epistemic Concepts Reducible to Ethical Concepts?", in Alvin Goldman and Jaegwon Kim, eds., *Values and Morals* (Dordrecht: D. Reidel): 215–29.

Glynn, Luke (2010). "Deterministic Chance", *British Journal for the Philosophy of Science* 61: 51–80.

Goldman, Alvin (1979). "What is Justified Belief?" in George Pappas, ed., *Justification and Knowledge* (Dordrecht: D. Reidel): 1–25.

Harman, Gilbert (1986). *Change in View* (Cambridge, Massachusetts: MIT Press).

Kahneman, Daniel (2011). *Thinking Fast and Slow* (New York: Farrar, Straus, and Giroux).

Lasonen-Aarnio, Maria (forthcoming). "Perspectives and Good Dispositions", *Philosophy and Phenomenological Research*.

Lehrer, Keith (1974). *Knowledge* (Oxford: Oxford University Press).

Millar, Alan (1991). *Reasons and Experience* (Oxford: Oxford University Press).

Neta, Ram (2019). "The Basing Relation", *Philosophical Review* 128 (2): 179–217.
Peacocke, Christopher (1986). *Thoughts: An Essay on Content* (Oxford: Blackwell).
Pollock, J. L., and Cruz, Joseph (1999). *Contemporary Theories of Knowledge*, 2nd edition (Lanham, Maryland: Rowman and Littlefield).
Siscoe, R. W. (2021). "Belief, Rational and Justified", *Mind* 130 (517), 59–83.
Smithies, Declan (2015). "Ideal Rationality and Logical Omniscience", *Synthese* 192 (9), 2769–93.
Sosa, Ernest (2007). *A Virtue Epistemology* (New York: Oxford University Press).
Staffel, Julia (2019). *Unsettled Thoughts: A Theory of Degrees of Rationality* (Oxford: Oxford University Press).
Tang, Weng Hong (2016). "Reliability Theories of Justified Credence", *Mind* 125 (497): 63–94.
Turri, John (2010). "On the Relationship between Propositional and Doxastic Justification", *Philosophy and Phenomenological Research* 80 (2), 312–26.
Wedgwood, Ralph (2002). "The Aim of Belief", *Philosophical Perspectives* 16: 267–97.
Wedgwood, Ralph (2007). *The Nature of Normativity* (Oxford: Oxford University Press).
Wedgwood, Ralph (2017). *The Value of Rationality* (Oxford: Oxford University Press).
Wedgwood, Ralph (2020). "The Internalist Virtue Theory of Knowledge", *Synthese* 197: 5357–78.
Williamson, Timothy (2000). *Knowledge and Its Limits* (Oxford: Oxford University Press).
Worsnip, Alex (2018). "The Conflict of Evidence and Coherence", *Philosophy and Phenomenological Research* 96 (1): 3–44.

14 Intersubjective Propositional Justification[1]

Silvia De Toffoli

The distinction between propositional and doxastic justification is commonly accepted (if not uniformly understood) among epistemologists. It was introduced by Roderick Firth in 1978 in the context of a metaepistemological inquiry on whether epistemic concepts could be reduced to ethical concepts (which he concludes with a negative answer). Firth sets out to answer that question by focusing on one central epistemological concept, that of "epistemic justification" or, (in his terminology) equivalently, of "warrant." He observes that although it is common to speak of justification (or warrant) *tout court*, this concept is ambiguous:

> Although I have referred in the singular to the epistemic concept expressed by the term "warranted" there are in fact two such concepts. For there is an important respect in which a belief may be warranted although we are subject to epistemic criticism for having that belief. We may be criticized on the ground that our doxastic state is not psychologically based on or derived from the relevant evidence in a rational way.
>
> (Firth, 1978, p. 217)

These are cases in which a subject's evidence sufficiently supports a proposition, but the subject believes such a proposition for reasons other than the ones offered by her evidence. For instance, Sarah might have enough evidence for believing that Till is a thief, but she actually believes that Till is a thief because she is biased against the minority group to which Till belongs. She can therefore be critiqued for holding the belief that Till is a thief even if it is true and she has enough evidence for it.

According to Firth, and to what has become the most widely held view on the matter, *a subject has propositional justification to believe that p if and only if she has sufficient epistemic reasons to believe that*

---

[1] Special thanks to Paul Silva for detailed feedback on previous versions of this chapter. Thanks are also due to Anne Meylan for comments and to Hilary Kornblith for multiple discussions about the relationship between propositional and doxastic justification.

DOI: 10.4324/9781003008101-19

p. Propositional justification is thus detached from actual beliefs. In our example, Sarah has propositional justification to believe that Till is a thief even if she is subject to epistemic criticism for holding such a belief. Moreover, she would still have propositional justification to believe that Till is a thief even if she did not actually believe it.

What does attach to actual beliefs is another type of justification: *doxastic justification*. *A subject is doxastically justified in believing p if and only if (i) she has propositional justification for p, (ii) she believes p, and (iii) she bases her belief that p on her sufficient epistemic reasons to believe that p.* According to this widely held picture, propositional justification is fundamental and doxastic justification is a derivative notion. Silva and Oliveira (forthcoming) call it the *reasons-first picture*: "The reasons-first picture characterizes propositional justification in terms of epistemic reasons and doxastic justification in terms of propositional justification." This picture groups together a cluster of theories that cash out in different ways certain central notions, such as *sufficient epistemic reasons* and *basing relation*.[2]

Doxastic justification is attached to existing psychological states whereas propositional justification is not. Nonetheless, propositional justification depends on the subject's evidence, and thus on "evidential psychological states" that is, those states that determine a subject's evidence:

> this assessment of propositional warrant is a judgment about the evidential relationship between certain psychological states and the proposition .... With appropriate qualifications we might want to call this a 'logical' relationship.
>
> (Firth, 1978, pp. 218–219)

Among the qualifications, we should include the assumption that logical relationships are not only deductive relationships, but also inductive. Essentially, it must be in principle possible to rationally infer p from one's evidence. Crucially, however, it does not have to be *actually* possible for a particular subject to perform such an inference:

> an assessment of doxastic warrant requires psychological information that is irrelevant to assessments of propositional warrant.
>
> (*ibid.*, p. 219)

According to the reasons-first picture, whether a subject S has propositional justification for p depends exclusively on the evidential support relations between p and S's evidence. What's more, these evidential support relations are a priori knowable (Chisholm, 1989; Kornblith, 2017).

---

2 For a discussion of the epistemic basing relation see (Neta, 2019).

Being not contaminated by our psychological idiosyncrasies, this conception of propositional justification is simple and clear. But is it perhaps too simple and clear to be of use in our epistemological theorizing? Hilary Kornblith (2017) thinks so. In (2017) and in a chapter of the present volume, Kornblith casts doubt on the adequacy of this conception of propositional justification to evaluate ordinary inferential beliefs. He argues that adopting this notion would lead to skepticism. He then proposes to break away from the reasons-first picture and to consider doxastic justification to be fundamental (more on this below).

In this chapter, I focus on beliefs that derive from going through deductive arguments. In keeping with Kornblith, I suggest that even for these kinds of beliefs, the apsychological notion of propositional justification introduced by Firth can hardly be reconciled with the idea that justification is a central component of knowledge. In order to propose an alternative notion, I start with an analysis of doxastic justification. Like Kornblith, I thus argue for the fundamentality of doxastic justification. My strategy is, however, different insofar as it operates within the reasons-first picture. The fundamentality claim that I endorse is not a metaphysical claim, but rather a conceptual claim according to which it is only by starting with doxastic justification that we can formulate a notion of propositional justification that is adequate for epistemological theorizing.

One might think that a way to make this notion of propositional justification more useful in epistemology is to impose subjective constraints on it. As will become clear in the following, however, this poses the risk of ending up with a notion of justification that is too idiosyncratic and thus unable to perform its characteristic normative role. I will propose a notion of propositional justification, *intersubjective propositional justification*, that is neither entirely apsychological nor idiosyncratic. To do so, I will argue that in order to be able to attribute propositional justification to a subject, we will have to consider her social context as well as broad features of our human cognitive architecture.

The organization of the chapter is as follows. In Section 14.1, I discuss the notion of propositional justification that arises naturally when taking propositional justification as fundamental, *objective propositional justification*. In Section 14.2, I describe Kornblith's take on ordinary inferential beliefs and his reasons to think that doxastic justification is fundamental. In Section 14.3, I dive into the logical and mathematical case and show that the notion of objective propositional justification cannot play a substantial role in logical and mathematical knowledge. In Section 14.4, I argue that propositional justification should satisfy a specific doxastic constraint—namely, the *idealized capacity principle*. In Section 14.5, I introduce a new notion, that of *intersubjective propositional justification*, and suggest that this is the right one to use in an epistemological analysis of science and mathematics. I then explore how this notion can be honed for the case of mathematics.

Ordinary Inferential Beliefs

Alvin Goldman challenges the reasons-first picture and defines propositional justification in terms of doxastic justification (in his terminology, he defines *ex-ante justification* in terms of *ex-post justification*). In his seminal paper introducing reliabilism, he explains:

> the bulk of this essay was addressed to ex-post [doxastic] justifiedness. This is the appropriate analysandum if one is interested in the connection between justifiedness and knowledge, since what is crucial to whether a person knows a proposition is whether he has an actual belief in the proposition that is justified.
>
> (Goldman [1976], 2000, p. 345)

He then goes on to propose a way to define propositional justification in terms of doxastic justification:

> Person S is ex ante [propositionally] justified in believing p at t if and only if there is a reliable belief-forming operation available to S which is such that if S applied that operation to this total cognitive state at t, S would believe p at t-plus-delta (for a suitably small delta) and that belief would be ex post [doxastically] justified.
>
> (*ibid.*)

By appealing to the reliability of belief-forming operations, Goldman defines propositional justification in terms of doxastic justification. Therefore, he considers doxastic justification to be fundamental.

Kornblith (2017) takes Goldman's suggestion further. On a first pass, Kornblith's argumentative strategy is to show that if we conceive of propositional justification as fundamental, we end up with a theory of justification that is too demanding and would lead to skepticism (which is rejected from the get-go). His focus is on ordinary inferential beliefs. According to a large body of literature on reasoning heuristics in the tradition of Tversky and Kahneman,[3] such inferential beliefs are not formed, as one would think, by approximating the laws of deductive or inductive logic. Instead, they are formed with the aid of various reasoning heuristics and rely on assumptions about our environment. This result can be interpreted (and has been interpreted) as a fault of our inferential practices. How can it be rational, for example, to use the law of *small* numbers rather than the law of *large* numbers?[4]

---

3 See (Kahneman, 2011).
4 See (Kahneman and Tversky, 1971) and (Kornblith, 2017, p. 73).

However, such heuristics are so widespread that, on pain of skepticism, they must produce justified beliefs, at least according to Kornblith. This thought is then at the basis of the project of articulating a model different from the one of inductive logic to evaluate our ordinary inferential beliefs. And this model can be developed only when focusing on what makes actual beliefs justified, that is, on doxastic justification. According to Kornblith, ordinary inferential beliefs should not be conceived and judged as based on arguments, but rather as originating from belief-producing mechanisms that can be, or fail to be, reliable.

Like Kornblith, I am not a skeptic. And, like Kornblith, I want to argue for the conceptual fundamentality of doxastic justification. I consider, however, highly reflective beliefs, beliefs formed by deductive reasoning rather than ordinary inferential beliefs. Thus, unlike Kornblith, I focus on justified beliefs that are formed on the basis of *good reasons*.[5]

The novelty of Kornblith's approach is to deny that justified ordinary inferential beliefs are based on good reasons. The novelty of my approach lies in proposing a novel conception of a *good reason*, one that is not entirely apsychological, but one that is itself tailored to our human cognitive capacities. To do so, it will be useful to first give a more detailed account of the apsychological notion of propositional justification as introduced by Firth.

Objective Propositional Justification

According to Firth and other epistemologists that take it to be fundamental, propositional justification concerns the "objective degree of support that a subject's evidence confers on a proposition" (Ichikawa and Jarvis, 2013, p. 163). Propositional justification, so conceived, is indexed to a subject's evidence, but crucially it does not depend on the subject's cognitive limitations and psychological make-up. Call this conception of propositional justification *OPJ*, *Objective Propositional Justification*.[6] Consider the following example.

> POKER. You, Ben, and I are playing poker. The fact that BF=<Ben is moving his feet>, which both you and I notice, provides strong evidential support for, and propositionally justifies believing that BB=<Ben is bluffing>. You believe BF and form an inferential belief in BB from it. I also believe that BF, but I fail to infer BB from it.

In this case, both you and I have (objective) propositional justification for BB. Our epistemic status, however, is different. This is possible because

---

5 In Kahneman's (2011) terminology, Kornblith centers his attention on the intuitive *System 1* while I handle the case of slow *System 2*.
6 This terminology is introduced in (Melis, 2018).

propositional justification does not entail belief. Consider another example:

> **CHESS.** We are in Bryant Park in New York City, witnessing a game of speed chess. You realize that B3=<Black can mate in three moves>, I don't. We have the same evidence (i.e., the position of the chessboard at time t).

We both have OPJ for B3, but I fail to appreciate it. Thus, I do not form the relevant belief. Apart from the fact that, in CHESS, the evidence entails your conclusion, the two cases are analogous. In both of them, our epistemic status is different because, while we both have OPJ, you also have *doxastic justification*. As we have seen, according to the reasons-first picture, *doxastic justification* is obtained from propositional justification by forming the relevant belief and basing it on sufficient epistemic reasons.[7]

So construed, doxastic justification depends on propositional justification. The latter tracks objective support relations while the former is impinged upon by our psychological idiosyncrasies—for the cases at hand, your superior skill at poker and chess. It is for this reason that most epistemologists consider propositional justification to be fundamental. Nonetheless, doxastic justification cannot be disregarded since, without it, propositional justification could not perform its role in underwriting knowledge. Knowledge not only requires justification but *justified belief*. We can see the entailment relations between knowledge and these two types of justification schematically:

Knowledge → Doxastic Justification → Propositional Justification

Let's take stock. According to the view articulated here, while doxastic justification is crucial to connect justification with knowledge, it is a derivative notion. Propositional justification is fundamental. This seems right since propositional justification, when contrasted with doxastic justification, is an objective notion, uncontaminated by the idiosyncrasies of our cognition, perspective, and abilities.

This view is endorsed by a number of epistemologists. In their classical defense of evidentialism, Feldman and Conee (1985) write:

> The doxastic attitude that a person is justified in having is the one that fits the person's evidence. More precisely: EJ [Epistemic

---

7 Note that most externalists allow for doxastically justified beliefs that are not based on reasons (e.g., proprioceptive beliefs, beliefs that were formed on evidence which is now forgotten, etc.). For a discussion of a range of such cases, see (Silva, 2021).

Justification]: Doxastic attitude D toward proposition p is epistemically justified for S at t if and only if having D toward p fits the evidence S has at t.

(Feldman and Conee, 1985, p. 15)

Propositional justification perfectly tracks evidential support relations between propositions. In their view, there are no constraints in terms of abilities to form beliefs. And in fact, they admit that "epistemic justification might have been normally unattainable" (*ibid.*, p. 19). Declan Smithies (2015) discusses the case of logical truths and endorses a similar position:

If rationality requires one to be certain of all logical truths, then it follows that one has sufficient reason or justification to do so.

(Smithies, 2015, p. 2776)

Again, the notion of epistemic justification is indexed to a subject's evidence but has nothing to do with cognitive limitation of the subject.

I now turn to considering inferential beliefs deriving from deductive reasoning. In some cases, these beliefs constitute knowledge. What will emerge is that OBJ is not the main ingredient of such knowledge. This in turn implies that this conception of propositional justification is not poised to play a role in an analysis of knowledge that arises from sophisticated deductions in domains such as logic and mathematics.

Mathematical Beliefs

If we apply it to the realm of deductive inquiries, OPJ offers the very best kind of epistemic likelihood: entailment. If propositional justification concerns the "objective degree of support that a subject's evidence confers on a proposition," then, for example, my proof that proposition p follows certain axioms, should license *prima facie* certainty of this conditional claim.

But what is the *epistemic* role of deductive reasoning? Consider CHESS. You correctly *see* that Black can mate in three moves (B3), and thus you form the relevant belief. Even if we share the same evidence (i.e., the configuration of the chessboard at a particular time), I don't form this belief. With enough patience, perhaps if you explain to me your reasoning step-by-step, I will reach the same conclusion and form the belief that B3 as well. The initial evidence is enough to justify your belief. The need for the explanation resulted only from my lack of competence. When I challenge you or simply ask you for an explanation, you can then give me a story of how to put together the evidence *I already have*.

Logical and mathematical beliefs are similar. They are prototypical deductive beliefs. For the present purpose, it will be useful to consider the beliefs in theorems or other mathematical propositions as conditional on certain starting points (i.e., the axioms) in order to avoid controversial assumptions about our knowledge of such starting points. Your explanation in CHESS is then analogous to a mathematical proof. Suppose that, by way of explanation, you are extraordinarily talented and well-trained in mathematics. Further, suppose that you correctly *see* that a complicated number-theoretic conjecture, C, follows from the Peano Axioms (PA). You then form the doxastically justified belief that PA → C. Even if your reasoning is obscure to me, we both have OPJ for the conditional proposition PA → C, even in the absence of a proof. Actually, we also had it before you discovered that PA → C was the case.

In line with these considerations, Smithies (2015), claims that *all* subjects have OPJ for all logical truths:

> consider a case in which I believe some complicated logical theorem T on the basis of sheer guesswork. If T is true, then I have propositional justification to believe that T is true.[8] (2783)

In this passage, to have reasons or (propositional) justification can be interpreted in two distinct ways: (i) A substantive claim about us: something along the lines of "we grasp the reasons or justification and its validity." (ii) A claim independent of us, simply stating that "there are reasons, or there is justification." Both alternatives are problematic for Smithies: (i) is not consistent with Smithies' view of propositional justification. Not all logical truths are sufficiently short and simple enough to have a justification we can grasp, yet for any logical truth T, "I have propositional justification to believe that T" is true; (ii) is not consistent with the ordinary meaning of "we have a reason or justification" which implies that it is something about us, since "we have it." In this case, it is even misleading to say, like Smithies, that *we have [objective] propositional justification*. We should instead say that *there is [objective] propositional justification*.

Basically, in the logical and mathematical domains (and the a priori domain more generally), what OPJ is picking out is not a notion of justification we can use to understand knowledge but the logical and mathematical facts themselves. These considerations suggest that, in some sense, notwithstanding the name, OPJ is not justification at all, *epistemic* justification, *bien entendu*. This is because it does not play a central role

---

8 Smithies puts leverage on the asymmetry between the a priori and empirical domains to argue that logical omniscience is a requirement of rationality. He then argues that this fact implies that we have sufficient justification for all logical truths.

in knowledge.⁹ Let me take this a bit more slowly. The conceptual role characteristic of justification is connected to knowledge. More precisely, propositional justification is the main component of knowledge. But OPJ is not the main component of logical and mathematical knowledge, at least if we consider, as I assume most do, knowledge as *human* (as opposed to divine or of extra-terrestrial creatures) knowledge. This implies that OPJ is not justification at all.¹⁰ This does not mean that it is not useful in epistemology. Of course it is! As a matter of fact, in the case of mathematics OPJ perfectly tracks mathematical facts, and we need to refer to such facts to epistemically assess our beliefs. Besides being connected to knowledge, justification must be truth-conducive (albeit not truth-entailing). Therefore, it is only with respect to logical and mathematical facts that we can evaluate whether a putative notion of justification is at all appropriate.

One possible strategy to overcome this problem and articulate a different notion of propositional justification is to invert the order of explanation and start by considering doxastic justification first:

Knowledge → <u>Doxastic Justification</u> → Propositional Justification.

If the new notion of propositional justification that will be developed below will earn its keep, then it will support the fundamentality of doxastic justification. We already have indirect evidence. This is because it is by considering propositional justification to be fundamental that we arrived at a conception of propositional justification that won't do.

My contention is that the domain of OPJ is at the same time too large and too small. That is, that it presents two problems:

> **PROBLEM ONE:** According to the characterization of objective propositional justification above, we have objective propositional justification to believe mathematical propositions whose proofs are beyond our ability to understand.¹¹ But this can seem counterintuitive.

---

9 One could argue, like Smithies, that all the difference is carried exclusively by doxastic justification. Actual beliefs are justified if and only if they co-vary reliably with truth. Pure reliability would then be the only criterion for doxastic justification. In particular, a reliable clairvoyant would be as justified as a reliable mathematician developing good reasons for her beliefs. This view, however, cannot lead to an adequate epistemology of mathematics. What we need for mathematical justification are good reasons, at least for first-hand justification. And good reasons, in mathematics, are good mathematical arguments.

10 Similarly, Kornblith (2017, p. 77) argues that it is exactly because propositional justification must play this central role in knowledge that there cannot be different types of it. That is, in the present terminology, why we cannot just be ecumenical and add another notion of propositional justification along with OPJ.

11 Moreover, it also implies that we have propositional justification to believe propositions that are too long and complex for us to understand.

PROBLEM TWO: According to the characterization of objective propositional justification above, we cannot have objective propositional justification in virtue of a fallacious deductive argument. But this can seem counterintuitive.

I develop and address PROBLEM ONE and PROBLEM TWO in the following sections. I present two cases to support the claim that these are indeed problems of OPJ.

Idealized Capacity Principle

In the previous section, we saw that PROBLEM ONE is indeed a problem. This is because if propositional justification is to be a central component of knowledge, it should not be reduced to logical and mathematical facts.

One way to address PROBLEM ONE is to impose a doxastic constraint on propositional justification. Giacomo Melis (2018) contrasts OPJ with what he calls *ordinary propositional justification*, which restricts propositional justification to reasons that are within reach of the subject.[12] A subject has "ordinary propositional justification only for the subset of propositions that her cognitive and doxastic abilities enable her to believe with justification" (p. 371).[13] I re-name this notion *subjective propositional justification* (SPJ) because it is indexed to the doxastic abilities of the subject—still, SPJ is not subjective in the sense that what looks like a good justification for p to the subject necessarily subjectively propositionally justifies p. As a matter of fact, SPJ can be constructed from OPJ by imposing the following principle:

> **SUBJECTIVE CAPACITY PRINCIPLE**: X provides S with propositional justification for p only if S's cognitive abilities enable her to form a doxastically justified belief that p on the basis of X.[14]

The SUBJECTIVE CAPACITY PRINCIPLE has been motivated in various ways in the literature. One cluster of arguments relies on some version of the *ought-imply-can* principle coupled with a deontological conception of justification. If S has propositional justification X for p, S ought to believe p on the basis of X. But, by the ought-implies-can principle, this cannot be correct since S cannot believe p on the basis of X. Of course,

---

12 Melis (2018) argues that we should just keep both notions of propositional justification. But as argued above, this is not a viable position if we take justification to be the main component of knowledge. See Footnote 9.
13 To be sure, it is not clear how these abilities should be identified and how modally stable they should be—but let me gloss over this issue.
14 Adapted from (Smithies, 2010, p. 14).

this principle is rejected by friends of OPJ.[15] Moreover, the SUBJECTIVE CAPACITY PRINCIPLE seems to deliver counterintuitive verdicts. Here is a case in point.

> JEALOUSY: Cate, a renowned mathematician, proves conjecture C. She sends her proof to her colleagues. All except one, Jason, grasp the proof and applaud Cate. In normal circumstances, Jason would recognize Cate's argument as a proof as well, but he secretly has the aspiration to prove the conjecture himself and is jealous of Cate. This jealousy activates a psychological defense mechanism that prevents him from grasping Cate's proof.

In this case, Jason cannot form a doxastically justified belief on the basis of Cate's proof.[16] But something seems to have gone wrong here. For there is a perfectly natural sense in which Jason *has* evidence that gives him justification to believe p, even though he lacks the ability to properly respond to that evidence and thereby form a justified belief. He has enough evidence but is unable to put it together correctly. This intuition is elicited by the fact that abstracting from a very idiosyncratic feature of his psychology (i.e., his jealousy), Jason would form a doxastically justified belief in the conjecture. This case demonstrates that SPJ is too idiosyncratic to play the role propositional justification should play in our epistemological theorizing. Thus, while OPJ should be rejected on the ground that it is entirely apsychological, SPJ should be rejected on the ground that it is overly psychological.

Kornblith (2017) thinks otherwise. Although he does not explicitly endorse SPJ, he envisages an alternative notion of OPJ that is sensitive to subjective differences:

> When the order of explanation is reversed, however, and propositional justification is defined in terms of doxastic justification, psychological matters become directly relevant to matters of propositional justification. If I have some psychological peculiarities which you lack, then even if you and I share all of the same beliefs, and all of the other nonbelief potential justifiers as well, assuming there are such justifiers, a different set of propositions may be propositionally justified for the two of us.
>
> (Kornblith, 2017, p. 68)

---

15 See (Feldman and Conee, 1985). Smithies (2010) points at the problem of over-intellectualization—which, however, does not apply in this context because we are focusing on reflective beliefs.
16 We can construe Jason's defense mechanism to be a more or less robust feature of his psychology.

This position, however, seems to give the wrong verdict in cases such as JEALOUSY.

The challenge is then to find a middle level of idealization, that is, a notion of propositional justification that can be placed between OPJ and SPJ. According to Smithies (2015), however, it is fine to abstract away from human cognitive abilities completely:

> But if there are requirements of rationality that apply to individual human beings who are incapable of meeting them, then why can't there be requirements of rationality that are beyond human capacities in general?
>
> (Smithies, 2015, p. 2779)

Smithies' move is to go directly from a denial of the Subjective Capacity Principle to the endorsement of no capacity principle at all, and thus to OPJ. But this is a mistake. As we saw in the previous section, OPJ is not the main component of mathematical knowledge. In other words, claiming that logical omniscience is a requirement of rationality does not help understand the epistemology of human logic and mathematics.

Let me now tweak JEALOUSY into a case that shows that, *pace* Smithies, it is reasonable to think that the requirements of rationality are bounded by our human capacities.

> **ALIEN-CATE**: Jason is now not affected by jealousy, and Cate is an alien disguised as a human. Her cognitive abilities far outstrip ours. Alien-Cate proves the conjecture with a deduction that no human being would be able to grasp, and she tries to share it with Jason, who inevitably fails to form an appropriately doxastically justified belief.

In this case, it is plausible to think that Jason does *not* have propositional justification. This is because Alien-Cate's deduction is beyond our capacity. For example, it might have as many inferential steps as atoms in the universe. If we endorse OBJ as the right notion of propositional justification, then, like any other subject, he would have (objective) propositional justification since the conjecture is indeed true. But I gave reasons to think that OBJ is not the right notion to work with if we want to articulate an epistemological account of mathematics. So, while in JEALOUSY Jason has propositional justification, it is plausible that in ALIEN-CATE he does not. The following intermediate principle can help to make sense of these different verdicts:

> **IDEALIZED CAPACITY PRINCIPLE**: X provides S with propositional justification for p only if an idealized human agent with the appropriate training would likely be in a position to form a doxastically justified belief that p on the basis of X.

What is the type of idealization at play? The idealized human agent is not a logically omniscient subject. In the case such as the ones at issue here, the idealization will have to be indexed to a specific domain D. If D is mathematics, an idealized human agent is a person of ordinary cognitive abilities belonging to a legitimate mathematical community operating around the time of S's life.[17] But what is a *legitimate mathematical community*? It is one that constitutes what Sanford Goldberg (2017) calls a *legitimate practice*:

> it is an ongoing and recognized practice, its standards are widely acknowledged, there have been no serious questions as to the propriety of either the practice or its standards.
> (Goldberg, 2017, p. 2867)

In normal circumstances, S's community will be a legitimate mathematical community, but this is not necessarily the case because S could be part of a deficient epistemic community, similar to the flat-earthers of mathematics.[18] We should then conceive of our idealized mathematician only considering S's background knowledge and appropriate training.[19] Note that the IDEALIZED CAPACITY PRINCIPLE is indexed to a particular time. If in the future our cognitive abilities will be drastically enhanced, we will be able to form doxastically justified beliefs on the basis of a larger body of arguments, and the IDEALIZED CAPACITY PRINCIPLE is sensitive to this. Moreover, the IDEALIZED CAPACITY PRINCIPLE is modulated according to general features of our human cognitive architecture. In this more moderate sense, I agree with Kornblith that the notion of propositional justification should not be entirely apsychological:

> what is propositionally justified for typical humans, given a certain body of potential justifiers, may be quite different from what is propositionally justified for typical members of a different species with the very same body of such justifiers.
> (Kornblith, 2017, p. 68)

---

17 In special cases, it could be that no such community is available. In such cases, the idealization would have to be characterized in terms of the capacities an average agent would have in S's broad circumstances.
18 Thanks to Neil Barton for discussion on this issue.
19 This accounts for cases in which S is ahead of her time and no member of her actual mathematical community can grasp her arguments due to lack of background knowledge.

To be sure, the IDEALIZED CAPACITY PRINCIPLE gives some leeway on how to interpret it, and it does not draw sharp lines. This is not a problem. What matters is that it is a tool we can use to eliminate requirements that are clearly beyond us and that are posed when adopting OPJ, like the one of logical omniscience. Further work is needed to spell out how the IDEALIZED CAPACITY PRINCIPLE operates in particular contexts.[20] In the context of this chapter, the important point is that this principle inherits some of the advantages of the subjective capacity principles, but skirts some of its problems. In particular, it makes sense of the fact that Jason, and any other human, does not have propositional justification for all logical truths (in CATE-ALIEN), but it is not overly psychological and remains an idealized principle that can be used for normative theorizing in epistemology (in JEALOUSY). This provides us with an answer to PROBLEM ONE, according to which endorsing OPJ as the right notion of propositional justification implies that we have propositional justification to believe propositions on the basis of proofs that are beyond our ability to understand.[21]

Let us now turn to PROBLEM TWO, according to which endorsing OPJ as the right notion of propositional justification implies that we cannot have justification in virtue of a fallacious deductive argument.

Good Arguments That Are Not *Ideally* Good

In light of the previous discussion, we have as a working hypothesis that in order for a reason to provide propositional justification, it has to satisfy the IDEALIZED CAPACITY PRINCIPLE. In the case of mathematics, these reasons are good mathematical arguments, that is, proofs. The IDEALIZED CAPACITY PRINCIPLE roughly says that proofs must be within our ken if they are to provide us with propositional justification.

But there is another issue. Proofs entail their conclusions. This leads to an infallibilist notion of justification in the realm of logic and mathematics, which, I suggest, is at odds with compelling cases. It is widely accepted among epistemologists that justification (both propositional and doxastic) allows for cases in which well-functioning agents do everything right but fail to achieve knowledge. For instance, this happens when a justified belief is false or when some sort of epistemic luck is involved. In POKER, it may very well be that while you were justified in believing that Ben was bluffing, it turned out that he was not bluffing. In CHESS, the situation is not so straightforward. In certain circumstances, it is plausible to think that you could count as justified in believing that Black could mate in

---

20 For an articulation of acceptability criteria in different mathematical communities see (De Toffoli, 2021b).
21 Once again this also implies that we have propositional justification to believe propositions that are too long and complex to understand.

three moves, even having made a mistake in reasoning. Suppose that due to the time constraint, the reliable process that forms your chess-related beliefs has missed a subtle defense available to White. Given the circumstances, you reasoned pretty well (most likely Black *is* going to mate in three moves since the defense was hard to spot) but not impeccably.

Also in logic and mathematics, it is plausible to think that a subject can be mathematically justified in believing a false proposition or in believing in a true proposition in virtue of a fallacious argument. This is, however, controversial. Justification in mathematics has been associated, since Frege, with genuine proof. Note that here I am considering *mathematical justification* to be (i) first-hand and inferential (and thus not testimonial), and (ii) *direct*, that is deriving from a mathematical argument.[22] Frege explains:

> It is not uncommonly that we first discover the content of a proposition, and only later give the rigorous proof of it, on other and more difficult lines; and often this same proof also reveals more precisely the conditions restricting the validity of the original proposition. In general, therefore, the question of how we arrive at the content of a judgement should be kept distinct from the other question, Whence do we derive the justification for its assertion?
> (Frege, 1960, p. 3)

Frege considers arithmetical truths to be a priori in the sense that their justification is a priori. Moreover, he adds that "An a priori error is thus as complete a nonsense as, say, a blue concept" (*ibid*). This makes it clear that fallacious arguments cannot, according to Frege, justify mathematical claims. Deploying our terminology, it is safe to say that Frege's focus was propositional justification alone. He aimed at shunning any question related to psychology. Frege's position is then endorsed by Hempel (1945) and the logical positivists. Moreover, it remains common among philosophers of mathematics to this day. The distinction between the context of discovery and the context of justification to which Frege alluded is widely considered to be a sharp distinction and it is taken for granted that proofs alone are to provide justification.[23] Moreover, they provide indefeasible a priori justification. In this respect, it is worth noticing that Kitcher (1984) pushes an empiricist account of mathematics exactly because he works with a conception of the a priori according to which a priori justification

---

22 An *indirect* type of inferential justification for a mathematical claim could be something of the following form. I have justification that my deduction p → q is correct because you told me so (r), and I believe p. Now I can infer q from r and p. Thanks to Paul Silva for suggesting me this clarification.
23 See, for example, (Burgess, 2015, p. 8).

is infallible and he realizes that such a conception cannot make sense of mathematical practice.[24]

Cases from mathematical practice seem to call for a fallible notion of mathematical justification, at least if we consider doxastic justification. Here is an example. It has to do with the famous 4-color conjecture. Roughly, the 4-color conjecture states that four colors suffice to color a planar map (such as a map of the world) in such a way as no two neighboring regions have the same color. It is simple to gather inductive evidence for this conjecture; it suffices to take different maps and start coloring them. The conjecture became of interest for the mathematical community in the middle of the 19th century, especially when it reached the attention of University College London professor Augustus De Morgan. The first accepted putative proof was found by Kempe.

> **KEMPE.** Alfred B. Kempe published an argument for the 4-color conjecture in 1879. This was a careful argument that divided the problem into several subcases. In 1890, Percy Heawood found a counterexample to one of the subcases.

It took roughly a century to find a genuine proof—and it still used Kempe's ideas.[25] When Kempe published his argument, it was reasonable for him to believe (and take himself to know) the 4-color conjecture because of it.[26] After all, not only did he check it, but other members of the mathematical community, starting with his reviewers, checked it as well—with none dissenting until 11 years later. Kempe could have done more. We can always do more. In practice, however, it is crucial to divide our time between innovation and verification.[27]

Epistemologists favoring OBJ will claim that Kempe had OBJ—just because the 4-color conjecture is true. But the clear problem is that, in this case, OBJ is not a path to knowledge because it is disconnected from Kempe's actual argument and thus from doxastic justification (allowing that he was indeed justified). What matters for doxastic justification is instead that Kempe had a *good argument even if it is not an ideally good argument*. That is, an argument that looked good to him and to the legitimate mathematical community to which he belonged, even if it failed to be a genuine proof.

---

24 However, nowadays many epistemologists accept that a priori justification is not infallible. See, for example, (BonJour, 1998; Casullo, 2003).

25 Said proof is generally considered to be the first computer-assisted proof. It was published in 1976 by Wolfgang Haken and Kenneth Appel.

26 Note that when I claim that Kempe did not have a proof but was nevertheless justified, I am treating justification as a full-on notion. To be sure, this notion is naturally graded.

27 It has been recently pointed out that incessant checking is epistemically problematic even if each check brings epistemic benefits (Friedman, 2019).

One epistemological position that endorses this intuition is *phenomenal conservatism*. According to Huemer, this philosophical position can be defined as follows:

> If it seems to S that p, then, in the absence of defeaters, S thereby has at least some degree of justification for believing that p.
> (Huemer, 2007, p. 30)

A key factor is that Kempe's argument not only looked good *to him*, but to the mathematical community at large. That is, not only did he have no defeaters, but he also had testimonial evidence that his argument was correct.

We can better spell out Kempe's epistemic situation by distinguishing between different types of undermining defeaters.[28] Kempe's argument admits an undermining defeater that cannot be defeated in turn. After all, his argument was fallacious. Neither Kempe nor his contemporary mathematicians were, however, aware of it. Stephen Cohen (1987) appeals to undermining defeaters to argue that standards that determine whether we should attribute knowledge to a subject are social in nature. He observes that defeaters of an argument can be obvious or very subtle and hard to spot. For instance, some arguments contain blatant mistakes. Even if they are not spotted by the subjects themselves, average members of the relevant community will have no problem pointing them out. In Cohen's words, those defeaters are *subjectively opaque* but *intersubjectively evident*. The defeaters of Kempe's original argument are instead both subjectively *and* intersubjectively opaque because they are very hard to spot even for the idealized mathematician (of course they are easy to spot now, with hindsight). In short, Cohen's thought is that arguments are candidates for supporting knowledge, and thus are *good arguments* on which doxastically justified beliefs are based, only if they do not admit intersubjectively evident defeaters for which the subject does not have a counter-defeater. More precisely:

> If knowledge does not entail ideally good reasons, then the intersubjective standards determine the level of opacity up to which a possessed undermining defeater (that is itself undefeated) will undermine knowledge.
> (Cohen, 1987, p. 11)

I have been concerned with justification rather than knowledge. In logic and mathematics, I conjecture that knowledge does indeed require ideally

---

28 It is customary to distinguish between two different types of defeaters for your belief that p: *undermining* and *rebutting* defeaters. The former are evidence that your reason for believing p is not a good reason, the latter are evidence for not-p.

good arguments, that is, truth-entailing arguments.[29] But I have given reasons to think that justification does not. Cohen's considerations, when applied to justification, can help us in making sense of Kempe's epistemic situation: there is an indefeasible defeater of his argument, but this defeater is both subjectively and intersubjectively opaque, and thus it does not undermine justification. As discussed in the previous section, the social context should be generally identified with a legitimate mathematical community.[30]

With this terminology in place, we can characterize a new notion of propositional justification.

Intersubjective Propositional Justification (IPJ): X provides S with propositional justification for p if and only if:

(1) X belongs to S's evidence,
(2) an idealized human agent with the appropriate training would be in a position to form the belief that p on the basis of X, and
(3) X does not admit intersubjectively evident defeaters that are subjectively undefeated.

Some clarifications are in order. We do not need to work with a particular conception of evidence.[31] In the case of logic and mathematics, X will be a logical or mathematical argument. The first condition is supposed to accommodate cases like JEALOSY. That is, cases in which a subject does not actually form the belief—but could have (because of condition 2). Condition 2 is the IDEALIZED CAPACITY PRINCIPLE we discussed before. Condition 3 is a social condition that restricts what can confer propositional justification to reasons that do not admit intersubjectively evident defeaters that are subjectively undefeated.

I grant that friends of OPJ will not be convinced that IPJ is the right notion to use. I do not claim to be able to convince them. My aim here is merely to suggest that IPJ gives rise to a more capacious notion of propositional justification, one that could be attractive to someone who is already skeptical of OPJ. For instance, Kornblith (2017) rejects OPJ and looks for a notion of propositional justification that is not entirely

---

29 I agree with Cohen that even in the case of knowledge there would be a social component at play: If knowledge does entail ideally good reasons, then intersubjective standards will determine the level of opacity up to which a possessed undermining defeater will undermine knowledge without the possession of a subjectively evident restoring defeater (Cohen, 1987, p. 2).
30 Cohen (1987) identifies it with the community of the person who attributes knowledge.
31 See (Kelly, 2016) for different options.

apsychological—he aims to find a notion that is sensitive to broad features of our cognitive architecture. I think IPJ is a contender at least for cases of believing for a reason.

In mathematics, IPJ is conferred by what I called elsewhere (2021a) *simil-proofs*. These are arguments that seem to be proofs but may or may not be proofs. With the terminology introduced here, we can define them as follows:

> **Simil-Proofs.** Mathematical argument X for p provides S with propositional justification, that is, is a *simil-proof* for S if only if:
>
> (1) X is part of S's evidence,
> (2) An idealized human agent with the appropriate training would be in a position to form the belief that p on the basis of X, and
> (3) X does not admit intersubjectively evident defeaters that are subjectively undefeated.[32]

Simil-proofs are arguments that look like proofs to the relevant audience but might fail to be. Kempe's proof was a simil-proof in his time but ceased to be a simil-proof when the gap was spotted. Being a simil-proof is, therefore, a time-sensitive property. No doubt, there is much to be said on how to characterize the relevantly trained subjects, and more generally, the relationship between a mathematical argument and its audience. But this is a matter for a different paper.

From the practitioners' perspective, simil-proofs are likely to be proofs. As a matter of fact, proofs do not wear their correctness on their sleeves. Whether a simil-proof is a genuine proof is a matter of logic and not of our understanding. If a simil-proof is fallacious, the self-checking activity of the mathematical community is likely to discover the fallacy, so belief would then be suspended or turned into disbelief. In (2021a), I have argued that simil-proofs are the type of justification that is generally required in practice. According to my account, Kempe has a true justified belief that does not amount to knowledge. Although mathematical knowledge necessitates proof, well-functioning mathematicians can be justified and

---

32 One difference with my previous definition is the following. In (2021a), I defined simil-proofs independently of a particular subject. In particular, a simil-proof could be such only for a group of individuals. Here I am focusing exclusively on individual justification, and I have glossed over the existence of good arguments that only a group of individuals could grasp. A well-known mathematical case of this is the proof of the classification of finite simple groups. Another difference is that in (2021a), I focused on doxastic justification alone. And I took the expression "having a simil-proof X for p" to be synonymous of "basing one's belief that p on the simil-proof X."

still mistaken about whether a given argument really is a proof. The criterion for justification is given by simil-proofs.

Conclusion

To argue for the fundamentality of doxastic justification, Kornblith (2022) argues against the reasons-first picture.[33] I also argue for the fundamentality of doxastic justification. To do so, I endorse the reasons-first picture, at least in a restricted form, for highly reflective beliefs which are formed by performing conscious inferences. I, however, proposed a specific interpretation of it. I suggested that in logic and mathematics, being ideally good (that is, being a correct deductive argument) is neither a necessary nor a sufficient condition for being a good argument—that is, correct deductive arguments may fail to confer propositional justification and in turn propositional justification may be in place without a correct deductive argument.

In logic and mathematics, good arguments are simil-proofs. I arrived at the notion of simil-proofs by trying to characterize the arguments on the basis of which mathematicians form doxastically justified beliefs. This perspective led me to impose an idealized capacity principle on propositional justification. Simil-proofs are the sort of things that can be scrutinized by appropriately trained subjects in normal circumstances. Because of this, they guarantee the possibility of self-checking activity both by the subject as well as by the community at large. To be sure, restricting the domain of proofs to *humanly graspable* proofs would be overly restrictive from the point of view of logic and, in particular, of proof theory. But it is not overly restrictive from the point of view of epistemology. Likewise, considering fallacious arguments might not be fruitful in other contexts, but it is in epistemology.

I discussed the case of logic and mathematics in detail. My suggestions, however, generalize to reflective activities in general (and not only to deductive reasoning)—activities that are carried out by what Daniel Kahneman (2011) calls *System 2*. In particular, to beliefs that require good arguments. No doubt there are disputes on how to delimit these, but uncontroversially, they include the domain of empirical sciences (as well as philosophy). Mathematics is a good testing ground because it is the hardest and cleanest case. In mathematics, ideally good arguments can be characterized in terms of logic. The contrast between ideally good arguments and intersubjectively good arguments is therefore particularly clear. While in empirical sciences beliefs can be false even if

---

33 Kornblith calls a variant of the reasons-first picture the *Arguments on Paper Thesis*. According to this thesis, a subject S is propositionally justified in believing proposition p if and only if either p requires no argument, or there exists a good argument for p from hypotheses that S already believes.

based on an ideally good argument, this is not the case in mathematics (at least if we consider mathematical propositions to be conditional on their axioms).

Doxastic justification, then, is conceptually fundamental because it is only by considering it first that we can articulate an adequate notion of propositional justification, one that can, in good cases, underwrite knowledge.[34] It is precisely starting from doxastic justification that I developed an alternative to both objective and subjective propositional justification: intersubjective propositional justification.

---

34 This is compatible with a conception of propositional justification as *theoretically* fundamental:

> [A] notion F has theoretical priority over a notion G when the role played by G in philosophical theorizing is, in some important sense, subordinate to the role played by F (Melis, 2018, p. 368).

References

BonJour, L. (1998). *In Defence of Pure Reason*. Cambridge University Press.
Burgess, J. P. (2015). *Rigor and Structure*. Oxford University Press.
Casullo, A. (2003). *A Priori Justification*. Oxford University Press.
Chisholm, R. M. (1989). *Theory of Knowledge* (3rd ed.). Prentice-Hall.
Cohen, S. (1987). Knowledge, Context, and Social Standards. *Synthese*, 73(1), 3–26. https://doi.org/10.1007/BF00485440
De Toffoli, S. (2021a). Groundwork for a Fallibilist Account of Mathematics. *The Philosophical Quarterly*, 7(4), 823–844.https://doi.org/10.1093/pq/pqaa076
De Toffoli, S. (2021b). Reconciling Rigor and Intuition. *Erkenntnis*, 86, 1738–1802. https://doi.org/10.1007/s10670-020-00280-x
Feldman, R., & Conee, E. (1985). Evidentialism. *Philosophical Studies*, 48, 15–34.
Firth, R. (1978). Are Epistemic Concepts Reducible to Ethical Concepts? In A. Goldman, & Kim Jaegwon (Eds.), *Values and Morals* (pp. 215–229). Kluwer.
Frege, G. (1960). *The Foundations of Arithmetic* (J. L. Austin, Trans.; 2nd Revised Edition). Harper Brothers.
Friedman, J. (2019). Checking Again. *Philosophical Issues*, 29(1), 84–96. https://doi.org/10.1111/phis.12141
Goldberg, S. C. (2017). Should Have Known. *Synthese*, 194(8), 2863–2894. https://doi.org/10.1007/s11229-015-0662-z
Goldman, A. (2000). What is Justified Belief? In E. Sosa, J. Kim, J. Fantl, & M. McGrath (Eds.), *Epistemology. An Anthology* (2nd Edition, 2008, pp. 333–347). Blackwell Publishing.
Hempel, C. G. (1945). Geometry and Empirical Science. *The American Mathematical Monthly*, 52(1), 7–17.
Huemer, M. (2007). Compassionate Phenomenal Conservatism. *Philosophy and Phenomenological Research*, 74(1), 30–55. https://doi.org/10.1111/j.1933-1592.2007.00002.x
Ichikawa, J., & Jarvis, B. (2013). *The Rules of Thought*. Oxford University Press.
Kahneman, D. (2011). *Thinking fast and slow*. Farrar, Straus and Giroux.

Kahneman, D., & Tversky, A. (1971). Belief in the Law of Small Numbers. *Psychological Bulletin*, 76(2), 105–110.

Kelly, T. (2016). Evidence. *Stanford Encyclopedia of Philosophy*. Retrieved May 17, 2021.

Kitcher, P. (1984). *The Nature of Mathematical Knowledge*. Oxford University Press.

Kornblith, H. (2017). Doxastic Justification Is Fundamental. *Philosophical Topics*, 45(1), 63–80.

Kornblith, H. (2022). What Does Logic Have To Do With Justified Belief?: Why Doxastic Justification is Fundamental. In P. Silva, & L. R. G. Oliveira (Eds.), *Propositional and Doxastic Justification: New Essays on Their Nature and Significance*. (pp. 40–58). Routledge.

Melis, G. (2018). The Intertwinement of Propositional and Doxastic Justification. *Australasian Journal of Philosophy*, 96(2), 367–379.

Neta, R. (2019). The Basing Relation. *The Philosophical Review*, 128(2), 179–217. https://doi.org/10.1215/00318108-7374945

Silva, P. (2021). Basic Knowledge and the Normativity of Knowledge: The Awareness-First Solution. *Philosophy and Phenomenological Research*, 1–23. https://doi.org/10.1111/phpr.12754

Silva, P., & Oliveira, L. R. G. (forthcoming). Propositional Justification and Doxastic Justification. In Maria Lasonen-Aarnio & Clayton Littlejohn (Eds.), *The Routledge Handbook of Evidence*. Routledge.

Smithies, D. (2010). Why Justification Matters. In D. Henderson, & J. Greco (Eds.), *Epistemic Evaluation: Point and Purpose in Epistemology* (pp. 224–244). Oxford University Press.

Smithies, D. (2015). Ideal rationality and logical omniscience. *Synthese*, 192(9), 2769–2793.

15 Knowledge-First Theories of Justification

Clayton Littlejohn

Let's revisit an exchange between Brueckner and Williamson. Williamson (2000) thinks that a thinker's evidence consists of all and only the things that she knows (E=K). On this view, a thinker's evidence should be understood as the objects of propositional knowledge (the knowledge-identification thesis). The possession of such knowledge is necessary and sufficient for the possession of this evidence (the knowledge-possession thesis). Brueckner (2009) thinks that this proposal runs into trouble in cases of non-inferential knowledge. If a thinker comes to know something non-inferentially (e.g., that the light is green, that she's thinking about Tennessee, that he's making an apple pie), this thinker presumably has a justified belief. Knowledge involves believing and the relevant belief has to be doxastically justified in order to constitute knowledge. To have a justified belief, in turn, she must have had justification to believe. Doxastic justification requires propositional justification. But to have a justification to believe something that she doesn't yet believe, she must possess evidence that supports this belief. The possession of this evidence cannot depend upon the possession of this belief that she hasn't yet formed. Propositional justification requires supporting evidence. The possession of the evidence to believe, say, that the light is green cannot require knowledge that the light is green because it is the possession of this evidence that is supposed to explain how we've met certain conditions necessary for knowing.

Brueckner has identified a real tension between the way that Williamson thinks of the connections between evidence, knowledge, and justification, and the way that most epistemologists prior to (and after) Williamson's (2000) defence of his knowledge-first approach to evidence. Brueckner's objection will probably seem compelling to many epistemologists because many seem to accept a familiar account of basing and some further assumptions about justification and knowledge. The standard story about basing is that we can have justification to believe p even if we do not believe p. Having this justification requires having

DOI: 10.4324/9781003008101-20

evidence that supports this belief and, crucially, believing p is not required for possessing the evidence that supports believing p. If we do form the belief that we have justification to believe, we then only have doxastic justification and justifiably believe p if our belief is properly based on evidence that gave us the justification to believe. We can think of doxastic justification as a matter of having propositional justification to believe and believing on the basis of the relevant evidence, whereas knowledge is thought to require doxastic justification and all that comes with that.

Brueckner's objection raises lots of interesting questions about what a knowledge-first theory of justification would look like. Ultimately, I think that the lesson to take from this is not, as Brueckner suggests, that E=K is mistaken. The lesson to take from this is that we should reject the evidentialist assumptions operative in Brueckner's discussion. I'll review some strategies for responding to Brueckner's objection and explain why we should be sceptical of the operative evidentialist assumptions. They are far from innocent. These assumptions commit us to claims about the nature of experience and belief and about the possession of evidence that I think we have good reason to reject.

First Response: Knowledge without Justification

One way to respond to Brueckner's objection might be to concede that doxastic and propositional justification require evidence but allow that knowledge doesn't require supporting evidence. On this view, we'd preserve the connection between evidence and justification but allow that there might be knowledge without supporting evidence or justification. On this view, Brueckner's objection to E=K would be undercut.

While Audi (1995) doesn't defend E=K, he has defended this sort of view. While we'll see that there might be good reasons to accept something in the neighborhood of what Audi proposes, I don't (yet) want to say that we can have knowledge without justification. I also don't want to say that this is what we find in the case of perceptual knowledge or knowledge via introspection. Audi's position seems to be based on two ideas, the first being that we lack evidence in some of these cases of knowledge and the second being that we cannot have justification if we don't have evidence. As someone who thinks that E=K is plausible, I have to be open to the idea that there's knowledge without evidence because I'd have to be open to the idea that there are processes that produce non-inferential knowledge as an output that don't take any kind of propositional evidence in as an input. What I don't see is why we should prefer to think of these cases as cases of knowledge without justification and evidence, rather than knowledge and justification without evidence. When we compare two beliefs and judge that one is justified and one is not, we should do so because we see some normative difference between them. It's hard to see, however, what normative difference there might be between them if they're both alike in terms of constituting knowledge.

One difficulty with the idea of knowledge without justification is that justification, in this setting, is a status. A justified belief is properly held, one that you don't need to abandon or revise. If we think of justification as a status, justified beliefs have a status such that it's not true that you should abandon them. On its face, knowledge would seem to be sufficient for such a status. On its face, it seems that knowing the answer to a question, say, means that you don't need to inquire further in order to take that question to be settled. There might be special contexts in which knowing is *not* sufficient for settling some question (e.g., settling questions about the defendant's guilt on the basis of knowledge which is itself based on things you shouldn't know as a juror seems inappropriate), but these special contexts are special. What makes them special, I take it, is that there are some non-epistemic reasons that bear on whether to take some question to be settled (e.g., whilst jurors might have to ignore certain considerations in trying to settle a question properly, the public at large doesn't have a similar responsibility to suspend judgment when given information that a judge says should be disregarded) that would give us reason to take a question to be unsettled even if our answer to that question has excellent epistemic credentials.

A second difficulty with this idea that we might have knowledge without justification emerges if we think about the normative significance of knowledge. While this is controversial, some of us believe that knowledge is the norm of belief. The idea that we shouldn't believe what we don't know because we don't know but should believe what we can know is one that seems to make sense of a considerable amount of puzzling data that alternative views don't seem to account for.[1] On its face, it seems that if a belief isn't justified, it's one that we shouldn't hold, but it's hard to see why we shouldn't hold a belief that constitutes knowledge if indeed knowledge is the norm of belief.

Perhaps the main difficulty with taking on the view that there might be knowledge without evidence while insisting that each instance of knowledge involves a justified belief is this idea that there might be two ways for beliefs to be justified, by the evidence and without evidence.

---

1 More carefully stated, I think we should say that we should believe when we're in a position to know and we have an interest in having an opinion about whether p. It might be that we have an interest in having an opinion about p because having an opinion might serve us well in our practical reasoning, but it might simply be that we are curious about whether p. It might be that having this interest has to do with the way we're related to others (e.g., someone has told us that p and our relationship to them gives us our interest in settling the question whether p). The position that I would want to avoid is one on which we ought to believe any proposition simply because it's known or knowable.

Ultimately, I think this isn't a terrible position to take, but since some epistemologists reasonably worry about this sort of view, let's consider an alternative line of response.

Second Response: Evidence without Knowledge

The most straightforward response to Brueckner's objection is to take it as it was intended, a successful objection to the idea that the only evidence we can possess consists of things we know. By rejecting the view that knowledge is necessary for the possession of evidence, the puzzles about how we acquire knowledge and evidence don't arise.

In this section, I shall argue that this is an unpromising response to Brueckner's objection. We should reject this approach to the justification of belief that treats the inferential and non-inferential case alike:

> **Common Support**: There is evidence that is essential to the justification of inferential and non-inferential belief and this evidence is constituted by the same kind of thing.

The idea behind the common support thesis is this. First, there is a common story that we should tell about how our beliefs can be justified regardless of whether they are formed inferentially or non-inferentially and that story should be told in terms of reasons for (and against) belief. They are justified by, and only by, the support of reasons and cannot be justified without this support. Second, we shouldn't complicate this story by saying that the stuff that constitutes the evidence that supports one sort of belief differs in kind from the stuff that supports a different sort of belief. This is supposed to rule out a kind of pluralist view on which, say, inferential beliefs are justified by evidence that's constituted by things that might be the objects of belief or knowledge when the things that justify our non-inferential beliefs must be something else entirely (e.g., sensations, experiences). If we say that all reasons for belief are pieces of evidence and all pieces of evidence are essentially the same sort of thing (as most contributors to these debates do) their views about the ontology of reasons will commit them to the common support thesis provided they accept some standard views about the role of reasons in justifying our beliefs.

The philosophers who accept the common support thesis think that there are ways of possessing evidence or reasons that doesn't require knowledge. On the views we're interested in, these views will need to identify some way of possessing propositionally specified evidence that doesn't require knowledge because we're focusing on views on which the evidence that justifies inferential belief consists of either propositions or facts and, in keeping with the common support thesis, says that the same must hold true for the evidence that justifies non-inferential belief. For some, we possess evidence by virtue of perceiving things. For others, we possess evidence by virtue of being aware of things. I shall identify some problems that I think arise for these accounts of possession, problems that give us some reason to think that the right response to Brueckner's objection is *not* to conclude that we don't need knowledge to possess evidence.

For Silva (Forthcoming-a, Forthcoming-b), the possession of reasons or evidence is understood in terms of awareness. We possess p as part of our evidence iff we're in a position to be aware that p is true. He thinks we can have awareness of facts without knowledge.[2] For McDowell (1998), perceiving is a way of acquiring propositionally specified reasons. It is by virtue of acquiring such reasons that perceptual knowledge is made possible. While he thinks that when we perceive, we're in a position to know that something is so, perceiving does not require knowing or believing that something is so. When we perceive, we don't have to accept the "invitation" to believe that things are as they appear to be. So, while believing and knowing involves, *inter alia*, being convinced that p, McDowell thinks that perceiving that p does not involve being convinced that p.

One issue that separates Williamson from those who defend non-doxastic accounts of possession is that they disagree about the following:

Neutrality: A thinker can possess p as part of her evidence and be neutral with respect to p.[3]

---

2 While I think it's clear that we can have awareness without knowledge when the object of awareness is a particular (e.g., aware of the kids playing the recorder outside the window), I don't think we can have awareness without knowledge in the cases that matter, cases in which a thinker is aware that something is so. I discuss the epistemic significance of difference kinds of awareness in Littlejohn (2015). In contrast, Huemer (2001) and Silva Jr (Forthcoming-a, forthcoming-b) argue that awareness of facts and knowledge can separate in some cases. Unger (1975) provides linguistic evidence for the view that ascriptions of propositional awareness are true only if corresponding ascriptions of propositional knowledge are true. I think some authors (e.g., Schroeder 2021) are within their rights to ask whether there might be mental relations between thinkers and facts that don't require knowledge or belief that differ from the ones that English speakers talk about using terms like "aware." Silva makes room for this as he treats "aware that" stipulatively, to refer to a generalization of the knowledge relation.

3 Not everyone who rejects the neutrality thesis accepts Williamson's identification of knowledge and evidence. For doxastic accounts of the possession of evidence that differ in significant ways from Williamson's, see Hofmann (2014), Mantel (2013), and Mitova (2015).

We'll say that someone is (attitudinally) neutral with respect to p iff they are neither right about p nor right about $\sim p$.[4] On Williamson's view, the neutrality thesis is mistaken. If you know p, you're right about p, and being right about p is incompatible with being agnostic about both p and $\sim p$. (By way of contrast, on a view like McDowell's (1998), a thinker that possesses p as part of her evidence by virtue of what she perceives might be neutral with respect to p if she doesn't accept the invitation to believe that experience gives us.)

Here is a second issue that separates Williamson from his critics who accept the common support thesis. Williamson's view doesn't commit us to the view that there are mental states or events that take the same objects as belief or knowledge but aren't themselves states or events that constitutively involve belief or knowledge. Someone sympathetic to Williamson's approach might think, for example, that actual or possible knowers come to know that the bird's head is red or positioned just so even if there is *no* propositional attitude or mental event involving propositional content that precedes this belief and explains its formation.[5] Williamson does defend the highly controversial view that knowledge is the most general factive mental state, but this is not something that we're committed to if we accept E=K. What we are committed to, however, if we accept the common support thesis, is a thesis about mind and its connection to reality:

> **Common Objects:** We possess propositionally specified evidence or reasons by virtue of being in certain mental states or undergoing certain mental events that do not constitutively involve either belief or knowledge.

For McDowell, perceiving is supposed to be similar to knowledge in that we can perceive that something is so or be aware that something is so and these perceptions and states of awareness take the same kinds of objects as propositional knowledge or belief. Thus, on these views, an antecedent to belief and knowledge might be something that is quite similar to belief and knowledge insofar as being in these states or undergoing these events

---

4 Following Collins (1996), I think that a thinker believes p or believes $\sim p$ iff they are right or wrong about p given their attitudes and the way the world in its relevant respects happens to be. There are ways of being right about p that don't involve belief. Guessing is a good example. Guessing, however, is an action, not an attitude, so it doesn't cause trouble for the way Collins characterises belief. On this way of thinking about belief, it's harder to understand how there might be knowledge without belief since, presumably, anyone who knows p is right about p.
5 It seems that Millar (2019), McGinn (2012), and Travis (2013) think that this might be true of actual knowers when the knowledge in question is perceptual.

constitutively involves the exercise of the capacities needed to be related to the objects of propositional knowledge and belief. That the cup is chipped, for example, is something that we're supposed to think we can know only because this object of knowledge is available as an object of non-doxastic states or events that precede the formation of beliefs that constitute knowledge.

I shall explain why I'm sceptical of the neutrality and common objects theses.

On Neutrality

The issue we want to address is whether someone can possess p as part of her evidence if she neither believes nor knows p. In other words, can she possess something as evidence without that piece of evidence being an object of a committal attitude, one that ensures that she's either right or wrong about p? According to the neutrality thesis, a thinker can be agnostic about whether p and still have p as part of her evidence. It's this combination of neutrality and possession that's key to understanding how it's possible in the non-inferential case for the fact or apparent fact that p to be the subject's reason for coming to believe p, for judging p, and so on. And it's by believing for the fact or apparent fact that p that explains, at least in part, how the subject's belief could be doxastically justified or constitute knowledge. If the subject had to first believe p or know p in order to possess p as part of her evidence, the subject couldn't possess p as a piece of evidence and be neutral. Further, in such a case someone like Brueckner would want us to say what, if anything, could have justified this thinker's non-neutral stance.

If every justified doxastic commitment has to be supported by independently possessed evidence and every instance of knowledge requires a justification to believe the target proposition, there must be a suitable neutral mental state or event that has propositionally specified objects. Being in this state would mean that there's some sense in which this content is in the subject's mind, but it wouldn't follow from the fact that this content is in the subject's mind that the subject would be right about p or wrong about p. Consider imagining and supposing. If Agnes were to imagine that the paint is chipped or suppose that the floor is scratched, she would be neither right nor wrong about the paint or the floor regardless of how the walls or floor were. One question, then, is whether the transition from a neutral state (e.g., supposing, imagining) to belief could be one in which the state's content is or captures the subject's reason for forming the belief, concluding, inferring, or judging.

I don't think that the typical defender of the neutrality thesis believes that the transition from imagining that p to believing that p (or some suitably related content) is one that might potentially justify believing this content. They wouldn't think that this would be a case in which the subject's reason for believing this content would be that *p*. The problem wouldn't be down to the fact that we're dealing with the wrong contents, but down to the fact that we're dealing with the wrong attitude types—supposing and imagining might have the right objects to be attitudes that gave us reasons, but they relate us to these objects in the wrong way to enable us to believe things for these reasons.

I suspect that the reason that neither imagining and supposing that *p* enables a subject to believe something for the reason that *p* is that a thinker can be neutral with respect to *p* when they imagine or suppose.[6] If this is right, this points to an obvious problem for the common support thesis. When it comes to *inferential* belief, it's possible for a thinker's reason for concluding that the walls hadn't been painted in a while to be the (apparent) fact that the paint is chipping because by virtue of believing that the paint is chipping, the thinker is committed to this (apparent) fact being so. In the inferential case, we seem to all agree that nothing could be the subject's reason for concluding something unless they were *not* neutral about whether it's so. In the non-inferential case, of course, there is no similar commitment to the fact or apparent fact that constitutes the (supposed) evidential basis for the relevant belief because if the subject were non-neutral with respect to this (apparent) fact, they'd believe that the target proposition was true and this content's being the subject's reason would mean that we were in fact dealing with an inferential case in which the subject's state of belief is grounded in a further belief.

The main difficulty, as I see it, is this. The defenders of the common support thesis have to say that in the non-inferential case, our beliefs are only justified if there's some propositionally specified reason that is the subject's reason for forming the relevant belief. They also presumably want to say that many of these beliefs *are* justified, so they want to say that it's often the case that when we come to believe non-inferentially that something is so, there's some propositionally specified reason that's our reason for forming this belief. On the one hand, this propositionally specified reason must be the object of some non-doxastic state because otherwise we're dealing with an inferential case. The non-doxastic state

---

6 There might be clear differences between perceiving on the one hand and imagining or supposing on the other. Any connection between supposing and imagining and the truth is accidental. The same cannot be said for perceiving. That's true, but the issues about neutrality are about the internally specified features of those things that provide the subject's propositionally specified reasons and those that do not. Thanks to Paul Silva for raising this issue. There are interesting questions about accidentality to consider, but we'll discuss them under a different heading as they seem to concern the environmental conditions that must be in place for some fact about the environment to be the subject's reason for responding in some way.

must be compatible with the thinker being neutral with respect to the relevant content because otherwise the state would be doxastic. But it's hard to see how it could be that our reason for believing something could be something that we're neutral about. If, say, I'm neutral about whether God exists, how could the (apparent) fact that God exists be my reason for concluding that naturalism is false? (Or, alternatively, if I'm neutral about whether God exists, how could the (apparent) fact that God doesn't exist be my reason for concluding that the ontological argument must be unsound?)[7]

My point is not that imagining and supposing couldn't differ from perceiving or experiencing in any interesting ways. My point is that one of their similarities is sufficient to establish that they do not provide us with propositionally specified reasons that might be our reasons for concluding things. The worry, in short, is about how we have to be

---

7 Someone might raise the following worry. Consider a different case. You look at a hen that seems to you to have five spots on it. You might not believe that it has five spots since you know you could easily have made a mistake. You look longer and count them. You only then believe after counting. If seemings are distinct from beliefs, then this is a possibility. In this case, if the initial seeming were suitably non-accidentally related to the fact that the hen has five spots, that fact (or your awareness of that fact) could be evidence you have for believing that the hen has five spots. Let's suppose the fact in question is the fact that seems true: that the hen has five spots. Could this be the subject's reason for believing that it has five spots? If it is, it's what convinced the subject that the hen has five spots. McDowell (2006) insists that the fact that p cannot be the subject's reason for believing p, but let's brush aside his concerns for the time being. One concern that I have about this is that the response assumes something that I don't believe—it assumes that there is a propositional attitude that is distinct from belief (e.g., because it's a neutral state) that has the content of the relevant belief and is how we're able to believe something for the reason that the hen has five spots. Here's a reason to be suspicious of this proposal. Suppose the subject expected the hen to have an even number of spots. (The short version of this is that the thinker is in the grips of the strange theory that spots always develop in pairs.) Could this subject, by virtue of having this seeming, be surprised where the subject's reason for being surprised is that the hen has five spots if this subject also doesn't believe that the hen has five spots? I don't think so. But this is strange. We know that this fact is the kind of thing that would be, if in the agent's possession, the kind of thing that *would* be the subject's reason for being surprised. (We know this because as soon as the subject believes it, he's surprised.) If it's not possible to be surprised that p by virtue of having some expectations and seemings that don't fit without believing that things are as they seem, it seems we have some reason to think that it's seeming that p to you is not, by itself, sufficient to put you in a position to have p be your reason for responding. Of course, if there are seemings (and I have no idea if there are) that are propositional attitudes distinct from belief, they *might* help explain what we believe, but we know that explanatory reasons aren't the same thing as the subject's reason. A pain, for example, could explain why I believe that I need to see a dentist, but it couldn't be my reason for believing that I need to see a dentist. An experience might be why I believe I need to see an optometrist, but it wouldn't be my reason for believing that I need to see an optometrist.

related to *p* mentally for *p* to be the subject's reason for believing.⁸ The transition from a neutral state to belief is *not* one in which first come to possess the evidence by means of being in the neutral state because the content of a neutral state wouldn't be our reason for making a transition from being neutral to being committed. Think about the standard gloss on the notion of the thinker's reason. As McDowell (1978) puts it, when we specify the agent's reason (i.e., the agent's basis for responding in some way), we have to show the "favourable light" in which this agent viewed this response. If we capture this light by means of specifying a proposition when the agent in question didn't take this proposition to correctly represent anything about the situation that made the response favorable, it couldn't be the agent's reason for responding, not on this conception. How could the agent take the relevant proposition to be true and capture what was desirable about their response if the agent is agnostic about this proposition?⁹

As I see it, the neutrality thesis is both essential to the common support thesis and clearly mistaken. Someone who either doesn't believe or disbelieves *p* couldn't be moved by the apparent fact that *p* to believe something, so *p* couldn't be the subject's reason *precisely* because the agent is neutral about *p*. This is in no way surprising if we remember the points that Unger (1975) tried to impress upon us, which is that the subject's reasons for responding (whether that response is an emotion, a

---

8 When it comes to things that are *not* the subject's reason (e.g., explanatory reasons), there's no plausible case for thinking that any belief would be required because explanatory reasons don't need to capture how things were from the subject's perspective to do their explanatory work. Recall Davidson's (2001: 141) remark that only a belief could be a reason for another belief. I'm defending a related idea. Only what's believed (or known) could be the subject's reason for believing or judging. When Davidson was asked to say something about the rational role of experience, he said that these non-doxastic antecedents to belief were not reasons but causes. Such causes could be reasons why a subject believes, things that connect a thinker to the facts in non-accidental ways so that the acquisition of knowledge isn't magic. Davidson could have said more here, but I don't think that what he's said is wrong.

9 Someone might object that this passage presupposes an overly intellectualist way of thinking about believing, acting, or feeling for reasons that are propositionally specified. Sylvan (2018), for example, tries to defend a view that's not overly intellectualist insofar as it drops the requirement that a propositionally specified reason is only a subject's reason for believing or acting if it appears to be an objective reason to the subject. I agree that we should drop this requirement, but I don't see that requirement as part of McDowell's gloss. McDowell's gloss seems to be compatible with the less demanding view that Sylvan favours. It's not McDowell's view, as I understand it, that in treating *that the bird's head is red* as a reason requires thinking of it as a reason. The gloss only seems to require that the subject's response is made sense of by specifying this fact and adding in some further details about how such facts move agents. It's this further account that Sylvan gives a virtue-theoretic account of. Thanks to Paul Silva for discussion of this issue.

belief, or an action) is *always* something that the subject knows. Unger's evidence for this is linguistic. He notes that regardless of whether we plug in for "X" something to do with the agent's feelings, believings, or doings, it is contradictory to assert, "Agnes's reason for Xing was that p, but she didn't know that p." I have not tried to defend this thesis in full generality. In fact, I don't care to. There is an aspect of this that's worth noting, which is that we have independent reason to think that the commitment that's necessary and sufficient for believing p must be in place for the agent's reason for Xing to be that p. Given the standard gloss on what the subject's reason is, that which the subject doesn't believe or disbelieves couldn't capture what *this* subject took to make their response sensible or desirable.

This is clear, I think, when we think about emotion and feeling. A question that the defenders of the neutrality thesis should answer but haven't answered is this. If we're able to *believe* things for propositionally specified reasons when we don't believe the relevant proposition (e.g., when we have an experience and are, prior to forming the belief, neutral about the proposition), why can't we *feel* things for the propositionally specified reason if we don't believe the relevant proposition? Why, for example, wouldn't a suitable slice of experience and a set of pro-attitudes make someone who either doesn't believe or disbelieves that their lover has returned after a long trip be pleased that their lover has returned from a long trip? Why couldn't a slice of experience and a set of aversions make someone upset that the house is a mess if they are agnostic about whether the house is a mess? Why would we need committal or non-neutral stances to be able to X for the reason that p when we're dealing with emotion if it's possible for our reason for believing to be something that we're agnostic about? Some answer must be given.[10]

On Common Objects

The defenders of the common support thesis might think that there's some way around the problems of the previous section, some way of expanding our conception of what it is to respond on the basis of a reason in such a way that we can base our responses on things that we

---

10 In fairness, I am assuming that all cases in which a subject's response is an instance of responding for a propositionally specified reason will have some common features. My opponent might question this, but it still seems fair to ask them why it's impossible for someone to be upset that p if they neither believe nor disbelieve p and I'd like to know what the story is and why we should think non-inferential belief is the *only* exception to the general view that if S's reason for Ving is that p, S believes that p. Thanks to Paul Silva for discussion of these points.

don't take to be true (e.g., the contents of neutral attitudes). I doubt it, but who's to say which doubts are reasonable and which ones aren't? Let's consider new reasons to doubt a popular view that I never understood the motivation for. Let's discuss the common objects thesis. The defenders of the common support thesis need the common objects thesis to understand how inferential and non-inferential beliefs might be based on the same sorts of things. This requires, in turn, that the objects of perception and experience are the same as the objects of belief and knowledge. I doubt that they are. I also doubt that they'd have to be. I think actual knowers and perceivers aren't like this and I'm even more certain that possible knowers and perceivers aren't like this. Either way, we'd have the resources we needed to reject the common objects thesis.

The pressures that lead people to endorse the common objects thesis might differ from philosopher to philosopher. McDowell (1998), for example, endorses a picture of knowledge according to which it's only possible to know when the bases for our beliefs make it impossible for us to fail to be in a position to know. He doesn't see how a belief based on anything but a fact made manifest could provide this sort of security. Once we acknowledge that the subject sees that *p*, for example, it's supposed to be impossible for the subject to fail to be in a position to know that *p*, provided that the subject accepts the invitation that experience provides and comes to believe that things are as they appear to be.[11] Schroeder (2021), to give another example, endorses a picture of knowledge according to which we know when we believe for sufficient objective and subjective reason. It wouldn't be possible to believe for reasons as he understands them if there were not non-doxastic states that we could be in that had the right sorts of objects so that we might come to believe non-inferentially on the basis of reasons.

---

11 McDowell no longer believes that *that the light is green* is something that might be there in the world waiting for us to perceive. Instead, the *that the light is green* gets into the picture when we interact with coloured lights in our environment because of the joint operation of sensibility and understanding. Since the senses don't (by McDowell's admission) come into contact with any that-such and such, we're left wondering how the transition from an initial contact with the senses and the environment that has no propositional input yields a propositional output that meets the non-accidentality requirement that he says all knowledge must meet. Let's call his answer to this challenge, "the answer." I don't believe we need non-doxastic propositional attitudes (e.g., experience conceived of as a state with propositional content) antecedent to perceptual beliefs for those beliefs to be non-accidentally connected to the facts in the way they must in order to be knowledge. And if readers want to know how I'd explain the possibility of beliefs being non-accidentally connected to the facts that we seem to know without the assistance of these propositional states, I'll refer them to the answer. We all need it. See Littlejohn (2017) for discussion.

To understand the case against the common objects thesis, it helps to understand a distinction that Travis draws between the *conceptual* and the *historical*. The conceptual, in his terminology, has to do with ways for things to be (e.g., red, on the rug, rusty, disappointing, filthy, unloved, etc.). The conceptual is thus intrinsically general. For any given way a particular might be, there might be more than one thing that instances it (and more than one way to instance it).[12] The historical, on the other hand, is not instanced. It has to do with the things that make up a shared environment that might (or might not) fall under some generality. On a naïve view of perceptual awareness, there are things that are historical found in a shared environment that we can perceive when we're properly related to them. On this view, nothing on the conceptual side of the divide would be an object of perceptual awareness since perception only relates us to the sorts of things that might be in our surroundings for us to perceive. Pigs, for example, are the sorts of things that we might stumble upon and see. That the sun has risen, however, is not the sort of thing that we might stumble upon and see. Why not? Well, among other things, that the sun has risen is not something that would be in Germany. Nor would it be in London, Los Angeles, or any other place you might care to look. That the sun has risen might be something known, so it's a perfectly fine object of knowledge. Since that the sun has risen has no location and emits no rays, however, it's hard to believe that it's something that we might see just as it's hard to believe that it's something you might touch or kick. Frege, quoted here by Travis, offers these remarks:

> But don't we see that the sun has risen? And don't we thus also see that this is true? That the sun has risen is no object which sends out rays that reach my eyes, no visible thing as the sun itself is. That the sun has risen is recognised on the basis of sensory impressions. For all that, being true is not a perceptually observable property.
>
> (2013: 123)

---

12 Some readers might not appreciate Travis's prose as much as I do (and thus fail to see exceptional writing when it's right before them). Maybe this talk of the conceptual and historical is non-ideal, though I struggle to find better terms for this. If you're struggling to get what he's driving at, reflect on his remark, "If Sid has crumbs on his face, one would not need to be *just* as Sid is in order to have crumbs on his face. Nor would Sid ... A way for things to be thus ranges over an indefinitely extensive range of particular cases" (2018: 339). Once we remember that there are many ways to have crumbs on a face, Sid's or yours, we can see the virtue of distinguishing this from the faces and crumbs out there in the wild waiting for us to spot them. Thanks to twitter user @sidandpia for the reference.

If this is right, doesn't this show that perception and knowledge take different objects?[13]

Perhaps, but it doesn't quite show that experience and knowledge take different objects. Even if the objects of the perceptual relation should be understood as historical rather than conceptual, there might be an understanding of perception and experience that would seem to give the defenders of the common objects thesis a line of response. It's true that some philosophers have seemed to say (and some still say) that things like *that the sun has risen* is something that we perceive or see, McDowell's views on this have shifted. It's worth considering the possibility that while there's a sense in which the things that are there in our common environment to be perceived all fall on the historical side of Frege's line, it still might be that the objects of *experience* include things that fall on the conceptual side.

McDowell thinks of perceptual experience as the upshot of the joint operation of sensibility and the understanding. Both the sensory contact with particulars (here we might think of this as one way of understanding some ways of thinking about perceiving) and the exercise of our conceptual capacities play an essential role in experience. So even if, say, when we're describing the objects that our senses afford us awareness of, we're going to describe these as particulars and report them in such a way that the reports are extensional, perhaps experience involves the exercise of conceptual capacities and has the same sorts of objects as belief. In effect, the naïve realists might be right about sensibility involving relations to particulars that doesn't involve concepts, but wrong to deny that there's more to experience than awareness of the particulars that we sense.

The main problem with this response is it puts the defenders of the common objects thesis in an awkward position. Think about this

---

13 French (2012) argues on linguistic grounds that when we see that *p*, we know that *p*. I think he's right, but there's a response (e.g., in Schroeder 2021: 91) that cases of perceiving without believing show that there are perceptual relations that relate us to the objects of knowledge even if we don't use familiar expressions (e.g., "sees that") to pick them out. But there's a response to this, too. He assumes that perceptual relations are representational, but some of us are highly sceptical of this view. But even if nature happens to furnish us with representational perceptual relations, I have argued there are possible creatures that are (a) introspectively indiscernible from us that (b) form perceptual beliefs that are non-accidentally correct in response to the very same environmental features that are responsible for our perceptual beliefs. *These* creatures (which might be counterfactual, but I think are actual) are knowers. And if there are possible knowers who don't base their perceptual beliefs on objects of knowledge possessed non-doxastically, we can set aside these questions about language and recognise the possibility of knowing without supporting propositionally specified reasons. See Littlejohn (2017) for these arguments. In turn, Schroeder would argue that views that posit the possibility of knowledge without supporting reasons suffer from the difficulty that they cannot explain various facts about defeat, but I've tried to address this concern in Dutant and Littlejohn (2021) and Littlejohn (2020).

suggestion that experience involves sensibility and the understanding where the understanding functions to apply general concepts to the particulars we encounter in our surroundings.[14] If perceptual knowledge is possible, it must be that the concepts that are applied to these particulars are not just applied correctly, they must be applied in such a way that their correct application doesn't happen by accident. Moreover, since what they're applied to in the first instance is historical and not conceptual, there must be something about these particulars that doesn't just make the application of some concepts correct but also something that triggers the correct application so that it's possible that their correct application is non-accidental. If there is some such historical trigger, something beyond the conceptual that ensures that concepts are applied correctly and reliably, it's hard to then see why it's so vitally important to insist that there are non-doxastic states that have the same objects as doxastic states.

Once we see that the things in our surroundings that our senses put us in contact with are historical and not conceptual (i.e., the shining sun is in our surroundings, but that the sun is setting is not in our surroundings) and see that the defenders of the common objects view have to recognize something historical that triggers the correct application of concepts in a reliable way, it's not at all clear why it should matter that the concepts are applied in the first instance by a doxastic state as opposed to some non-doxastic antecedent.

The defenders of the common objects view might remind us that there's more to knowledge than reliability. Knowledge, they might say, also requires intelligibility, that the beliefs we form make sense or fit with our perspective on things. I don't disagree, but I don't see a major advantage for a view that posits non-doxastic antecedents to doxastic states that have the same kind of content as belief to ones that do not. They might say that if there is no non-doxastic state in which, say, some generality is applied to the historical case at hand, the application of the relevant concept in belief would be arbitrary. This is unconvincing. The picture we're being handed by the defenders of the common objects thesis is that something beyond the understanding triggers the application of concepts in experience. If the triggering is, according to the defenders of the common objects view, something that takes place beyond the conceptual, the intelligibility worries would seem to arise for both sides equally. It seems

---

14 This is McDowell's (2009) revised picture of experience. He has backed off from the view that things like *that the bird on the post is a cardinal* is itself something that might be in the world for us to perceive but nevertheless thinks that when we have a visual experience, say, we can have an experience with this content. In this way, he hopes to take on board the point that Travis finds in Frege without abandoning the idea that in experience we find a basis for belief that consists of some fact such that in being aware of it, we're guaranteed to be in a position to know that it is so.

it's a wash and their view enjoys no advantage over a view on which experience isn't itself any sort of propositional state.

Here's a way of pressing my concern about the (alleged) superiority of the common objects view. Imagine two creatures who navigate their environments equally well. They believe the same things and are disposed to believe the same things when placed into sufficiently similar situations. The first creature is wired up in such a way that it applies the same concepts in experience and the beliefs that it realizes so that when it forms perceptual beliefs, there's a transition from a non-doxastic state that is accurate iff *p* to the belief that *p*. The second creature has no non-doxastic states with this kind of content as its experiences do not involve the exercise of conceptual capacities. The trigger that triggers the application of the concepts in the first creature at the level of non-doxastic states (and so indirectly triggers the application at the level of belief) just triggers the application at the level of belief in the second creature. Provided that the subjective character of their experiences is similar and their dispositions are as I've described, I can't see any reason to credit the first creature with knowledge we'd deny the second. But if it's plausible that these creatures might know the same things, that has to be a problem for the common support thesis since, by hypothesis, we find that support in the generation of only one creature's beliefs.

Third Response: Knowledge and Being Justified without Evidence

We have looked at two ways of responding to Brueckner's objection. According to the first, we should recognize that perceptual beliefs are not based on evidence and conclude from this that they cannot be justified but still insist that they might constitute knowledge.

> **Response 1**: Perceptual beliefs are not justified because they are not based on evidence, but they might nevertheless constitute knowledge.

My main concern about this proposal is that it seems that if a belief constitutes knowledge, it shouldn't need to be supported by evidence to be properly held, so it's more natural to conclude that *if* such a belief might constitute knowledge, it could also be justified without being based on evidence. According to the second line of response:

> **Response 2**: Perceptual beliefs can be justified and can constitute knowledge because they can be based on propositionally specified evidence that provided by perception or experience.

One of my main concerns about this proposal is that there seems to be no compelling reason to think that only processes that take in something propositional as an input at the first stage could yield doxastic states that might be justified or might constitute knowledge. Once we acknowledge that the ultimate inputs to these processes are things found in the environment (e.g., the particulars we can touch, taste, or see and the conditions that they're in) that interact with our senses that are not themselves propositional, we have to acknowledge that the outputs could only be knowledge if there was, at some stage in the process, a non-accidental way of applying concepts to something historical where something historical triggers the application of the concept. And once it's clear that this is a commitment of every non-sceptical view concerning perceptual knowledge, the crucial question becomes this.[15] Why should it matter if the concepts are applied so that some antecedent non-doxastic state has the content of the beliefs produced as output instead of the beliefs themselves being the first state that has this content? There seems to be no good answer to this question, so we seem to have no good reason to insist, in keeping with Response 2, that all knowledge be constituted by belief that's based on independently possessed propositional evidence.

The response that I favor would be this:

Response 3: Perceptual beliefs can be justified without being based on evidence because of how they're related to knowledge.[16]

This response avoids any commitment to the idea that we could possess propositionally specified evidence just by virtue of being in some sort of non-doxastic state. It thus frees us from taking on controversial assumptions about the nature of perceptual consciousness in order to defend our non-sceptical view of perceptual knowledge (as Response 1 does). It also allows that there might be some necessary connection between knowledge and justification (as Response 2 does). I think this combines the best of both approaches and avoids difficulties that arise for these views.

Ultimately, some knowledge must have a basis that differs in kind from the sort of basis we have for our inferential beliefs. The basis for

---

15 As Silva (Silva Jr, Forthcoming-a, Forthcoming-b) argues (correctly, in my view) there's room for safe non-doxastic propositional states and so that might help my opponent formulate a plausible anti-sceptical view, but the thing that I would stress is that the things that ensure that these states are safe could ensure that doxastic states were safe even without the presence of any intermediary propositional state. Thus, I see the reasons or evidence that some see as justifying perceptual belief as dispensable when it comes to acquiring knowledge. In turn, this makes them dispensable when it comes to the justification of belief. Even if we have them, some possible knowers might not.

16 Sylvan (2018) also takes this line, but I don't think he's committed to the idea that there's knowledge that isn't based on the kinds of reasons that our inferential knowledge would be based on. For a response to Sylvan, see Silva Jr (Forthcoming-b).

our perceptual beliefs might either be the experiences themselves or the things revealed by experience, but if the basis is nothing at all like the premises or considerations that figure in inferential reasoning, no terrible epistemological consequence seems to arise. In this final section, I would like to say something about the connection between knowledge and justification so that readers might have a better idea of what a knowledge-first theory of justification might look like.

The knowledge-first theory of justification that I like says that evidence might matter for justification, but only if it somehow matters for knowledge. In cases where knowledge is possible without supporting evidence, we should assume that justification is also possible without supporting evidence. And that's because what makes justified beliefs justified is that they bear the right relation to knowledge. This suggestion might offend the sensibilities of epistemologists who have held, following Goldman (1979), that we shouldn't use certain epistemic notions in our theories of justification. It's true that if justification were a constituent or ingredient in knowledge, it wouldn't do to say that justified beliefs are justified because of how they're related to knowledge, but it's important to realize that not everyone thinks that this is how justification and knowledge are related. That's not how I think of it, at any rate.

When I think of non-human animals, for example, I think that they might see things and know things without it being the case that they have justified beliefs. I take it that it only makes sense to say that an individual's responses are justified (or unjustified) if this individual can be held accountable for those responses. If an individual can be held accountable and their responses meet a standard, we should say that they are justified. If they don't meet it, their responses are not justified. I happen to think that the standard that we use when evaluating beliefs is a knowledge standard. We believe what we should (in an objective sense) if our beliefs constitute knowledge. We believe something we shouldn't believe (in this objective sense) if our beliefs fail to constitute knowledge. On the simplest way of thinking about justification and normative standards, our beliefs are justified iff they conform to those standards, so they're justified iff they constitute knowledge.

On this way of thinking about justification, the possibility of having justified beliefs that aren't based on evidence isn't any more mysterious than the possibility of having knowledge that's the output of a process that doesn't take propositional inputs. That's because the justification property is the property that attaches to responses (e.g., beliefs) that meet a standard (e.g., conform to the knowledge standard). If it helps, think of the connection between justification and belief in the way that we might think of the connection between legal and action. That's how I think of it, at any rate. At an abstract level, the legal acts don't violate the laws. Tell us what the laws are and we can tell you something more concrete about what it takes to live within the bounds of the law.

At this point, two sorts of question arise. It's important to see that these questions are concerned with slightly different issues. The first question is a question about the proper specification of the standard. Why, someone might ask, should we think of that standard as concerned with knowledge rather than truth? The second question is concerned with the relationship between justification and the standard whatever it might be. Why should we think that justification requires conforming to the norm? Why couldn't it be something else?

In response to the first question, I'd say a few things. The first is that when we think about the various cases that we'd want a theory of justification to address, the knowledge-centered views do better than any alternative view that I'm aware of. It explains the intuitive differences between ordinary cases of justification from fallible sources (e.g., experience, testimony) and lottery beliefs. It also further explains why knowledge of the fallibility of a source (e.g., the knowledge that a book contains an error) does not prevent the source from providing knowledge and justification whilst preserving the intuitive difference between these cases and lottery cases where high probability doesn't seem to put us in a position to know or to justifiably believe.[17] This, though, is just data that we can use to try to justify the claim that the knowledge norm is the best candidate for being the ultimate epistemic standard. It doesn't explain why it should be knowledge rather than something else. Here, I would say that beliefs have a distinctive virtue when, but only when, they constitute knowledge. The only source of reasons that consists of facts is belief when it constitutes knowledge. If this is right, these facts about belief's function and when it can fulfill it (i.e., that its function is to provide facts as reasons and that it does so iff it constitutes knowledge) can explain why the fundamental standard should be understood in terms of knowledge.[18]

In response to the second question, I would say that even if we all agreed that bearing some relation to knowledge is ultimately what determines whether a belief is justified, we might doubt that the relation in question is quite as intimate as I've suggested. My main reason for thinking that a belief is justified iff it constitutes knowledge is that I think that justification is a normative notion and that a belief is justified iff it is properly held. It should be justified if it's not the case that it shouldn't be held. It should not be justified if it shouldn't be held. Assuming that a belief is permissible to hold iff it constitutes knowledge, this is the account we're left with.[19]

---

17 For an extensive discussion of the differences between lottery cases and preface cases and how they relate to mundane cases involving perception or testimony, see Dutant and Littlejohn (2021).
18 For elaboration and defence of this idea, see Littlejohn (2018a, 2018b).
19 See Sutton (2007) for an important defence of this view.

One might object that this view is problematic because justification is a normative notion that bears an intimate connection to reasons. This view is particularly appealing if you have sympathy for the reasons-first view. We might say, for example, that justified beliefs are beliefs that are held for sufficient reason(s). It's not clear whether the notion of "believing for sufficient reason" is conceptually connected to knowledge in such a way that "S believes that p for sufficient reason iff S knows that p."

A full response to this sort of worry would require extensive discussion. First, one could follow the lead of McDowell (1998) in saying that it's part of the nature of knowledge to involve the kind of connection to reasons the objector envisages. Having argued against this view of knowledge, however, this is not the route that I want to go. Second, the knowledge-centered view of justification sketched here *is* compatible with a reasons-first approach to justification (but not Schroeder's (2021) reasons-first account of knowledge). I take reasons-firsters to say things like this: whenever a subject ought to X (or ought not X), this is because the reasons (in combination) make this the case. I'm skipping over the difficulty of stating how reasons have to be related to an option to make it forbidden and required. Here's a reasons-centered way of stating my theory of justification. The reasons that bear on whether to believe are provided by knowledge norms (e.g., norms that enjoin us to believe what we can know and to refrain from believing what we cannot know). If we say that we should believe because we're in a position to know, this is because there's a normative reason that favors believing. And if we say that we shouldn't believe, it's because we're not in a position to know and there's a decisive reason against believing.[20]

While I would deny that a belief is justified only if based on a propositionally specified reason, I don't have to deny that normative reasons explain why justified beliefs are justified and unjustified ones are not. What I have to deny is that all the reasons that matter to justification are accessible to us, within our ken, or things we're in a position to know and that justifiably believing (or acting, feeling) requires a correspondence between our reasons for believing (or acting, feeling) and the reasons that, say, figure in our one, true theory of why people ought to respond in some way. To justifiably believe, say, we don't need to believe where our reason for believing is that we're in a position to know. We just need to believe in a way that results in our knowing.

Some fans of the knowledge-first approach seem to think that justification doesn't depend upon the objective factors that knowledge does. If

---

20 I don't see any reason why reasons-firsters would deny that the reasons that matter are connected to norms like the knowledge norm (or the greatest happiness principle, the categorical imperative, etc.). I've never seen an argument for the reasons-first view that wasn't, in effect, an invitation to accept this approach because it's more fruitful than alternatives. But this would seem to require the reasons-firsters to be comfortable with the existence of norms or principles since they don't, to my knowledge, ever argue that such things are mistaken.

this is because they think that all legitimate normative notions somehow depend upon the agent's perspective, I think this is mistaken (Littlejohn 2012: 202–222).[21] If, however, the idea is that there are legitimate normative notions more sensitive to the agent's perspective, I agree. One might say, for example, that there is a notion of justification that's more closely connected to what we *subjectively* ought to believe. It doesn't seem plausible that we subjectively shouldn't believe something simply because we don't know it to be true. We need some other approach.

A popular approach is to say that some belief is justified iff it is sufficiently similar to some possible case of knowledge.[22] For example, the similarity in the ways of coming to believe that you have hands in the normal case and in the BIV's case is sufficient to ensure that the BIV's belief is justified on the assumption that the belief in the normal case is knowledge. The fact that beliefs about lottery propositions aren't sufficiently similar to cases of knowledge in terms of how they're formed is supposed to explain why those beliefs aren't knowledge.

One worry that I have about this approach is that any belief that constitutes knowledge is going to be maximally similar to some case of knowledge, so this similarity approach will inevitably lead to the conclusion that a subject's belief is justified in this more subjective sense if that belief constitutes knowledge. This doesn't seem right to me. Suppose you're watching a football match and the ball goes out of play. If the ball goes out ten yards from the goal line, many of us could know that the ball did not go out at the fifty-yard line. Few of us could know that it didn't go out at the nine-yard line. When we think about the strongest thing that we could know in such a case about the ball's distance from the goal, it seems very improbable given our total evidence that this and not something nearby is the strongest thing we can know.[23] Given the risk of believing in violation of the knowledge norm, it seems that it wouldn't be rational for a thinker to believe this proposition. However, given the view that a belief is rational or justified if it's sufficiently similar to a case of knowledge, we couldn't deny that such a risky doxastic gambit would be rational or justified.[24]

---

21 Kiesewetter (2017) and Lord (2018) develop the view this way, but I think that *if* reasons (understood as facts that include fact about the situation) determine how we ought to respond, this is an objective "ought" not a subjective one and that any theory of the prospective "ought" should be told in terms of credences about objective reasons (not, as they think, sets of objective reasons that we know or are in a position to know).
22 See, for example, Bird (2007), Ichikawa (2017), Rosenkranz (2021), and Smithies (2019).
23 This case is inspired by Williamson's (2014) discussion of the unmarked clock, which he uses to argue for the possibility of improbable knowing (i.e., cases in which someone can know *p* even though it is nearly certain given their evidence that they don't know that *p*). See Rosenkranz (2021) for an important dissenting view on such cases.
24 See Lasonen-Aarnio (2010) for a discussion of unreasonable knowledge. I don't know if she thinks that cases of improbable knowledge are cases of unreasonable knowledge, but we agree that such cases should be possible.

In my view, the best approach to subjective justification in the knowledge-first framework is one that tells us that we're subjectively justified in believing those things that wouldn't be too risky to believe given the twin aims of believing what we can know and refraining from believing what we cannot. We can determine whether a belief would be too risky by thinking about how objectively wrong it would be to fail to believe what can be known and how objectively wrong it would be to believe what we don't know. On this view, subjective justification wouldn't be sufficient for knowledge for obvious reasons and subjective justification wouldn't be necessary for knowledge because there can be situations in which it's not worth the risk even if things would have turned out well for you.

This combined theory of objective and subjective justification is, in my view, the best knowledge-first theory of justification we could hope for. As it happens, I also think that the knowledge-first approach is the right one.[25]

---

25 Thanks to Paul Silva for extensive comments on a previous draft. While I cannot reasonably hope to persuade him, I hope that they helped improve the discussion.

References

Audi, Robert. 1995. Memorial justification. *Philosophical Topics* 23: 31–45.

Bird, Alexander. 2007. Justified judging. *Philosophy and Phenomenological Research* 74: 81–110.

Brueckner, Anthony. 2009. E=K and perceptual knowledge. In P. Greenough and D. Pritchard (ed.), *Williamson on Knowledge*. Oxford University Press, pp. 5–11.

Collins, Arthur. 1996. Moore's paradox and epistemic risk. *The Philosophical Quarterly* 46: 308–319.

Davidson, Donald. 2001. *Subjective, Intersubjective, Objective*. Oxford University Press.

Dutant, Julien & Littlejohn, Clayton. 2021. Defeaters as indicators of ignorance. In J. Brown and M. Simion (ed.), *Reasons, Justification, and Defeat*. Oxford University Press, pp. 223–246.

French, Craig. 2012. Does propositional seeing entail propositional knowledge? *Theoria* 78: 115–127.

Goldman, Alvin. 1979. What is justified belief? In G. Pappas (ed.), *Justification and Knowledge*. Reidel, pp. 1–25.

Hofmann, Frank. 2014. Gettier for justification. *Episteme* 11: 305–318.

Huemer, Michael. 2001. *Skepticism and the Veil of Perception*. Rowman & Littlefield.

Ichikawa, Jonathan. 2017. *Contextualising Knowledge*. Oxford University Press.

Kiesewetter, Benjamin. 2017. *The Normativity of Rationality*. Oxford University Press.

Lasonen-Aarnio, Maria. 2010. Unreasonable knowledge. *Philosophical Perspectives* 24: 1–21.

Littlejohn, Clayton. 2012. *Justification and the Truth-Connection*. Cambridge University Press.

Littlejohn, Clayton. 2015. Knowledge and awareness *Analysis* 75: 596–603.
Littlejohn, Clayton. 2017. How and why knowledge is first. In A. Carter, E. Gordon & B. Jarvis (ed.), *Knowledge First*. Oxford University Press. pp. 19–45.
Littlejohn, Clayton. 2018a. The right in the good: A defense of teleological non-consequentialism in epistemology. In K. Ahlstrom-Vij and J. Dunn (ed.), *Epistemic Consequentialism*. Oxford University Press, pp. 23–48.
Littlejohn, Clayton. 2018b. Evidence and its limits. In C. McHugh, J. Way and D. Whiting (ed.), *Normativity: Epistemic and Practical*. Oxford University Press, pp. 115–135.
Littlejohn, Clayton. 2020. Do you see what I know? On reasons, perceptual evidence, and epistemic status. *Philosophical Issues* 30: 205–220.
Lord, Errol. 2018. *The Importance of Being Rational*. Oxford University Press.
Mantel, Susanne. 2013. Acting for reasons, apt action, and knowledge. *Synthese* 190: 3865–3888.
McDowell, John. 1978. Are moral requirements hypothetical imperatives? *Proceedings of the Aristotelian Society* 52: 13–29.
McDowell, John. 1998. *Meaning, Knowledge, and Reality*. Harvard University Press.
McDowell, J. 2006. Reply to Dancy. In C. Macdonald and G. Macdonald (ed.), *McDowell and his Critics*. Blackwell, pp. 134–142.
McDowell, John. 2009. *Having the World in View: Essays on Kant, Hegel, and Sellars*. Harvard University Press.
McGinn, Marie. 2012. Non-inferential knowledge. *Proceedings of the Aristotelian Society* 112: 1–28.
Millar, Alan. 2019. *Knowing by Perceiving*. Oxford University Press.
Mitova, Veli. 2015. Truthy psychologism about evidence. *Philosophical Studies* 172: 1105–1126.
Rosenkranz, Sven. 2021. *Justification as Ignorance*. Oxford University Press.
Schroeder, Mark. 2021. *Reasons-First*. Oxford University Press.
Silva Jr, Paul. Forthcoming-a. Possessing reasons: Why the awareness-first approach is better than the knowledge-first approach. *Synthese* 199: 2925–2947.
Silva Jr, Paul. Forthcoming-b. Basic knowledge and the normativity of knowledge: The awareness-first solution. *Philosophy and Phenomenological Research*. doi: 10.1111/phpr.12754
Smithies, Declan. 2019. *The Epistemic Role of Consciousness*. Oxford University Press.
Sutton, Jonathan. 2007. *Without Justification*. MIT University Press.
Sylvan, Kurt. 2018. Knowledge as a non-normative relation. *Philosophy and Phenomenological Research* 97: 190–222.
Travis, Charles. 2013. *Perception: Essays After Frege*. Oxford University Press.
Travis, Charles. 2018. Reply to Keith A. Wilson. In J. Collins and T. Dobler (ed.), *The Philosophy of Charles Travis: Language, Thought, and Perception*. Oxford University Press, pp. 338–351.
Unger, Peter. 1975. *Ignorance*. Oxford University Press.
Williamson, Timothy. 2000. *Knowledge and its Limits*. Oxford University Press.
Williamson, Timothy. 2014. Very improbable knowing. *Erkenntnis* 79: 971–999.

16 Epistemic Consent and Doxastic Justification[1]

Luis R.G. Oliveira

In various recognizable ways, we hold ourselves and each other accountable for the things that we believe. Though not typically obsessive about it, most of us sometimes reflect on our own beliefs and cognitive powers, especially when under pressure from other beliefs, sensations, feelings, testimony, disagreement, and so on. Most of us can tell when something seems "epistemically off"—though not always and not always correctly—and most of us are at least somewhat disposed, in varying degrees of seriousness, to do something about that bothersome impression.[2] No doubt we are industrious in communicating any perceived epistemic foibles in our peers. What others believe and how they manage their cognitive lives, especially on sensitive topics or topics near and dear to us, is often the very target of our criticism, the cause of our resentment, and the grounds for sanctions such as social exclusion and public shaming.

My starting point in this chapter is a commitment to understanding the property of "being doxastically justified in believing that p" as the inchoate ideal that is behind these familiar (but hard to describe) *practices of epistemic accountability*. When we try to understand the proper grounds for evaluating someone's state of believing that p as being justified or unjustified, I take it that we are trying to understand the proper grounds for engaging with ourselves and each other in ways that we are already disposed to engage. In my view, this gives a clear purpose and a clear value to this kind of philosophical investigation. We are beings who are inextricably engaged in, and dependent on, these private and collective practices of epistemic

---

1 For invaluable discussions of the ideas in this chapter, and for comments on previous drafts, I'm grateful to Justin Coates, David Phillips, Hilary Kornblith, Joshua DiPaolo, Timothy Perrine, Ed Ferrier, Paul Silva, Miles Tucker, Bob Gruber, Jonathan Weid, and Laura Callahan.
2 See Zagzebski (2012, 27–33) for a discussion of the epistemic fundamentality of a pre-reflective "experience of dissonance."

DOI: 10.4324/9781003008101-21

accountability; by better understanding and by improving on these practices, we better understand and improve ourselves.³

There are three dominant conceptions of doxastic justification in the literature: one focusing on whether the mechanisms responsible for the relevant belief are connected to truth in the right way, one focusing on whether that belief is based on adequate grounds, and one focusing on the relation between that belief and character traits of the believer. Consider three traditional and representative articulations:

> If S's belief in p at t results from a reliable cognitive process, and there is no reliable or conditionally reliable process available to S which, had it been used by S in addition to the process actually used, would have resulted in S's not believing p at t, then S's belief in p at t is [doxastically] justified.⁴
>
> (Goldman 1979/1992, 123)

> S's doxastic attitude D at t toward proposition p is [doxastically justified] if and only if (i) having D toward p [fits the evidence S has at t]; and (ii) S has D toward p on the basis of some body of evidence e, such that (a) S has e as evidence at t; (b) having D toward p fits e; and (c) there is no more inclusive body of evidence e' had by S at t such that having D toward p does not fit e'.⁵
>
> (Feldman and Conee 1985/2004, 93)

> A justified belief is what a person who is motivated by intellectual virtue, and who has the understanding of his cognitive situation a virtuous person would have, might believe in like circumstances.
>
> (Zagzebski 1996, 241)

---

3 My commitment to relating doxastic justification to our practices of epistemic accountability does not reflect a sociological belief that epistemologists working on this topic are, by and large, also seeing things this way. See Plantinga (1990, 45–49), Alston (2005, 12–15), Silva (2017, 28–29), and Goldberg (2018, 13–47) for discussion of the variety of different conceptions of justification found in the literature, and for very different suggestions for what to do about it. Following some work on externalism about knowledge, moreover, I here take it that knowledge does not require justification (cf., e.g., Armstrong 1973, Nozick 1981, Audi 1993, Sosa 2007, Pritchard 2005, Audi 2020). I also do not assume that *justification* and *rationality* amount to the same thing (cf. Siscoe 2021).

4 I have inserted "doxastically" to clarify the kind of justification at stake. Goldman's preferred term for this property, a term he introduces soon after the quote just above, is "*ex post* justification" (cf. Goldman 1979, 124).

5 I am substituting "doxastically justified" for Feldman and Conee's preferred term for the same property, "well founded," and I am inserting "fits the evidence S has at t" in place of their place holder use of "justified," which they define earlier as fitting the evidence (cf. Feldman and Conee 1985/2004, 83).

Different accounts have been developed along similar or hybrid lines. Yet if these accounts—or any other—are about the property that *properly grounds* our practices of epistemic accountability (their original intentions notwithstanding), then they must be taken as more than simply the articulation of a concept, a point of view, a natural kind, or some such: they must be taken as expressing *epistemic norms* as well, norms about the formation and maintenance of doxastic states, norms that we can hold and be held accountable by. In particular, we must be able to derive from them true claims of the form "S ought not φ at t," claims whose truth explains why it can be appropriate to criticize, resent, and sanction those who do, regretfully, φ at t. Even more, given the various kinds of norms we are ordinarily familiar with—moral norms, prudential norms, conversational norms, norms of etiquette, and so on—the epistemic norms derived from these and other accounts of doxastic justification must have *normative authority* over us: it must be truly appropriate to criticize, resent, or sanction someone for flouting *them*.[6]

What I have as my guide in this chapter, therefore, is what we can call the *Normative Authority Conception* of justification:

> **NAC:** S is justified in their belief that p at t (to some degree n) if and only if their believing that p at t is not ruled out by epistemic norms that have normative authority over S at t.

This is not a particular *account* of doxastic justification, one that by itself rivals the traditional views just mentioned. This is instead a guiding *conception* indicating what accounts of doxastic justification are supposed to be about and, therefore, a guide for how to judge their plausibility.[7] We get particular accounts of justification out of this conception, of course, by endorsing an account of normative authority—an account of what makes the violation of a norm in general, or an epistemic norm in particular, the proper ground for criticism, resentment, and sanctions. No substantive account of justification is therefore eliminated by *fiat* on this conception, even if accepting it imposes substantive and controversial constraints on what could count as a plausible candidate.

Pleasant ecumenicism aside, it is very much unclear to me whether the epistemic norms expressed by the accounts just above, and the particular

---

6 See Brown (2019, 2020) for a similar claim about "epistemic blameworthiness." We need not assume, however, that epistemic norms have *independent* normative authority, so long as their authority can be derived from norms that do, indeed, have normative authority over us. I won't discuss this kind of indirect approach here. That said, see Oliveira (2017) for a criticism of accounts connecting epistemic norms to moral norms (cf., e.g., Grimm 2009), and see Cote-Bouchard (2015) for a criticism of accounts connecting epistemic norms to prudential norms (cf., e.g., Kornblith 1993).
7 See Alston (1985) for the distinction between conceptions and accounts and for the theoretical priority of the former. See Silva (2017) for discussion and application.

prescriptions we can derive from them, have normative authority over us. It is unclear to me, that is, whether epistemic norms enjoining us not to have unreliably formed beliefs, improperly based beliefs, or unvirtuous beliefs, can properly ground our practices of epistemic accountability. That said, I will not argue for this claim today. Instead, with this concern in mind, in this chapter I develop an alternative account of doxastic justification by looking for an explanation for the normative authority of epistemic norms—for why flouting them can make criticism, resentment, and sanctions appropriate. In a reversal that has Strawsonian and Alstonian connections, I will argue that our practices of epistemic accountability have explanatory priority over the grounds of their own propriety.[8]

Drawing from work in political philosophy, I will argue that (a) the cognitive and evaluative commitments and concerns behind our actual practices of holding each other and ourselves accountable for our beliefs reveal which epistemic norms we have *consented to be under*, and that (b) it is because we have consented to be under the authority of these norms—by actually holding ourselves and others accountable to them—that they in turn indeed have normative authority over us. In other words, it is by doing well or poorly with respect to our own epistemic commitments, collectively and interpersonally thus understood, that we are justified or unjustified in our beliefs and, consequently, properly subject to criticism, resentment, and sanctions for them. What I offer here, to be clear, is but a sketch. My aim is to identify a particular difficulty, motivate a potential solution, and outline a program for its further development.

Attributability and Ownership

I want to begin by quickly surveying some work that is motivated by a similar concern to mine. The concern here is with what makes our practices of epistemic accountability appropriate. I will argue, however, that there are two dimensions to this question of propriety and that these views only address one of them – successfully or not.

Working from within the Feldman and Conee general approach, Adam Leite has argued that we can only be the proper targets of criticism for our beliefs if we have the power to directly determine, through private or public deliberation, the reasons for which we hold our beliefs. This is because our reasons for believing that p—which are the target of criticism, on views like Feldman and Conee's—must be *attributable* to us,

---

8 See Strawson (1962) and Alston (1989, 1991). For some difficulties for this explanatory reversal regarding "moral responsibility," see Todd (2016). For a way out of those difficulties—a way out that is available for my proposal here about "doxastic justification"—see Beglin (2018).

and because "states of a sort which are never directly determined by a person's conscious deliberation, the commitments incurred through her conscious deliberation, or her best explicit evaluation of reasons, are not attributable to her in the relevant sense" (Leite 2004, 231). This concern with attributability as a requirement for proper criticism is certainly not unique to Leite. The kinds of evaluations behind our ordinary practices of accountability—epistemic or not—seem to presuppose that we are, in some relevant sense, the sources of whatever it is we are being criticized, resented, or sanctioned for. It would certainly be odd to behave in this way toward someone in virtue of something that merely happened to them.[9] Leite's view on what it takes for a state to be attributable to someone, however, where one must be involved in *directly determining* that state, is indeed somewhat unique.

Yet if we take the Feldman and Conee approach to doxastic justification, and if we think of justification as the inchoate ideal behind our practices of epistemic accountability, and if we moreover accept such a tight connection between direct determination and attributability, we are then led to something like the view that q is S's reason for believing that p only if S "endorses its adequacy as a reason for believing that p, and is committed to responding in appropriate ways if q proves to be an inadequate reason" (Leite 2004, 237). Failing this condition, then, whatever else is true of q, it is not my reason for believing that p. This is not, of course, an account of what it takes for something to be a *good* reason, nor is it an account of what it takes for S to be justified in believing that p. It is simply an account of one's *actual* reasons, one that follows from substantive views about what it takes for someone to be a proper target of criticism by virtue of their reasons for believing that p.[10]

In defending some such view, as you might expect, Leite is not suggesting that we only have reasons for our beliefs and are therefore capable of being justified in holding them or criticized in the relevant ways, after having explicitly committed ourselves to them in private or public deliberation. Even though criticizing someone as unjustified is, for Leite (2004, 233), to criticize them for their "*endorsement* of certain considerations as adequate reasons" (my emphasis), that endorsement can be tacit and dispositional. One counts as endorsing q as their reason for p, according to Leite (2004, 234), if one *would* "appropriately manifest, express, or acknowledge one's reasons in one's explicit thinking or attempts to justify one's belief," *were* the appropriate situations to present themselves. This is all well and good; we would have implausibly too few justified beliefs otherwise.

---

9 For broader discussions of the connection between normative evaluation and attributability see Scanlon (1998), Watson (2004), and Smith (2012).
10 For an evaluation and critique of Leite's full epistemological project, see Perrine (2018).

Less stringent accounts of what it takes for a state to be attributable to someone are friendlier to Goldman's approach to justification. On this approach, recall, justification is not determined by one's reasons for believing some p but rather by properties of the mechanisms that produced the belief, mechanisms that are sub-personal, typically involuntary, and almost always opaque to introspection. Nonetheless, the states that are outputs of these mechanisms can be attributable to us—in the sense that makes us proper targets of normative evaluation for having them—if we *take ownership* for those mechanisms and those outputs. If we identify these sub-personal mechanisms with ourselves, and identify their outputs as our own, then we are properly criticizable when these outputs don't look good.[11]

There are at least two kinds of proposals regarding this ownership-relation in the literature.[12] One proposal takes ownership for a belief as primarily a matter of recognizing oneself, through a historical and developmental process, as the source of beliefs formed by that mechanism, and as a matter of accepting that one is a fair target of criticism for having those beliefs (cf. Breyer and Greco 2008; Breyer 2010, 143; McCormick 2011, 173–4). The other proposal takes ownership for a belief as a matter of one's reflective attitude over one's reasons: either the attitude of taking oneself to have better reasons for endorsing that belief than not (cf. Duke-Yonge 2012, 246), or the attitude of recognizing the judgment that one's reasons support that belief as reflecting one's values (cf. Osborne 2021). Once again, these are not accounts of what it takes to be justified in believing that p, but rather accounts of what it takes to own up to one's beliefs—of what it takes for the belief that p to be attributable to S, in the relevant sense—such that one can be a proper target of criticism on account of having them.

None of these accounts, moreover, requires an explicit and conscious act behind the fact of ownership. From the mechanism side, McCormick (2015, 121) tells us that "even if we never consciously endorse a mechanism, we can still have ownership of it ... if *my practices* reveal that I have accepted the expectation that I keep beliefs of this kind in line with my higher order judgments of how I ought to believe" (my emphasis). From the reasons side, Osborne (2021, 8) tells that S owns a belief "just in case she holds it for reasons she takes *or is disposed* to take herself to possess, and the attitude reflects an evaluative judgment that she regards *or is*

---

11 For a broader discussion of the connection between normative evaluation and ownership, see Fischer and Ravizza (1998).
12 Some have discussed belief ownership in connection with doxastic justification (Breyer and Greco 2008, Breyer 2010, Duke-Yonge 2012), others in connection with doxastic responsibility (McCormick 2011, Osborne 2021). For the purposes of this chapter, I am ignoring these differences. See Oliveira (2018), however, for an argument that epistemic justification should not be understood as an evaluation of an agent as responsible in their belief.

disposed to regard as her own, i.e., *she is disposed* to reflectively endorse it as expressing her values" (my emphasis). Once again, it is hard to see how this could be otherwise, our practices of epistemic accountability being so profligate, and our time spent on actual discussion and actual deliberation being so limited.

Despite their various differences, what all of these views have in common is their focus on the conditions required for S to be a *proper target* of criticism for believing that p, in particular the requirement that S's belief be attributable to S. In this way, however, all of these views focus on what it is *on the subject's side* that makes doxastic evaluations appropriate. What they leave out, in turn, is a discussion of the conditions required for *a norm* to be an appropriate standard for the evaluation of that subject's state. What gives normative authority, after all, to certain norms as the proper standards for evaluating the beliefs and/or reasons that are properly attributable to me? In owning up to certain beliefs, or in committing to certain reasons, what makes me accountable for flouting *these* epistemic norms and not others? There are two dimensions, in other words, that together constitute the propriety of our practices of epistemic accountability. What is being evaluated positively or negatively must be properly attributable to me, on the one hand, and the grounds for that evaluation must have authority over me, on the other. I can define a host of properties and evaluate you on whether you instantiate them, but that won't automatically make it appropriate for me to criticize, resent, or sanction you for falling short, even if they are attributable to, or owned by, you.[13]

Consider an analogy. When Magnus Carlsen evaluates a complicated chessboard position as "winning for black"—where this does not mean, of course, that black will in fact win—the evaluation is appropriate because Carlsen is both (a) evaluating a game of chess and (b) applying to it the appropriate standards for that kind of evaluation. It would be quite irrelevant if Carlsen were to evaluate a game of backgammon by those same standards, or were to evaluate a game of chess by the standards appropriate to backgammon instead. Appropriate evaluations require a match between proper targets and proper standards. And when those standards are behind practices of accountability, then an account of what makes them *proper* just is an account of what makes gives them *normative authority*. Without some such account, however, our understanding

---

13 To be clear, none of these authors is trying to answer the question I'm pursuing here, so I am not imputing their arguments with this failure. My claim is that even if we take them as having achieved their aims—i.e., take them as having correctly identified the conditions under which we are the proper targets of evaluation for having the belief that p—we are still in the dark as to which norms are such that violating them makes criticism, resentment, and sanctions appropriate.

of our practices of epistemic accountability, and our search for an account of doxastic justification that can ground them, is incomplete.[14]

Constitutivism and Normativism

I now want to consider a kind of account of epistemic normativity that, by focusing on the source of epistemic norms, "promises to explain, in a relatively straightforward way, the authority of epistemic norms" (Nolfi 2015, 181). On this kind of account, "beliefs will be appropriately evaluated with respect to epistemic norms simply by virtue of being the sorts of mental attitudes that they are" (ibid). Despite their recent wide support, however, I will argue that these accounts fail to deliver on that promise. I begin by distinguishing between two minor variants of this view.

One variant is often called *constitutivism*. The general suggestion here is that we can extract norms for engaging in any kind of activity by examining the non-normative constraints on what counts as performing that activity in the first place. One only counts as playing chess, for example, if one is moving certain kinds of pieces in certain kinds of ways. This is to say that it is constitutive of the activity of playing chess—as opposed to playing some other game or no game at all—that one refrains from doing certain things at certain times (e.g., from moving one's rook diagonally during a match). These constitutive constraints are non-normative in the sense that they are merely claims about certain actions and certain activities, and not yet claims about norms. Nonetheless, from these claims about what counts as chess playing, we can *indirectly* extract norms of the kind "if S is playing chess at t, then S ought not φ at t," where φ-ing at t is incompatible with counting as playing chess at t.

We can derive epistemic norms in a similar way. The classic, if imprecise, statement of this view is Bernard Williams' (1973, 136) famous claim that "beliefs aim at truth," which is intended as a non-normative description of the role a mental state must actually play in one's psychology in order to count as a belief in the first place. Statements along these lines abound. According to Scott-Kakures (1994, 87), "no one believes that p if she also believes that the belief that p is unsupported by any consideration having to do with the truth of p." According to Street (2009, 225), "S believes that p if and only if (as a routine matter or when she thinks about the matter in full consciousness) S takes considerations that S regards

---

14 Discussions of normativity and attributability in moral theory typically ignore the issue I'm highlighting for a very natural reason: there is a strong presumption, in the moral case, that the relevant norms are indeed authoritative in the sense of properly grounding criticism, resentment, and sanctions. I have two comments here. First, whatever we say about the appropriateness of this presumption in the moral case, there is no similarly strong presumption in the epistemic case. Second, I'm of the view that such presumptions, of whatever strengths, must ultimately be backed up by arguments anyway.

as bearing on the truth of p to be reasons for and against believing that p." These are not simply (alleged) empirical observations or predictions; these are substantive non-normative constraints on what kinds of mental states can count as a belief. They are analogous to the claim that "no one is playing chess if they are moving their rooks diagonally on the board." Yet, from such constraints on what counts as a belief, we can indirectly identify epistemic norms of the kind "if S is believing at t, then S ought not φ at t," where φ-ing is incompatible with counting as believing that p at t. Identifying a plausible and satisfying non-normative constraint on the mental state of belief, of course, has proved to be tricky business.[15]

Another variant of this kind of account is often called *normativism*. Here the suggestion is not that we derive epistemic norms indirectly by first identifying the non-normative constraints on what count as a belief, but rather that we do so directly: it is part of the very nature of the mental state of belief that it is subject to certain norms. On one development of this view, for example, our concept of belief has a constitutive standard of correctness, namely, that "S's belief that p is correct iff p is true" (cf. Shah and Velleman 2005). On another development, the mental state of believing that p "is correct if and only if it is disposed to inform our actions by serving as a kind of map so that our actions successfully achieve the ends that our actions are meant to achieve" (Nolfi 2015, 197–198). Despite the differences between these two developments—one focusing on our concept and one focusing on a mental state—and despite the differences between this variant and the previous—one being indirect and one being direct—the central move is nonetheless the same. From the very nature of belief, we can extract norms of the kind "if S is believing at t, then S ought not φ at t," this time where not being subject to this norm is itself incompatible with counting as believing that p at t. Of course, arriving at a plausible and satisfying formulation of this norm has proved to be tricky business just as well.[16]

For my present purposes, it matters very little which variant, or which development of which variant, is correct. Constitutive normativity of whatever kind is rather cheap. The norms extracted from the nature of chess playing (directly or indirectly) don't really carry, by themselves, any normative authority over us. I can at any time decide to stop playing chess and make whatever moves I wish, or no moves at all, and—provided I have not thereby flouted any *other* norms of, say, respect, or promise keeping, and so on—no kind of criticism of my behavior would be appropriate on those grounds. The constitutive norms of chess may well properly ground evaluations of chess playing, but those evaluations don't by themselves

---

15 For relevant discussions, see Winters (1979), Bennett (1990), Scott-Kakures (1994), and Frankish (2007).
16 For relevant discussions, see Shah and Velleman (2005), Hieronymi (2008), McHugh and Whiting (2014), and Nolfi (2015).

properly ground criticism, resentment, and sanctions. To be sure, epistemic norms are different from the norms of chess in that we have no way of begging off from the activity of believing, no way to decide not to form or hold beliefs, and so no way to remove ourselves from the domain of application of the norms governing that kind of activity. Perhaps, then, this difference grants them the normative authority lacked by the norms of chess and the norms of similarly contingent activities.

But this is to misunderstand the problem. From the fact that I cannot escape a certain activity, it doesn't follow that the norms governing that activity have normative authority over me—that it is proper to criticize, resent, and sanction me for flouting them. This is because the following generalization is not true: for all activities φ, if S is engaged in φ-ing then S ought to φ well. If this were true and I truly couldn't help but φ, then it would be inescapably true of me that I ought to φ well. And since flouting the constitutive norms of φ-ing counts as a particularly egregious way of not φ-ing well—either by not φ-ing at all or by necessarily φ-ing incorrectly—it would follow from all of this that those norms have normative authority over me, that I am inescapably *bound* by them in the sense capable of grounding proper criticism, resentment, and sanctions. I ought to φ well if I φ at all; I φ-ed badly; shame on me. But the relevant generalization is not true. From the fact that I am engaging in a certain activity, it may follow that my performance is evaluable by the norms of that activity, but it does not follow that those norms have normative authority over me and that I can be properly held accountable for my shortcomings. So if the norms of belief have normative authority over us, it is not *because* they are the constitutive norms of something, even if it is something we can't escape.[17]

This worry applies to any bare appeal to constitution, no matter how involved. Recently, for example, A.K. Flowerree (2018) has defended a view that locates the source of epistemic normativity not in the nature of belief but rather in the nature of agency. Following Korsgaard's (2008) account of action, Flowerree (2018, 305) suggests that "our understanding of an action is intelligible only if we see it as the agent engaging

---

17 Osborne (2021, 9) says that "the holding of a belief by default makes one answerable for that belief. The intuitive justification for this claim is that if someone e.g., professes to believe *that* p, it always is apt (if not *appropriate*) to ask them *why*" (emphasis original). But the question, once again, is not whether the norm applies; the question is whether it has normative authority. It is always appropriate to evaluate a chess move by the rules of chess, but this doesn't make those rules authoritative over me (in the relevant sense of accountability). See Enoch (2006, 2011) for a related and influential criticism of constitutive accounts of "agency." The key difference between the challenge Enoch presents and mine is that mine is not looking for what reasons one has to *care* about constitutive norms. See McHugh and Whiting (2014, 707–708) for a discussion of this challenge in terms of hypothetical vs instrumental norms. My challenge is orthogonal to that distinction. See Perrine (forthcoming) for discussion of similar issues regarding *epistemic value*.

in movement that is *guided* by her representation of the world. So any description of what the agent is doing will have to include what the agent took to be true when she acted. It is part of what makes the action the action it is" (emphasis original).[18] With belief and action thus intertwined, the constitutive norms of belief can inherit the normative authority of the constitutive norms of agency. As Flowerree (2018, 305–306) puts it, "believing well is constitutive of acting well."

The success of this account of epistemic normativity, of course, depends on the success of the supporting constitutive account of practical normativity. The constitutive norms of belief have authority over us, on this picture, only if the constitutive norms of agency have authority over us *by virtue of being constitutive of agency*—and not on the basis of something else. Yet constitutive accounts of practical normativity—those that extract the norms of action from what is constitutive of agency—face precisely the challenge outlined above. What gives the constitutive norms of agency *their* normative authority? The answer cannot be an appeal to the mere fact that they are *the constitutive norms* of agency. We have already seen that it is false that, for all activities ψ, if S is engaged in ψ-ing then S ought to ψ well. What is constitutive of some activity, by itself, is neither here nor there for the matter of normative authority. Even if Flowerree is correct that "believing well is constitutive of acting well," we have not yet been told why it is the case that we ought to "act well," such that it would follow that we ought to "believe well" too. Whatever gives the constitutive norms of agency—if indeed there are any some such—their normative authority, such that they can pass it along to the norms of belief, must be some further fact not yet described.

Neither constitutivism nor normativism, therefore, delivers on the promise "to explain, in a relatively straightforward way, the authority of epistemic norms" (Nolfi 2015, 181). To do so, they must either insist, implausibly, on the generalized claim that, for all activities ψ, if S is engaged in ψ-ing then S ought to ψ well, or identify some fact other than the fact of constitution that explains why we ought to ψ well in this or that case. Either way, we better look elsewhere for what we're after.[19]

---

18 There is an echo here of Nolfi's (2015, 197) claim that "the proper function of belief is to inform our decisions to act by serving as a kind of map of the way things are so that we achieve whichever ends our actions aim to achieve," though the views they develop differ in important ways.

19 Constitutivists sometimes insist that questioning the authority of the constitutive norms of agency is incoherent (see Velleman 2009, Flowerree 2018). Since *all* normative authority derives from the constitutive norms of agency, in their view, to ask for the source of *their* normative authority is to pose an ill-formed question. This strikes me as objectionably self-confident. Of course, if constitutivism is true, then the challenge is misguided; that's a simple logical entailment of the claim that, if the challenge is not misguided, constitutivism is false. But to say that there is no challenge in the first place, that its very statement is incoherent, precisely *because* of what is postulated by the theory being challenged, that's theoretical navel-gazing at its worst.

Consent and Authority

I want to suggest that we can make progress toward an account of the normativity of justification by paying attention to work on political legitimacy instead.[20] There is a long tradition in political philosophy behind the idea that a government's legitimate rule depends somehow on the consent of those being ruled by it. This connection between consent and legitimacy, as I see it, is largely parasitic on the fundamental intuition that only the act of consent can transfer the authority we have over ourselves to something or someone who does not have that authority of necessity. "The ultimate authority over oneself," I here agree with Zagzebski (2012, 136), "is oneself." What I want to suggest, therefore, is that the *normative authority* of epistemic norms is very much like the *legitimacy* of a government's rule over a people. Both properties arise when groups of people voluntarily organize their lives together under common rules, and both properties can attach themselves, at different times, to a varied and sometimes even incompatible set of rules. By examining the relation between consent and political legitimacy, at any rate, I hope to draw lessons about the connection between consent and normative authority as well. In this section, I describe Amanda Greene's work on political authority and I extract from it a general principle outlining a connection between consent and normative authority.

Connecting consent to a plausible theory of political legitimacy is no mean feat. While the *actual* consent of all individuals does not seem necessary for a government's legitimate rule over them, the *hypothetical* consent of all individuals does not seem sufficient for legitimate rule either. One of the obvious problems of requiring actual consent for legitimacy is that it would turn out that no government is, or has ever been, or can ever be expected to be, legitimate. This seems implausible.[21] But merely requiring hypothetical consent for legitimacy seems inadequate too. If an entire group of people objects to a particular government policy, it is not enough for a government official to reply—even if truly—that the policy is legitimate since they *would* consent to it, under ideal conditions of information, rationality, and evaluative orientation. Actual dissent can have consequences for legitimacy, even if against a policy that "all citizens as free and equal may reasonably be expected to endorse in the light of principles and ideals acceptable to their common human reason" (Rawls 1996, 137). Any plausible theory of how consent contributes to legitimacy, therefore, must somehow find a middle way.

---

20 Drawing general lessons about normativity—or particular lessons about epistemic normativity—from work in political philosophy is not unusual. See, e.g., Raz (1988) and Zagzebski (2012).
21 Some, of course, accept this result as true (e.g., Huemer 2012).

Bearing in mind these worries, Amanda Greene (2016, 2017, 2019, 2020) has recently articulated and defended a "Weberian" account of political legitimacy, one where "a state is legitimate to the degree that it is regarded by its subjects as having a valid claim to rule" (2017, 314). The heart and burden of this kind of account, of course, is specifying the conditions under which such acknowledgment of validity—such consent[22]—truly contributes to legitimacy. In short, Greene takes any kind of authority to have an essential function and takes legitimacy as a status that some authority can have by virtue of being recognized as performing its essential function well. Consent that is disconnected from such *telic recognition*, as I will call it, fails to contribute to the attainment of this status.[23]

In the case of governments, the key characteristic of what Greene calls *quality* consent—consent that truly contributes to legitimacy—is that the consent is based on a positive evaluation of the government's success with respect to the essential function of governance: benefiting its subjects through the exercise of power and authority (cf. Greene 2016, 84, 2019, 69). This is the sense in which the kind of evaluative attitude behind quality consent has a *fixed target*. Consenting to the authority of a government on the basis of something that is unrelated to the essential function of governance does not contribute to that government's legitimacy since it fails the Weberian requirement of telic recognition—it fails to be a "recognition of a political order as a political order" (Greene 2019, 72). But the relevant evaluative attitude, while having a fixed target, also has a *flexible content*. As Greene puts this at different times:

> On the basis of what a subject considers relevant and valuable *by her own lights*, she forms an overall subjective assessment of governance and, on that basis, consents to her political order.
>
> (2016, 84, my emphasis)

> The judgments that are involved rely on *subjective valuations of apparent goods* that have been achieved by the regime, at either the individual or collective level.
>
> (Greene 2019, 70, my emphasis)

---

22 In her 2016, Greene speaks in terms of "consent." In subsequent work, Greene speaks in terms of "assent." I will use "consent" throughout, however, except for direct quotes from her later work, since "assent" already features prominently in other debates in epistemology (e.g., Owen 2003, Williamson 2007, Baxter 2018).

23 The term "recognition" here is factive. As Greene (2020, 214 fn 2) puts it, "legitimacy consists of an objective element (*fulfilling* a promise to be valuable) and a subjective element (being seen as such by the relevant audience)" (my emphasis).

What is flexible here, to be clear, are the terms of the evaluation behind quality consent: what *I* consider beneficial in a government's exercise of power and authority. It is this combination of a fixed evaluative target with a flexible evaluative content, in an act of telic recognition, that gives quality consent its legitimacy-producing power.

Greene's neo-Weberian connection between political legitimacy and quality consent is attractive for a variety of reasons. I want to highlight three reasons in particular that will be presently relevant. First, Greene's account respects the fundamental intuition, mentioned above, that the authority of a government is somehow derived from the authority we have over ourselves, an authority that is guided and expressed by our actual, subjective, and variegated evaluative and cognitive states. In this way, her account correctly prevents the co-existence of legitimate authority and widespread alienation of the kind that arises when "one cannot authentically affirm the regime to which one is subject as in any sense worthwhile, i.e., as providing at least some benefits that one values subjectively" (Greene 2019, 78). Second, despite locating the ultimate source of political legitimacy in the individuals themselves, Greene's account nonetheless respects the social and collective nature of this status. A government does not fail to have legitimate authority over me simply because I fail to consent to it, even though my consent or dissent matters for its legitimacy. Third, Greene's connection between political legitimacy and quality consent avoids narrow-minded parochialism: it does not consider a state as illegitimate simply because it does not conform to the value judgments of my culture (e.g., with the fundamentality of personal freedom) or the political ideals of my time (e.g., with democratic liberalism); rather, it allows legitimacy to obtain despite variations in value systems (cf. Greene 2017, 315). If an illiberal and undemocratic state is benefiting its subjects through the exercise of power, and if its subjects recognize it as such and consent to its authority despite lacking a degree of personal freedom that we ourselves would find minimally adequate, then that state counts as legitimate by Greene's neo-Weberian lights. All of this seems right to me.[24]

Just as we have seen above with one's commitment to reasons or one's ownership of mechanisms and beliefs, however, actually consenting to a government's authority does not require either overt expressions with a specific affirmative content or similarly structured occurrent thoughts. Instead, one typically expresses one's consent in behavior that expresses the relevant evaluative and cognitive attitudes. "Normally," as Greene (2019, 71) puts it, "the disposition to comply and readily cooperate with

---

24 What I have presented here, of course, is not a detailed and careful defense of Greene's views. For a fuller picture, see Greene (2016, 2017, 2019, 2020).

exercises of power and authority is a good indicator of this acceptance [i.e., quality consent]." A bit later,

> Quality assent stands for a combination of a volitional state (acceptance) and a belief state (judgment). A decent proxy for this combination of willing and believing is a set of behavioral dispositions—to obey, first and foremost, but also to evince general support for the order upheld by the regime.
>
> (Greene 2019, 76)

The qualifiers "normally" and "decent" are unavoidable here since non-consenting subjects may have prudential reasons to comply and cooperate with their governments that are unrelated to consent. But what is important for our present purposes is the fact that our dispositions can instantiate our consent, and not so much the difficulties that beset illuminating the correct connection between the two and the precise conditions for when the property is or is not instantiated. Much as I can count as valuing X and believing Y by virtue of my behavior and dispositions, without ever consciously considering the relevant propositions (cf., Audi 1994, Schwitzgebel 2002, Zagzebski 2003/2020), I can count as consenting to an authority by virtue of behavior and dispositions that express the relevant evaluative and cognitive attitudes.[25]

I now want to draw on Greene's account of the legitimacy of governments and produce a general account of legitimacy for norms—or, as I will prefer to put it, an account of their normative authority. Take *quality consent* to mean the kind of consent to be under the authority of a certain norm that comes from recognizing its success in fulfilling its essential function (i.e. consent that is based on telic recognition). Take a norm to have *normative authority* when it is appropriate to criticize, resent, or sanction someone for flouting them. I propose the following principle connecting *consent* and *authority*:

> **Consent and Authority (C&A):** Norm N has some degree of normative authority over S at t if (a) S is a member of community C, and (b) a sufficiently large number of the members of C have quality-consented to be under the authority of N.

Notice that C&A only lays down a sufficient condition for when it is appropriate to criticize, resent, or sanction someone for flouting a certain norm. I am here only identifying one way in which a norm can come to

---

25 This is not, notice, to make quality consent merely hypothetical. The reliance on dispositions is not the same as the claim "he *would* consent, if only ..." but is rather the claim "he *does* consent, because..." There is an enormous amount of complexity behind the idea of non-explicit consent. I ignore that complexity for the purposes of the present sketch.

have normative authority over us.[26] Also notice how C&A identifies individuals as the *source* of normative authority but identifies the communities composed of these individuals as its *grounds*. According to C&A, my quality-consenting to be under the authority of some norm is not enough for it to have normative authority over me, just as my quality-dissenting from some norm is not enough to remove me from under its rule. On this point, C&A contrasts with other claims about authority that take individuals as *both* source and ground, for example:

> The authority of another person is justified for me by my conscientious judgment that if I do what the authority directs (or believe what the authority tells me), the result will survive my own conscientious self-reflection better than if I try to figure out what to do/believe myself.
> (Zagzebski 2012, 148)

C&A is more radically social than this. It claims instead that the normative authority of some norm can be derived from a similar source but without really depending on it. In other words, C&A harnesses the power that we have as individuals to sometimes imbue normative force to previously neutral rules or policies, but it filters that power through the social structure that a collection of such powers can create.[27]

Finally, notice how C&A takes normative authority to come in degrees and how it leaves unspecified what is the precise function that goes from some ratio of quality consent within C to some degree of normative authority for N over the members of C. This is by design.

With C&A in hand, I will propose below an account of doxastic justification that is tied to what I will call "epistemic consent" and that shares in the three attractive features of Greene's account mentioned above. By connecting the authority of epistemic norms to the authority we have over ourselves, the account explains why it can be appropriate to criticize, resent, or sanction someone for having unjustified beliefs and it avoids, in this way, both the phenomenon of normative alienation and the phenomenon of normative parochialism. All of this, of course, while respecting the social and collective nature of epistemic justification and thereby avoiding the slide into an implausible kind of subjective normative relativism.

---

26 In particular, C&A does not purport to identify a mechanism by which *normative reasons* are generated. I myself deny that there is a necessary connection between the normative authority of N over S (and the consequent propriety of criticizing, resenting, or sanctioning S for flouting N) and S's normative reasons for Φ-ing. (cf., Oliveira 2021). Whether I am right or wrong about this, the point is that this matter is substantive and independent of C&A.

27 For more on this normative power of individuals, see, e.g., Zagzebski (2005/2020, 2012) and Chang (2013a, 2013b).

Epistemic Consent and Doxastic Justification

Recall the *Normative Authority Conception* of justification I identified at the beginning of this chapter as my guide:

> **NAC:** S is justified in their belief that p at t (to some degree n) if and only if their believing that p at t is not ruled out by epistemic norms that have normative authority over S at t.

Differently from traditional conceptions, NAC prioritizes the way in which the state of being justified grounds the appropriateness of our practices of epistemic accountability: proper criticism, resentment, and sanctioning *on the basis of someone's flouting an epistemic norm*. To be doxastically justified in believing that p, in other words, is for it to be *epistemically inappropriate* to criticize, resent, and sanction me (though not necessarily inappropriate on other grounds).

But NAC is not yet an account of justification. For that, we first need an account of normative authority—an account of what makes the violation of a norm the proper ground for criticism, resentment, and sanctions. In the previous section, however, we have identified a source of normative authority that is a candidate for this post:

> **Consent and Authority (C&A):** Norm N has some degree of normative authority over S at t if (a) S is a member of community C, and (b) a sufficiently large number of the members of C have quality-consented to be under the authority of N.

My suggestion now is that C&A explains the kind of normative authority that is had by the epistemic norms of justification. I call the resulting account the *Epistemic Consent Account* of justification:

> **ECA:** S is justified in their belief that p at t (to some degree n) if and only if, for any epistemic community E that S is a member of, there is no norm N such that (i) a sufficiently large number of the members of E have epistemically quality-consented to be under the authority of N, and (ii) S's believing that p at t is ruled out by N.[28]

---

28 ECA is an account of "doxastic justification." As such, it purports to describe the conditions under which someone's state of believing that p is epistemically justified. Epistemologists, however, have often found useful to distinguish between *being justified in believing that p* and *having justification for believing that p*. To give an account of this later state is to give an account of "propositional justification." On some views, propositional justification is the more fundamental notion, with doxastic justification defined partly in terms of it. My view reverses the order of explanation (cf. Goldman, 1979/1992). On my view, propositional justification is a relation between S and a proposition, at a time, that is defined in terms of the epistemic status S's belief in p *would have*, at that time, given ECA. See Kornblith's (2022) contribution to this volume for a defense of this reversal and see Silva and Oliveira (forthcoming) for a discussion of these and related issues.

According to ECA, facts about doxastic justification are social facts: they are facts about a relation that holds between individuals and their communities. This kind of social-constructivism about epistemic normativity is not new.[29] What is unique to ECA, however, is the claim that the ultimate source of the normative authority of epistemic norms is *epistemic quality consent*: consent to be under the authority of epistemic norms that comes from recognizing their success in fulfilling their essential function (i.e., epistemic consent that is based on telic recognition). If epistemic norm N is to have normative authority over anyone, according to ECA, then a significant number of individuals must have endorsed N on account of recognizing that N's rule achieves what it essentially purports to achieve. I conclude by saying something about this central and distinctive element.

I take a broad view of the essential function of an epistemic norm—similar to the broad view Greene takes of the essential function of governance—namely, delivering truth-related benefits. Just as an individual's consent-producing endorsement of governance has a fixed target with a flexible content, an individual's consent-producing endorsement of epistemic norms can be based on a recognition that it delivers a variety of epistemic goods. Some may endorse norm N on account of recognizing its increase of our access to truth, others for its production of knowledge, and others for its connection to understanding; still others may endorse it out of a concern for coherence, reflective endorsement, evidential support, reliability, intellectual virtue, and so on. In each case, an individual is recognizing that N's rule delivers truth-related benefits and, by endorsing it on these different but related grounds, instantiates epistemic quality consent to be under its authority. The same individual, of course, may also endorse different norms for different truth-related benefits. There is no presumption here that each of us has one and only fundamental epistemic commitment and concern.

Telic recognition, however, is factive. Epistemic quality consent—consent to be under the authority of an epistemic norm—only occurs when the relevant norm's rule in fact delivers some truth-related benefit, aside from being recognized as such by some individual. This is why it is important to resist the temptation to reduce the essential function of epistemic norms to the delivery of one or another of the epistemic goods we are variously concerned with. Norm N's rule can succeed in delivering truth-related benefits (and be correctly recognized as such) without delivering all of them, and without delivering any particular one of them as well.[30] What makes these benefits "truth-related," in other words, is not their objective relation to a more "fundamental" good of truth—indeed, the

---

29 See, e.g., Brandom (1994) and Goldberg (2018).
30 This suggestion is in tension with a common way of thinking about epistemic goods, a way that is well represented by Pritchard (2014, 113) when he says that "from a purely epistemic point of view it is ultimately only truth that we should care about."

fact of the matter seems to be that many of these goods are not so related anyway (cf., e.g., Kornblith 2012)—but rather that our non-instrumental commitment and concern for them is *motivated* by a commitment to, and a concern for, truth.[31] In this way, a religious leader, or a philosophical mentor, may be factually misguided in their teachings and yet deliver the truth-related benefits of coherence, reflective endorsement, evidential support, intellectual virtue, and even understanding, such that the endorsement of an epistemic norm N respecting their authority can be based on the proper kind of telic recognition that grounds epistemic quality consent, despite N's rule failing to deliver truth.[32]

Importantly—indeed, most importantly—it is precisely by *engaging* in practices of epistemic accountability—by holding ourselves and others accountable to certain epistemic norms—that we instantiate our epistemic consent to be under the normative authority of those norms. Just as ownership or commitment to reasons, and just as political consent, epistemically consenting to be under the authority of some epistemic norm does not require explicit and overt affirmative expressions—or similarly structured thoughts. I can count as having the required cognitive and evaluative states behind consent merely by actually holding myself and others accountable to an epistemic norm, provided I do so out of a commitment to, and concern for, the truth-related benefits I endorse.[33] The idea here is that when I sense that something is *epistemically* off and feel the pull to do something about it, I am thereby revealing that by my own epistemic lights—lights that come from my commitments to, and concerns for, truth—I seem to be in violation of norms that deliver truth-related benefits (broadly construed). Similarly, when I hold you accountable for being *epistemically* off, I am expressing my judgment that you have flouted a norm that delivers truth-related benefits as well—a judgment

31 My commitment and concern for coherence or reflective endorsement, for example, is non-instrumentally truth-related, in this sense, when (a) I do not value coherence or reflective endorsement *as a means to* the further end of truth, and yet (b) the motivational structure that causes such a non-instrumental concern is itself grounded in a prior commitment to, and concern for, truth.
32 For arguments suggesting that understanding is possible with and through falsehoods (and, indeed, sometimes *only* through them), see Zagzebski (2001/2020) and Elgin (2017). For an argument that the kind of reflective equilibrium we find in Hume, Popper, Goodman, and Quine disconnects justification from likelihood of truth, see Johnsen (2017).
33 There is, of course, much in our practices of accountability that are not based on a concern for truth-related benefits. These do not count, on my terminology, as practices of *epistemic* accountability, even when their targets are doxastic states. How to properly characterize the relevant commitment to, and concern for, truth that gives rise to practices that are non-instrumentally attuned to truth-related benefits—in order to distinguish those that are practices of epistemic accountability from those that are not—is a complex issue that I also leave open another day. See, however, Zagzebski (2003/2020, 178–781) for a discussion of "epistemic motivation," and Zagzebski (2005/2020, 186–192) for a discussion of the "logic of caring" for epistemic goods.

that arises out of my commitment to, and concern for, truth. Here, notice, there is no reason to worry about the imperfect match between overt behavior (be it internal or external) and quality consent. The behavior we are considering here is not my *mere obedience or compliance* to the relevant norms (as if by accident or by virtue of some other concern), but rather my *motivated obedience* and *voluntary enforcement* of those epistemic norms on myself and others.

We finally have in view the full nature of the explanatory reversal I mentioned at the beginning of the chapter. According to NAC, to be doxastically justified in my believing that p (to some degree n) is for it to be *epistemically inappropriate* to criticize, resent, or sanction me. There are, therefore, facts about the propriety of holding me epistemically accountable in these ways—facts that determine whether I am justified in my belief. The surprising claim we get from combining NAC with C&A, however, is that what grounds and explains these facts about the propriety of epistemic accountability are simply further facts about our practices of epistemic accountability themselves. For it to be epistemically inappropriate to hold me accountable for believing that p at t, after all, is just for me to be part of an epistemic community that has *epistemically quality-consented* to be under epistemic norms that do not rule out my believing that p at t. And, on the view I am urging here, an epistemic community epistemically quality-consents to be under certain epistemic norms simply by expressing their fundamental commitment to, and concern for, truth in practices of epistemic accountability in the first place. For better or for worse, this is truly epistemic normativity from the ground up.[34]

Of course, a satisfying defense of ECA requires saying much more than this about consent and other matters. How do we individuate epistemic communities?[35] How do we extract "the norms that I am hold-

---

34 In similar but different ways, both Strawson and Alston take the relevant practices in their purview to be explanatorily prior to the grounds of their propriety. For Strawson, as Beglin (2018, 618) tells us, "our responsibility practices are an expression of certain concerns, and they thus reflect these concerns and are answerable to them." For Alston (1991, 158), "what is, factually, a more or less fixed habit of going from inputs of type I to a belief output of correlated type B, is also, evaluatively, a principle of justification for beliefs so formed. The principle says that when a belief of type B is formed on the basis of an input of type I, that belief is thereby (prima facie) justified." My view owes much to theirs. Goldberg (2018, 147–149) endorses a similar reversal, explaining epistemic standards by way of the epistemic expectations we are entitled to have of each other. By constraining the normative power of our actual practices with the normative notion of "entitlement," however, Goldberg's view is not, normatively speaking, "practices-first" all the way down.
35 In order to avoid a worry similar to the one I raised for constitutivists in section 3, answering this question requires attention to how membership into an epistemic community is itself an expression of an individual's fundamental commitment to, and concern for, truth. In particular, it requires attention to the difference between epistemic dissent and epistemic defection.

ing myself and others accountable to" from the complex patterns of internal and external behavior that constitute our practices of epistemic accountability?[36] What are the norms, after all, that have normative authority over me and most of us?[37] I do not have the space to address these and other questions here. But there are clearly different possible answers. I hope this chapter is just the beginning of a conversation on how to give ECA its most plausible articulation.

Conclusion

If we take doxastic justification as the inchoate ideal behind our practices of epistemic accountability, then we are faced with the problem of explaining how the norms of justification have the kind of normative authority over us that makes it appropriate to criticize, resent, and sanction someone for flouting them. I have argued here that we can make progress on this problem by paying close attention to work in political philosophy connecting the legitimacy of governments to consent to be ruled. The resulting account of doxastic justification—ECA—has four features that I find attractive in an account of doxastic justification.

First, and most obviously, ECA produces an account of justification that is connected to an account of normative authority that I find plausible. It explains, to my liking, why it is appropriate to criticize, resent, and sanction me when I have an unjustified belief: I belong to an epistemic community, I contributed to the grounds of the normative authority of our shared epistemic standards (by having truth-related commitments and concerns and by expressing them through various internal and external practices of accountability), and I have failed them. This is the sense in which ECA avoids the phenomena of normative alienation.[38]

---

36 Answering this question requires the careful work of understanding how our fundamental commitment to, and concern for, truth is *actually expressed* in our various practices of epistemic accountability. And while for the moment I stand with Strawson (1962, 2)—"I can give no simple description of the field of phenomena at the centre ... for the field is too complex"—a good start is Brown's (2019, 2020) work on epistemic blame and Goldberg's (2018, ch. 5) work on epistemic social expectations.
37 ECA represents a kind of naturalistic approach to epistemology. There is no telling what the norms of justification are *in advance*, as it were, of doing the careful and empirical work of examining and understanding our practices of epistemic accountability. That said, my sense is that this approach reveals that all norms of justification are what Josh DiPaolo (2019, 2049) calls "norms of compensation." See the second feature of ECA that I highlight in the conclusion below.
38 *Subjective permissivists* about evidential support also suggest ways in which individuals can play a role in determining the details of their epistemic situations (see, e.g., Schoenfield 2014, Callahan 2019). Their views, however, typically take for granted the normative authority of evidentialist norms and only give the subject enough powers to affect the particular prescriptions that apply to them. ECA, on the other hand, takes the normative authority of no epistemic norm for granted.

Second, ECA achieves this without imposing the normative authority of certain norms as "universal," "self-evident," or "brute" facts. The similarities between our natures, our fundamental concerns, and our circumstances no doubt ensures a great amount of overlap between the kinds of epistemic norms that have normative authority over the members of different epistemic communities—even at different times and places. But finer differences in our cultural upbringings, or finer differences in our concerns and contexts, may well produce some amount of divergence on their details. This is not a matter of some communities endorsing implausible anti-inductive norms or some such. (Would a group's commitment to, and concern for, truth really ever be expressed in practices of accountability that are guided by anti-inductive norms?) Instead, this is a matter of different communities having different evidential standards and thresholds, different views on the proper place for trust on epistemic authorities, different practices regarding disagreement, different habits for tolerating uncertainty, inconsistency, groundlessness, and so on. Much like the non-subjectivist relativism of Greene's account of political legitimacy, we here have the appropriate kind of normative flexibility: understanding what I am properly accountable for, epistemically speaking, requires first understanding the norms of the epistemic communities I am embedded within. This is the sense in which ECA avoids the phenomena of normative parochialism.[39]

Third, ECA delivers a view of doxastic justification—and a related understanding of our practices of epistemic accountability—that respects the fact that we lack sufficiently meaningful doxastic agency. There is no reason to think that we cannot consent to be under the authority of norms that govern states of ours for which we have minimal amounts of agency. Those of us, like myself, who think that our degree of doxastic agency is closer on the spectrum to our degree of digestive agency than to the degree of agency we typically have over our bodily movements should welcome this result.[40]

---

39 The worry about parochialism is not political. What would be the grounds for excluding some set of epistemic norms *a priori* as unacceptable if not the privileging of another set of norms? And what non-arbitrary, non-infinitely-regressable, and non-circular grounds could one have for privileging one set of epistemic norms over another (cf. Alston 1989, 10–11, 1991, 149–153)?

40 In Oliveira (2015), I resisted an argument against the basing requirement on justification (found in Silva 2015), by drawing an agential contrast between the epistemic and moral domain and by articulating a notion of "non-agential permissibility" that made the norms of epistemic evaluation more like the norms for evaluating clocks than the norms for evaluating actions. I take the present chapter to be a development of that central notion and a correction of some claims I made in its defense. In particular, I was wrong in thinking that non-agential permissibility made talk of praise and blame inappropriate, and incorrect in thinking that doxastic justification necessarily has basing requirement. See Silva's (2022) contribution to this volume for discussion. In Oliveira (2021), however, I argued that our lack of sufficiently meaningful doxastic agency means there are no such things as doxastic obligations or even normative reasons to believe. The account of epistemic normativity developed here is intended as complimentary to those results.

Fourth, and this is perhaps the most controversial of these attractive features, ECA allows for the possibility of "unclear" and "borderline" cases. These kinds of cases may arise in at least two kinds of circumstances: when it is unclear whether the number of members of a certain epistemic community who have epistemically consented to N is sufficiently large, and when one is a member of two or more communities with conflicting norms. Yet I think unclarity about whether I am doxastically justified in certain circumstances is precisely the right result. If there is a case for imprecision regarding the very concept of belief (cf. Schwitzgebel 2002, 252), there is certainly a strong case for imprecision in our concept of justification. In my view, we shouldn't expect exactness in matters of normative evaluation—the kind of exactness that tends to come, for example, from modeling the norms of justification on mathematical or scientific (probabilistic) reasoning. Caution and modesty in our attributions of justification should not only be recommended on account of our poor access to the relevant facts, it should also be recommended on account of the nature of the facts we purport to make claims about.[41]

---

41 This does not mean that ECA entails relativism about attributions of justification—where whether S is justified in their belief that p depends on which community we explicitly or contextually select as providing the standards for evaluation. See Goldberg (2018, 239–243) for a discussion of this issue.

References

Alston, William (1985). "Concepts of Epistemic Justification," *The Monist* 68(1): 57–89.
Alston, William (1989). "A "Doxastic Practice" Approach to Epistemology," in *Knowledge and Skepticism*, edited by Marjorie Clay and Keith Lehrer. Routledge: 1–29.
Alston, William (1991). *Perceiving God: The Epistemology of Religious Experience*. Cornell University Press.
Alston, William (2005). *Beyond "Justification": Dimensions of Epistemic Evaluation*. Cornell University Press.
Armstrong, David (1973). *Belief, Truth, and Knowledge*. Cambridge University Press.
Audi, Robert (1993). *The Structure of Justification*. Cambridge University Press.
Audi, Robert (1994) "Dispositional Beliefs and Dispositions to Believe," *Nous* 28: 419–434.
Audi, Robert (2020). *Seeing, Knowing, and Doing: A Perceptualist Account*. Oxford University Press.
Baxter, Donald (2018). "A Pyrrhonian Interpretation of Hume on Assent," in *Skepticism: From Antiquity to the Present*, edited by Diego Machuca and Baron Reed. Bloomsbury Academic: 380–394.
Beglin, David (2018). "Responsibility, Libertarians, and the "Facts as We Know Them": A Concern-Based Construal of Strawson's Reversal," *Ethics* 128: 612–625.

Bennett, Jonathan (1990). "Why is Belief Involuntary?" *Analysis* 50: 87–107.
Brandom, Robert (1994). *Making it Explicit: Reason, Representing, and Discursive Commitment.* Harvard University Press.
Breyer, Daniel (2010). "Reflective Luck and Belief Ownership," *Acta Analytica* 25: 133–154.
Breyer, Daniel and Greco, John (2008). "Cognitive Integration and the Ownership of Belief: Response to Bernecker," *Philosophy and Phenomenological Research* 76(1): 173–184.
Brown, Jessica (2019). "Epistemically Blameworthy Belief," *Philosophical Studies* 177: 3595–3614.
Brown, Jessica (2020). "What is Epistemic Blame?" *Nous* 54(2): 389–407.
Callahan, Laura (2019). "Epistemic Existentialism," *Episteme* 1–16. doi:10.1017/epi.2019.25
Chang, Ruth (2013a). "Grounding Practical Normativity: Going Hybrid," *Philosophical Studies* 164(1): 163–187.
Chang, Ruth (2013b). "Commitments, Reasons, and the Will," in *Oxford Studies in Metaethics (Vol. 8),* edited by Russ Shafer-Landau. Oxford University Press: 74–113.
Cote-Bouchard, Charles (2015). "Epistemic Instrumentalism and the Too Few Reasons Objection," *International Journal of Philosophical Studies* 23(3): 337–355.
DiPaolo, Joshua (2019). "Second Best Epistemology: Fallibility and Normativity," *Philosophical Studies* 176: 2043–2066.
Duke-Yonge, Jennifer (2012). "Ownership, Authorship and Externalist Justification," *Acta Analytica* 28: 237–252.
Elgin, Catherine (2017). *True Enough.* MIT Press.
Enoch, David (2006). "Agency, Shmagency: Why Normativity Won't Come from What is Constitutive of Action," *Philosophical Review* 115(2): 169–198.
Enoch, David (2011). "Shmagency Revisited," in *New Waves in Metaethics,* edited by Michael Brady. Palgrave Macmillan: 208–233.
Feldman, Richard and Conee, Earl (1985/2004). "Evidentialism," reprinted in *Evidentialism: Essays in Epistemology.* Oxford University Press: 83–100.
Fischer, John and Ravizza, Mark (1998). *Responsibility and Control: A Theory of Moral Responsibility.* Cambridge University Press.
Flowerree, A.K. (2018). "Epistemic Shmagency," in *Metaepistemology: Realism and Anti-Realism,* edited by Christos Kyriacou and Robin McKenna. Palgrave Macmilllan: 289–310.
Frankish, Keith (2007). "Deciding to Belief Again," *Mind* 116(463): 523–548.
Goldberg, Sanford (2018). *To the Best of Our Knowledge.* Oxford University Press.
Goldman, Alvin (1979/1992). "What is Justified Belief?" Reprinted in *Liaisons: Philosophy Meets the Cognitive and Social Sciences.* MIT Press: 105–126.
Greene, Amanda R. (2016). "Consent and Political Legitimacy," *Oxford Studies in Political Philosophy* 2: 71–97.
Greene, Amanda R. (2017). "Legitimacy without Liberalism: A Defense of Max Weber's Standard of Political Legitimacy," *Analyse & Kritik* 39(2): 295–323.
Greene, Amanda R. (2019). "Is Political Legitimacy Worth Promoting?" *NOMOS: Journal of the American Society for Political and Legal Philosophy* LXI: 65–101.

Greene, Amanda R. (2020). "When Are Markets Illegitimate?" *Social Philosophy and Policy* 36(2): 212–241.
Grimm, Stephen (2009). "Epistemic Normativity," in *Epistemic Value*, edited by Adrian Haddock, Alan Millar, and Duncan Pritchard. Oxford University Press: 243–264.
Hieronymi, Pamela (2008). "Responsibility for Believing," *Synthese* 161: 357–373.
Huemer, Michael (2012). *The Problem of Political Authority*. Palgrave Macmillan.
Johnsen, Bredo (2017). *Righting Epistemology: Hume's Revolution*. Oxford University Press.
Kornblith, Hilary (1993). "Epistemic Normativity," *Synthese* 94(3): 357–376.
Kornblith, Hilary (2012). *On Reflection*. Oxford University Press.
Kornblith, Hilary (2022). "What does Logic Have to do With Justified Belief? Why Doxastic Justification is Fundamental," in *Propositional and Doxastic Justification: New Essays on Their Nature and Significance*, edited by Luis Oliveira and Paul Silva. Routledge.
Korsgaard, Christine (2008). *The Constitution of Agency: Essays on Practical Reason and Moral Psychology*. Oxford University Press.
Leite, Adam (2004). "On Justifying and Being Justified," *Philosophical Issues* 14: 219–253.
McCormick, Miriam S. (2011). "Taking Control of Belief," *Philosophical Explorations* 14(2): 169–183.
McCormick, Miriam S. (2015). *Believing Against the Evidence: Agency and the Ethics of Belief*. Routledge.
McHugh, Conor and Whiting, Daniel (2014). "The Normativity of Belief," *Analysis* 74(4): 698–713.
Nolfi, Kate (2015). "How to be a Normativist About Belief," *Pacific Philosophical Quarterly*, 96(2): 181–204.
Nozick, Robert (1981). *Philosophical Explanations*. Harvard University Press.
Oliveira, Luis R.G. (2015). "Non-Agential Permissibility in Epistemology," *Australasian Journal of Philosophy* 93(2): 389–394.
Oliveira, Luis R.G. (2017). "Deontological Evidentialism, Wide-Scope, and Privileged Values," *Philosophical Studies* 174(2): 485–506.
Oliveira, Luis R.G. (2018). "Ampliative Transmission and Deontological Internalism," *Pacific Philosophical Quarterly*. 99(2): 174–185.
Oliveira, Luis R.G. (2021). "Evading the Doxastic Puzzle by Deflating Epistemic Normativity," in *Epistemic Duties: New Arguments, New Angles*, edited by Scott Stapleford and Kevin McCain. Routledge: 44–62.
Osborne, Robert (2021). "Doxastic Responsibility, Guidance Control, and Ownership of Belief," Episteme 18(1): 82–98.
Owen, David (2003). "Locke and Hume on Belief, Judgment, and Assent," *Topoi* 22(1): 15–28.
Perrine, Timothy (2018). "Justification, Justifying, and Leite's Localism," *Acta Analytica* 33(4): 505–524.
Perrine, Timothy (forthcoming). "Conceptions of Epistemic Value," *Episteme*. doi:10.1017/epi.2021.17
Plantinga, Alvin (1990). "Justification in the 20th Century," *Philosophy and Phenomenological Research* 50: 45–71.

Pritchard, Duncan (2005). *Epistemic Luck*. Oxford University Press.
Pritchard, Duncan. (2014). "Truth as the Fundamental Epistemic Good," in *The Ethics of Belief*, edited by Jonathan Matheson and Rico Vitz. Oxford University Press: 112–129.
Rawls, John (1996). *Political Liberalism*. Columbia University Press.
Raz, Joseph (1988). *The Morality of Freedom*. Oxford University Press.
Scanlon, T. M. (1998). *What We Owe Each Other*. Harvard University Press.
Schoenfield, Miriam (2014). "Permission to believe: Why permissivism is true and what it tells us about irrelevant influences on belief," *Nous* 48(2), 193–218.
Schwitzgebel, Eric (2002) "A Phenomenal, Dispositional Account of Belief," *Nous* 36(2): 249–275.
Scott-Kakures, Dion (1994). "On Belief and the Captivity of the Will," *Philosophy and Phenomenological Research*, 54: 77–103.
Shah, Nishi, and Velleman, David (2005). "Doxastic Deliberation," *Philosophical Review* 114(4): 497–534.
Silva, Paul Jr. (2015). "Does Doxastic Justification Have a Basing Requirement?" *Australasian Journal of Philosophy* 93(2): 371–387.
Silva, Paul Jr. (2022). "Does the Basing Demand on Doxastic Justification have any Dialectical Force? A Response to Oliveira," in *Propositional and Doxastic Justification: New Essays on Their Nature and Significance*, edited by Luis Oliveira and Paul Silva. Routledge.
Silva, Paul Jr. and Oliveira, Luis R.G. (forthcoming). "Propositional Justification and Doxastic Justification," in *Routledge Handbook of the Philosophy of Evidence*, edited by M. Lasonen-Aarnio and C. Littlejohn. Routledge.
Siscoe, Robert Weston (2021). "Belief, Rational and Justified," *Mind* 130(517): 59–83.
Smith, Angela (2012). "Attributability, Answerability, and Accountability: In Defense of a Unified Account," *Ethics* 122(3): 575–589.
Sosa, Ernest (2007). *A Virtue Epistemology*. Oxford University Press.
Strawson, P. F. (1962). "Freedom and Resentment," *Proceedings of the British Academy* 48: 1–25
Street, Sharon (2009). "Evolution and the Normativity of Epistemic Reasons," *Canadian Journal of Philosophy* 39(suppl 1): 213–248.
Todd, Patrick (2016). "Strawson, Moral Responsibility, and the 'Order of Explanation': An Intervention," *Ethics* 127: 208–240.
Velleman, David. 2009. *How We Get Along*. Cambridge University Press.
Watson, Gary (2004). *Agency and Answerability*. Oxford: Oxford University Press.
Williams, Bernard (1973). "Deciding to Believe," in *Problems of the Self*. Cambridge University Press: 136–151.
Williamson, Timothy (2007). *The Philosophy of Philosophy*. Wiley-Blackwell.
Winters, Barbara (1979). "Believing at Will," *The Journal of Philosophy* 76(5): 243–256.
Zagzebski, Linda (1996). *Virtues of the Mind*. Cambridge University Press.
Zagzebski, Linda (2001/2020). "Recovering Understanding," reprinted in *Epistemic Values*. Oxford University Press: 57–77.
Zagzebski, Linda (2003/2020). "Intellectual Motivation and the Good of Truth," reprinted in *Epistemic Values*. Oxford University Press: 168–185.

Zagzebski, Linda (2005/2020). "Epistemic Value and the Primacy of What We Care About," reprinted in *Epistemic Values*. Oxford University Press: 186–203.

Zagzebski, Linda (2012). *Epistemic Authority*. Oxford University Press.

Zagzebski, Linda (2020). *Epistemic Values: Collected Papers in Epistemology*. Oxford University Press.

Index

Page numbers followed by n indicate notes.

accountability *see* epistemic accountability
agency 61, 62, 133, 134, 295, 296, 307
Alston, William 131, 186, 289, 305n34
Arguments-On-Paper Thesis: challenges to 48–52; coherentism and 41; defenses of 52–54; definition of 40, 41, 260n33; doxasticism and 40, 41, 55, 56; empirical support and 45–48, 52; foundationalism and 41; illusions and 50–52; inferential justification and 42, 44, 45, 51, 52; justification as empirical and 42–45; language of thought and 47, 48; laws of logic and 42, 45, 48, 49; overview of 40–42; perceptual system and 49, 50, 53, 54; performance errors and 46, 47; reflection and 53, 54
Aristotle 45, 226
Audi, Robert 2, 7, 8n2, 13n7, 162n2, 264
authority 67, 68, 288, 289, 292, 293, 296–304, 307; *see also* normativity

Bach, K. 87n16
basing relation: agency and 133, 134; Bayesian epistemology and 224, 225; betterness and 124, 125; causal accounts of 79n2; coherentism and 32, 33, 132; constraints on 110n18; definition of 1, 131, 221; demand for 131–136; doxastic justification and 1, 41n3, 131–136; doxastic rationality and 220–226, 239; epistemic accountability and 307n40; faith and 212; goodness and 133, 134; higher-order evidence and 109–112; hope and 212; importance of 122–124, 129, 131, 132; instrumentalism and 126, 127; overview of 109–112; parity argument and 132–136; procedural justification and 135, 136; properly based beliefs 33, 123–128, 153, 289; responsibility and 128, 129; seemings and 223; suspension and 152–157; virtue epistemology and 153, 154
Bayesian epistemology 1, 36, 224, 225
Beglin, David 305n34
bifurcationism 103, 104
Bird, Alexander 187–191, 195, 196
Boole, George 40
Born, Einar 205
Brandom, Robert 45n7
Brown, Jessica 306n36
Brueckner, Anthony 3, 263, 264, 266, 267, 269, 278

Carter, J. Adam 3, 181
Chignell, Andrew 205
Chisholm, Roderick 31, 43, 44
Christensen, David 97n2, 98n3, 102, 103
Cohen, Stephen 80n6, 257, 258
coherentism: Arguments-On-Paper Thesis and 41; basing relation and 32, 33, 132; doxasticism and 41; foundationalism and 33, 41; holism and 31–33; inferential justification and 32; objections to 32; rise of 31
Coliva, Annalisa 3, 162, 167, 169, 170–173, 178, 179
collective epistemology; *see also* intersubjective propositional justification; acceptance view

and 182–186; automaticity of belief and 184; challenges to 181–183, 190, 191; collaboration and 189, 190; defenses of 184–186; dispositions and 190n16; distributivism and 187–191, 195; divergence arguments and 197; functionalism and 187–190, 194–197; Gettier problems and 181; individualism and 183, 192, 193; inflationism and 197; joint acceptance account of 183n6; knowledge-first account of 191–198; overview of 3, 4, 181, 182, 198; rejectionism and 181–186, 191, 193, 198; skepticism and 182; summativism and 181, 191

Collins, Arthur 268n4
Comesaña, Juan 132
commitment 65–68, 165, 167, 168, 170
Conee, Earl 15n8, 80n4, 143–145, 220–222, 236, 246, 247, 287n5, 289, 290
confirmation, theory of 30, 31, 34
consent 297–308
constitutivism 65, 293–296, 305n35
contextualism 233, 236, 237
Cruz, Joseph 132, 223

Davidson, Donald 272n8
degrees of belief 35, 36, 219, 220, 224, 230–234
De Morgan, Augustus 255
De Toffoli, Silvia 3, 241
DiPaolo, Joshua 306n37
disjunctivism: access problem of 90, 91; discriminative rational support and 92, 93; distinguishability problem for 91–93; favoring rational support and 92, 93; hinge assumptions and 168n7; internalism and 2, 83–86, 89–94; propositional justification and 2, 23–25, 80; suspension and 153; virtue epistemology and 148
distributivism 187–191, 195
Dogramaci, Sinan 238
doxasticism: Arguments-On-Paper Thesis and 40, 41, 55, 56; challenges of 27, 28, 38; coherentism and 41; defenses of 55, 56, 243–246, 260, 261; definition of 27; doxastic constraint and 112, 113; epistemic blindspots and 28; essential cognitive admirability and 27, 28; foundationalism and 41; laws of logic and 40; *a priori* reasoning and 55, 56; propositionalism and 27; psychological factors and 55, 56; reasons relation and 34–36
doxastic justification: accessibility and 14; basing relation and 1, 41n3, 131–136; definition of 1, 7, 8, 141, 287; explanatory justification and 86–89, 94; externalism and 246n7; faith and 211–214; hope and 211–214; inferential justification and 8, 9; internalism and 79–82, 87, 88; knowledge and 7, 8, 10–12, 246, 249; limits of 3; memorial justification and 14–17; overview of 8–10; procedural justification and 135, 136; responsibility and 128–129; stative justification and 135, 136
doxastic rationality: basing relation and 220–226, 239; Bayesian epistemology and 224, 225; challenges to 234–237; contextualism and 233, 236, 237; defenses of 234–237; degrees of belief and 219, 220, 230–234; dispositions and 226–230, 233, 239; internalism and 234, 235; overview of 219, 220; probabilism and 237–239; rationality as virtue and 226–230; reliabilism and 234, 235; seemings and 223; unified account of 224; virtue epistemology and 226–230, 233, 239
Durkheim, Émile 187
Dutant, Julien 276n13
Dynamical Systems Theory 189

Elga, A. 97n2, 103n11
Engel, M. 87n16
entailment 8, 23–25, 100, 101, 247
epistemic accountability: agency and 295, 296, 307; attributability and 289–293; authority and 288, 289, 292–302; basing relation and 307n40; consent and 297–308; constitutivism and 293–296, 305n35; normativity and 288, 289, 292–297, 302–305; overview of 286–288, 306–308; ownership and 289–293; subjective permissivism and 306n38

epistemic normativity *see* normativity
epistemic rationality *see* doxastic rationality propositional rationality rationality and reasons
epistemology; *see also* collective epistemology; virtue epistemology; holism and 30–33; landscape of 28–30; overview of 28–34; search for fundamentality in 30–34
error theory 107, 108, 182n5
evidence, higher-order *see* higher-order evidence
evidential defeat 99–102, 118
evidentialism 102, 103, 113, 114, 142–145, 152
ex ante justification: agency and 61, 62; attitudes and 61–69, 74; commitment and 65–68; community with differing norms and 67, 68; constitutivism and 65; definition of 60, 61; epistemic reasons and 157; *ex post* justification distinguished from 60–62, 71; importance of 61; normativity and 61–69; rationally determinable conditions and 63–66; suspension and 143–145, 152, 153; well-formedness and 66–68
explanatory justification 86–89, 94
ex post justification: competence and 70–73, 146; definition of 60, 61, 73; epistemic reasons and 157; *ex ante* justification distinguished from 60–62, 71; explaining attitudes and actions and 69–74; importance of 61; normativity and 61, 62, 69, 74; reasons first about 158; suspension of judgment and 145, 146, 153
expressivism 182n5
externalism 1, 81, 89, 94, 246n7, 287n3

factive reasons 2, 79, 80, 84, 85, 90, 91, 93
faith: basing relation and 212; belief and 203–206; definition of 202–204; dimensions of 203–206; doxastic justification and 211–214; fundamental mental states and 206, 207; hope and 204, 205, 208; normativity and 207–210; overview of 202, 203, 214; propositional justification and 211–214

Feldman, Richard 80n4, 99, 143–145, 220, 221n2, 222, 236, 246, 247, 287n5, 289, 290
Firth, Roderick 60n1, 109n17, 201n2, 220, 222, 241, 243, 245
Flowerree, A.K. 295, 296
Fodor, Jerry 47, 48, 177
Foley, Richard 41n3
foundationalism 27, 31, 33, 41
Frege, Gottlob 34, 35, 255, 275, 276, 277n14
French, Craig 276n13
Friedman, Jane 141, 142, 150n6, 158–160
functionalism 187–190, 194–197

Gerken, Mikkel 166n5
Gettier problems 159, 181
Glynn, Luke 232n17
Goldberg, Sanford 253, 305, 306n36
Goldman, Alvin 15n8, 40n2, 60n2, 79n2, 112n20, 142, 234, 244, 280, 291
Greene, Amanda 297–300, 303
group belief *see* collective epistemology

Hakli, Raul 183, 184, 186
Harman, Gilbert 31, 40n2, 42n4, 163, 165, 167
Hawthorne, John 98n3
Hempel, C. G. 255
higher-order evidence: basing relation and 109–112; bifurcationism and 103; conciliation option and 116–118; conflicts among evidence and 102–106, 118, 119; defeaters and 99–102, 110, 118; definition of 2, 98; entailment and 100, 101; evidentialism and 102, 103, 113, 114; knowledge and 106–109, 118; level splitting option and 116, 117; meta-coherence and 102–106; normativity and 114–116; overview of 97–99; probablistic accessibilism and 100–104; rationality and 103, 104, 113–119; steadfastness option and 116, 117; suspension and 145, 148, 149
hinge assumptions: commitment and 165, 167, 168, 170; definition of 3, 162; disjunctivism and 168n7; doxastic hinge assumptions 163–167;

316 *Index*

externalism and 168; overview of 162, 163; perceptual justification and 162, 164–169, 172, 173; propositional hinge assumptions 163–167; rationality and 176–179; skepticism and 169; varieties of 167–170

holism 30–33

hope: basing relation and 212; definition of 202, 203; despair distinguished from 205, 206; dimensions of 205; doxastic justification and 211–214; faith and 204, 205, 208; fundamental mental states and 206, 207; normativity and 207–210; overview of 202, 203, 214; propositional justification and 211–214

Horowitz, Sophie 105n12, 115, 116

Huemer, Michael 131, 132, 257, 267n2

Hume, David 33, 169–170, 175, 176

Hutchins, Edwin 185

individualism 183, 192, 193

inferential justification: Arguments-On-Paper Thesis and 42, 44, 45, 51, 52; coherentism and 32; doxastic justification and 8, 9; inductive inference 51, 52; knowledge and 263; laws of logic and 42; propositional justification and 8, 9, 242–245; psychological inference 42, 44, 45; statistical inference 51, 52

instrumentalism 126, 127

internalism: accessibilist account of 80; access problem and 91; classical account of 80–85, 93; disjunctivism and 2, 83–86, 89–94; doxastic justification and 79–82, 87, 88; doxastic rationality and 234, 235; explanatory justification and 86–89, 94; factive states and 83–86, 89–94; implicit justification and 15n8; mentalist account of 80; new evil demon intuition and 80–90, 93, 94; non-factive states and 79–84, 89, 90, 93, 94; normativity and 83, 85–88; perceptual justification and 164, 165; propositional justification and 2, 79–82; rationality and 83, 85–88; reasons and 82–88, 94

intersubjective propositional justification; *see also* collective epistemology; definition of 243, 258; idealized capacity principle and 250–254; inferential justification and 244, 245; mathematical beliefs and 247–250, 253–256, 259, 260; non-ideal good arguments and 254–260; overview of 241–244, 260, 261; phenomenal conservatism and 257

Jackson, Elizabeth 3, 201, 205, 207

judgment suspension *see* suspension of judgment

justification *see* doxastic justification *ex ante* justification *ex post* justification memorial justification perceptual justification propositional justification

Kahneman, Daniel 51, 244, 245n5, 260

Kantianism 3, 142, 145, 148, 149, 153–156, 158

Kaplan, M. 45n7

Kelp, Christoph 3, 181

Kempe, Alfred 256, 257, 258

Kiesewetter, Benjamin 283n21

Kitcher, P. 255

knowledge: doxastic justification and 7, 8, 10–12, 246, 249; higher-order evidence and 106–109, 118; indefinite expandability of 23–25; inferential justification and 263; memorial justification and 17; normativity and 29; overview of 10, 11; propositional justification and 7, 8, 10–12, 23–25, 246, 249; requirements of 7, 8; unreasonable knowledge 106–109, 118

knowledge-first accounts: awareness without knowledge and 267n2; challenges to 263, 264; collective epistemology and 191–198; common objects and 273–278; evidence without knowledge in 266–269; justification without evidence in 278–284; knowledge without evidence in 278–284; knowledge without justification in 264–266; neutrality and 269–273; non-inferential knowledge and 263;

Index 317

normativity and 282; overview of 3, 263, 264; reasons-first approach and 282, 283; subjective justification and 283, 284
Kornblith, Hilary 2, 40, 243–245, 249n10, 251, 253, 258, 260
Korsgaard, Christine 295, 296
Kotzen, M. 101
Kulkarni, Sanjeev 31
Kvanvig, Jonathan 2, 27, 29, 30, 32–34

language of thought 47, 48, 229
Lasonen-Aarnio, Maria 106, 107, 109, 111, 114n22, 117
law of large numbers 51, 52
laws of logic 40, 42, 45, 48, 49
Lehrer Keith 80n6, 230n15
Leite, Adam 45n7, 289, 290
Lewis, David 206
liberalism, epistemic 1, 21, 132, 136
Littlejohn, Clayton 3, 263, 267n2, 276n13
logic, laws of 40, 42, 45, 48, 49
Lord, Errol 3, 74n6, 141, 144–146, 283n21

Mackie, J.L. 33
Malmgren, A.-S. 40n2
Martin, Adrienne 205
mathematical beliefs 3, 247–250, 253–256, 259, 260
McCormick, Miriam 291
McDowell, John 168, 267, 268, 271n7, 272, 274, 276, 277n14, 282
McGinn, Marie 268n5
McGrath, Matthew 132
Meirav, Ariel 205
Melis, Giacomo 250
memorial justification: doxastic justification and 14–17; false propositions and 16; information base and 15; knowledge and 17; memorial images and 16; overview of 2, 7, 14–17; propositional justification and 14–19; seemings and 20–23; self-ascriptions and 17
mentalism 15n8, 37, 80
Menzel, Christopher 27
Meylan, Anne 2, 3, 121
Millar, Alan 268n5
Miracchi, Lisa 141–142, 147–148, 153

Nagel, J. 185n9
Neta, Ram 2, 59, 132
Nolfi, Kate 296n18
non-factualism 1, 132
normativism 293–296
normativity: agency and 295, 296, 307; attributability and 293n14; epistemic accountability and 288, 289, 292–297, 302–305; *ex ante* justification and 61–69; *ex post* justification and 61, 62, 69, 74; faith and 207–210; higher-order evidence and 114–116; hope and 207–210; internalism and 83, 85–88; knowledge and 29, 282; propositional justification and 19, 83; reasons and 83, 85–88; suspension and 149; virtue epistemology and 153–156

Oliveira, Luis R.G. 1, 3, 4, 41n3, 132–135, 242, 286, 307n40
Osborne, Robert 291, 295n17

Palermos, O. 187, 189–191, 196
Palmira, M. 178
perceptual justification: conservative accounts of 163–165, 169, 170–172; forms of 163–170; hinge assumptions and 162, 164–169, 172, 173; internalism and 164, 165; liberal accounts of 163, 164, 169–172; moderate accounts of 163–166, 167–179; objections to moderate accounts of 170–179; overview of 162; perceptual systems and 49, 50, 53, 54; rationality and 164, 173, 174; skepticism and 172, 174–178
phenomenal conservatism 1, 20, 21, 132, 257
Plantinga, Alvin 32
Pollock, John 32, 99, 100, 132, 223
Pritchard, Duncan 2, 30, 79, 80n3, 82n12, 168, 303n30
probabilism 237–239
proper basing *see* basing relation
propositionalism: atomism and 33–38; defenses of 27–30, 37, 38, 55, 242, 244–246; definition of 27; doxasticism and 27; epistemic landscape and 28–30; holism and 33; laws of logic and 40; mental

states and 37, 38; *a priori* reasoning and 55, 56; psychological factors and 55, 56; reasons relation and 34–38

propositional justification; *see also* intersubjective propositional justification; accessibility and 14, 15; apsychological conception of 42, 55, 243, 245, 258, 259; conceptual conditions for 18, 19; definition of 1, 7, 8, 141, 245; dialectical nature of 19; disjunctivism and 2, 23–25, 80; eliminationism and 24; entailment and 23–25, 247; faith and 211–214; free-floating justification and 10; fundamentality of 242, 244–246; higher-order justification and 12, 13; hope and 211–214; inferential justification and 8, 9, 242–245; internalism and 2, 79–82; knowledge and 7, 8, 10–12, 23–25, 246, 249; memorial justification and 14–19; normativity and 19, 83; overview of 8–10; possession conditions for 9, 11–14; realizationist conception of 21–23; reasons-first approach to 242–244, 246, 260, 282; retentional account of 24; scope of 7; seemings and 20–23; skepticism and 244, 245; sources of 19–23; structural justification and 13n7

propositional rationality 224, 230–232, 235, 238, 239

Pryor, J. 163

Quine, Willard Van Orman 31

rationality and reasons: factive reasons 2, 79, 80, 84, 85, 90, 91, 93; *see also* doxastic rationality; higher-order evidence and 113–119; hinge assumptions and 176–179; ideal and non-ideal rationality and 113–119; internalism and 83, 85–88; motivational reasons 82–88, 94; perceptual justification and 164, 173, 174; propositional rationality 224, 230–232, 235, 238, 239; reasons, theory of 30, 34–36; responsiveness to 134n4; skepticism and 174–179

rejectionism 181–186, 191, 193, 198

reliabilism: contextualism and 236, 237; doxastic rationality and 234, 235; forms of 234; generality problem for 236; implicit justification and 15n8; objections to 236; process reliabilism 80, 145, 235; virtue epistemology and 129, 234

Rips, Lance 46

Scanlon, Thomas M. 34, 35
Schoenfield, Miriam 114n22, 117
Schroeder, Mark 134n4, 274, 276n13
Scott-Kakures, Dion 293
seemings 20–23, 223
Sellars, Wilfrid 31
Silins, Nicholas 132
Silva, Paul, Jr. 1, 3, 41n3, 123, 124, 131–136, 242, 267, 279n15
Simion, Mona 3, 181, 197
skepticism: collective epistemology and 182; hinge assumptions and 169; Humean form of 175, 176, 178, 179; perceptual justification and 172, 174–178; propositional justification and 244, 245; Pyrrhonian form of 178; rationality and 174–179
Skyrms, B. 100n6
Smithies, Declan 2, 97, 109n16, 247, 248, 249n9, 252
Sorensen, Roy 28
Sosa, Ernest 73n5, 125, 141, 142, 145, 147, 148, 168, 234
Stanley, J. 98n3
Strawson, P. F. 289, 305, 306n36
Street, Sharon 293, 294
Sturgeon, S. 149
summativism 181, 191
suspension of judgment: basing relation and 152–157; challenge of 142–149; as committed neutrality 149; competence and 147, 148; disjunctivism and 153; epistemic reasons and 151–153; evidentialism and 142–145, 152, 157; *ex ante* justification and 143–145, 152, 153; *ex post* justification and 145, 146, 153; forms of 149–151, 155; Gettier problems and 159; higher-order evidence and 145, 148, 149; importance of 141,

142; justification for 148, 149; normativity and 149; overview of 141, 142; rational profile of 149–151; relegation approach to 142–149; respect and 152–157; restructuring approach to 142; virtue epistemology and 152, 153, 157; zetetic turn and 142, 158–160

Sylvan, Kurt 3, 74n6, 82n12, 141, 144, 145, 146, 272n9, 279n16

Talbott, W. 40n2
Tang, W. 145
Toffoli, Silvia De 3, 241
Travis, Charles 268n5, 275, 277n14
Turri, John 112n20, 122, 135, 221
Tversky, A. 51, 244

Unger, Peter 267n2, 272, 273

Veritism 143n1, 146, 153, 154
virtue epistemology: basing relation and 153, 154; competence and 146, 153; definition of 29; degrees of virtue in 230–234; disjunctivism and 148; doxastic rationality and 226–230, 233, 239; early forms of 142–149; evidentialism and 145; Kantian virtue epistemology 149, 153–158; normativity and 153–156; rational parity and 147, 148; reliabilism and 129, 234; respect for truth and 156–158; suspension and 152, 153, 157; teleological virtue epistemology 142, 146–148, 153, 157; veritist virtue epistemology 146, 153

Weber, Max 299
Wedgwood, Ralph 3, 219
Wegner, M. 189
Wietmarschen, H. 109n16
Williams, Bernard 45n7, 293
Williamson, Timothy 3, 61, 192, 193, 223, 263, 267, 268, 283n23
Wittgenstein, L. 174, 175, 178
Worsnip, Alex 225n9
Wright, Crispin 163, 170–179

Zagzebski, Linda 297

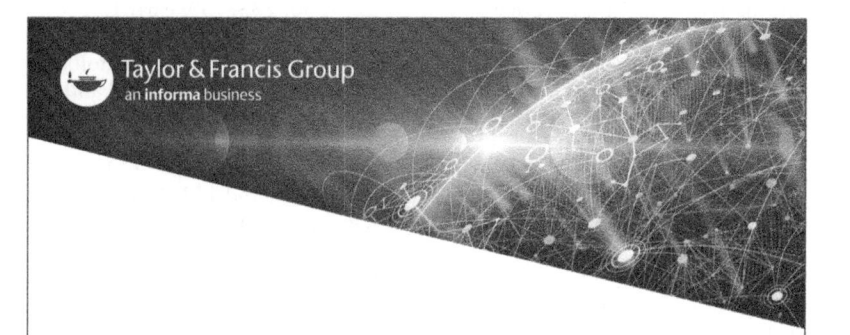

For Product Safety Concerns and Information please contact our EU representative GPSR@taylorandfrancis.com Taylor & Francis Verlag GmbH, Kaufingerstraße 24, 80331 München, Germany

Printed and bound by CPI Group (UK) Ltd, Croydon, CR0 4YY